THIRUKKURAL RESEARCH 2021

DR. M.P Chockalingam

INDIA • SINGAPORE • MALAYSIA

ISBN 979-8-88986-911-5

CONTENTS

PART - III

PERSONAL LIFE: NOTES ON FAMILY LIFE (LOVE-LIFE / BLISSFUL LOVE / DESIRE FOR PLEASURE)

APPENDIX A-1 TO A-15

PREFACE BY AUTHOR

Some 62 year ago, Dr.Mu.Varatharajanaar (1949)[1], an eminent academician authored a detailed interpretation of Thirukkural, under the title "ThirukkuRaL-TheLivurai" (descriptive notes), in order to popularize Thirukkural among the students. He used to believe that there are rich contents in Thirukkural which can be selected and taught to young children during their formative years of their school age, so as to help them to grow as responsible citizens with good conduct/character and capabilities! Value education and knowledge development must go together simultaneously! The idea of the child growing with good conduct and capabilities was revealed and reiterated by Poet Pattukkottai-Kalyanasundaram in the year 1959, through a movie-song[2], insisting that "a child must grow as a good person, and at the same time, as a capable (knowledgeable) person, to bring happiness to elders"!

"yeNNa-th-thil una-k-ku, yidam nhaan tharu-vae-n! yenakku, yini nhee, yenna-yenna tharu-vaai? ...nhalla-va-naaka, vallamai sae-ra,

vaLar-nh-thaa-lae pOthu-madaa! vaazh-nh-thaa-lae pOthu-madaa!!"

A few years earlier, the same poet highlighted the concept that the growth of a child must take care of two aspects, namely, i) physical growth and ii) absorption of knowledge. *"aaLum-vaLaraNum; aRivum-vaLaraNum; athu-thaaN-daa-vaLarchchi":* These concepts are in resonance with kural couplets 67 to 70! The poet advised a child to study Thirukkural, as a duty-bound exercise, every day! *('ThirukkuRaL-nhoolai, chiRanhtha-mup-paalai, karuththudan-kaalai, padippathu, unathu-vaelai".*

Research on Thirukkural is a continuing phenomenon, in many countries around the world! Tamil publications of Thirukkural Interpretations by many scholars like Pulavar Kuzhanthai[2], Navalar Dr.R.Nedunchezhian[3], Dr.Kalaigner M.Karunanithi[4], and Dr.Va.Su.Pa.Manickam[5], and English translation by Sri C.**Rajagopalachariar** (Rajaji)6 have been helpful for maintaining the awareness about Thirukkural among the student-community!

Writer Sujathaa[7], in his "Thirukkural -PuthiyaUrai 1995", observed that there is sufficient material available in Thirukkural in relevance to the requirements of the youths of the 21st Century, citing Kural couplets in Chapter 48: "Knowing of one's own strength", and, in Chapter 62: "Firmness in Strenuous Acts", having relevance to Entrepreneurship! He felt that translation of Thirukkural must be made available in prose-form, in order to promote popularization of Thirukkural around the world, among the English- speaking people, as it was felt that translation of Thirukkural, in poetry form, in English would not correctly convey the original concepts of Thiruvalluvar, the poet!

Gopalakrishna Gandhi, a bureaucrat in Indian Administrative Service, Diplomat, and former Governor of West Bengal (India), has authored a poetry-form of Thirukkural in English, translating all the 1330 couplets, and dedicating it to: "The Interwoven.. Memories of Chakravarti Rajagoplachari and Periyar E.V.Ramasamy". It must be mentioned that the two leaders, namely, Rajaji and Periyar E.V.Ramasamy were both appreciative of the genius of Thiruvalluvar.

From the year 1928 onwards, awareness about Thirukkural started increasing, especially among the social reformers like Periyar E.V.Ramasamy, Perarignar Annaa (C.N.Annadurai), *KalaivaaNar* N.S.Krishn*an, Kalaignar*

-Dr.M.Karunanithi, Poet (Puratchikkavignar) Bharathidasan, Thavaththiru Kundrakkudi Adigalar, *Kavignar* Kannadaasan, and among some academic scholars / dignitaries like Thiru.V.Kaliyanasundaranar, Maraimalai Adigalaar, Devaneya Paavaanar, *Muththamizhkkaavalar* Ki.Aa.Pe.Viswanatham, *Panmozhippulavar* Ka.Appadurai, '*Thirukkuralaar*'- Munusamy, *Rajah* Sir Muthiah Chettiar and many others.

Dr.V.Irai Anbu[9], a bureaucrat in Indian Administrative Service, has authored a book on "Comparing Titans Thiruvalluvar and Shakespeare", highlighting the concepts of management science described by Thiruvalluvar being echoed in the Shakespearean Plays, in the form of situational quotes!

Also, it is explained as to how the two literary giants of the world, namely, Thiruvalluvar and Shakespeare have brought out the core ideas of Management Science which remain relevant during the 21st century! University-level research is being pursued by many learned Professors, like A.A.Manavaalan.[20]

Dr.R.Krishnamurthi[10], a specialist in Corporate Management Training Programs has published a book on "Thirukkural: A Management Treasure", bringing out the fact that there are guidelines indicated in the contents of Thirukkural which remain relevant to the latest management practices of the 21st Century.

Nobel Laureate Herbert A. Simon's11 theory on management concepts, consisting of three elements, namely, 'intelligence-activity', 'design-activity', and 'choice-activity', related to the decision-making process that are 'prophesied' in three Thirukkural couplets, 465, 462 and 467, respectively.

It is to be remembered that there have been 260 publications of Tamil translations of Thirukkural, from the year 1812 to 2006, done by more than 250 eminent Tamil scholars[13]. and 61 publications of English translation of Thirukkural from the year 1794 to 2018, with contributions from several eminent scholars from Tamil Nadu, and foreign countries[14]. Thirukkural happens to be the book largely translated into many languages of the world, (up to the year 2001), next only to the Bible and the Quran! Thirukkural has been translated into 41 languages of the world[15]! These details reinforce and reiterate the belief of Writer-Sujathaa that Thirukkural has got relevance to the 21st Century and beyond, serving as a lighthouse of knowledge to guide the youth-population, around the world! Rev.Fr.Constanzo Beschi (*Veera-Maa-Munivar*, 1680-1747), was the first European-Tamil scholar to inform the European intellectuals about the richness of Tamil Literature, including the wisdom behind Thirukkural[16]. Francis Whyte Ellis (1777-1819), a British Civil servant, and scholar in Sanskrit and Tamil, initiated the hypothesis of Dravidian Languages and translated some selected (160) couplets from the first two parts of Thirukkural into English, in the year 1812, and also released a gold - coin with the image of Thiruvalluvar[17].

An unpublished manuscript of Malayalam-translation of Thirukkural 'existed' in the year 1595.18 The first Thirukkural and 'Naladiyar (Naaladiyar)' were released in 1812 by Gnanaprakasam (printed by Masadinacarital Printers, in Madras (Chennai).[19] In the year 1956, *Periyar* E.V.Ramasamy appealed to the public, in a public function, in the presence of '*Mahasannidhanam*'-*Thavaththiru*- Kundrakkudi- Adigalaar that the contents of Thirukkural must be studied with an analytical approach to assess the sociological impacts on which the great poet lays stress, especially on discipline, morality, and self-respect! At that time, myself (the author of this book) was a high-school student, in Bishop Heber High School, Puthur, Tiruchirapalli. Therefore, it has become my life's ambition to explore the treasure of knowledge available in Thirukkural, in greater depth, and to write a book.

Professor Solomon Pappiah[12], the author of 'Thirukkural- Uraiyudan' (2006) has described all the 1330 Kurals, and has made an appeal to the Tamil-speaking people that they should study and enjoy the wisdom of their world-renowned ancestor called Thiruvalluvar!

Being encouraged by these inspirations, I have made a humble effort during the past twenty years, in translating the 1330- couplets, and compiling them under the caption "Thirukkural Research 2021", aiming at popularizing Thirukkural among the students at the global level! I hope that this book will be useful as a reference book for younger generation, in India, and abroad, on topics of multi-disciplinary interests!

AN APPEAL TO STUDENT-READERS:

I wish to conclude that the youngsters may undertake further research on various aspects of their interests, from the ocean of Thirukkural! The students in Tamil Nadu may feel proud that one of their ancestors, namely, Poet Thiruvalluvar, for having created a world-renowned literature on preaching about kindness, virtues, avoidance of hatred and enmity, on the one side, and on the other hand, to guide his descendants (the youth of the world) to come up in life, by acquiring good human qualities, with the required endurance, perseverance, to upgrade the status of themselves, bringing fame and wealth to their families! Kindly appreciate the fact that Thiruvalluvar has devoted one full chapter on "Promoting Family Welfare", in Chapter-103! Thiruvalluvar will be delighted to watch your response, as your well- wisher and guide!! Thiruvalluvar happens to be the only poet in the whole world who has taken extraordinary efforts to convince an individual human being to acquire virtuous qualities to come up in life, through hard work and enthusiasm, never losing heart at times of crisis, and to function with goodwill towards others, and hatred towards none! At the same time, he wants good persons to remain vigilant about bad elements in the society (in Chapter-108 (Unscrupulous Persons)!

The beauty lies in the fact that, Thirukkural written some 2000 years ago, remains relevant to meet the challenges of the 21st Century and beyond, thus bringing fame to Tamil Literature! Tributes to Thiruvalluvar from world leaders is presented in Annexure-2. Comparison of Thirukkural ideology, as reflected in international literature has been attempted in Annexures-3A to 3H, for the benefit of researchers! Quotes from philosophers,poets,world-leaders, and business-magnates around the world have been appended, to demonstrate how well the quotes fit-in with the ideology of Thirukkural! Quotes from international businessmen of Indian origin have been added to motivate the students in India!

The great poet wants to be your adviser and consultant, by guiding you in all your efforts to elevate yourself, i) by absorbing good habits, conduct and character, ii) by remaining steady and smart to make endeavors in qualifying yourself in field of your choice, iii) by avoiding laziness and lethargy, iv) by making friendship with the right kind of people, v) by taking care to earn the patronage of elders to achieve your goals, vi) with determination and will-power while facing hardships, and vii) while remaining vigilant to avoid acquaintance with bad persons, or evil forces!

Every child can familiarize himself or herself with the following Kurals, selecting one poem from each chapter of Thirukkural, learning them slowly, right from class-one of elementary education! It will be fun, like reciting rhymes! By the time, the child passes the school- final class, the following kurals can be learned, so as to understand the objectives of the self, and climb up the ladder of higher education: (vide Kural-numbers detailed below):

2, 34, 45, 71, 100, 108, 115, 121, 131, 151, 161, 177, 190, 200, 202, 215, 225, 236, 250, 282, 294, 303, 314, 317, 324, 355, 385, 391, 396, 412; 423, 434, 439, 443, 460, 466, 475, 490, 497, 504, 517, 527, 540, 562, 575, 595, 605, 616, 621, 636, 647, 656, 666, 672, 691, 703, 706, 717, 724, 731, 737, 754, 786, 828, 891, 942, 948, 960, 969, 978, 985, 994, 1018, 1021, 1031.

College / University level students, in all disciplines, will find the contents of Thrukkural, to be applicable to their personal lives, as well as to understand the broad outlines of information related to professional norms, whatever be the walk of life they happen to choose! There is so much of information in Thirukkural as relevant to areas such as Philosophy, Sociology, Human Psychology, Ethics and Spiritualism, Human Rights, Political science, General Administration, Business Management, Financial Management, Defense of a Country, Criminal Justice, Professional Ethics, Charity, Medical and Health Sciences, Agricultural Sciences and Food Production, Hydrology and Climatology, Architecture and Construction activity, Entrepreneurship, Personality Development, Labour Management, Poverty-Alleviation, etc. This book will serve as a companion/guide, not only to the students, but also, to the general public.Thirukkural must be popularized among the masses, in order to promote unity, kindness and goodwill, at village levels, through Youth Forums, throughout India. Similar efforts are being supported in *Tamil Sangams* established all over the world, through voluntary efforts. This is an encouraging trend to promote universal brotherhood. Comparison of the ideology of Thiruvalluvar with the philosophies of international intelligentsia will broaden the knowledge of the youth.

Quotes from great personalities can shape up the growth of youngsters in a big way:

1. "Success is measured not so much by the position that one has reached in life, as by the obstacles which he has overcome"- Booker T. Washington (1856-1915), Educator, Writer, U.S.A., author of "Character Building", "The story of My Life and Work", etc. (This concept is revealed in kural 1026).

2. "Do unto others what you want others to do unto you! Do not do unto others what you do not want others to do unto you"... aslogan often told to his students by Rev.Fr.Ehrhart, S.J., FormerPrincipal of St.Joseph's College, Tiruchirapalli, Tamil Nadu, India. (This concept is found in kurals 206, 311, 316, 318, 320).

It must be the ideal of youngsters to remain good throughout their lifetimes in order to be useful to the society and the country. That is the core ideology of the poet Thiruvalluvar, to create a harmonious and peaceful society.

REFERENCES:

1. Dr.Mu.Varadarajanaar, 1949, "ThirukkuRaL-TheLivurai", The South India Saiva Siddhantha Publishing Society Tinneveli Ltd., 522, T.T.K.Salai, Chennai-600018.

2. Pattukkottai Kalyana Sundaram, Poet, 1959, movie Song in KalyanaParisu, *"unnaik-kaNdu-nhaan-aada, ennaikkaNdu nhee- yaada, ullaasam pong-kum... deepaavaLi...enakku nhee enna-enna thauvaai?..... nhallavan-aaga -vallamai -saera, vaLarnh-thaalaey pOthumadaa! vaazh-nh-thaalaey*

pOthumadaa!". "*nhallavanaaga*" means "as a good person". "*vallamai saera*" means "with capabilities/ skills/intelligence/ wisdom". In another song, the poet reiterated that "*aaLum- vaLaraNum; aRivum-vaLaraNum; athu-thaaNdaa- vaLarchchi*", meaning that the child- growth must comprise of physical growth and knowledge-wise growth.

3. Dr.R.Nedunchezhian, 1991, "Thirukkural-Thelivurai", Nedunchezhian Educational Trust, No.4. Masilamani street, SeethammalKudiyiruppu, Alwarpet, Chennai-600 018.

4. Dr.Kalaignar M.Karunanithi, 1996, "Thirukkural-Kalaignar-Urai", Thirmagal Nilayam, Sucons Apartments, No.13, Sivaprakasamsalai, T.Nagar, Chennai-600 017.

5. Dr.Va.Supa.Manickam, 2016, "Thirukkural-Thelivurai", Manivasagar-Pathippagam, 31,Singer street, Chennai-600 108.

6. Thiru C.Rajagopalachari (Rajaji), 1965, "KURAL-THE GREAT BOOK OF TITU-VALLUVAR", Bharatiya Vidya Bhavan, Kulapati K.M.Munshi Marg, Mumbai-400 007.

7. Sujatha, Writer, 1995, "Thirukkural-Puthiya-Urai", Uyirmmai-Pathippagam, 11/29, Subramaniam Street, Abiramapuram, Chennai-600 018.

8. Gopalakrishna Gandhi, 2015, "Thiruvalluvar: The Thirukkural: A New English Version,Alpha Book Company, 7/16, Ansari Road, Darya Ganj, New Delhi-110 002.

9. Dr.V.Irai Anbu, 2015, "Comparing Titans Thiruvalluvar and Shakespeare", Viva Books Private Limited,, 4737/23, Ansari Road, Darya Ganj, New Delhi-110 002.

10. Dr.R.Krisnamurthy, 2018, "Thirukkural: A management Treasure", Notion Presss, No.6, McNichols Road, Chetpet, Chennai-600 031

11. Herbert A. Simon-Facts, Nobel Prize.org. Nobe Media AB 2020 Mon.28 Sep. 2020<https://www.nobelprize.org/prizes/economic- sciences/1978/ simon Publication /facts/(cited in Reference 9; pages-128 & 129).

12. Professor Solomon Pappiah, 2006, "Thirukkural-Uraiyudan", Kavitha, P.O.Box No. 6123, No.8, Masilamani street, T.Nagar, 600 017.

13. ThirukkuralUraiAchchetrappattiyal-tamil(ta.m.wikipedia.org/ wiki/%EO; (https://www.valaitamil.com)

14. English Translation of Thirukkural: (https://En.m.wikipedia.org/ wiki/ Thirukkural_ Translation_ into_English).

15. Thirukkural Translations-Wikipedia: (https:// www. en.m.wikipedia. org/ wiki/Tirukkural_Translation

16. 17.https://www.en.wickipedia.org>wiki>Constanzo Beschi).

17. https://www.en.m.wokipedia.org>wiki>Francis Whyte Ellis.

18. (https://www.en.m.wikipedia.org/wiki/HistoryofTirukkural_Translations

19. "What are some mind-blowing facts about Thirukkural", by Advocate AnanthakrishnanRamanujam, in "Are non-Tamil Indians aware of Thirukkural and Thiruvaluvar" in Quora website, https:// www.quora. com, 16th May 2019.

20. "A Compendium of Tirukkural Translation in English" (set of 4-books), by Prof.A.A.Manavalan, Central Institute of Classical Tamil, Chennai, 2010.

PUBLISHER'S NOTE

Thirukkural is the most prestigious literature on human virtues, righteousness and ethics. This has been widely recognized at the global level. Many versions of interpretations of Thirukkural have been authored by eminent scholars, in Tamil and English. In this book, interpretations of kural couplets havebeen made in English, in a simpler style, for all the 1 3 3 0 - kural-couplets.

Appendix-1 to Appendix-9 describe the various aspects of research, as indicated, in the respective headings. Citations from global literature, and quotes from world leaders including Abraham Lincoln, world philosophers including Confucius, Aristotle, Plato, business- magnates including Henry Ford, Bill Gates, Warren Edward Buffet, Ratan Tata, Mukesh Ambani, Gautam Adani, Shiv Nadar, N.R.Narayana Murthy, and persons of eminence, including Dr.Nelson Mandela, Leo Tolstoy, Dr.B.R.Ambedkar, are indicated with reference to the corresponding couplet of Thirukkural, matching with the ideology behind the quotes! Comparison of Thirukkural with quotations from William Shakespeare corresponds to a special feature.

Appendix-7 compares Thirukkural with major religious philosophies of Christianity, Islam, Jainism, Buddhism, Sikhism, and Hinduism.This deserves the attention of universal brotherhood. Appendix-9 discusses factors related to human equality. Appendix-11 presents the highlights of Thirukkural relevant to WORLD PEACE! Appendix-13 gives some details about the book,followed by CITATION INDEX which enlists the world leaders, thinkers, ancient philosophers, writers, business-magnates and other luminaries who have been quoted in this book, to bring out the concepts of Thirukkural embedded in the quotes!Appendix -14 describes the key to pronunciation of kural couplets in English.

Multi-disciplinary relevance of Thirukkural is explained. The richness of Thirukkural will be a guiding factor for those students interested in Entrepreneurship, Management Sciences, Law, Psychology, Philosophy, Political Science, Sociology, Professional Ethics, Professional Practice,

Theology, etc., in conceiving a core-idea. Their efforts to acquire the necessary skills needed for personality-development will become a reality! The specifics related to career development can be easily visualized! We hope that this book will deserve the appreciation of the student community at the international level Prof.M.P.Chockalingam,Plot No.3, Second Cross Street,

Dr.Radhakrishnan Nagar, Thiruvanmiyur, Chenna-600-041, TamilNadu, India. Email: chockalingammp@gmail.com. Phone: +91-8838901884.

PART – I

(VIRTUE / RIGHTEOUSNESS / ETHICS)

CHAPTER-1

PRAISE OF SUPREME FORCE

1. akara muthala yezhuth-th(u)-yellaam aathi
   pakavan muthatRae ulaku.

   The first alphabet "A" marks the origin for all letters in a language! Similarly, for all activities of the world, the origin is the blessings from the Ancient God.

   (If the term '*aadhi-bakavan*' is taken as '*aadhi- bakalavan*', it can be inferred as: 'all activities of the world are dependent on the Sun, meaningthe predominance of solar energy'). There are interpreters who claim that the term '*aadhi-bakavan*' straightaway means the Sun-God!

2. katRatha-naal aaya payan-yen –kol vaal-aRivan
   nhatRaaL thozhaar yenin?

   What is the benefit of learning, if a learned person does not worship the noble feet of the Almighty who possesses the absolute (pure /ultimate) knowledge?

3. malar-misai yaekinaan maaNadi sae-rnh-thaar
   nhilamisai nheedu- vaazh- vaar.

   All persons embracing the noble feet of the Almighty who has already ascended the flower of wisdom (heart) of human beings will live longerin this world.

4. vaeNduthal vaeNdaamai ilaan –adi saer-nh-thaar-k-ku
   yaaNdum idumbai ila.

   For those who reach the feet of the Almighty who is free from feelings oflikes and dislikes, there will never be any sufferings.

5. iruL- saer iru-vinai-yum saeraa iRaivan
   poruL-saer pukazh -purinh-thaar maattu.

For those who have understood the meaningful glory of the Almighty, the long-lasting miseries arising out of ignorance will not occur.

6. poRi-vaayil ai-nh-thu.aviththaan poi-theer ozhukka
   nheRi- nhindRaar nheedu vaazhvaar.

   The Almighty has abandoned the desires of the five senses, and followsa code of conduct free from falsehood. Those who steadfastly follow a similar code, will live longer. Their fame will remain longer in this world!

7. thanakku –uvamai illaa-thaan thaaL- saernh-thaar-kku-al-laal
   manak-kavalai maatRal arithu.

   The Almighty does not have any equal or parallel entity. Except for those who worship the noble feet of the Almighty, it becomes difficult for others to liberate themselves from mental- worries.!

8. aRa-(v)aazhi anh-thaNan thaaL- saer-nh-thaarkku al-laal
   piRa-(v) aazhi nheenh-thal arithu.

   The Almighty is like the deep ocean of virtues. It is possible to swim across the sea of the present life (full of miseries and testing- times), for those who follow the virtuous path, similar to that of the Almighty; For others who live in this world, and yet, do not follow the virtuous path of the Almighty, it is not possible to swim across the sea of life, containing sufferings and tribulations! (Also, interpreted as 'sea of rebirths'). Please see Appendix-1.

9. koL-il poRi-yil kuNam-ila-vae, yeN-kuNath-thaan
   thaaLai vaNang-kaa- th- thalai.

   The Almighty is the possessor of the considerate and gracious traits of sensation, worth being contemplated by humans as admirable! The head of a person, not worshiping the noble feet of the Almighty, will not have the right objective or full-benefit of the five senses, namely, Taste, Sight, Touch, Hearing and Smell.

10. piRavi-p- perung-kadal nheenh-thuvar, nheenh-thaar
    iRaivan- adi sae-raa- thaar.

Those who embrace the noble feet of the Almighty, will find it easier to cross the great sea of birth. For those who do not embrace the feet of the Almighty, it becomes impossible to cross the sea of testing times during this birth. (Alternatively, the sea of birth is also interpreted as the Next Birth or Subsequent Births).

CHAPTER-2

BLESSING OF RAIN

11. vaan- nhindRu ulakam vazha-ngki varuthal-aal
    thaan- amizhtham yendRu- uNaraR- paatRu.

    Life in the world prevails based on the sky-dominated rains. Therefore, the rainwater is understood as the divine food for all living-species (beings).

12. thuppaar-kku-th- thuppu- aaya, thuppu- aakki, thuppaarkku
    thupp(u) –aaya, thoo-vum mazhai.

    Rainwater occurs as a droplet in the sky and falls as spray (or snow) on to the land. This water helps to produce (edible) food which is safe enough to eat (by promoting agriculture), in addition to itself (water) serving as a safe food to all those who consume it.

13. viN-(N)indRu poi-ppin viri-nheer viyan- ulakath-thu
    uL- nhindRu udatRum pasi.

    In this wide world surrounded by vast expanse of sea-water, if the atmospheric process fails to produce the rainwater, a long- lasting (distressing) hunger and famine will prevail, and make the life miserable! (Note: Sea water is available in plenty; and hence, it is referred to as vast resource, but yet not fit for direct-use!).

14. yaerin uzhaa-ar uzhavar puyal-yennum
    vaari vaLam-kundRi-k- kaa-l.

    Farmers cannot plough their lands (to cultivate), if the water-carrying clouds lose their abundance of moisture in the sky, and fail to pour down from the sky (over land) as rainwater.

15. keduppathoo-vum, kettaar-kku-ch-chaarvaai- matRu-aang-kae
    yeduppathoo-vum yellaam mazhai.

    Excessive rain causes damage to the farmers, as well as failure of rainfall, causing loss to the farmers. To compensate the losses, it does rain againat appropriately-sufficient quantities, to rescue and enrich the farmers, and to uplift them.

16. visumbin thuLi- veezhin allaal- matRu aang-kae
    pasum- pul thalai- kaaNbu arithu.

    If the rain-droplet from the sky does not fall down as rain, to the land, it will become rare to see even the leaves of green grass showing up above the ground, to enlighten our hopes.

17. nhedum –kadalum than- nheermai- kundRum thadinth(u)- yezhili
    thaan- nhalkaa th(u)-aaki vidin.

    Even the vast/ expansive ocean will lose its water-resources content, if the water vapour does not rise up as dense clouds, to yield rain! (Rainfall over the ocean and rainwater through rivers reaching the ocean, enrich the ocean with regard to the quantity and quality of water).

18. siRappodu poosanai sellaathu vaanam
    vaRakku-mael, vaanOr-kkum yeeNdu.

    If the sky ever dries up, resulting in failure of the rains, even the ritualistic worship of the heavenly (celestial) gods will not (cannot) take place, in the process of praying to them.

19. thaanam, thavam –iraNdum thang-kaa, viyan- ulakam
    vaanam- vazhang-kaa- thu, yenin.

    If the sky does not donate rainwater, any activity related to performing ritualistic sacrifices (Yagas) cannot take place; and the resources for supporting the poor cannot be sustained, in this wide world. (The farmers will not be able to feed the ascetics; nor offer financial support to the ascetics to conduct the ritualistic sacrifices (yagas) and to sustain piety!).

20. **nheer- indRu amai-yaathu ulaku-yenin, yaar- yaar-kkum vaan- indRu amaiyaathu ozhukku.**

If it can be assumed that the process of life cannot be supported, for any one, without the contribution of rain, falling from the sky, it is to be said that the regulation of orderly life-process itself (conduct, character, human-interactions) will suffer in sthis world. Confusions in sharing of water will disturb orderliness in society! (Another interpretation:There would not be any flow of water (*ozhukku*), without the aid of the atmospheric reactions(leading to the cloud-condensation-phenomena, taking place in the sky!).

(There is a hidden scientific hint in the phrase: "*vaan-indRu- amaiyaathu ozhukku*", implying that no downpour of rainfall can take place, without contributions from the sky (atmosphere)! G.U.Pope gives importance to this factor, namely, the role of the sky in causing the rainfall, and the consequent flow over the land! (Rainfall helps to cleanse the Environment and to give the life-supporting moisture, to the elements of the environment, namely,air,water, and soil,benefiting the living- organisms and vegetation. The sky (atmosphere) supports the reactions among the moving air-masses (air-parcels, eddies), causing the occurrence of winds, with varying temperatures and pressures of warmer-air mass versus cooler-air mass, vertical re-distribution of temperatures in air (in upper air layers versus lower air layers), cloud formation, the occurrence of colder winds moving over the clouds, and thus, helping the cloud-condensation process, and the consequent rainfall). (Ref:: https:www. weather.govhydro NWS JetStream-The Hydrologic Cycle).

CHAPTER-3

MERIT OF ASCETICS

21. ozhukkaththu nhee-ththaar perumai vizhuppath-thu
vaeNdum panuval thuNivu.

It is the firm conclusion of ancient literature on human virtues that the determination of ascetic persons/saints to renounce the worldly pleasures deserves praise/ exaltation / glorification..(Note: The ancient literature is cited to support the concept).

22. thuRanh-thaar perumai thuNai-k- kooRin vaiyaththu
iRanh-thaarai yeNNi-k- koNd(u)- atRu.

Narrating the greatness of those who have renounced the worldly life in this world is of infinite magnitude, as huge as the counting of dead- persons in this world, up to date! (Note: The concept of infinity, as a number, is implied!).

23. irumai vakai- therinh-thu yeeNdu- aRam- pooNdaar
- perumai piRang-kitRu ulaku.

The greatness of saintly persons will shine brighter in this world, if they decide to resort to ascetic life, after assessing (analyzing) the pros and cons of ascetic life in contrast with married-life, as the two different paths of life have got different forms of sufferings and pleasures!!

24. uran-yennum thOtti-yaan, Or-ai-nh-thum kaap-paan
varan-yennum vaippiRku- Or vith-thu.

An ascetic (saintly person) who controls his/her five senses of the organs, using his/her wisdom as the weapon, will be considered as the seed for the very discipline of asceticism itself, bringing fame to the very ascetic order! (Note: It applies to both genders).

25. ai-nh-thu-aviththaan aatRal akal- visumb(u) uLar- kO-maan
inh-thira-nae saalum kari.

The moral strength of a person who can control over his/ her five senses is tremendously great! The negative example is Lord Indiran, the chief of the inhabitants of heaven (who violated the norms and got a perennial punishment!!). (* according to ancient puranic hint; hearsay-belief of people).

(Note: The poet does quote Lord Indiran as a positive example of good character. The puranic story could not have been known during the poet's lifetime! This needs a debate, and further research!).

26. seyaRku- ariya seivaar periyar, siRiyar
seyaRku- ariya sei-ka-laa -thaar.

Great persons are those who are capable of doing greater things, which are difficult for others to do. Small persons are those who are not capable of doing such greater deeds.

27. suvai, oLi, ooRu-Osai, nhaatRam- endRu, ai-nh-thin
vakai therivaan kattae ulaku.

The entire world can be controlled by a person who is capable of evaluating/ assessing the pros and cons of controlling the five senses of human organs, namely, touch, taste, smell, sight and sound, and keeping them under control!

28. nhiRai mozhi maanh-thar perumai nhilaththu
maRai- mozhi kaatti vidum.

The glory (greatness/fame) of philosophers will be exhibited by the words of wisdom that they have left behind, in the form of any recorded evidence! (Note: This applies to great persons, both during their life- times, as well as 'afterwards'). Their good words will become 'quotes', after their demise.

29. kuNam –yennum kundR(u)- aerRi nhindRaar, vekuLi
kaNa-maeyum kaath-thal arithu.

The anger of persons who have ascended the mountain of good virtues will last only for a few seconds! (realizing and fearing that such an anger will produce harmful effect on the recipient!).Such persons will have their anger under their control; thereby, deserving a great merit!

30. anhthaNar en-bOr, aRav-Or, matRu ev-vuyir-kkum
senh-thaN-mai pooNdu ozhuka-laan.

An ascetic /saintly person is considered to be an embodiment of virtues, as the requirement is to show, in action, a noble attitude/ universal kindness towards all forms of life,living in this world! Such a person will be designated as an "*anh-thaNar*"! (The term becomes meaningful,based on the excellence in (human)qualities, and 'not' by any other consideration). Please See Appendix-1.

CHAPTER-4

INSISTENCE ON VIRTUE

31. siRappu yeenum, selva-mum yeenum, aRaththin-oong-ku
aakkam (y)evanO uyirkku.

Following the virtuous path (*aRam*) in all actions will bring glory and wealth. For a living person, there could be no other strength which could prove to be better than the force of righteousness/virtues/ethics! (Note: The integrated concept of the three qualities is called: "*aRam*": Righteousness/ Virtues/Ethics). Kurals 34 & 35 describe the term.

32. aRaththin -oongku aakkam-um illai; athanai
maRath-thalin oong-ku illai kaedu.

There is no other greater strength, for a living-person, except following the path of virtues. There is no other greater harm which would result, if virtuous path is ignored. (Following the virtuous path becomes one's own strength; and ignoring it, will produce harm to the self (him/her)!

33. ollum vakaiyaan aRa-vinai Ovaa-thae
sellum vaai yellaam seyal.

In an acceptable way, any virtuous act must be done, without fail, without violating the codes of norms, in whatever possible ways it can be affordably done (by words, or deeds or thoughts)!

34. manaththu-kkaN maas(u)-ilan aathal anaith-thu aRan;
aakula nheera, piRa.

Absence of bad thoughts in one's own mind is the sum total of all forms of virtues. Other attitudes (traits) correspond to vanity (showiness/ pretentious acts) only.

35. azhu-kkaaRu, avaa, vekuLi, innaa-ch-chol, nhaan-kum
izhukkaa iyandRathu aRam.

Virtue is defined as the acts free from four aspects, namely, jealousy (envy), greediness (avarice), anger and bitter words (evil-speech) which are not pleasant.

36. andRu- aRivaam yennaathu aRam-seika; matR(u)athu
pondRung-kaal pondRaa-th- thuNai.

Do not postpone any act of virtue (of helping others), by saying, 'let me do it some other day'. As a matter of fact, this act of generosity will be considered as an undying boon-companion when the process of death approaches a person.

37. aRaththu-aaRu ithu yena- vaeNdaa; sivikai
poRuth-thaan-odu oornh-thaan idai.

Any effort of preaching the details of benefits of following the virtuous path becomes unnecessary, to be explained, both to the persons carrying the palanquin, and to the person(s) riding inside it! (Any amount of preaching does not convince them, on virtues, as violation of virtues and human rights have already occurred in their acts. (Please See Appendix-1).

38. veezh-nhaaL padaa-mai nhandRu-aatRin, ah-thu- oruvan
vaazh-nhaaL vazhi adaikkum kal.

Do good things every day, without wasting even a day! This practice will correspond to a big stone/boulder to be placed to permanently close the path leading to next birth (rebirth)!

39. aRaththaan varuva-thae inbam; matRu yellaam
puRaththa; pukazhum -ila.

The pleasure coming to a person, in return for one's virtuous action (carried out to the benefit of others), is the only genuine pleasure/ happiness. All other pleasures are in vain, and those pleasures may not bring forth fame!

40. seyar-paala thO-rum aRanae; oruvaR-ku,
uyaR-paala thO-rum pazhi.

Any action recommended for usefulness must be a virtuous act/ righteous deed. Any other act, contrary to this effect, will bring bad reputation (blame) to a person! Any offensive (evil/wicked) act must be avoided!

CHAPTER-5

MARRIED LIFE

41. il-vaazh-vaan enbaan iyalb(u)-udaiya moovar-kkum
nhallaa-tRin nhindRa thuNai.

    A person who has chosen the path of married-life, by definition, is considered as a protector of the three categories of people, namely, wife, children and parents who are considered as natural dependents on him!

42. thuRanh-thaar-kkum, thuvva- thavarkkum, iRanh-thaarkkum,
il-vaazhvaan enbaan thuNai.

    The person who has chosen the family life, has got a bounden-duty to stand as a solid support to i) ascetics/saints, ii)poor people without a reliable support of income, and iii) the old people who do not have anybody else to support them.

43. then-pulath-thaar, theivam, virunh-thu –okkal, thaan-endRu – aang- ku
ai-m-pulathth(u)-aaRu Ombal thalai.

    The principal duty of a person in the married life is to extend hospitality to five categories of people, namely, i) vagabonds/ wise persons, ii) deceased-ancestors, family-gods, iii)guests, iv) relatives, and v) self and family!

44. pazhi-anchip-paaththooN udai-th-thaa-yin, vaazh-kkai
vazhi-yenj-chal ye-gn-gnaa-ndRum il.

    If those persons in married-life avoid any actions related to wickedness/ crime (but do things in accordance with prescribed code of norms), and practice the habit of sharing food with others, prosperity will not be disrupted in their lives. They will not face any hardship.(It is also interpreted that their descendants will not become childless!).

45. anbum aRanum udaiththu)u)-aayin, il-vaazh-kkai
paN-bum, payanum, athu.

The married-life of a person will be considered to have achieved the very purpose of life, commensurate with culture, grace, and benevolence (gain), if such a married-life possesses the merit of practicing love (kindness) and virtuous actions.

46. aRathth(u)- aatRin il-vaazh-kkai aatRin, puRaththu- aatRil
pOi-p- peRu-vathu ye-van?

Could there be any better benefits, if a family-man switches over to ascetic life (renouncing all the worldly pleasures), when he is presently leading the family-life, happily, in accordance with the virtuous path? (No additional benefit; no necessity to switch over, whatsoever!). (NOTE: This can be considered as a rebuttal to the belief that only persons who lead their lives in the ascetic order could reach the heaven. Refer to kural 50 which states that the heaven is kept open to those persons who lead a virtuous life, in the domestic way of life (family-life)!). Also, see kural 58.

47. iyal-bi-naan, il-vaazh-kkai vaazhbavan yenbaan
muyalvaar-uL- yellaam—thalai.

The person who leads the family-life in the virtuous path, with good personal qualities, deserves to be placed on the top of all those persons who (desire and) endeavour to lead a decent life in this world.

48. aatRin ozhukki aRan-izhukkaa il-vaazh-kkai
nhO-R-paarin nhO-n-mai udaiththu.

Persons in family-life who practice virtuous path in all their actions, and carefully avoid doing any action opposed to the virtuous path, will deserve equal merit, on par with those persons who have chosen the path of penance and who perform it correctly!

49. aRan-yena-p- patta-thae il-vaazh-kkai; a-h-thum
piRan -pazhip-pathu -illaa-yin nha-ndRu

Married life is extolled/glorified as the only virtuous path. It will be better appreciated, if actions blamed by others can be avoided!

50. vaiyath-thuL vaazh-vaang-ku vaazh-bavan vaan-uRaiyum
thei-vaththuL vaikka-p- padum.

A person (he/she) who leads a married life in this world, in accordance with the prescribed norms of the virtuous path, (as expected of any living-person), will be considered as one among the godly persons living in the heaven!

CHAPTER-6

VIRTUES OF A WIFE (LIFE-PARTNER)

51. manaith-thakka maaNb(u)-udaiyaL aaki-th- thaR- koNdaan
    vaLath-thakkaaL - vaazhkkai-th -thuNai.

    An ideal wife is as person who exemplifies in the domestic virtues, commensurate with the pride of the family, and controls the financial management of the family, within the limits of income-resources of her husband. (Note: In the modern concept, 'within the limits of family-income' is the criterion. There are people who exceed this limit!).

52. manai-maatchi illaaL-kaN il-laayin- vaazh-kkai
    yenai-maatchi-th- th(u)-aayinum il.

    If the honourable quality of moral values are absent in a wife, the husband will lose the merit, whatever be the greatness of the family, in other aspects!

53. illathu-yen illavaL maaNbu-aanaal; uLLathu—yen
    illaval maaNaak kadai?

    No other merit will be lacking in a man, if his wife has got the meritorious strength of virtues! If virtuous calibre is lacking in his wife, the husband will not have any praiseworthy possession of merit!

54. peNNiR perunh-thakka yaa –(v)uLa; kaRpu-yennum
    thiNmai uNd(u)-aaka-p- peRin?

    What other valuable blessings could be there, if a woman has got the meritorious strength of chastity (moral purity)?

55. theivam -thozhaaL; kozhu-nhan thozhuthu - yezhuvaaL;
    pei-yena-p – peiyum mazhai.

    A wife who does not even worship any god, but takes pleasure in giving prominence to her husband, always with respect, thereby earning the special regards for that value in society, will be considered as a beneficial person, just like a rain which rains (occurs) on being requested (commanded) to rain!

56. thaR-kaaththu-th- thaRkoNdaan paeNi-th- thakai-saandRa
soRkaaththu, sOr-v(u)-ilaaL peN.

An ideal woman is a person who protects herself in the life- style, and takes good care of her husband, and who controls her words to be pleasant, and who remains active always, avoiding lethargy. (Note: The term '*thar-kaath-thu*' means protecting her self-interest, including personal honour, safety, peace of mind, health, etc., as a member of the family).

57. siRai-kaakkum kaappu yeven sey-yum? makaLir
nhiRai - kaakkum kaa-p-pae thalai.

Who will prefer to keep women in confinement in the house? A woman has to protect her honour/chastity, herself, by her own will-power! That brings her the highest glory and self pride!

58. petRaal perRin peRuvar peNdir! perum-siRappu-p-
puththae-Lir vaazhum ulaku!

A woman, who gets a husband blessed with virtuous qualities in their family life, will get a prestigious fame in the heaven, where gods survive!

(Alternatively: If a woman practices all virtues expected of an ideal wife, in guiding the family towards prosperity, she will deserve a praiseworthy fame in heaven where gods survive!).(Note: In both versions of interpretations, it is established that both women and men will be rewarded equally, for their virtues practiced during their life-times!).

59. pukazh-puri-nh-tha il-illOr-kku illai ikazhvaar-mun
yaeRu- pOl- peedu nhadai.

For a man whose wife's moral qualities are not good, the pride of walking in style, like a prestigious lion, will not be possible for him! Others will not respect him!

60. mangalam- yenba manai- maatchi, matRu athan
nhan-kalam nhan-makkat paeRu!

The wife's wholesome excellence in virtues is considered as the splendour and pride of the family; and will be further glorified by the treasure of good children!

CHAPTER-7

CHILDREN AS A TREASURE

61. peRum- avatRuL yaam-arRivathu illai, aRivu-aRinh-tha
    makkat- paeRu; alla piRa.

    There cannot be any better benefit for the parents than having intelligent children in their lives. (poet's testimony).

62. yezhu- piRappum theeyavai- theeNdaa; pazhi piRang-kaa-p-
    paNpudai makkat peRin.

    Any evil effect will not occur to the parents, even during their seven births, if they have got children who lead their lives in the virtuous path, free from any evil act! (Second version: Any evil- effect will not happen to the parents, at any stage of their life-times, if they have got children who lead their lives in the virtuous path, free from any evil act!).

63. tham-poruL yenba- tham- makkaL, avar- poruL
    tham-tham vinai-yaan varum.

    Parents will claim that their children are their wealth, as that wealth comes to them through good deeds they perform, on behalf of their children!

64. amizh-thinum- aatRa inithae; tham makkaL
    siRu-kai aLaa-viya koozh.

    The simple food, such as gruel, made of boiled grains (or flour), dabbled and splashed in playfulness, by the tiny fingers of their babies, will be far far tastier to them, than even 'ambrosia', the divine food of the gods in heaven!

65. makkaL-mei theeNdal udarRk(u) –inbam; matRu –avar
    sol- kaettal inbam sevikku.

To the parents, the touch of their own babies is blissful to their bodies and mind, and listening to the words of their own-babies is blissful to the ears, and they will get elated in their feelings, as proud parents!

66. kuzhal- inithu, yaazh inithu, yenba, tham makkaL
mazhalai-ch – chol kaeLaa- thavar.

Those parents who have not enjoyed the blissful experience of listening to the infantile words of their own babies would only say that the sound of music coming from the flute (air-instrument) and lyre(*Yaazh*, a string-instrument) are pleasant to the ears!

(Note: '*Yaazh*';is a traditional music- instrument, in the category of string-instruments, which was being used in ancient Tamil-land, 2000 years ago. The string instrument was made out of fine iron-wire. The body of *Yaazh* was a harp-like fabrication carved out of a selective wood!). The term "*kuzhal*" may mean the musical instrument called "*Naadhaswararam*",or flute.

67. thanh-thai makaRku- aatRum nhandRi, avaiya-ththu
munhthi- yiruppa-ch- cheyal.

The primary duty of a father to the child is to do the needful to make sure that the child is placed in the fore-front of any forum of learned-people (by giving him/her an opportunity to learn and earn the required-merit through education).

68. thammin tham-makkaL aRivudaimai, maa-nhi-laththu
man-nu-yirkku yellaam inithu.

The knowledge earned by the children is more useful to others, living in this wide world, than the measures of happiness felt by the parents themselves.

(Another version: The intelligence of the next generation off- springs will be higher than the intelligence of the parents. It is a positive benefit for the society). It will bring happiness to parents, as well as to others. (Please see Appendix-1). Their brilliance must serve the welfare of the society. The poet fixes the responsibility on the persons who are blessed with a higher knowledge than their parents. Their brilliance is a societal- treasure. They must remain dedicated to societal benefit.

69. yeendRa- pozhuthiR perithu- uvakkum than-makanai-ch-
chaandROn yena-k- kaetta thaai.

The mother will have a higher degree of happiness when she hears her son/daughter being praised by others as a fair and wise person,than the happiness which she would have enjoyed at the moment of time of giving birth to the child.

70. makan – thanh-thaikku aatRum uthavi yivan-thanh-thai
yen-nhO-tRaan - kol-yenum chol

The primary duty of a son towards his father is to earn a praiseworthy word of appreciation from others, through his achievements, to the extent of others wondering as to how this father managed to get such blessings from the Almighty, to deserve getting such a meritorious child, and what kind of penance the father could have performed to appease the Almighty God? (Note: This concept applies to the female child also!)

CHAPTER-8

POSSESSING KINDNESS

71. anbiRkum uNdO adaikkum- thaazh? aarvalar
    pun-kaN- nheer poosal tharum.

    Is it possible at all to have a bolt to stop the true love (kindness) being shown to others? The sympathetic tears of an affectionate person appearing over the eyes, on seeing the distress of another person- in- grief, will reveal the true love (kindness) which is in store!

72. anbu-ilaar yellaam thamakku uriyar; anb(u)- uadai-yaar
    yen-bum uriyar piRar-k-ku.

    Persons who do not possess love (kindness) will acquire everything for themselves. But, those persons who do practice love (kindness), will dedicate everything to the welfare of others, including the very bones of their bodies!

    (Note: '*Enbum-uriyar-piRarkku*', as a phrase could mean that they would even be prepared to face bodily-injuries,for the sake of a person whom they love, if he/she gets into trouble at the hands of others! There are recorded evidences in this cruel world, to prove this point).

73. anbO-du yiyai-nh-tha vazhakku- yenba, aar-uyirkku
    yenbO-du iyai-nh—tha thodarpu.

    It is said that the human body and the soul are united firmly in the natural way, so as to function as a system. Similarly, our kindness in the mind and our actions in reality must be closely linked in our lives!

74. anbu-yeenum aarvam- udaimai; athu-yeenum
    nhaNb(u-y)ennum nhaadaa-ch- chiRappu.

    Kindness (love) towards another person yields a desire, towards the link, which, in turn, emerges as a friendship called a rare asset, for any person to acquire!

75. anbu-tRu amarnh-tha vazhakku – yenba, vaiyaka-ththu
inbu-tRaar yeithum chiRappu.

It is said that the honour which anybody living in this world would get is due to the benefit of having lived a successful life, happily, by sharing the affection / kindness towards every one!

76. aRaththi-Rkae anbu – saarbu yenba, aRiyaar;
maRath-thi-R-kum a-h-thae thuNai.

It is said that practicing of virtuous path is related to kind ness; Many people do not know that the same 'kindness' serves as the source of support for the acts of valour needed to remove evils! (Note: '*Rasigamani*'-T.K.C (Chidambaranathan Mudaliar) comes up with another interpretation: Kindness towards dependents makes a person to commit a crime and earn wealth, to remove the poverty of the beloved-ones! The reason is his love for his dependents. Thus, his 'love' becomes responsible for his 'non-virtuous' acts (*maRam*)! However, this needs further research, in the light of criminal psychology!). Kural 656 has to be compared!

77. yenb(u)-il athanai veyil- pO-la-k- kaayu-mae
anbu ila-tha-nai aRam.

Any creature without bones (invertebrates) in its body-structure will be burnt up by the scorching sun. Similarly, human beings without the tendency to show love and kindness towards others will be destroyed by the code of Virtuous Path which functions as a 'force' by itself.!

78. anbu –akaththu illaa uyir- vaazhkkai, vanpaaR-kaN
vatRal-maram thaLirth-th(u) -atRu.

The person leading a life without any kindness in the heart will not flourish (prosper), just like a decaying tree which does not sprout (put forth shoots), in a hard desert land!

79. puRaththu-uRuppu yellaam yeven- cheyyum; yaakkai
akath-thu-uRuppu anb(u) - ilavarkku.

What is the use of external parts of the human body, if the quality of kindness in one's mind towards others is totally absent? (Note: The poet considers that the body and soul, put together, constitutes the structure (a system)). The living status of a human body must be based on the path of love (kindness).

80. anbin- vazhi-yathu uyir-nhilai; a-h-thu –ilaar-kku
yenbu-thOl pOrththa udambu.

The living status of a human body must be based on the path of love/kindness. For those who do not possess the quality of love (kindness), the surviving human body will only be considered as a structure of bone (skeleton) covered with skin.

CHAPTER-9

DOMESTIC HOSPITALITY

81. irunh-th(u)- Ombi il-vaazhva- th(u)-yellaam, virunh-thu-Ombi vaeLaaNmai seitha-R- poruttu.

    The very purpose of taking care of the family-properties and leading a family-life is for the purpose of practicing hospitality extended to guests!

82. virunh-thu puRaththa-thaa-th- thaan-uNdal, saavaa maru-nh-th(u)-yeninum vaeNda-R-paatR(u) andRu.

    When a guest is waiting outside the house (waiting to see you), eating your food in privacy, all by yourself, is prohibited, even if it happens to be a medicinal food which would (/could) save your life!

83. varu-virunh-thu vaika-lum Ombu-vaan vaazhkkai paru-vanh-thu paazh-paduthal indRu.

    A family-man who extends hospitality to guests every day, will not be affected by any sufferings related to poverty!

84. akan-amar-nh-thu seyyaaL-uRaiyum, mukan-amar-nh-thu nhal-virunh- thu Ombu-vaan il.

    The goddess of wealth will reside in his house with her wholehearted happiness, if a person extends hospitality to his guests, with a cheerful face! (*'sey-yaaL'* = Goddess Lakshmi).

85. vith-thum idal- vaeNdum kollO, virunh-thu-Ombi mich-chil misai-vaan pulam.

    Would it be necessary to sow the seeds in the land owned by a person who maintains the habit of hosting the guests and eating the food from whatever remains (as left over) in the bowl. (Alternatively: A generous person will not hesitate to use the seeds of grains to host a guest, instead of safeguarding it, to be kept in reserve, for sowing in the land! (Ref:KalaignarUrai).

(Note: A host will not hesitate to use the grain which has been kept in reserve as 'seed', when a guest comes in, unexpectedly. It means an utter poverty of having exhausted all the grain-reserves in the house. Failure to host the guest will reveal the poverty. In that situation, the host does not hesitate to utilize the seed-grain for cooking, instead of saving it for being sown in the cultivable land, when the season begins. This couplet highlights the importance of domestic hospitality, as a duty- bound obligation, on the part of a family-man).

86. sel-virunh-thu Ombi, varu-virunh-thu paarthth(u)-iruppaan
nhal-virunh-thu vaanath- thavarkku

The person who has extended hospitality satisfactorily to an outgoing guest, and is looking forward to receive a forthcoming guest, will become eligible to be a guest to the gods, the occupants of the heaven!

87. inaith-thuNaiththu yenbathu-ondRu illai; virunh-thin
thuNai-th-thuNai vaeLvi-p- payan.

It is not possible to quantify the benefit that would reach the person who extends hospitality to guests. Extending hospitality is like performing a rigorous penance (or performing a ritualistic sacrifice)! The benefit coming to the host will depend upon the importance of the guests.

88. parinthu-Ombi –p- patRu-atRaem yenbar, virunh-thu-Ombi
vaeLvi thalaip-padaa- thaar.

Those who did not take efforts to entertain hospitality to guests, and relatives, when they were wealthy, will later on regret for having lost touch with relatives and friends, and it is a pity that this realization comes to them only when they lose all their wealth, and become poor!

89. udaimai-yuL inmai virunh-thu-Ombal Ombaa
madamai madavaar-kaN uNdu.

Poverty of a wealthy person is nothing but the unwillingness of a rich person to extend hospitality to guests. Failure to practice hospitality, in spite of their wealth, can be found in the attitude of stupid- persons.

90. mOppa-k- kuzhai-yum ani-ch-cham; mukam-thirinh-thu
nhOkka-k- kuzhai-yum virunh-thu.

'*Anichcham*' flower, being soft and delicate, would get withered, if it is being held near the nose to enjoy its fragrance.

Similarly, the guest will get upset, if the host reveals an unpleasant gesture (by facial expression, or by the nature of words uttered, while receiving the guest!)

CHAPTER-10

UTTERING PLEASANT WORDS

91. in-solaal yeeram-aLaiyi-p- padiRu-ilavaam
sem-poruL kaNdaar- vaai-ch- chol.

The pleasant words coming from the mouth of the learned and wise persons will emerge out of the warmth and love contained in their hearts, and will be free from falsehood/mischief/ill-will/deceit

92. akan-amarnh-thu yeeathal-in nhandRae; mukan-amarnh-thu-
in-solan aaka-p- peRin.

Uttering pleasant words, with a cheerful face, to a person is considered to be better than giving a gift of material value, to a person with the wholehearted -willingness!

93. mukath-thaan amarnh-thu,inithu nhOkki, akath-thaan-aam
in-sol in-athae aRam.

The virtue is defined as the practice of uttering sweet (pleasant) words coming from the bottom of the heart, with a pleasant-look emerging from the face (countenance)!

94. thun-puRoo-um thuvvaamai yillaakum, yaar-maattum
inbuRoo-um in-sol- avarkku.

The painful poverty will not come to any person who makes it a point to utter only pleasing words to all persons.

95. paNivu-udai-yan, in-solan, aathal oruvarkku
aNi; alla-matRu-p- piRa.

Becoming a person, well-known for the virtue of humility, and pleasant words, is considered as an ornament to the person concerned. All other ornaments are of no value!

96. allavai thaeya, aRam-perukum; nhallavai-
nhaadi, ini-ya solin.

If a person makes it a point to seek good objectives, and to practice using only pleasant words, the genuine virtue will flourish in him, and any adverse effect will recede (go away) from him!

97. nhayan-yeendRu nhan-adRi payakkum; payan yeendRu
paNpin thalai-p-piriyaa-ch- chol.

Words which are capable of extending benefit to others which are uttered pleasantly, without deviating from courtesy/culture, will yield profit to the person who practices it, in addition to benefit of merit (fame)/ happiness!

98. chiRumai-yuL nheeng-kiya in-sol, maRumai-yum
immai-yum inbam tharum.

Sweet words, free from insulting effect on others, will yield happiness during this birth and subsequent births! (Also,interpreted as happiness during lifetime and thereafter). Good words of great persons become 'quotes', after their,demise!

99. in-sol inithu - yeendRal kaaNbaan, yevan-kolO
van-sol vazhang-ku vathu.

Why should a person utter cruel words, especially when the person knows about the pleasant effects produced by the kind words to all?

100. iniya uLavaaka, innaatha kooRal
kani-yiruppa-k- kaai-kavarnh-thu -atRu.

Uttering unacceptable (unpleasant) words when pleasant- words are readily available, is similar to a person being attracted by unripe fruits, when the fully-ripe fruits are readily available. (In eating the unripe fruits, the taste may not be enjoyable).

CHAPTER-11

SENSE OF GRATITUDE

101. seyyaamal-seitha udhavikku vaiyakam-um
vaanakam-um- aatRal arithu.

A person extends a help to the another person without having received any help from the benefited-person! In such a case, if the benefited person wants to pay back (the debt/gratitude), even the entire world and the sky above will not be considered as a sufficient compensation (to clear the debt!)! (The word '*vai-ya-gam*' implies the earth-planet, and '*vaa-nagam*' implies the universe!).

102. kaalaththi- naal- seitha nhandRi, siRithu-yeninum
gnaa-lath-thin maaNa-p- peri-thu.

A help extended to any person at the hour of need will be considered as bigger than this planet earth itself, even if the size of such a help received is smaller in value/magnitude. (Note: It (the sense of gratitude) depends on the attitude of the person who received the help).

103. payan-thookkaar seitha udhavi, nhayan-thookkin
nha-nmai kadaliR perithu.

The help rendered by any person without expecting any help in return (from the beneficiary), is a great help. If the worth of the act is assessed, its value is far more larger than the vast sea itself.

104. thinaith-thuNai nhandRi seyinum, panai-th-thuNai-yaa-k
koLvar payan-theri- vaar.

Although the value of help received is smaller than the size of a millet-grain, persons who receive it, will consider that help to be equivalent (equal) to be of the size of the seed of a palm tree which is several times larger than the size of a millet grain! (Note: Millet-seed will yield benefit whenever it is sown to the field during every season! But, a seed of palm- tree, if planted once, will grow into a big tree, and will start giving many benefits to the planter, during his/her lifetime, and beyond! The benefit will continue for many generations! This is the basis of comparison between the two seeds!

(Note: There are other interpreters who compare the size of a millet grain with the size of a palm tree itself! This needs a debate!

However, it is logical to compare the size of one seed with that of the other seed).

105. uthavi varaiththu-andRu uthavi; uthavi
se(i)ya-p-pattaar saalbin varaith-thu.

The value of help rendered is not the real value. The deserving wor thiness of the recipient will stand for the value of the help rendered! (Note: If the beneficiary is a poor person, the help rendered is considered larger!).

106. maRavaRka maasu-atRar kaeNmai; thuRavaRka
thunbath-thuL thuppu-aayaar nhatpu.

Do not forget the acquaintance with the great people who are free from abuses/blames. Do not discontinue your friendship with those who did not desert you when you were in trouble.

107. yezhumai yezhu-piRappum uLLuvar; tham
kaN vizhumam thudaith-thavar nhatpu.

A wise person will recollect, with pleasure, during his/her seven births (seven generations/ during times of elevated prosper ity) about the greatness of friendship of those good people who had wiped out tears from his/her eyes at the time of his/her sufferings!

108. nhandRi maRappathu nhandRu-andRu; nhandRu-allathu
andRae maRappathu nhandRu.

It is not beneficial to forget the sense of gratitude for the benefit received by you from others. On the contrary, a bad occurrence needs to be forgotten on the very same day of its occurrence, itself.

109. kondRu-anna innaa se(y)yinum, avar-seitha
ondRu-nhandRu uLLa-k- kedum.

If a person has committed a bad act, such as an act equivalent to committing a murder, or a heinous crime, it will get nullified, if the affected person recollects one single good act done to him, during the past, by the alleged offender, to the benefit of the affected- person.

110. yen-nhandRi kondRaar-k-kum uivu-uNdaam; uivu-illai
sei-nhandRi kondRa makar-R-ku.

There is no hope for betterment in future life for a person who has erased (killed) in his mind, the very memory of the help received by him from others. In contrast, there is hope for betterment in future life, even for anyone who has violated any other virtue! (Also interpreted as: A son or daughter who does not take care about the welafare of parents will not prosper/flourish in life).

CHAPTER-12

NEUTRALITY

111. thakuthi yena- ondRu nhandRae pakuthi-yaal
paaR-pattu ozhuka-p- peRin.

Practicing impartiality (neutrality) is the only one virtuous policy, in situations warranting the interactions with people who remain divided among themselves on issue-based problems! (It implies one's response in a secular-society)

112. seppam udaiyavan aakkam sithaivu-indRi
yech-chaththiRku yae-maappu udaiththu.

The wealth of a person well-known for neutrality/rectitude/ honesty, will not perish, and will bring glory to his/her descendants, for generations!

113. nhandRae tharinum nhaduvu-ikanh-thu-aam aakkaththai
andRae ozhiya vidal.

Avoid forthwith accepting any treasure, if it comes to you for relaxing/ overlooking your determined will-power in maintaining your neutral stand! (even if you are made to believe that it would bring benefits to you).

114. thakkaar thakavu-ilar yenbathu avar-avar
yech-chath-thaal kaaNa-p- padum.

The quality of the person, whether the person is virtuous or non-virtuous will be known, depending on the fame left behind by him/her, after his/ her death!

115. kaedum perukkamum il-alla; nhenj-chaththu-k-
kOdaamai saandROrkku aNi.

Affluence and poverty are not uncommon in the real-world- scenario. Whether they are in affluence or in poverty, the wise persons will not deviate from neutrality in their minds, and it is considered that it is a proud ornament for such persons!

116. keduval-yaan yenbathu aRika; than nhenj-cham
nhadu-oree-yi alla seyin.

When a person knows that he/she is deviating from the path of neutral stand (neutrality), let that person realize that he/she is destroying himself/herself by that deviation!;

117. keduvaaka vai-yaathu ulakam; nhaduvaaka
nhandRikkaN thang-kiyaan thaazhvu.

The people of the world will not find fault with the poverty of a person who maintains the honour of dwelling in (maintaining the path of neutrality! The society will only admire (adore) him/her.

118. saman-seithu seer-thookkum kOl-pOl, amainh-thu –oru-paal
kOdaamai saandROr-kku aNi.

A weighing balance decides the true weight of an object by balancing the two pans, with reference to a neutral mark. Similarly, wise persons maintain a fair stand without deviating from neutrality. Such an act is considered as a prestigious ornament to wise persons.

119. sol-kOttam il-lathu seppam; oru-thalai-yaa
uL-kOttam inmai peRin.

If the internal mind system does not deviate from neutrality, while doing mediation/arbitration, the words spoken out, externally, will not deviate from neutrality!

(Note: The poet insists on the neutrality of responsible persons en trusted with authority).

120. vaaNikam sei-vaarkku vaaNikam paeNi-p-
piRavum thama-pOl seyin.

Business transactions will ever flourish, if those persons involved in business take care of the commodities, as their own,until selling it to buyers!

CHAPTER-13

SELF CONTROL

121. adakkam amarar-uL uikkum; adang-kaamai
aar-iruL uith-thu- vidum

Persons who practice the virtue of humility/modesty will earn the status of salvation, on par with the dwellers of heaven! Those who violate humility/ modesty will earn the destination of deep darkness/unending sufferings!

122. kaakka poruLaa adakkath-thai; aakkam
athanin-oong-ku illai uyirkku.

Humility/modesty is considered as a treasure. For any per son, there is no other treasure worthy enough to possess!

123. seRivu-aRinh-thu seermai payakkum; aRivu-aRinh-thu
aatRin adang-ka-p- peRin.

Any action performed with modesty, after having understood the details of the norms, will be appreciated, being weighed upon the richness of value which the action deserves.

124. nhi-layil thiri-yaathu adang-kiyaan thOtRam
malai-yinum maaNa-p- perithu

The greatness of a person who practices humility/modesty, without deviation from the prescribed code of norms, will be valued far larger than the greatness (loftiness) of a mountain.

(Note: The loftiness of the Himalayan-Mountain is poetically cited to highlight the virtue of a human being, in the literary tradition in India!).

125. yellaarkkum nha-ndRaam paNithal; avar-uLLum
selvar-kkae selvam thakai-ththu.

Practicing humility is good for all persons. Among them, it is more important for rich persons, to be valued as wealth within wealth (which corresponds to additional wealth).

126. orumai-yuL aamai-pOl ainh-thu –adakkal aatRin
yezhumai-yum yae-maappu udaith-thu

If a person exercises control over the five senses, like the Tortoise controlling its limbs, within its shell, it will bring merit (glory) during all the seven births. (Alternatively, interpreted as. the merit (glory) will continue, even after attaining advanced progress in life!). (*yezhumai*= upheaval to prosperity in life).

127. yaa-kaa-vaar aayi-num nhaa-kaakka; kaavaa-k-kaal
sO-kaappar sol-izhukku-p- pattu.

Even if it is not possible to have a control over anything else, at all, it is a must that a person exercises a complete control over the words of the tongue. If not, the defaulter will suffer in distress, due to the evil effects of disgrace of the words, so uttered.

128. ondRaa-num thee-ch-chol poruL-payan uNdaa-yin
nh-andR (u)-aakaathu aaki vidum.

Even if one bad word is uttered, in the cluster of words spoken out by a person, for a well-meaning benefit, the benefit conveyed by other good words will also be distorted! Misunderstood!

129. theeyi-naal chutta-puN uL-aaRum; aaRaa-thae
nhaa-vi-naal chutta vadu.

A wound caused by fire may get healed on the inside. But the scar produced by a burning-word of the human tongue will never get healed! (Note: The difference between a wound and a scar is brought out clearly).

130. katham -kaaththu-k- katR(u)- adangkal aatRuvaan chevvi
aRam-paarkkum aatRin nhu-zhainh-thu.

The divine quality (personified-force) called virtue will be looking forward to join the person who has got the maturity of practicing modesty, commensurate with his/her good learning, and applying restraint (control) over his/her anger!

CHAPTER-14

GOOD CONDUCT/CHARACTER

131. ozhukkam vizhuppam thara-laan, ozhukkam
uyiri-num Omba-p- padum.

Good conduct/character yields greatness/eminence/majesty, and hence, it must be truly practiced dearer than one's own life itself.

132. parinthu – Ombi-k- kaakka ozhukkam; therinthu-Ombi-th-
thaeri-num a-h-thae thuNai.

Good conduct must be practiced with liking and devotion, (even during hard times)! On analysis of benefits availed by practicing all the various other virtues, it is confirmed that good conduct is the best virtue which can offer a firm protection for one's own life!

133. ozhukkam udaimai kudimai; izhukkam
izhi-nh-tha piRappaa-i vidum.

Owning the strength of good conduct will reflect the birth in a good family. Bad conduct will reflect a mean (low) birth. (Note: Good conduct is claimed to enjoy a honour for the family in which the person is born!).

134. maRappi-num Oth-thukkoLal aakum; paa-r-ppaan
piRappu -ozhukkam kundRa-k- kedum.

If a priest, born in a Brahmin family, loses the memory of the vedic-scriptures, it is possible to learn it again. If the priest does not practice good conduct, he will lose the benefit of his birth in a good family. Please see Appendix-1.

(Note: Sri C.Rajagopalachari (Rajaji) adds, in his translated version of "Kural; The Great Book of Tiru-Valluvar", Bharatiya Vidya Bhavan, 1965, in page 20, as follows: "What is lost in learning may be made up for, but what is once lost in the way of life is lost for ever". He adds: "The caste-system regulated the society in the days of 'our-poet'. The Brahmin had the duty of study and teaching. If the scripture was forgotten by the Brahmin, he lost the purpose of his elevated rank. But this, says the poet, could be made up for, by fresh study! Not so, however, could the Brahmin regain his position, once he fell into the error of neglecting the regulation of the life prescribed for him. Ignorance or the neglecting of prescribed study was a great offence in the Brah min. But a greater offence was the neglect of the discipline of life prescribed for him!:").

135. azhukkaaRu udaiyaan-kaN aakkam-pO-ndRu, illai
ozhukkam yilaan-kaN uyarvu.

A person who possesses jealousy will not get any wealth, or the wealth that he gets will be dissipated. So also, a person without good conduct/ character will not get any betterment in life!

136. ozhukkath-thin olkaar uravO-r; izhukkath-thin
yae-tham padu-paakku aRinh-thu.

Those who have got a firm determination in the mind, will not practice anything contrary to good conduct, as they are aware of the distress that would result due to non-compliance of good behaviour!

137. ozhukkath-thin yeithuvar mae-n-mai; izhukkath-thin
yeithuvar yeithaa-p- pazhi.

Those who practice good conduct will attain betterment in life. Those who practice bad conduct will get blame and abuse which cannot be erased for ever.

138. nhandRikku vith-thaakum nhal-ozhukkam; thee-(y)ozhukkam
yendRum idumbai tharum.

Good conduct/character is the seed for producing beneficial results in one's life. Bad conduct/character will yield perennial distress.

139. ozhukkam udai-ya-var-kku ollaa-vae, thee-ya
vazhukki-yum vaayaal solal.

Bad words will not be uttered, even by the slip of the tongue, in the case of those who practice good conduct!

140. ulakath-thOdu otta ozhukal pala- katRum
kallaar aRivu -ilaa- thaar.

Those who do not learn to live with the other people of the world, in agreement with the prescribed norms of the society are considered as ignorant persons, lacking worldly wisdom, even if they have learned many things.

CHAPTER-15

AVOIDANCE OF IMMORAL DESIRE

141. piRan -poruLaaL pett(u)-ozhu-kum pae-thai-mai gnaa-la-ththu
aRam-poRuL kaNdaar-kaN il.

A righteous person will not be attracted by another person's wife, as he has understood the norms of the world relating to virtues and human bonds.

142. aRan-kadai nhi-ndRaaruL yellaam piRan-kadai
nhi-ndRar-in paethai-yaar il.

A person will be a greater fool, if he stands near the door of a neighbour with bad intentions and immoral desires, when com pared to a person who violates other virtuous norms.

143. viLinh-thaar-in vaeRu -allar; mandra theLinh-thaar-il
theemai purinh-thu- ozhuku- vaar.

A person will be considered as a dead person, if he devel ops an immoral desire towards the wife of another man who believes the person undoubtedly.

144. yenaith-thuNaiyar aayinum yen-naam; thinaith-thuNaiyum
thae-raan piRan-il pukal.

Whatever be the greatness of a person in all respects, if he enters another man's house with immoral intentions, the person becomes worthless; his human value being diminished to lesser than the size of a millet seed!

145. yeLithu-yena il-iRappaan yeithum; ye-gn-gnaa-ndRum
viLi-yaathu nhi-Rkum pazhi.

If a person commits an immoral act with another man's wife, thinking that the act is easy to be done, the sense of guilt will haunt his conscience and the blame will stay imperishable with him, through out his life-time, and beyond! (Note: The blame will persist until his death, and afterwards too, in peoples' memory about him! Bad reputation!!).

146. pakai-paavam ach-cham pazhi- yena nhaa-n-kum
ika-vaa-vaam il-iRappaan kaN.

If a person commits an immoral act with another man's wife, he will be inheriting the four curses, namely, enmity with many others, the effects accruing for committing a sinful act, a permanent fear in the mind affecting his tranquility, and a life-long blame against his name as a scar on his personality!

147. aRan-iyalaan il-vaazhvaan yenbaan piRan-iya-laaL
peNmai nha-ya-vaa- thavan.

A person will be regarded and respected as a virtuous per son in the family- life, if he is free from the temptation of being at tracted by the beauty of another man's wife!

148. pirRan-manai nhO-kkaa-tha pae-raaN-mai saandROr-k-ku
aRaN- ondRO! aandRa ozhukku!

If a man maintains a moral strength of not being attracted by another man's wife, the merit reflects not only the strength of virtue, but also the greatness of an exemplary character.

149. nhalakku – uriyaar, yaar-yenin, nhaa-ma-nhee-r vaippin
piRarkku-uriyaaL- thOL- thO-yaa- thaar.

If a question is asked as to who will be eligible to be called as the most pleasant and praiseworthy person in this wide-world surrounded by the noise-producing seas (which induce fear in the mind), the answer will be the person who has never embraced the shoulders of another man's wife, for a lustful act!

150. aRan-varaiyaan alla se(i)-yi-num piRan-varai-yaaL
peNmai nha-ya-vaamai nha-ndRu.

Even if a person cannot fulfill the obligations related to vir tuous acts, to qualify for beneficial effects, or happens to commit some non-virtuous acts, these defaults will be forgiven, if a person could avoid developing an immoral desire towards another man's wife!

CHAPTER-16

PATIENCE AS A VIRTUE

151. akazh-vaarai-th- thaa-ngku-m nhi-lam-pO-la-th thammai
ikazhvaar-p- poRuththal thalai.

Land (earth) bears the weight of those persons who dig it,, and deface it! Therefore, it becomes the duty of any one person to bear with any other person who causes insult to the self. In that case, it becomes a virtue of patience!

152. poRuth-thal iRappi-nai, yendRum; athanai
maRath-thal athani-num nha-ndRu.

If someone oversteps the norms, either by word, or deed, it is better for the affected person to bear with (endure) the offence, when it happens! Forgetting the episode is far better!!

153. inmai-yuL inmai virunthu -oraal; vanmai-yuL
vanmai mada-vaar-p- poRai.

Poverty within poverty corresponds to one's inability to extend hospitality to guests. In contrast, the strength within strength (for any person) corresponds to the patience in bearing with (forgiving) the foolish acts of the ignorant folks.

154. nhi-Rai-yudaimai nhee-ng-kaamai vaeNdin, poRai-yudaimai
pO-tRi ozhuka-p- padum.

If a person decides that the wholesomeness of greatness should not depart from the self, it becomes necessary, for that person, to practice patience, with pride and conviction, in his/her life!

155. oRuth-thaarai ondRaaka vaiyaarae, vaippar
poRuth-thaarai-p- pon-pO-l pothi-nh-thu.

Persons causing offence to others will not be considered as equals to others in the society. Persons practicing patience will be placed in high esteem by the people, similar to the gold being carefully embedded (laid) with perfection!.

156. oRuth-thaar-kku oru –nhaa-Lai inbam; poRuth-thaar-kku
pondRum thuNai-yum pukazh.

The joy of those causing harm to others will remain with them, giving them cheer, only for a day! On the contrary, the fame of those persons bearing with the ordeal will remain forever, until the time of their demise!

157. thiRan-alla, thaR-piRar sei-yi-num nhO-nho-nh-thu
aRan-alla sei-yaamai nha-ndRu.

Even if others do something unlawful and harmful to you, do not do anything opposed to virtuous norms, to them, in retaliation, after brooding over the pains of being hurt. (That response of yours will be good for your own interests!).

158. mikuthi-yaan mikkavai sei-thaarai-th- thaam-tham,
thaku-thi-yaan vendRu vidal.

If the mightier persons, induced by arrogance and muscle- power, cause harm to others, in violation of the code of virtues, the intelligent way of responding to them, will be better appreciated, if the susceptible person decides to win over the offenders, by up- grading the worthiness/status of the self (by hard work and perse verance!).

159. thuRa-nh-thaarin thooy-mai udai-yar, iRan-thaar- vaaii
innaa-ch-chol nhO-R-kir- pavar.

Persons who endure the bitter words by the unruly persons, will be considered nobler than those who have renounced this worldly lives, having reputation of living in virtuous path! (Note: Those unruly persons will be branded as dead persons, as indicated by the word '*iRa-nh-thaar*').

160. uNNaa-thu nhO-R-paar periyar; piRar-sol-lum
innaa-ch- chol nhO-R-paar–in pin.

Those good persons who practice fasting without eating food, as a ritualistic penance, will be considered great only next to those who endure the insulting words of others. (Note: Persons who endure the insulting-words of others deserve more merit!).

CHAPTER 17

AVOIDANCE OF ENVY

161. ozhukk(u)-aaRaa-k- koLka; oruvan-than nhe-nj-chath-thu
azhu-kk-aaRu il-aatha, iyalbu.

Every person must make it a practicing-principle to make it a natural quality (firm belief in the mind) to be free from jealousy.

162. vizhupp(u)-aetRin a-h-thu, oppathu illai,yaar-maattum
azhukkaatRin- an-mai peRin.

For any person, there is no other virtue to be acquired which would be equal (or superior), in merit, to the absence of jealousy, in the mind! Absence of jealousy deserves more merit.

163. aRan- aakkam vae-Ndaa-thaan enbaan, piRan-aakkam
pae-Naathu azhu-kkaRu-p- paan.

A person who does not appreciate the wealth of another person, and harvests jealousy, instead, will be considered as a person who does not aspire for moral strength of virtues or prosperity for himself /herself! (If you want virtue to remain with you, and if you want prosperity to come to you, please do not develop jealousy!).

164. azhukkaatRin alla-vai sei-yaar, izhukkaatRin
yae-tham padu-paakku aRi-nh-thu.

Nobody will dare to cause any evil deed to others, out of jealousy, knowing well, fully, that the after-effects of such an act would bring misery to the self (to his/her life)!

165. azhukkaaRu udaiyaar-kku, athu-saalum, onnaar
vazhukki-yum, kaedu yeen-pathu.

If any person practices jealousy, the jealousy itself will be sufficient to destroy that person, even if enemies fail to cause destruction to that particular person.

166. koduppathu azhukk-aRup-paan chutRam(um), udup-pathoo-vum uNbathoo-vum indRi-k- kedum.

A person who, out of jealousy, prevents others from giving monetary/ material help to the needy, will be destined to suffer without food and clothes! The offender will lose all links with his kith and kin!.(Note: The word 'chutRam(um)' has been used in the couplet, to convey the correct sense which the poet would have meant). Three adverse effects are mentioned: i) loss of link with kith and kin; ii) suffering without food, and iii) suffering without clothes!). This needs a debate.

167. av-viththu azhuk-kaaRu udai-yaanai- ch- cheyya-vaL, thavvai-yai-k- kaatti- vidum.

Out of jealousy, if a person develops bad thoughts in the mind, the goddess of wealth will send (forward) the person to the goddess of poverty! (before the person starts initiating bad deeds)!

168. 'azhuk-kaaRu' yena- oru 'paavi', thiru-ch-chetRu-th- theey-uzhi uy-ththu- vidum.

A contemptible (sinful) force called 'jealousy' will destroy the wealth of a person who practices jealousy, and it will drive the person to commit evil acts, and get ruined.

169. avviya nhe-nj-chath-thaan aakkamum, chevvi-yaan kae-dum, nhi-nai-kka-p- padum.

The great wealth of a person who practices jealousy, on one side, and poverty of a virtuous person on the other side, are the two issues which deserve to be remembered for a deeper analysis, as those situations do not correspond to normalcy!?

(Note: It is a reality which cannot be justified logically. This needs research as to what the poet wants to say on this topic!). The poet thinks that virtue in a person must be rewarded, instead of being punished to suffer in poverty? The poet does not seem to believe in the Fate-Theory to justify the sufferings of the righteous persons! Hence, he raises a question about it!). This needs a debate, comparing it with kural 37.

170. azhukkaatRu* akand-Raar-um illai; ah-thu-ill-aar
perukkath-thil theer-nh-thaar-um il.

No record exists to show that persons practicing jealousy enjoyed greater prosperity, or to show that persons free from jealousy would have a reduced (lesser) prosperity! (It is better to avoid jealousy!) (Note: * '*azhu-k-kaatRu* = persons who follow the path of "*azhukkaaRu*= jealousy).

(The first word of the couplet "*azhukkatRu*" was modified, as "*azhukk-aa-tRu*", to suit the meaning given by Parimael-azhakar). Please note that "*azhukk-aa-tRu*" = "*azhukk(u)-aa-tRu*",

CHAPTER-18

AVOIDANCE OF COVETING/COVETOUSNESS

171. nha-duvu- indRi nha-n-poruL veh-kin kudi-pondRi-k-kutRam-um aang-kae tharum.

    Without a justified approach, if a person desires to possess another man's legitimate property, the offender's family will get destroyed, and will be subjected to a permanent blame!

172. padu-payan- veh-ki pazhi-p-paduva, sei-yaar nhaduvu-anmai nhaaNu- pavar.

    Those who shy away from planting violence, because of their deep conviction (belief) in virtues, will not commit the blunder of desiring for snatching away the property of another person, (although knowledge of benefits coming from some relaxation in their firm-policies is already known to them). They will not be attracted by those 'rewarding-worldly-benefits', which would come to them through their wrong-doings! This implies that they are well-aware of the probability of adverse effects which would follow them, if they commit any wrong doings!

173. chitRinbam veh-ki, aRan–alla seiyaa-rae matru-inbam vae-Ndu- pavar.

    Those who aspire for eternal bliss will not desire to be attracted by small pleasures which are opposed to virtuous path!

174. ilam- yendRu veh-kuthal chey-yaar pulam-vendRa pun-mai-yil kaatchi- yavar.

    Those good persons who have overcome the temptations of their five senses, and have earned a bright reputation (fame) for themselves, will not stoop down to develop a desire for acquiring another person's property, on the excuse (pretext) that they are poor!

175. ah-ki- akan-dRa aRivu - yen-naam, yaar-maattum
veh-khi veRiya se(y)-yin.

What is the use of intensive,exhaustive and extensive knowledge of a person, if he/she desires to acquire the property of any other person,in methods opposed to the fame of such a great knowledge!? If a highly educated person happens to violate the norms, it will result in a self-insult on him/her!(whoever does it).

176. aruL- veh-ki aatRin-kaN nhi-ndRaan poruL- vehki
poll-laatha choozha-k- kedum.

A person who wishes to earn divine blessings and sustain himself in virtuous path,will get destroyed, if he/she wishes to have materialistic gains through illegitimate means!

177. vae-NdaRka, veh-ki aam-aakkam; viLai-vayin
maaNdaRk(u)- ari-thaam payan.

No person should aspire for acquiring another person's property/wealth! If a person uses it after becoming the owner of that property/wealth, by violating the norms, and if it starts growing, the yields will not bring glory to that person. On the contrary, it will prove to harmful to that person!

178. a-h-kaamai sel-vath-thiRku yaathu-yenin, veh-kaamai
vae-Ndum piRan- kai-p- poruL.

If a person desires that his/her wealth must not get reduced, the desire of that person will get fulfilled,only if that person does not desire for acquiring another person's wealth by fraudulent means!

179. aRan-aRinthu veh-kaa aRiv(u)-udaiyaar-ch chae-rum
thiRan- aRi-nh-thu aang-kae thiru.

Wealth will reach those honest persons who practice the virtuous path, in not developing a desire for another person's wealth, as the wealth itself knows the moral strength of such persons (who deserve to be honoured and rewarded!).

180. iRal-yeenum yeNNaathu ve-h-kin viRal-yeenum
vae-Ndaamai yen-num serukku.

If a person desires eagerly to secure another person's prop erty in an illegitimate move,such a coveting-act would cause destruction (ruin) to the offender! If a person has got the proud conviction that he/she will not develop any desire for acquiring another person's property, that conviction itself will yield all successes in whatever act he/ she carries out!

CHAPTER-19

AVOIDANCE OF SLANDERING /BACK-BITING

181. aRam-kooRaan alla seyi-num oruvan
puRam-kooRaan yendRal inithu.

If any person who does not indulge in back-biting (slanderous talk) against anybody, such a person must be appreciated, even if he does something bad, which deserves to be branded as non- virtuous!

182. aRan-azhee-yi alla-vai seitha-lin thee-thae
puRan-azhee-yi poiy-th-thu nakai.

To talk something ill about a person to others, in the absence of the person concerned, and to exhibit a deceitful (false) smile, while meeting the same person, is far more evil than doing things against the dictates of thevirtuous path!

183. puRam-kooRi-p- poiy-ththu- uyir- vaazh-tha-lin, saathal
aRam-kooRum aakkam tharum.

If a person indulges in back-biting (slanderous talk) against others, and utters lies for the purpose of shameless survival, it will be concluded that death will be preferable than survival, for such a person, as death would offer (/bring) all benefits to him as ensured in the codes of virtue.

184. kaN-nhi-ndRu kaN-aRach- chollinum, choll-aRka
mun-nhindRu pin-nhOkkaa-ch- chol.

Even if you utter a merciless word to another person, while facing him face to face, in front of his eyes, you must not speak out anything bad about him, in his absence (behind his back), using any adverse-word without examining the ill-effects produced by such words!

185. aRam- sollum nhe-nj-chath-thaan anmai puRam-sollum
pun-mai-yaal kaaNa-p- padum

The genuineness of truthfulness in the heart of a person who habitually praises the virtuous path, will be revealed, if he/she indulges in the shameful habit of back-biting (talking bad about a person behind his/her back).

186. piRan- pazhi kooRu-vaan than-pazhi- yuLLum
thiRan-theri-nh-thu kooRa-p- padum.

If a person highlights the faults of others, the faults of that person will be selectively chosen, for being told to others.

187. paka-ch-cholli-k- kae-Lir-p- pirippar, nhakach-cholli,
nhatp(u)-aadal thae-tRaa- thavar.

Some persons who do not have a liking for the humorous and friendly way of interacting with one another, among friends, will take fancy in spreading back-biting words to cause breaking of friendship, so that the group collapses. Such persons can never maintain a good friendship. (This will happen even among relatives).

188. thunni-yaar kutRam-um thootRum marabi-naar
yennai-kol yae-thilaar maattu.

If those persons who propagate, with bad taste, the short- comings of their own intimate friends, it is wondered as to what they would do to unknown strangers?.

189. aRaN- nhO-kki aatRung-kol vaiyam puRan-nhOkki-p-
pun-sol uraippaan poRai.

To bear the body-weight of those persons who indulge in speaking out slanderous words, about any person in the absence the concerned person, the planet earth considers that it is its bounden duty to bear the weight of such (shameless) persons also, out of charity/merciful considerations!? (Such persons do not deserve that mercy!).

190. yae-thialaar kutRam-pOl, tham-kutRam kaaN-kiR-pin
theethu - uNdO mann-um uyirkku.

In the matter of back-biting, if the faults committed by others are treated on par with the faults of one's own self, will there be any harmful effects, at all, on any living person who desires to live long in this world? (Analyse your own fault, in practicing the bad habit of back-biting! Do not talk about the faults of others. Then, all things will be safe for every one, in this world, including yourself!)

CHAPTER 20

AVOIDANCE OF USELESS WORDS

191. pallaar muni-ya-p- payan-ila sollu-vaan
yellaar-um yeLLa-p- padum.

A person who speaks out useless words, earning a displeasure (resentment) from many other persons, will finally end up being ill-treated by all.

192. payan-ila pallaar-mun sollal nhayan-ila;
nha-ttaar-kaN sei-thalin thee-thu.

Speaking useless words in the presence of many others is far worse than doing unkind (offensive) things against one's own friends!

193. nha-yan-ilan yenbathu sollum payan-ila
paarith-thu uraikkum urai

If a person speaks out useless words, in elaborate conversations, it will be understood (inferred) that the person does not have any virtue or intelligence!

194. nha-yan-saaraa nhanmai-yin nheekkum; payan-saaraa-p-
paNbu-il –sol pallaar- akaththu.

If a person speaks out useless words which do not have any relevance to any benefit, or if his/her words lack good culture, it would end up affecting the impression about his/her virtue or worthiness! Good benefits will not reach that person.

195. seermai- siRap-podu nheeng-kum; payan-ila
nheer-mai- yudai-yaar solin.

If persons of good conduct utter useless words, their importance/fame and dignity/grace will disappear (in the minds of others, about those persons)!

196. payan-il-sol paaraatu-vaanai, makan-yenal
makkat- pathadi yenal.

A person who practices the usage of useless words deserves to be called as worthless person, such as a chaff-of-men, instead of being known as a wholesome man!

197. nhayan-ila solli-num sollu-ka; saandRO-r
payan-ila sol-laamai nhandRu.

Virtuous persons must not utter useless words, even if they happen to utter 'not-so-good' words (which will not be commensurate with their praiseworthy-quality!).

198. arum-payan aa-yum aRivi-naar sol-laar
perum-payan illaa-tha sol.

Wise persons who are used to examine the valuable benefits of words, will not utter words which will not have larger ben efit / meaning / value / significance!

199. poruL-theernh-tha, poch-chaanh-thum sol-laar; maruL-theer-nh-tha
maas(u)-aRu kaatchi- yavar.

Wise persons who are free from confusion, and blessed with faultless enlightenment, will not utter useless words, even by absent-mindedness!

200. sollu-ka; sollil payan-udaiya; sol-laRka
solli-l payan-ilaa-ch chol.

Do utter words, after choosing the meaningful and beneficial words. Do not utter words which will not yield any benefit, among the many words known to you!

CHAPTER-21

FEAR FOR EVIL ACTS

201. thee- vinai-yaar anj-chaar; vizhumi-yaar anj-chu-var;
thee-vinai yennum cherukku.

Persons of wholesome character will be afraid of commit ting any evil act! Bad elements who are capable of enacting evil acts out of arrogance, will not be afraid of committing any evil act, without knowing that the false pride coming out of it is a deceitful/ misleading belief!

202. theeyavai theeya payath-tha-laal, theeya-vai
thee-yi-num anj-cha-p- padum.

Evil acts will yield evil effects, and hence, the evil acts will be feared for, more than the fear for fire!

203. aRivin-uL yellaam thalai-yenba; theeya,
cheRu-vaar-kkum seyyaa vidal

The most important form of wisdom is to practice the avoidance of causing harm to even an enemy who had caused harm to you in the past!

204. maRa-nh-thum- piRan- kaedu soozhaRka; soozhin,
aRam -soozhum; soozh-nh-thavan kaedu.

Even in forgetfulness, no person should devise a plot (plan) to cause any harm to another person! If this principle is violated, the force of Virtue (justice/righteousness/ethics) will plan causing destruction to the person who violates!

205. ilan - yendRu theeya-vai sei-yaRka; sei-yin,
ilan-aakum; matRum peyarth-thu.

Do not do any harm to a person, thinking that the recipient is a poor person who cannot retaliate. If you do any harm, you will become a poor person,yourself, in return for what you did! Your position will revert itself from abundance (wealth, riches) to poverty!!)

(Note: This interpretation needs further research). Please see kural 174 to examine the difference between the word "*ilam*' used in kural 174 and the term "*ilan*" used in kural 205. Please see Ap pendix-1.

206. thee-p-paala thaan- piRar-kaN sei-yaRka; nhOi-p-paala
thannai adal- vae-Ndaa- thaan.

If a person who does not want any form of distress to occur to himself/ herself, then, he/she must not cause anything injurious to another person. (Similarity: Do not do unto others, what you do not want others to do unto you!: This is a rhyming couplet often taught by teachers in schools to their students!)

207. yenai-p-pakai utRaarum uy-var; vinai-p-pakai
vee-yaa-thu pin- sendRu adum.

Any person having a severe enmity with another person, may even survive; But the aftermath of any evil act, as a force, will chase the offender, without break to cause destruction to the offender!

208. thee-ya-vai sei-thaar keduthal, nhi-zhal-thannai,
vee-yaa-thu adi -uRai-nh-thu- atRu.

Distress will attach itself at the very heels of those who committed evil act to others, similar to the shadow of the self, getting attached to the feet!

209. thannai- th-thaan kaathalan aayin, enaithth(u)-ondRum,
thun-naRka thee-vinai-p- paal.

If a person possesses love for the self, then, he/she must not commit any evil act (unworthy act/sinful act) which would cause harm to others. The policy should be to keep away from evil- path.

210. arung-kae-dan yenbathu aRika; marung-ku- Odi-th
thee-vinai sei-yaan yenin.

If a person avoids deviating from the right path to cause an evil act to others, let it be known that, even the rarest of rare-evil effect will not happen to him!

CHAPTER-22

DESIRE TO HELP THE NEEDY

211. kaim-maaRu vae-Ndaa-k- kada-p-paadu, maari-maattu
    yen-aatRum -kollO ulaku.

    How can the people of the world pay back the Nature to compensate the donation of rainfall which enhances the prosperity of the world? Therefore, those good persons who practice philanthropy (charity) do not seek any favour, in return, for whatever they donate! (Please see kural 218).

212. thaaL –aatRi-th- tha-nh-tha poruL –yellaam thakkaar-k-ku
    vaeLaaNmai seithal poruttu.

    An ideal person will think that the purpose of earning wealth, through hard labour, will be to use it for distribution to deserving persons, for taking care of their benevolence/welfare! (It should be the objective of those privileged-persons who are blessed-with wealth).

213. puth-thae-L ulakath-thum yeeNdum peRal- arithae,
    oppurav(u)-in- nhalla piRa.

    It is difficult to find another act which will bring equal effect as one's willingness * to help others who are in need, in this world, and in the world of gods, in yielding benefits to the recipients, and in bringing fame to the donor! (* Note; service to society, act of benevolence / beneficence, charity, philanthropy, moral support to righteous persons, voluntary help to those who are in distress are covered in this aspect).

214. oth-thathu aRivaan uyir- vaazh-vaan; matRaiyaan
    seth-thaa-ruL vaikka-p- padum.

    A person will be considered as a living person only if he/she possesses the natural tendency to offer material (and moral) help to needy people!

Others, who do not practice this noble action (or attitude) are considered as dead persons!

215. ooruNi nheer-nhiRai-nh-th(u) -atRae, ulaku-avaam
paer-aRi- vaaLan thiru.

The accumulation of drinking water in the village tank, up to the brim, will benefit the people. It is comparable with the ever- growing wealth of the most generous, benevolent and wise person (who knows the needs of the people)!

216. payan-maram uL-Loor-p- pazhuth-thu- atRaal, selvam
nha-yan-udai- yaan-kaN padin.

If wealth is made (accumulated) by a benevolent person, who possesses the desire to use the wealth for good purposes, it is like a useful tree, bearing edible (sweet, ripe) fruits, being located in the middle of one's own village! (The benefit will reach the people in both cases!).

217. marunth(u)-aaki-th- thappaa maraththu-atRaal, selvam
peru-nh-thakai- yaan-kaN padin.

If the wealth accumulates with the most generous person, who believes in practicing philanthropy, it is like having a herbal tree which never fails to cure the illness of people!(That great person will help the needy, all the time!). (Note: Herbal use of vegetation is highlighted).

218. idan-il paruvath-thum oppuraviRku olkaar,
kadan-aRi kaatchi- yavar

The wise person who visualizes his obligations to the society around him will not hesitate to practice philanthropy even during time-periods when his wealth is dwindling.(Note: This moral is applicable to both genders. Such persons will be regarded as those who are enlightened with a clear vision about the purpose of life!).

219. nhayan-udaiyaan nhal-koor-nh-thaan aathal, seyum-nheera,
sei-yaathu amaika-laa- vaaRu.

The inability of a benevolent person to continue with the usual charitable/ philanthropic activities is felt as the real poverty of an erstwhile rich person! (The good person regrets, and the society loses the benefit!).

220. oppura-vinaal varum kaedu-yenin, a-h-th(u)- oruvan
vitRu-kkOL thakkathu- udaiththu.

If it is thought that philanthropy would lead to loss of wealth, then, it can be said that such a loss deserves (is worth) to be purchased by selling one's own self!

CHAPTER-23

CHARITY

221. vaRiyaarkku- ondRu yeevathae yeekai; matRu yellaam
kuRi- yethirppai nheera-thu udaith-thu.

Giving a material help to the poor persons, typically, qualifies for being called as charity! Giving material help to all others will correspond to reciprocal acts, enacted-in- anticipation of (expected) returns!

222. nhall-aaRu yeni-num koLal -theethu; mael-ulakam
il-yeni-num yeethalae nhandRu.

Begging is bad, although it is approved in the path of virtues! It is always beneficial to give material help to others, even if anybody says that the heaven (upper world) will be denied to a person who practices the art of giving! (Note: The poet is expressing fear that false propaganda could even be spread in the name of eligibility to enter the 'heaven after death', falsely theorizing that those who liberally give to others will not be eligible to enter the heaven! Ignorant people are there to believe in, whatever they are being told! That is why the poet gives a caution not to believe whatever is being told, without examining it, vide kural 423).

223. ilan –yennum yevvam urai-yaamai yeethal,
kulan-udai-yaan kaNN-ae uLa.

Giving materialistic help to others is a prestigious attitude, readily found in persons hailing from good family background (without outwardly revealing their situation of poverty-ridden in- ability to do such a help).

224. innaathu irakka-p-paduthal, ira-nh-thavar
in-mukam kaaNum aLa-vu

It is a painful experience for the giver, when a person comes for begging, until the giver is able to see the cheerful face of the receiver (the beneficiary)!

225. aatRuvaar aatRal pasi- aatRal; ap-pasi-yai
maatRuvaar aatRalin pin.

The power of those who are fasting to perform the ritualistic penance is ranked as meritorious, only next to those who quench the hunger of the poor people. (Giving food to the starving-persons is considered as the most meritorious service!).

226. atRaar azhi-pasi theerth-thal, a-h-thu - oruvan
petRaan poruL - vaip- puzhi.

The act of feeding the poor people with timely food, to save them from the killing-hunger, is considered as the store-house (repository/warehouse), for the safe-keeping of the material-wealth of the fortunate (wealthy) persons! (That is how the person will feel, if the person is good!).

227. paath-thooN maree-yi yavanai-p- pasi-yennum
thee-p-piNi theeNdal arithu.

Hunger, also known as a fiery (fire-like) disease, will not touch a person who has become habituated to share his/her food with others.

228. yeeth-thu- uvakkum inbam aRiyaar-kol, thaam-udaimai
vaith-thu –izhakkum- van-Ka- Na-var.

Those merciless persons who accumulate their wealth, without sharing with others, often happen to lose their wealth, due to some unknown reasons. Don't they know the value of happiness they would have enjoyed (cherished) in their minds, through the art of giving to others who are needy?

229. irath-thalin- innaathu; mandRa, nhi-rappiya
thaa-mae thami-yar uNal.

If a person eats the food out of his huge earnings, all by himself, without sharing the food with others (fearing that the wealth will get reduced), it can be said that his action is more miserable than the agony of begging from others!

230. saatha-lin innaatha-thu illai; inith(u) athoo-(v)um
yeethal iyai-yaa-k- kadai.

Nothing is more miserable than death! However, even death is considered to be pleasant when compared to the poverty which prevents a person from giving material help to others, thus, making the person unworthy of helping others! (This is how the person will feel, if the person is capable of respecting his own self-respect!).

CHAPTER-24

FAME

231. yeethal isai-pada vaazhthal, athu -allathu,
oothiyam illai uyirkku.

Apart from performing charity, and living a life of praise- worthy fame, there is no other benefit in human life, for a living per son.

232. urai-p-paar urai-p-pavai yellaam, ira-p-paarkku- ondRu
yeevaar-mae-l nhiRkum pukazh.

Those who talk about good things happening in this world, will be talking all about the standing-fame of the donor who readily gives moral help/ material help/alms to any deserving - person who begs for help!

233. ondRaa ulaka-ththu uyar-nh-tha pukazh-allaal,
pon-dRaa-thu nhiRpathu- ondRu il.

Excepting the lofty fame accumulated by a person through good deeds, there is nothing which remains as a treasure, without getting destroyed in this everlasting world.

234. nhila-varai nheeL-pukazh aatRin, pulavarai-p-
pO-tRaathu puth-thae-L ulaku.

If a person acquires a great fame which spreads beyond geographical boundaries of lands, in the planet earth, through good deeds, the heaven will praise him/her, more than praising the heavenly persons (who are immortal)! (Alternatively: Persons with great fame earned through selfless service will be respected more than wise persons with bookish knowledge only).

235. nhath-tham-pOl kaedum, uLath(u)-aakum saakkaadu-m,
vith-thakar-kku allaal arithu.

Paste made from rubbing a conch-shell is used as a medicine for children. Similar to it, wealth of a virtuous person is being given to the benefit of others, making the virtuous person poor, similar to the conch -shell becoming thinner. Fame for such a virtuous person increases. Facing a natural death with glory will only be possible for such great persons who make sacrifices for the welfare of others! That kind of glory will not be available to others!

236. thO-ndRin pukazhodu thO-ndRuka; ah-thu-ilaar
thO-ndRalin thO-ndRaamai nha-ndRu.

If any person is born in this world, the entry of the person will be better appreciated, if some contribution is going to be made by that person to the benefit of the society, so that the person may deserve a fame! In the case of others who are not capable of generating a similar fame for themselves, their entry or non-entry into this world may not produce any significance!

(Inference: If person enters a field/discipline/career, he/she must create a fame for the self, through sustained proficiency/excellence in knowledge, earning an undisputed fame! If people are not able to achieve that level of excellence, their entry or non-entry may not produce any significance in the chosen field!). (Note: Contribution of knowledge by an individual person is considered important to the field of study). (Please see Appendix-1)

237. pukazh-pada vaazhaa-thaar, tham-nhO-vaar, thammai
ika-zh-vaarai nhO-vathu yevan?

Those who live without earning fame start blaming others who happen to insult them. Why should they blame so? They have to blame themselves, for 'not-earning' the merit of fame through their own good deeds!

238. vasai –yenba vaiya-th-thaarkku yellaam, iasi-yennum
yech-cham peRaa-a- vidin.

All those who live in this world, have to remember that it will be considered as a disgrace, if no specific fame (renown) is left behind their names, as the overall-remains, which would be counted positively towards their fame, after their departure from this worldly life!

239. vasai- ilaa vaN-payan kundRum, isai-ilaa
yaakkai poRuththa nhilam.

The land (soil) which bears the body-weight of a person without any fame will be considered as a non-fertile land!

(Note: Fame comes to a land through the useful people born in the land!).

240. vasai- ozhi-ya vaazhvaa-rae vaazh-vaar; isai-ozhi-ya
vaazh-vaa-rae vaazhaa- tha-var.

Persons leading their lives, free from any kind of abuse/ disgrace, are considered to be enjoying their praise-worthy lives. Those who lead their lives, without earning any kind of fame (renown), whatsoever, are considered to leave no record of their ex istence.

CHAPTER-25

GRACIOUS ATTITUDE

241. aruL-selvam selvath-thuL selvam; poruL-selvam
poori-yaar kaNNum uLa.

Wealth of wealth is understood as the wealth of kindness/compassion, as the material wealth is available even with the wicked and cruel persons, or persons without any merit, whatsoever!

242. nhal-aatRaan nhaadi aruL- aaL-ka; pal-aatrRaal
thaer-inum a-h-thae thuNai.

Seek and practice the virtuous path in all your actions, by showing kindness (compassion) to all! In whichever stream a per son may be trained, the virtuous path will be the ultimate support for a living-person!

243. aruL sae-r-nh-tha nhenj-chinaar-kku illai; iruL-sae-r-nh-tha
innaa ulakam pukal.

The entry into the darkness-related distress (the Hell) is negated (denied) for those who possess a kind heart with a gracious compassion. (They deserve their places only in the heaven!). ('No - Entry' into the Hell, for good people).

244. mannuyir-Ombi aruL-aaL-vaar-kku, il-yenba
than-uyir anj-chum vinai.

For a person who takes care of all the forms of life on earth, and administers (shows) compassion, there is no necessity for any burden of worrying about the life (safety) of the self!

245. al-lal aruL - aaL-vaar-kku illai; vaLi-vazhang-kum
mallal-maa gnaa-lam kari.

There is no distress for a person who practices kindness and compassion, as witnessed (evidenced) by people living in the air-circulated world which is with full of abundance/affluence/wealth and fertility.

(Note: Movement of air in the atmosphere is described as a characteristic feature for the enrichment of the components of the Environment, namely, air,water, soil, and ecological factors).

246. poruL nheeng-ki-p- poch-chaa-nh-thaar yenba, aruL-nheeng-ki
alla-vai seithu- ozhuku- vaar.

Those who are deviating from the path of kindness and compassion, committing cruel acts prohibited by virtuous path are branded as persons who are hardened enough to deviate from the righteous path and who have forgotten the very purpose of their lives!

247. aruL ill-aarkku av-vulakam illai; poruL- ill-aarkku
iv-vulakam illaa-ki- yaang-ku.

This world is not meant (to live happily) for those who do not have enough wealth available with them! Similarly, there will be no place in the heaven,for those who do not have enough merit earned by performing good deeds of kindness and compassion during their life-times in this world! (Alternatively, it is also said that those persons who do not develop any objective to be pursued, will not be able to live a meaningful life in this world!)

248. poruL- atRaar pooppar, oru-kaal; aruL-atRaar
atRaar; matRu aathal arithu.

Those who are presently without wealth, may even become wealthy (prosperous) in future. But, those persons who have not practiced kindness and compassion during their life-times will never qualify themselves for any redemption/salvation. It becomes impossible to change it, at that stage.

249. theruLaathaan mei-p-poruL kaNdu-atRaal, thae-rin
aru-Laa-thaan sei-yum aRam.

If a person, not practicing kindness and compassion, tries to give material help to others, for the sake of publicity, and if the merit is assessed, it would be considered that it is as futile as a person without wisdom attempting to have a perception of the true beings (divine knowledge)!

(Note: perception means: ability to see or hear or become aware of 'something' through the senses! Ref: Greek Philosopher Plato's philosophy!).

250. vali-yaar- mun thannai-nhinaikka; thaan, than-nin
meli-yaar-mael sellum- idaththu.

Any man should remember, and contemplate, at the time of rushing upon a person who is weaker than himself, as to how he would tremble (get terrified), if persons mightier than himself ever come upon him! (This helps the person who wants to claim that he practices kindness and compassion).

CHAPTER-26

REFUSAL TO EAT FLESH

251. than-oon perukkaRku –th- thaan- piRithu oon-unbaan
ye-gn-gna-nam aaLum aRuL?

How would it be possible, for sure, for a person to show kindness and compassion when he is in the habit of eating the flesh of another creature for promoting the growth of his own flesh (body)!

252. poruL- aatchi pO-tRaa-thaar-k-ku illai; aruL-aatchi
aang-ku- illai oon-thin- pavar-kku.

For those who do not take care of their property, the benefits of the property will not be available. Similarly, the nature of administering kindness and compassion will not be possible for those who eat flesh of another creature!

253. padai-koNdaar nhenj-cham-pOl nhandRu-ook-kaathu, ondRan
udal-suvai- uNdaar manam.

The mind of a warrior in the battlefield will not encourage kindness and compassion. He will be worried about the performance of his weapons available on his hands to cause injury to his enemy. Similarly, the minds of the persons who are used to enjoy the body-taste of flesh of another creature will not encourage showing kindness and compassion towards the living- creatures!

254. aruL -alla-thu yaathu-yenil kollaamai; kO-Ral
poruL- alla-thu av-voon thin(n)al.

Action related to enactment of kindness and compassion is nothing but avoidance of killing. Eating the flesh of any creature is not a virtuous (meaningful) act!

255. uNNaamai uLLathu uyir-nhilai; oon-uNNa
aNNaaththal seiyaa-thu aLaRu.

Avoidance of eating flesh of another creature by human being, if practiced, will have relevance to the very survival and multiplication of those species,in the dictates of nature's predominance! If a person practices the eating of flesh of any creature, the hell will finally swallow him,and will not let him out. (The wide mouth of the hell will be closed, once the food goes inside!).

256. thinaR-poruttaal kollaa-thu ulaku-yenin, yaarum
vilai-p-poruttaal oon-tharu-vaar il.

If the people of the world decide not to kill the living-creatures, for the purpose of eating, there will not be anybody to kill the living creatures, and offer it for sale!

257. uNNaamai vae-Ndum pula-al, piRithu-ondRan
puN; (N)athu uNar-vaar-p- peRin.

Determination not to eat flesh is recommended, as it becomes essential to realize that, after all, the flesh is the wounded- portion of the body of another living creature!

258. seyirin thalai-p-piri-nh-tha kaatchi-yaar uNNaar
uyi-rin thalai-p-piri-nh-tha oon.

Wise persons who have got liberated themselves from the act of causing harm to another living creature and making it to suffer, and subsequently acquired the enlightenment (vision), will never practice eating of flesh!

259. avi- sori-nh-thu aayiram vae-ttalin, ondRan
uyir-sekuth-thu uNNaamai nhandRu.

The practice of 'not-killing' a living creature, and 'not-eating' its flesh is far more beneficial than performing a thousand ritualistic sacrifices by pouring voluminous quantities of ghee(derivative of butter) to the burning fire to appease the deity to whom the sacrifice is offered!

260. kollaan pulaa-lai maRuth-thaanai-k- kai-kooppi
yellaa uyirum thozhum.

All living creatures on this earth will raise their hands up- ward and worship a person who refuses to either kill a living creature or to eat its sflesh!

CHAPTER-27

PENANCE

261. utRa- nhOi nhO-ndRal, uyir-kku - uRu-kaN seyyaa-mai
atR-ae thavath-thiR-ku uru.

The practice of genuine penance incorporates the endurance of sufferings of the self, and avoidance of causing harm to any form of life (to human beings or any other creatures)!

262. thavam-um, thavam-udai-yaar-kku aakum; avam, atha-nai
a-h-thu- ilaar maeR-koL- vathu.

The self-imposed penance is meant for those who can do it by observing the necessary restrictions, and by following the prescribed code of virtuous path. Let not those persons undertake penance,if they do not have any of these qualities, for the sake of pretentious looks! Shame upon those who pretend!

263. thuRa-nh-thaar-kku-th- thup-puravu vae-Ndi, maRa-nh-th-aar-kol
matRai- yavar –kaL thavam?

For the very purpose of feeding the ascetics/saints, those persons in domestic-life have forgotten to choose the path chosen by the ascetics! Could that be true?! (How great is their attitude?! It is really a life devoted to sacrifice).

264. onnaarth- theRa-lum, uva-nh-thaar-ai aakkal-um
yeNNin, thavath-thaan varum.

It is possible for an ascetic/saint to control the enemies, and uplift the useful persons, through his/her meditation, if he/she de sires so!

265. vae-Ndiya, vae-N-diyaang-ku yeitha-laal, sei-thavam,
yeeNdu muyala-p- padum.

Whatever is wished for is achieved as desired, in the life of an ascetic/saint, and hence, it is considered worthwhile to pursue the practice of Penance!

266. thavam-sei-vaar tham-karumam sei-vaar; matRu, allaar
avam-sei-vaar, aasai-yut-pattu. (ut-pattu=uL-pattu).

Ascetics are those who perform their assigned duty! All others commit certain unacceptable acts, being overcome by temptations!

267. chuda-ch-chudarum pon-pOl oLi-vidum, thunbam
chuda-ch-chuda nhOR-kiR- pavar-kku.

The more heated in the fire, the more will be the brightness of glow of the melting-gold. Similarly, repeated exposure to burning-hardships gives the refinement/elegance/wisdom to those who observe fasting and penance. (Note: An industrial process of melting gold was indicated 2000 years ago).

268. than-nuyir thaan-aRa-p - petRaanai, yae-naiya,
man-nuyir yellaam thozhum.

All other forms of life (souls) in this world will worship a person who has liberated himself from the sensation of 'me' and 'my life', from his mind, relinquishing all that belongs to the self, thus qualifying himself as an ideal ascetic/saint! (This applies to females also in the ascetic order).

269. kootRam kuthi-th-tha-lum kai-koodum, nhO-tRa-lin
aatRal thalai-p-pat- tavarkku.

Challenging and bypassing (routing/diverting/overcoming) death would even become handy, for an ascetic who pursues the power of penance! (Note: This applies also to females in ascetic- order!).

270. ilar-palar—aakiya kaaraNam, nhO-Rpaar
silar; palar nhO-laa thavar.

Those who practice penance, and become powerful are not many!Several persons are reluctant to (or fail to) take up the trouble of pursuing rigorous penance, thereby, lacking power and, thus, undergoing distress!!

CHAPTER-28

BAD CONDUCT

271. vanj-cha manath-thaan padi-tRu ozhukkam, boothang-kaL ai-nh-thum aka-th-thae nhakum.

    The five senses of the body system will ridicule (smile) in shame, within himself, about the lustful conduct of a bad person (pursuing penance) with a deceitful mind

272. vaan-uyar thO-tRam yeven-sei-yum?; than nhenj-cham thaan-aRi kutRap-p- padin.

    What is the use of a sky-high appearance (of an ascetic), if his own conscience laments (regrets) the guilt known to his own self?

273. vali-yil nhi-laimai-yaan val-luruvam petRam puli-yin-thO-l pO-rththu-mae-i-nh-thu atRu.

    A person in the ascetic discipline who has got a huge body without a strong control on the status of mind will be viewed as a person resembling a cow covered with the skin of a tiger, grazing (eating grass) in the field. (Note: Pretentious role is the objection).

274. thava(m)-maRai-nh-thu allavai-seithal puthal-maRai-nh-thu vae-ttuvan puL-simizh-ththu atRu.

    A person who hides himself in the outward appearance of an ascetic/ saint, indulging in bad (sinful) activities, is just like a hunter who hides himself behind a bush before striking at a bird, for catching it, in his hunting activity!

275. patRu atRae-m yenbaar paditR(u)- ozhukkam yetRu-yetRu-yendRu yae-tham pala-vum tharum.

    Anybody who proclaims that he has renounced all forms of desires, and yet indulges in lustful conduct, has to end up landing in a sequence of distresses, one after another, making him regret for his acts, for having committed a wrongful act, as if he committed this act without deep-thinking!committing the worst offence against humanity.

276. nhenj-chil thuRa-vaar, thuRa-nh-thaar-pOl vanj-chith-thu
vaazh-vaar-in van-ka-Naar il.

Those persons who do not renounce their worldly desires in their hearts, and yet, pretend as ascetics, living in a life of cheating and falsehood, are worse than cruel persons committing the worst offence against humanity!

277. puRam -kundRi kaNda-nai-ya rae-num akam-kundRi
mookkil kari-yaar udaith-thu

This world owns some persons, whose appearance is fair, resembling the red colour of the red berry (Abrus precatorius, '*kuNdumani*', crab's eye, rosary pea, jequirity bean). But their heart is as dark as the nose of the same-berry!

278. manath-tha-thu maas(u)-aaka maaNdaar-nh-eer aadi maRainh-thu-
ozhu-ku(m) maanh-thar palar.

It is surprising to note that there are persons living in this world, possessing dirt in their minds, and yet pretending as honourable persons in the society, doing cheap tricks such as disappearing in the flowing river-water to claim a show of strength, and, still, practicing a hideous conduct in the background! Unbelievable!!

279. kaNai-kodithu, yaazh-kOdu, sev-vithu; aang-ku anna
vinai-padu paa-laal koLal.

Arrow is of straight shape, but it produces harmful results, if used! Lyre (a string instrument, resembling Guitar) is of curved shape, but it gives a pleasant music! Therefore, let people be assessed by their deeds (usefulness), instead of their (pleasing) appearances!!

280. mazhi-th-thalum nhee-ttalu-m vaeNdaa; ulakam
pazhith-tha-thu ozhi-th-thu vidin.

Neither shaving of the head nor growing long hair will be required (needed), if it could be assured that all the actions forbid\den by the wise men in the world can be completely avoided, in one's actions, in the life of an ascetic, in this world!

CHAPTER-29

AVOIDANCE OF STEALING

281. yeL-Laa-mai vae-Ndu-vaan yenbaan, enai-th-thu - ondRu-m
kaLL-aamai kaakka - than nh-enj-chu

A person desirous of being free from abuse (blame) must protect himself/ herself, from the act of stealing anything from others.

282. uLLath-thaal uLLa-lu-m thee-thae; piRan poru-Lai-k
kaLLath-thaal kaL-vae-m yenal.

If a person permits an idea of stealing another person's property by fraudulent means to crop up in his mind, that 'thought' itself corresponds to an evil act.

283. kaLa-vi-naal aakiya aakkam, aLav(u) iRa-nh-thu
aava-thu pOla-k- kedum.

Any asset generated through fraudulent means will get destroyed, beyond normal limits, although it would appear as if it is growing! (Even a nominal portion may not remain!).

284. kaLa-vin-kaN kandRi-ya kaathal, viLai-vin-kaN
vee-yaa vizhu-mam tharum.

The callous (insensitive /cruel) desire stored in one's mind on acts related to robbery, will yield endless evil-effects, when it starts producing results (dividends), after such illegal acquisition!.

285. aruL-karuthi anbu-udaiyar- aathal, poruL-karuthi-p-
poch-chaappu-p- paarp-paar –kaN il.

Becoming a kind person in appreciation of mercy and grace,will be impossible, for any person who is waiting for the forgetfulness of others, for grabbing/stealing their properties.

286. aLavin-kaN nhi-ndR(u)- ozhukal aatRaar, kaLavin-kaN
kandRi-ya kaatha- lavar.

Those persons who practice callous/cunning desire in executing robbery will not be able to adjust their life-style in measured- bounds (within their affordable limits)!

287. kaLavu- yen-num kaar-aRi- vaaN-mai, aLavu- yennum
aatRal purinh-thaar-kaN il.

The obscured (dark /cunning) and hidden knowledge of fraudulent activity will be absent in those persons who have got renowned strength of practicing norms for earning their livelihood, within their limits (leaps and bounds!). The term *'kaar-aRiv(u)-aaNmai'*=dark knowledge. implying instinctive capacity to devise/design dark deeds.

(Note: Similarity in the core idea: Obscurus=dark; derived from Latin word).

288. aLavu- aRinh-th-aar nhenj-chath-thu aRam-pOla nhi-Rkum
kaLavu- aRinh-thaar nhenj-chil karavu.

Deceitful traits (characteristics) dwell (prevail) in the minds of robbers, similar to the manner in which virtuous qualities are stored in the minds of those wise persons (who are mindful about limiting their desires).

289. aLavu-alla seithu, aang-kae veevar, kaLavu-alla
matRai-ya thae-tRaa- thavar.

Those who are capable of involving only in fraudulent activities, and who do not put their faith in doing good works, are likely commit more and more crimes, and get ruined!

290. kaLvaarku-th- thaLLum uyir- nhi-lai; kaLLaar-k-ku-th
thaLLaa-thu puth-thaeL ulaku.

In the case of fraudulent persons, they will be hated by their own 'souls'! But the souls of those good persons free from any fraudulent activity, can find entry into the heaven! (Admission to the heaven will not be refused for those good souls!).

CHAPTER-30

TRUTHFULNESS

291. vaa-y-mai yena-p-paduvathu yaa-thu, yenin, yaathu-ondRum
theemai ilaa-tha solal.

Truthfulness means telling the words which are completely free from evil, in any form, whatsoever! To whomsoever, it may be!

292. poy-mmai-yum vaa-y-mai idath-tha, purai-theer-nh-tha
nha-n-mai paya-kkum yenin.

Uttering a lie will be treated on par with truth, if such an act produces benevolent result! (which is free from harm)!

293. than- nhenj-chu aRivathu poy-ya-Rka; poy-th-tha-pin
than- nhe-nhenj-chae, than-nai-ch chudum.

Let there be no falsehood by any person, on any matter, already known to one's own mind. If it happens, one's own mind (conscience) would cause a burning (scorching) fire to the mind of the self. (Peace of mind will be disturbed).

294. uLLath-thaal poyyaa-thu ozhukin, ulaka-th-thaar
uLLath-thuL yellaam uLan.

True to his/her heart, if a person maintains a virtuous path, free from falsehood (in words, thoughts and deeds), that person will dwell (remain) in the hearts/minds of all the people in the world.

295. manath-thodu vaa-y-mai mozhi-yin, thava-th-thodu
thaananj- chei- vaarin thalai. (thanam seivaarin thalai).

A person speaking the truth, true to his heart (conscience), is considered in status above those good- persons who practice self-imposed penance and compassionate charity!

296. poy-yaa-mai anna pukazh-illai; yey-yaa-mai
yellaa, aRam-um tharum.

There cannot be a better reputation (fame) for a person,than 'not uttering' falsehood. In that case, without any further effort of the person, all forms of virtues will be yielded to that person!

297. poy-yaa-mai poy-yaa-mai aatRin, aRam- piRa,
sei-yaa-mai sei-yaa-mai nhandRu.

If a person, takes care to implement, without fail, the avoidance of falsehood, all other duties may not be insisted to be done, as the avoidance of falsehood accommodates all other virtues!

298. puRam thoo-y-mai nheer-aan amai-yum; akam- thoo-y-mai
vaa-y-mai-yaal kaaNap- padum.

External purity of the human body is made possible by washing with water. The purity of the human mind can be made known by the truthfulness of words, deeds and thoughts of a person!

299. yellaa viLakkum viLakku- alla; saan-d-ROr-k-ku-p-
poyyaa- viLak-kae viLakku.

All lamps cannot be considered as useful lamps which could show the way, in one's life! For noble persons, avoidance of falsehood (implementation / practice of truthfulness) is the real (superior) lamp which can show the way in life!! All other lamps are rated below the meritorious virtue of truthfulness practiced by noble-persons.

300. yaam- mey-yaa-k- kaNda-vatRul, illai, yenaiththu- ondRum,
vaa-y-mai-yin nhalla piRa. (Poet's testimony).

Among all the forms of knowledge, we have seen and felt through literature, that there is no other superior (valuable) virtue, other than Truthfulness, in human life!. (The poet testifies, for upholding truthfulness!).

CHAPTER-31

AVOIDANCE OF ANGER

301. sel-idaththu-k- kaap-paan sinam-kaap-paan, al-idath-thu,
kaak-kil- yen? kaavaak-kaal yen?

Any person must take care to cautiously control the anger being shown towards a weaker person, as that anger would cause harm to the recipient. When the recipient is a stronger person, who cannot be harmed, it does not matter whether the person controls the anger or not! (The angry person will cause harm to the self!)..(Whether it is a 'he' or 'she'!).

302. sellaa- idath-thu-ch chinam theethu; sel-idath-thum
il, atha-nin theeya- piRa.

When anger is pointed towards a stronger person, the anger may not harm that person who is targeted; but it will cause harm to the self (the person who shows anger). When anger is directed towards a weaker person, it may cause harm to the person targeted; but the act of showing anger is considered as an evil act, worse than any other act. It will bring harm to the person who shows anger! The good name, so far maintained, will be marred. (Anger is to be controlled always, no matter whether it is being shown to wards a strong person or weak person!).

303. maRath-thal vekuLi-yai yaar- maatum; theeya
piRath-thal athan-aal varum.

Make it a point to forget developing anger towards any person, whomsoever it may be! Some evil effects will be yielded from it, affecting the person who exhibits the anger!

304. nhakai-yum uvakai-yum kollum sinath-thin
pakai-yum uLa-vO piRa?

Could there be any other enemy to a person when he/she practices anger which kills cheerful feelings, and happiness, together. Anger itself is the enemy to the self, capable of causing all possible harms!.

305. thannai-th-thaan kaakkin, sinam-kaakka; kaavaak-kaal
thannai-yae kollum sinam.

If a person wants to safeguard the self, he/she has to control the anger, applying the necessary restraint (self-control) in the mind! If not, the anger of the person will lead to self-destruction!

306. sinam- yennum sae-rnh-thaarai-k-kolli, inam-yennum
yae-ma-p- puNai-yai-ch- chudum.

Anger,which is known as the killer of its intimate companion (the person who develops anger), will burn the relationship with the close relatives of the angry person, whereas the link with these relatives is considered as a source of protection, similar to a life-saving boat, at times of crisis (while facing troubled-waters)! The term '*inam*' may mean friends, as well as relatives (kith and kin)!

307. sinath-thai-p- poruL- yendRu koNdavan- kaedu,
nhi-lath-thu- aRai-nh-thaan kai, pizhai-yaathu - atRu.

The palm will not escape from being hurt, if a person beats up the hard ground with force, with hand. Similarly, harmful effects would result on a person, who possesses (and exhibits) anger as the characteristic property!

308. iNar-yeri- thOy-vu-anna innaa se(i)-yinum
puNar-in, veku-Laamai nhandRu.

Even if a person has done harm to you, similar to the degree of exposing you to the horrors of a burning-flame, it is beneficial to you, if you can avoid showing anger, when the same person approaches you, seeking your friendship!

309. uLLi-yathu- yellaam udan yeithum; uLLath-thaal,
uLLaan vekuLi, yenin.

If a person does not give accommodation to anger in the mind, then, the person will readily obtain anything that he/she desires to have!

310. iRanh-thaar iRanh-thaar anai-yar, sinath-thai-th-
thuRanh-thaar, thuRanh-thaar thuNai.

Persons who show excessive anger are considered similar to the dead-persons. Those who abandon anger are considered respectable similar to the ascetics (saints)!.

CHAPTER-32

AVOIDANCE OF EVIL-ACT

311. siRappu -yeenum, selvam peRin-um, piRarkku-innaa
sei-yaamai maasu-atRaar kOL.

It is the policy (principle) of virtuous persons, who are free from blemishes in their minds, not to carry out any evil act which will harm another person, even if that act has got the prospects of bringing eminence and wealth to them!

312. kaRuth-thu -innaa sei-thavak- kaNNum, maRuth-thu-innaa
sei-yaamai maasu-atRaar kOL.

Virtuous persons who are free from any blemishes in their minds, believe in a policy (principle) not to cause any harm to another person, even in retaliation to the offender who had initiated harmful act on them earlier!

313. sei-yaamal chetRaark-kum innaa-tha seitha-pin
uyyaa vizhu-mam tharum.

Unprovoked, if any person does any harm, to any other person (treating the offended person as the enemy), the aftermath (consequent-effect) will yield untold (non-redeemable) misery to the offender! (Ref: KalaignarUrai).

314. innaa seitharai oRuth-thal, avar- nhaaNa,
nha-n-nhayam seithu vidal

The best way to punish a person who has done harm to you, will be to do something beneficial to that person, thus making that person to feel ashamed of his/her earlier act. Also, later on, you must forget all about it, to feel relieved (and to have peace of mind)!

315. aRivinaal aakuvathu uNdO? piRi-thin- nhOy
than-nhOy- pOl, pOtRaa-k- kadai.

There is no use of wisdom of a person, if the person does not consider the illness (suffering) of others as the illness (suffering) of the self, with regard to showing mercy or pursuing remedial measure!

316. 'innaa' yenath- thaan uNarnhth-thavai, thun-naamai
vae-Ndum piRan-kaN se(i)yal.

Any person, who had experienced whatever act is harmful to the self, must take care to avoid directing such an act towards others. (Note: This is similar to: "Do not do unto others, what you do not want others to do unto you! Do unto others what you want others to do unto you!". This is being taught to the children as a 'rhyming-couplet' in schools!).

317. yenai-th-thaa-num ye-gn-gnaa-ndRum, yaarkkum, manath-thaanaam
maaNaa sey- yaamai thalai.

If a person decides not to cause any harm which would hurt the feelings of others, causing mental strain, at any time, even in a small measure, that greatness of the person will be considered as the most important virtue among all other virtues which the person (he/she) may possess!!

318. than-uyirkku in-naa-mai thaan- aRivaan yen-kolO
mannuyir-kku innaa se(i)yal?

How does a person justify any harmful acts which he/she causes on the various forms of living creatures (including humans), knowing very well, by experience, that whatever is harmful to the own self would be harmful to others?

319. piRa-rkku innaa muR-pakal sey-yin, thama-kku- innaa
piR-pakal thaa-mae varum.

If a person carries out any act causing harm to any other person during the forenoon, a similar harm will be returned routinely in the afternoon, to that person(whoever initiated the offensive act)!

320. nhOy- yellaam nhOy- sei-thaar mae-la-vaam; nhOy- sei-yaar
nhOy- inmai vae-Ndu- pavar.

All sufferings will be coming forth upon those who cause suffering to others. Therefore, those who pray for freedom from sufferings, must not cause any sufferings to others. (Note: 'Do unto others what you do want others to do unto you'!) (Note: This is a rhyming-couplet, in English, often told by teachers to their students in school! The right time to practice-saying it out!).

CHAPTER-33

AVOIDANCE-OF-KILLING

321. aRa-vinai yaathu-yenil kollaa-mai; kO-Ral
piRa-vinai yellaam tharum

If virtuous act is to be defined, it relates to avoidance of killing. The act of killing a life will lead to harvesting the results of all other evils (without the person doing any other evil-act!).

322. pakuthth(u)- uNdu, pal-uyir O-m-buthal, nhoolO-r
thokuth-thavatRuL yellaam thalai.

Sharing the food with many forms of lives, in order to take care of them, corresponds to the principal virtue among the norms compiled by all the learned- scholars. (All forms of life is a highlight). (Note: The poet insists that human persons must show kindness to all forms of life, not only by practicing the avoidance of killing, but also by providing food to them! The term '*pal-uyir O-m-buthal' means protecting/conserving many forms of living-species!). A higher degree of mercy!!*

323. ondRaaka nha-llathu kol-laamai; matRu -athan,
pin-saara-p- poy-yaamai nha-ndRu.

First of all, the avoidance of killing is good. Further, to serve as a supplement, avoidance of falsehood is good (to strengthen the virtues to the self).

324. nhal-laaRu yena-p- padu-vathu yaathu- yenin, yaathu-ondRum
kol-laamai soozh-um nhe-Ri.

The good path is defined as the path encompassing the avoidance of killing any form of living- creature!

325. nhi-lai- anj-chi nheeththaar-uL yellaam, kolai- anj-chi-k-
kol-laamai soozh-vaan thalai.

Any person, as an ascetic, who practices the policy of 'not-killing any living creature', is considered to be given more prominence, above all the other ascetics/saints who renounced the worldly pleasures (fearing the intriguing/entrapping/challenging practices of worldly life)!

326. kol-laamai mae-R-kondu ozhu-ku-vaan vaazh-nh-aaL-mae-l,
sel-laathu uyir-uNNum kootRu.

Death, which takes away the life of all persons in the world, will hesitate to act upon the life of any person who practices the policy of avoiding the action of killing any creature!

327. than-uyir nhee-ppi-num sei-yarkka, thaan- piRithu
in-nuyir nhee-kkum vinai.

Let no person commit the act of taking away the valuable life of any other creature, even if it happens to lose his/her own life!

328. nh-andR(u)- aakum aakkam –perithu- yeninum, saandrO-r-kku-k-
kon-dRu- aakum aakkam kadai.

The benefit-yielding wealth, even if it could be huge, will be considered as inferior and sinful, by the virtuous persons, if it comes to them, through their involvement in the act of killing! (Note: This is a satire to the practice of killing an animal, and offering it to a deity, in the name of ritualistic sacrifice, with a hope of harvesting huge benefits from the deity to whom the sacrifice is being offered!).

329. kolai- vinai-yar aakiya maakkaL, pulai-vinai-yar
pun-mai theri-vaar akath-thu

Merciless human beings who are known for their act of killing will be placed in low rating of esteem, by those wise persons who know the meanness of the act of killing.

330. uyir-udambin nhee-kki-yaar yenba, seyir-udambin
sellaa-th- thee vaazhkkai yavar.

It is generally believed by people that those persons who indulge in the activity of killing (separating the life from the living- creatures) would be destined to suffer from a life of chronic sufferings, in the form of diseases and other hardships.

CHAPTER-34

IMPERMANENCE

331. nhill-aa-tha- vatRai nhilai-yina yendRu- uNarum
pullaRi- vaaNmai kadai.

Those persons will be considered to be foolish, if they exhibit their ignorance by firmly believing that certain non-permanent things would remain permanent and long-lasting!

332. kooth-thaattu avaik-kuzhaa-th-thu- atRae, perunj-chelvam
pO-k-kum athu- viLinth(u) atRu.

Similar to the manner in which the crowd gathers around a drama-theatre slowly in the beginning before the commencement of the show, the great wealth comes to a person in slow paces. When the drama-performance is over, the crowd departs immediately, and quickly. Similarly, the wealth disappears from the person suddenly (abruptly), at a faster pace.

333. aRkaa iyalpitRu-ch- chelvam, athu-petRaal,
aRkuba aang-kae seyal.

Wealth that accumulates, has got the characteristic nature of dissipating (without notice)! Therefore, if wealth is obtained, one should carry out certain good deeds of charity, while remaining rich, so that it yields long-standing benefits to many others, thus, bringing glory to the donor!

334. nhaaL –yena, ondRu-pO-l kaati, uyir- yee-rum
vaaL, athu, uNarvaar-p- peRin.

Pretending that one day is similar to the next day, (as if it is a single unit), the day (representing time), proves to be a life-cutting knife, if any person thinks about it deeply. (Note: It is a philosophy of uncertainty!).

335. nhaa-ch-chetRu, vikkuL-mae-l vaaraa-mun, nhal-vinai
maeR- sendRu, sey-yap padum.

Well before the tongue starts dying away, and hiccups start showing up, in the sequence of a dying-process, every person must think that it is better to go ahead in carrying out benevolent deeds of charity, speedily, to the benefit of others! (so that a permanent fame for the donor will remain in the life-history of that person!).

336. nhe-ru-nhal uLan-oruvan, indRu-illai, yennum
perumai udaith-thu-iv- vulaku.

A person who was alive yesterday, is not alive today! That kind of fame (pride/ excess/unpredictability) rests with this world, indicative of impermanence of human life! This great fact serves as a caution! (The world remains in-tact, perplexed, with freedom, only, to mourn the loss!).

337. oru-pozhuthum vaazh-vathu aRiyaar, karuthu-ba,
kO-di-yum alla, pala.

Those who do not know whether they are going to be alive during the next moment, or not, would be contemplating about acquiring material-wealth worth tens of millions of value! That is their mindset. What a pity?

338. kudambai thaniththu- ozhi-ya-p puL – paRanh- thatRae
udambOdu- uyir-idai nha-t-pu.

Egg-shell remains lonely, when the baby bird flies away, from the inside of the shell! Similar tie (link) exists between the body and soul of a human being!

339. uRang-ku- vathu-pO-lum saak-kaadu; uRang-ki
vizhip-pathu pO-lum piRappu.

The occurrence of death is like going to sleep! The birth of a person is like waking up from sleep (slumber)! (Both events are unpredictable). (Note: Does it describe the cycle of human births? It needs further research).

340. pukkil- amain-thinRu kollO, udambi-nuL
thuch-ch-il irunh-tha uyir-kku?

Could it be true that no home (abode) is available for the soul when it leaves the human body, where in it was sheltering so far/so long, in a small corner? (Note: A great philosophy is hidden behind the statement!).

CHAPTER-35

RENUNCIATION

341. yaatha-nin- yaatha-nin nheeng-ki-yaan nhO-thal
athanin- athanin ilan.

Whatever thing a person has renounced, it is for sure that no pain will originate from that 'thing' which has been renounced! (Note: It applies to 'human-desires' in the philosophical sense. The principle can be extended to allergy-causing food-items, as well; so also, to bad habits like smoking or chewing tobacco!!).

342. vae-Ndin- uNdaaka-th thuRakka; thuRanh-tha-pin
yeeNdu- iyaR- paala pala.

For experiencing true pleasure, it is desirable to renounce everything whatever is available with the self, to start with. After renouncing, there are many other naturally-pleasant blessings which would be available to enjoy (experience, relish) in the life of an ascetic! (Note: It applies to material objects, favourite-foods, personal-belongings, as well as habits and practices, and beliefs in hereditary-superstitions?! This principle applies not only to ascetics, but also to every one in domestic order! This needs research).

343. adal- vae-Ndum ai-nh-than pulath-thai; vidal-vae-Ndum
vae-Ndiya yellaam orung-ku.

The desires induced by the five senses of human body must be controlled (destroyed/won over/defeated) in the mind by an ascetic/saint, by self-determination/meditation/will-power. All desires relating to those five senses must be abandoned altogether! All at the same time!! Abruptly!!!

344. iyal-paakum nhO-nbi-Rku- ondRu inmai; udaimai
mayal-aakum matRum peya-rth-thu.

It is the natural requirement for any one person, who wishes to undertake penance, with preparedness to renounce everything, and to possess nothing! Possession will lead to confusion, with a probability of reverting back to temptation (which will prove to be a trap!).

345. matRum thodar-p-paadu yeven-kol; piRappu-aRukkal
utRaa-r-kku udambum mikai?

For those who desire to nullify the evils of this birth, their human body itself is a surplus burden to them! While this is so, is there a need for them to have any additional bonds/attachments in life? Not at all!

346. 'yaan'-'yenathu'- yennum serukku-aRuppaan, vaanO-r-kku
uyar-nh-tha ulakam pukum.

(Note: The phrase '*uganhtha- ulakam pukum*' : considered).

A person who eradicates (erases /wipes out) from his mind, the various human qualities such as the false-pride which would make a person utter words like "I", and "Me", "My belongings", will be elevated to the status of deserving entry into the higher world above the heavenly beings. (This is the benefit of earning freedom from human desires).

(Note: An abode superior to heaven, is indicated by the words "*vaanO-r-k-ku uyar-nh-tha ulagam*" The term '*uga-nh-tha-ulagam*' could be more appropriate, instead of '*vaanO-r-k-ku uyar-nh-tha-ulagam*'. The phrase '*uganhtha-ulagam*' means the heaven meant for heavenly-dwellers, whereas '*uyanrnhtha-ulagam*' means another heaven which could be superior to heaven itself, like the 'upper-house of the heaven'.

Heaven is the most superior abode. There is no other house superior to heaven. This needs research. The intention of the poet has to be understood that human persons in the ascetic order deserve to enter into the heaven, if they erase the feelings of self-pride, by shedding the sense of attachment, such as "I", "Me", "My belongings",etc., from their minds. The intention could not have been to place them in a status superior to heavenly-dwellers; but. only in equal status on par with them. (Please see Appendix-1).

347. patRi- vidaa-a idumbaikal, patRinai-p-
patRi vidaa- a- thavarkku.

If those persons (ascetics) cling to the bonds (desires), without loosening the grips, the consequence will be: the sufferings arising out of the bonds (desires) will also be attaching themselves to the persons, without loosening the grip! In such a case, the sufferings will continue.

348. thalai-p-pattaar theerath- thuRa-nh-thaar; mayang-ki
valai-p-pattaar matRai- yavar.

Those who renounce all their desires, totally, without leaving a residue, are placed in high esteem. Others get entangled in the net (web) of desires, after experiencing illusion/temptation!

349. patRu- atRa kaNNae- piRappu- aRukkum; matRu,
nhi-lai-yaamai kaaNa-p- padum.

The miseries of life will not occur, only in the case of those, who free themselves from all desires. For others, a situation of uncertainty would be experienced!

350. patRuka- patRu-atRaan patRi-nai; ap-patRai-p-
patRuka, patRu vida-R-ku.

Earn the bondage with the Almighty, in order to be able to renounce the worldly desires, because the Almighty is totally free from worldly bonds!

CHAPTER-36

REALIZATION OF TRUE KNOWLEDGE

351. poruL alla- vatRai-p- poruL-(y)endru uNarum
maruL- aanaam, maaNaa-p- piRappu.

If any person feels attracted towards things which are devoid of truth, and starts believing it as truth itself, such a person will be subjected to sufferings in life, because of his/her delusional (deceptive) act!

352. iruL- nheeng-ki, inbam payakkum; maruL-nheeng-ki
maa-saRu kaatchi yavar-kku.

Those who free themselves from delusion and come up with a clear vision, free from evil, will enjoy unlimited happiness, as darkness goes away from their minds!

353. aiyath-thin nh-eeng-kith theLinthaar-kku, vaiyaththin
vaanam nha-Ni-yathu udai-ththu.

For those persons who liberate themselves from delusion (false belief) and acquire a clear vision, the heaven will be nearer to them than the earth!

354. aiy-uNarvu yeithiya-k-kaNNum, payam-indRae
mei-uNarvu illaa-thavarkku.

Even for those persons who have successfully controlled their five senses, there could not be any use of it, if they lack the feelings of truthfulness (clarity on divinity/true knowledge)!

355. yep-poruL yeth-than-maith-thu aayinum, ap-poruL, mei-p- poruL
kaaNpathu aRivu.

Whatever be the substance, whatever be the nature of the substance, it will be ascertained as wisdom, if the true nature of it can be assessed/seen/evaluated.

356. katRu-yeeNdu mei-p-poruL kaNdaar, thalai- p-paduvar
matRu-yeeNdu vaaraa nheRi.

Those persons pursuing the path of ascetics, after going through the process of learning, and successfully having perceived spiritual knowledge, will not revert back to the path of worldly life! They will be seeking only salvation!

357. O-rth-thu -uLLam uLLathu uNarin, oru-thalai-yaa-p-
pae-r-ththu- uLLa vae-Ndaa-p- piRappu.

For any person who feels that the knowledge relating to truthfulness has been absorbed in the mind, and if it is being felt truly, there is no need for that person to believe that there is a re- birth for the self!

358. piRappu yennum pae-thai-mai nhee-ng-ka-ch- chiRappu- yennum
sem-poRul kaaNbathu aRivu.

Re-birth sounds like a myth or ignorance! To clarify the situation, it will be wise to seek the Almighty who is the very embodiment of Absolute knowledge! (Note: To liberate the self from the ordeal of rebirth, one must choose to live by virtuous path (Refer to kurals 50, 349, 361, 362).

359. saarbu- uNar-nh-thu saarbu-keda ozhukin, matRu azhi-ththu,
saar-tharaa saar-tharu nhO-y!

It is considered that the illness of captivity to desires must be overcome, by an ascetic, by knowing the intricacies of bondage, and by following the path of non-attachment, putting the faith on the ascetic path chosen, in order to realize the self from feelings of temptation. If freed from temptations, no suffering would come!

360. kaamam, vekuLi, mayakkam, ivai- moondRan,
nhaa-mam keda-k- kedum nhO-y.

When the very names of the three characteristic traits, namely, passion (for sensual pleasures), anger, and ignorance (non- clarity) are erased from one's mind, there would not occur any kind of evil to the ascetic-person concerned!

CHAPTER-37

CURTAILMENT OF DESIRE

361. avaa- yenba, yellaa uyirkkum, ye-gn- gnaa-ndRum
thavaa, ap- piRappu-yeenum viththu.

Excessive desire (Greed), they say, is the seed which yields re-birth, to all the forms of life, all the time!

362. vae-Ndung-kaal vae-Ndum piRavaamai; matRu, athu,
vaeNdaamai vae-Nda varum.

If a person opts for self-denial (freedom from human desires), any of his/ her prayer will be granted, if the prayer is for nullifying rebirth! (Note: It is rhyming couplet!).

363. vae-Ndaa-mai - anna, vizhuch-chelvam, yeeNdu illai;
yaaNdum, a-h-thu-oppathu, il.

There is no other prestigious (noble) wealth (blessings), other than freedom from desire (avarice/greed)! Anywhere and every-where, it is a priceless (valuable/ precious) wealth! There is no other wealth which is equal to it!

364. thooy-mai yenbathu avaa-inmai; matR(u)-athu,
vaay-mai vae-Nda varum.

Purity of mind is the absence of desire in the mind. This purity of mind will be granted, if truthfulness is prayed for (by practicing truthfulness!)

365. atRavar yenbaar, avaa- atRaar;
matRaiyaar, atRaa-ka, atRathu ilar.

Ascetics are typically those who have renounced all desires, and thereby deserving merit. Others are considered to be those who have not fully renounced their desires, thereby being unable to free themselves from the clutches of desires/temptations!

366. anj-chuvathu O-rum aRanae; oruvanai
vanj-chip-pathu O-rum avaa.

It is a virtue to exercise caution and fear against desire, be cause it is always a reality that a person will be deceived by the desire (temptation) which could prevail in the mind!

367. avaa-vinai aatRa aRuppin, thavaa-vinai,
thaan vae-Ndum aatRaan varum.

If a person completely curbs greediness (avarice), from his/ her mind, all stable situations, bringing benevolence, will come to him/ her, as he/she wishes.

368. avaa -illaar-k-ku, illaa-kum, thunbam; a-h-thu -uNdael,
thavaa-athu, mae-n-mae-l varum.

For those who do not have any greediness, there will not be any suffering. If greediness is possessed, sufferings will be coming forth, further and further!

369. inbam idai-yaRaa-thu yeeNdum, avaa -yennum
thunbath-thuL thunbam kedin.

Real happiness, without any interruption, will be made avail able to a person's life in this world, if he/she could get rid of any greediness in the mind, as the greediness is called 'suffering within sufferings'.

370. aaraa iya-Rkai, avaa nhee-ppin; anh-nhilai-yae,
pae-raa iyaRkai tharum.

If it is possible to curtail (curb) all the excessive natural desires (which could not be satisfied immediately), it can be expected that very great natural bliss will be yielded, as a perennial pleasure!

CHAPTER-38

DESTINY/FATE

371. aa-k(u)-oozh-aal thO-ndRum asaiv(u)-inmai; kai-p-poruL
pO-ku-oozh-aal thO-ndRum madi.

Favourable fate will produce perseverance, in a person, to enhance the value of wealth on hand. On the contrary, unfavourable fate will produce laziness (or absence of alertness) in a person, making the person lose whatever he has got!

372. pae-thai-p- padukkum, izhav(u)-oozh; aRiv(u)-akatRum,
aakal-oozh utRak- kadai.

Destructive fate produces folly (foolishness/stupidity) in a person, in spite of his knowledge-potentials. Constructive fate will produce expansive knowledge to his benefit!

373. nhuNNiya nhool- pala kaRpi-num, matRum- than
uNmai aRivae mikum.

Although a person has studied many books in detail, the fate will permit him/her to reveal only limited knowledge!

(Note: Ignorance, false beliefs and superstition may prevail in the mind, in spite of higher education! What remains will be dominated by surroundings, local culture,traditions, etc, (See kural 452 to 455).

(Bias embedded in the mind will block the new knowledge earned by further reading. The poet feels that such a mind will not accept reforms! Even superstitions will be continued to be believed in!)

374. iru-vaeRu ulakath-thu iyaRkai; thiru- vaeRu;
theLLiyar aatha-lum vaeRu!

There are two different (differently different) categories of destiny! Those who acquire wealth correspond to one category. Those who acquire wisdom (eminence) correspond to a totally different category! (The basis for the difference is still not known).

375. nhallavai yellaa-am theeya-vaam; theeya-vum,
nhallavaam, selvam se(i)yaR-ku.

In the process of earning wealth, due to the intervention of 'FATE', whatever is good is likely to work out as bad, or whatever is likely to be bad, is likely to work out as good!

376. pari-yi-num aakaa-vaam; paal-alla, uith-thu-ch-
chori-yi-num, pO-kaa, tha-ma!

Even if protected with utmost care, the property not 'destined' in one's favour, will not stay with that person. Property destined to be one's own, will not go, even if thrown out!

377. vakuth-thaan, vakuth-tha vakai-allaal. kOdi
thokuth-thaar-kkum thui-th-thal arithu

Even if a person accumulates wealth worth several millions in value, it may not be possible for the person to enjoy the wealth, if there is no provision for it, in the dictates of destiny designed for that person, as determined by the Almighty! (Corollary: There is a beneficial provision in favour of every human being in the dictates of Fate; It is up to the individual to work hard to earn that favour! Please see kural 620).

378. thuRap-paar,man, thuppuravu il-laar, uRaR-paala
oottaa kazhiyum yenin.

It is a dictate in 'Fate Theory' that poor persons must go through the long-lasting miseries in their lives. If that binding could be cleared, those poor persons (being frustrated with their inability to get the essential materials in life) will develop a natural desire to resort to the path of ascetics!

379. nhandRu- aang-kaal, nallavaa-k- kaanbavar, andRu-aang-kaal,
allal padu-vathu yevan?

When good things happen due to fate, people feel happy. When bad things happen due to the same kind of aspect, namely, fate, people feel bad and grumble/grudge/murmur/grieve! Why the difference in their response?

380. oozhiR- peru- vali, yaa-vuLa? matRu- ondRu,
soozhi-num, thaan, mu-nh- thuRum. (munthu uRum).

Could there be any other force stronger than the fate? Even if any other appropriate force, through man's effort, could surround the spot to his/her favour, the fate will overtake it to enforce its own design. (Note: Nobody needs to get worried. Some encouraging words are given in kural 620).

PART – II

GOVERNANCE/ HUMAN RESOURCES/ SOCIAL INTERACTIONS/FAMILY PROSPERITY

CHAPTER 39

GREATNESS OF THE RULER OF THE LAND

381. padai, kudi, koozh, amaichchu, nhatpu, aRaN—aaRum,
udai-yaan arasar-uL aeRu.

A king who possesses the six things, namely, powerful army, loyal subjects, decent wealth, capable ministers, reliable friends (allies) and a protected-fort (fortress) is considered as a lion among the kings!

382. anj-chaamai, yeekai, aRivu, ookkam, in(h)-nhaan-kumyenj-chaamai
vae-nh-tharkku iyalbu.

The requirement of a king must not fall short of the four things (traits/qualities), namely, fearlessness, philanthropy, wisdom and courage (with valour).(Note: These are the qualities desirable in each person, in the modern world, to claim leadership-potentials!).

383. thoo-ng-kaamai, kalvi, thuNiv(u)-uadaimai, im-moondRum
nhee-ng-kaa nhi-lan –aaL- bavaRku.

For a person who rules the land, three qualities are needed, namely, i) awareness (smartness/alertness), ii) education and iii) boldness (courage with self-confidence and valour).

384. aRaN-izhuk-kaathu, allavai nhee-kki, maRan-izhu-kkaa
maa-nam udaiya-thu arasu.

The king must uphold the honour for valour, and dignity of rule, by avoiding any evil act (which is considered to deviate from the ordained virtuous path), and avoiding any act which would invite insult to his rule.

385. iyatRal-um, yee-ttal-um, kaath-thal-um, kaath-tha,
vakuth-thal-um vallathu arasu.

A king must be capable of devising the methods of generating wealth, earning the wealth in the normal way, safeguarding the wealth so earned, and distributing the wealth equitably to the benefit of the citizens (subjects/people).

386. kaatchi-kku yeLiyan, kadunj-chollan -alla-nael,
meek-kooRum mannan nhi-lam.

The entire world will exalt (praise/glorify) the king, profusely, if he is easily approachable, and if he is free from using harsh words! (Easy access (approachability) is desired: i) for those who need material help from the king, and ii) for those who want justice for their sufferings caused by bad elements in society).

387. in-sol-aal yeeththu-aLikka vallaar-kku, than-sol(l)-aal,
thaan kaNdu anai-th-thu, iv-vulaku.

If a king practices the habit of i) speaking out pleasant words, ii) remaining affable/kind and courteous, and iii) giving financial assistance to the poor and the needy, the world of people will take pleasure in abiding by his words, and remain loyal, as the king himself could ever visualize to see!

388. muRai sei-thu kaap-paatRum mannavan, makkat-ku,
iRai- (y)endRu vaikka-p- padum.

A king who rules the land upholding the virtuous path, and protecting the people with care, will be remembered in the hearts of the people as their god in human form!

389. sevi-kaippa, sol-poRukkum paNbu-udaii vae-nh-than,
kavikai-k-keezh(th) tha-ng-kum ulaku.

The people will be delighted to stay under the shade of the umbrella of their honourable king who reigns (rules) the country, with tolerance to the bitter words of complaints uttered by the citizens (subjects) to the extent of straining his ears.

390. kodai, aLi, se-ng-kO-l, kudi-Ombal, nhaan-kum,
udai-yaa-naam vae-nh-tharkku oLi.

A king is considered to be the guiding light of all other kings, if he does carry out the four duties in ruling the land, namely, i) philanthropy/ charity/beneficence, ii) gracious attitude while interacting with people,

iii) righteous rule (depicted by the symbolic Sceptre, and iv) bestowing care for people's welfare and protection.

CHAPTER-40

LEARNING / EDUCATION

(Note: Thiruvalluvar takes special care to canvass for promoting public education, out of his genuine concern for societal benefit. This could imply that a historical necessity could have existed in the socio-political scenario prevailing in the land, at that time! He fixes the responsibility on the individual-person for earning education, knowing fully well that the King or his favourite 'wise-men' will not take steps to promote education among the masses). The poet's concern for poor persons and illiterate persons is reflected in kurals 404; 414; 1062 and 1046.

391. kaRka; kasadu- aRa; kaRpavai, katRa-pin
nhiR-ka, athaR-ku-th thaka.

Let every person learn; learning it thoroughly, without er rors; and after learning, whatever has been learned, must be put into practice, in accordance with what has been learned!

(Note: Educated persons must follow the norms they have learned, by putting into practice whatever they have leaned, by considering the privileges they enjoy! If not, the orderliness in the society will suffer. The educated persons are considered as a wealth for the country in kural 731. The brilliance of children is expected to benefit the society, in addition to bringing pride to parents, as believed by the poet, vide kural 68. If educated persons do not do their duties as custodians of the society, exercising all responsibilities, with integrity and dedication, the country will not prosper!).

392. yeN-yenba, (y)aenai yezhu-ththu yenba, iv-viraNdum
kaN-yenba vaazhum uyirkku.

It is said that Numbers and the other item called Letters are as important as the two eyes of a living person in this world. (An other interpretation:

Good thoughts and learning through letters are considered as important to a living person, as precious as the two eyes! Logic: a knowledge of numbers gets included in learning.

Thoughts are related to virtues, and hence the importance. Please see kurals 9; 424; 910). Good thoughts are insisted upon in character-building. Proficiency in letters and numbers will help a person to make a living. Good thoughts will ensure a meaningful personality. It has got a social- relevance.

393. kaN-udaiyar yenbavar katRO-r; mukathth(u)- iraNdu
puN-(N)udaiyar kallaa thavar.

Learned persons are said to have two eyes! The illiterate- persons will be considered to have two wounds (called eyes) on their faces!! (Note: The eyes of an illiterate person cannot acquire knowledge through letters and numbers, and have got, therefore, only limited functional uses of the eyes: Please see kurals 407; 410). The poet sympathizes with them, in kurals 404; 414; 1046).

394. uvappa-th thalai-k-koodi, uLLap- piri-thal,
anaith-thae, pulavar thozhil.

The traditional practice among the learned-scholars is to meet and interact joyously, sharing their knowledge with one an other; and at the time of parting, they will be emotionally longing for the next opportunity to meet and interact! That is their great culture and tradition, among the learned-scholars!

395. udai-yaar- mun, il-laar-pOl, (y)aek-kat-Rum katRaar,
kadai-ya-rae kallaa thavar.

Whoever did receive education, did not hesitate to stand in front of the teacher with all humility, for the purpose of receiving education (like a begging poor-person standing in front of a rich person) were able to learn, and receive education. (As a result, they earned the respects from the society). Those who missed the chance to learn are branded as illiterates (who, unfortunately, would lose all prominence in the society!).

396. thottanai-th-th(u) ooRum maNaR-kaeNi, maa-nh-thar-kku-k-katRanai-th-thu ooRum aRivu.

Water will rise up in a well, dug in the sand-bed, depending upon the depth up to which digging is done. Similarly, for the human beings, the more is the reading, the more will be the knowledge gained/stored/earned!

397. yaa-thaa-num nhaadaa-maal, ooraa-maal, yen-oruvan saa-nh-thuNai-yum kallaa-tha vaaRu.

The learned persons will get acceptability to live in any country, in any village, wherever they go! Why then, a person does not want to avail the benefit of learning until the time of death? (Note: The poet does not specify any age-limit for learning (receiving education); He seems to believe in 'adult-education' too!)

398. orumai-k-kaN thaan katRa kalvi, oruvaR-ku yezhumai-yum (y)ae-maappu udaiththu.

The learning of one person acquired during his/her present birth (lifetime) will have the reputation during the consecutive seven births! (Note:'seven-births' is interpreted as seven generations: Ref: KalaignarUrai). (Note: Refer to Heritability of IQ-Wikipedia: https:// en.m.wikipedia.org, wiki,Heritability of IQ...).

399. thaam –in bu-ruvath(u), ulaku-in buRak-kaNdu kaamuRuvar katRu aRi-nh-thaar.

The people of the world will find pleasure in reading and appreciating the ideas of the learned- persons revealed through their books, research findings, other writings and speeches. Encouraged by this reality, the learned persons do find (take) pleasure in reading more and more, for gaining advanced knowledge.

(Note: The concept of updating knowledge, by learned-persons, was highlighted, 2000 years ago! That too, being encouraged by the support of the people)

400. kae-du-il vizhu-ch-chelvam, kalvi; oruvaRku
maadu; alla, matRai yavai.

For any person,knowledge earned through learning (education) is the most precious wealth which cannot be destroyed! The other forms of wealth are not equal to it, in extending benefits to a living-person! (Note: Every person must receive education. That is the expectation of the poet.

Education is not perishable, and hence considered everlasting. Other forms of wealth are perishable / unstable and hence considered non-permanent).

CHAPTER-41

ILLITERACY

401. arangk(u)- indRi vatt(u)-aadi-yatRae, nhi-rambiya
    nhool- indRi-k- kO-tti koLal.

    Speech given by an illiterate person, without full knowledge learned from books, is meaningless like playing the game of chess without a pre-marked-board (chess-board)!

    (Note: The pre-marked board for chess-game is similar to the pre scribed syllabus for a course of study, and hence the example!).

402. kallaa-thaan sol- kaa muRuthal, mulai-iraNdum
    il-laathaaL peN- kaa-mutRu atRu.

    If an illiterate person develops a desire for acquiring power of words, it will be a useless effort. It is an effort-in-vain, like an immature-woman, who does not have the two breasts fully developed, longing for attaining womanhood/feminine charms!

403. kallaa-thavar-um nha-ni-nhallar, katRaar-mun,
    sol-laath(u) irukka-p- peRin.

    The presence of illiterate persons will be very good, if they remain silent (and listen) in front of learned persons, without making an effort to speak out their knowledge, whatever they know, by which action, they would only embarrass others! (Please see kural 405).

404. kallaa-thaan otpam kazhiya-nha-ndRu- aa-yinum,
    koLLaar, aRivudai- yaar.

    Although the knowledge of an illiterate person may be fairly good, it is a pity that the learned persons may not approve of it!

    (Note: The poet admires the natural (inborn) wisdom of an illiterate-person, and regrets the probable non-approval of such bright-ideas by learned persons!

(Note: The poet feels that a person must receive education for the purpose of being socially accepted by learned persons, if not for any other reason!).

405. kallaa- oruvan, thakaimai thalaip-peithu
sol-laada-ch chO-rvu padum.

The value of knowledge of an illiterate person, of which he might have been boasting of, will be revealed when the words are uttered by him, in front of the learned persons!

406. uLar-yennum maath-thirai-yar al-laal, payavaa-k-
kaLar- anai-yar kallaa- thavar.

The illiterate persons are said to be unproductive with regard to knowledge, similar to the unproductive (non-cultivable) wasteland. However, they are included in the list of 'living- persons!

407. nhuN-maaN- nhu-zhai-pulam, il-laan (y)ezhil-nhalam,
maN-maaN punai- paavai -yatRu.

The goodness of beauty of an illiterate person is like the beauty of a doll made out of an ornamental clay, as the mental assemblage of that person is not exposed to the fine details of any systematic academic discipline.

408. nhallaar-kaN patta vaRumai-yin, in-naa-thae,
kallaar-kaN patta thiru.

The wealth accumulating with an illiterate person is more harmful than the poverty inflicting upon good persons.

409. mae-l piRa-nh-thaar- aayinum, kal-laathaar, keezh-p-piRa-nh-thum
katRaar anaith-th(u)- ilar paadu.

An illiterate person, although having been born in the upper echelon of the society, will not be considered equal, in dignity, to a learned person born in the lower echelon of the society! (Note: The poet tries to propagate the merit of education among the under-privileged sections of the society! This needs research). (Please See: Kalaignar Urai).

410. vilang-kodu makkaL anai-yar, ila-ng-ku-nhool
katRaa-rOdu (y)ae-nai yavar.

The difference between animals and human beings can be compared, with regard to mental capabilities. Whatever difference is assessed, a similar difference will be revealed while comparing illiterate persons with persons who have earned exposure to celebrated books, with regard to the knowledge-base! (Note: Resourcefulness of intelligence-potential is earned through education. Refinement of the sixth sense, skill-development, and other human capabilities are enhanced through education. Out of concern and benevolent care, the poet cautions the illiterate person about the importance of education, so that he/she might deserve a better treatment and dignity in the society, as reflected in kurals 403, 404, 409, 397, etc.).

CHAPTER-42

KNOWLEDGE THROUGH HEARING

(Note: The poet gives a concession (suggestion) to persons who did not (and could not) earn exposure to the privilege of learning (formal education), in the sense that knowledge-base can be enriched through the art of hearing! By devoting time to listen to public speeches, music, literary discourses, drama, theatrical performances, etc.. a person can acquire knowledge!).

411. selvath-thuL selvam, sevi-ch-chelvam; ach-chelvam
selvath-thuL (y)ellaam thalai.

Knowledge of any person gained by listening through the ears is considered as the most precious wealth (top in the list) among all other forms of wealth.

412. sevikku uNavu il-laatha pOzh-thu, siRithu,
vayitRu-kkum yeeya-p- padum.

Some small quantity of food will be given to the stomach to satisfy the hunger, only when there is no food (listening-material) to be fed into the ears! (Listening material = music, speech by others). (Note: In the modern scenario, televised programs and cinema take care of this requirement).

413. sevi- uNa-viR- kae-Lvi yudai-yaar, avi-yuNavin
aa-ndR-aa—rOdu oppar nhi-lath-thu.

Persons who enjoy their food for thought, through the ears, although living on land in this world, are comparable, in status, to their ancestors who enjoy the divine food in the heaven!

414. katRilan aayinum kae-t-ka; a-h-thu- oruvaRku,
oRkath-thin ootR(u)-aam thuNai.

Even if a person remains without the benefit of learning, let that person lend the ears to hearing a lot of good information. It is like a propping-support to remain cheerful during physical weakness/ mental worries.

415. izhuk-kal udai-yuzhi ootRuk-kO-l atRae
ozhukkam udai-yaar vaai-ch- chol.

The words of those wise persons who follow the virtuous path are worthy of being listened to! That knowledge gained by ordinary persons will be useful to them, as a supporting staff (stick) while walking on a marshy land, thus preventing them from falling down! Those words will give a helping hand, to a poorly-informed -person (or ignorant person), preventing him/her from making a mistake, in the usage of proper words.

416. (y)enaith-thaanum nha-llavai kae-tka; anai-th-thaa-num
aa-ndRa perumai tharum.

If a person lends his/her ears to hear good information/material, even in a small measure, it will bring a dignified benefit derived through hearing.

417. pizhaith-th(u)-uNar-nh-thum pae-thaimai sollaar, izhaith-- th(u)-uNar-nh-thu
yeeNdiya kae-Lvi yavar.

Those persons who carefully and attentively accumulate the vast and rich knowledge through hearing, will not speak out opinion to others, on topics which they have only partially understood, when approached for advice. (They will not pretend as if they know everything. They will avoid giving advice on topics which they have only partially understood!).

418. kae-t-pinum kae-Laath-thakai-ya-vae, kae-Lvi-yaal
thO-t-ka-p- padaatha sevi.

The ears of a person capable of hearing well, will be considered deaf, if the message of good knowledge has not pierced through the ears so far (to be heard)! (The benefit of hearing will not give any benefit to such a person!).

419. nhu-Na-ng-ki ya kaeLvi-yar- allaar, vaNa-ng-ki-ya
vaai(y)-inar aathal arithu.

Persons, without a fine and sharp knowledge gained through hearing, cannot become successful in delivering eloquent/fluent speeches!

420. seviyin suvai- yuNaraa vaay-u-Narvin maakkaL
avi-yinum, vaazhi-num, yen?

Those persons who are not used to enjoy the taste of gathering knowledge through ears, but who are only used to the tasty food taken through the mouth, may not understand the benefits of being alive, in contrast to facing death! (They are the great losers of an enjoyable (blissful) experience of listening through ears, when they were alive!). (Note: The pleasure of listening to music enjoyed by a living-person can be visualized while interpreting this couplet!)

CHAPTER-43

POSSESSION OF WISDOM

421. aRivu atRam kaakkum karuvi; seRu-vaar-k-kum
uL-(L)azhikkal aakaa aRaN.

For any person, wisdom (knowledge) is the weapon which guards against destruction. It serves as a fortress which cannot be entered into, by any enemy to cause destruction.

422. sendRa idath-thaal sela-vidaa(thu), theethu oree-yi,
nha-ndRin-paal ui-p-pathu aRivu.

(One must try to acquire) wisdom which is capable of preventing the person's mind from going hither and thither (here and there), (as guided by the senses of organs),and regulating one's mind, towards a good path, thus preventing from committing evil acts.

423. (y)ep-poruL yaar-yaar vaai-k-kae-t-pinum, ap-poruL
mei-p-poruL kaaN-bathu aRivu.

Whatever is being heard from whomsoever it may be, the truth behind whatever is being heard must be ascertained (evaluated/investigated) to find out the true nature behind it. That is the wisdom.

424. yeN-poruLa - vaaka-ch- chela-ch-cholli-th- thaan-piRar vaai
nhuN-poRul kaaN-bathu aRivu!

Whatever thought is embedded in one's mind must be shared with others in an orderly way, in any forum, so that it is understood properly (to earn the admiration/appreciation of others), and the person must be shrewd (smart) enough to absorb (grasp) the minute thinking of others, as heard from their words! This is a part of wisdom!

425. ulakam thazhee-yi-ya-thu, otpam; malar-thalum,
koombal-um il-lath(u) aRivu

Wisdom of a person requires ability to make friendship at world-level, and manoeuvre it at a comfortable status, in such a way that the petals of the flower do not close down or get withered away!

426. (y)ev-vathu uRaivathu ulakam, ulakath-thO-du,
avvathu uRai-vath(u) aRivu.

Wisdom requires that a person must follow the path in life, synchronizing it with whatever path along which the people of the world align themselves. That is an element of wisdom!

427. aRivu udai-yaar aa-va- th(u) aRivaar; aRiv(u)-ilaar,
a-h-thu- aRi- kal-laa thavar

Wise persons will be able to know beforehand what ex actly is going to happen in future! Unwise persons will lack that knowledge!!

428. anj-chuvath(u) anj-chaamai pae-thai-mai; anj-chuvathu,
anj-chal aRivaar thozhil.

It will amount to be foolishness, if a person does not fear for whatever thing is to be feared for! It is the alert practice of a wise person which helps the self, to remain cautious about what should be feared for.

429. (y)ethir-athaak- kaakkum aRivinaar-k-ku illai,
athira varuvathO-r nhOy.

Those persons will not be affected by sudden calamities (mishaps, troubles), if they are capable of knowing, in advance, about the probable occurrence of any trouble, and if they are capable of taking (appropriately) preventive measures.

430. aRiv(u)- udaiyaar yellaam udaiyaar; aRiv(u)-ilaar
(y)en-nudai-ya rae-num ilar.

Wise persons will remain cheerful as if they have got all forms of sufficient wealth. Persons who lack wisdom will always complain that they possess 'nothing', even if they own unlimited wealth! (It all depends on the wisdom of a person! The sense of contentment is the criterion!!).

CHAPTER-44

CONDEMNING-FAULTS

431. seruk-kum sina-mum siRumai-yum il-laar,
perukkam peru-mitha nhee-r-th-thu.

The growth and prosperity of those persons who are free from arrogance, anger and meanness (unfairness) will deserve pride, with admiration of the society!

432. ivaRa-lum maaNbu-iRa-nh-tha maa-nam-um, maaNaa
uvakai-yum yae-tham iRai-kku.

Miserliness, arrogance without magnanimity, and shameless joy (related to personal pleasures) are considered as faults for the ruler of the land!

433. thinaith-thuNai-yaam kutRam vari-num, panai-th -thuNai-yaa-k-
koLvar, pazhi nh-aaNu - vaar.

Persons who fear guilt, would visualize a small offence committed by them, as small as a millet-grain, as if, it is offensive enough to be the size of a big seed of palm tree, while regretting for it!

(Note: The size of one seed is compared with the size of another seed, the difference being many orders of magnitude! The size of one seed of palm tree will be equal to many hundred times the size of a millet-seed!)

434. kutRamae kaakka poruLaaka; kutRa-mae
atRam tharoo-um pakai.

Crime (offence) committed by a person is like an enemy capable of causing death to that person. 'Therefore, prevent any offensive action against others, thus, making it a policy to be followed by you, throughout your lifetime'!

(Note: The term '*atRam*' means destruction/annihilation, implying that the crime committed by a person will cause 'total-destruction' to the person who commits the crime!).

435. varu(m) -munnar-k- kaavaa-thaan vaazh-k-kai, yeri-munnar
vaith-thooRu pO-la-k- kedum.

Life of a person who does not prevent an evil act before it could occur, will be destroyed just like a stack-of -straw placed in front of a glowing flame, at closer proximity!

436. than- kutRam neekki-p- piRar-kutRam kaaNkiR-pin,
yen-kutRam aakum iRai-kku?

For any ruler of the land, the 'modus-operandi' (the method of doing it) must be: that the ruler should examine the faults of others, after the ruler (the self) has ensured that he is 'proved-free' from any such fault. Then, the ruler will be admired as faultless, and his judgement on others would be considered fair!

437. seyaR-paala sei-yaath(u) iva-Riyaan selvam
uyaR-paa-lath(u) andRi-k- kedum.

The wealth of a stingy (miserly) person who does not perform any benevolent act within his affordability, will get destroyed, without any guarantee for sustainability of his wealth!

438. patRuLLam (y)ennum ivaRan-mai, yetRuL-Lum
yeNNa-p- paduvathu- ondR(u) andRu.

Sticking on to greediness, and practicing miserliness (not-spending on even duty-bound obligations to society) is considered as a crime-related offence!

439. viyavaRka- ye-gn-gnaa-ndRum, thannai; nhaya-vaRka
nhandRi paya-vaa vinai.

A person must neither indulge in praising one's own self, nor desire to do anything which would not produce a beneficial result.

440. kaatha-la kaathal aRi-yaa-mai ui-k-kiR-pin,
 (y)ae-thila, (y)ae-thilaar nhool.

If a person is capable of carrying out any activity related to conserving his/her wealth and enjoying personal comforts, without being let known to others, even his/her enemies cannot do any harm to that person through their bad-designs! (Note: Maintaining secrecy about personal programs is highlighted).

CHAPTER-45

LINK WITH GREAT PERSONS (AS PATRONS)

441. aRan-aRi-nh-thu mooth-tha aRivudai-yaar kae-Nmai
thiRan aRi-nh-thu thae-r-nh-thu koLal.

Practical wisdom (prudence) suggests that a smart person must select and earn the relationship of wise persons in consideration of their virtues and great wisdom, and earn their patronage (so that it is beneficial to the self!").

442. utRa-nhOy nhee-kki, uRaa-amai muR-kaakkum
petRi-yaar-p- pae-Nik- koLal.

An intelligent person must cherish and maintain the link with those persons who are capable of removing the present sufferings and preventing the future sufferings for the self!

443. ariyavatRuL yellaam arithae, peri-yaarai-p-
pae-Ni-th thamar-aa-k- koLal.

Maintaining a link with a great person, and making him/her to show interest in one's favour, is the rarest of rare-achievements that any one person could accomplish!

444. tham-min peri-yaar thamar-aa ozhuku-thal
vanmai-yuL (y)ellaam thalai.

It is the highest strength of any person to act in such a way that the elders who are at a higher level than the person concerned are appreciative of him/her, to the extent of their coming forward to show a keen interest in his/her progress.

445. soozhvaar- kaN (N)aaka ozhuka-laan, mannavan,
soozhvaarai-ch choozh-nh-thu koLal.

Virtually, the king functions as the eyes of the ministers and advisers who surround him all the time, and, through whom he sees the world, and governs his kingdom as per their advice! So, the king must closely (thoroughly) examine them before selecting them for the work!

446. thakkaar inath-than-aai-th- thaan-ozhuga vallaa-nai-ch-
chetRaar seya-k-kidanh-tha-thu il.

No harm could be caused to the king by his enemies, if the king has got the strength of acting upon the advice of (a team of) able-advisers, by building intimate and trustworthy relationship with them!

447. idikkum thuNai-yaa-rai aaL-vaarai yaa-rae
kedukkum thakai-mai yavar?

Who can do a harm to a king who rules the land, with assistants empowered with freedom of pin-pointing the errors (committed by the king), whenever committed, or likely to commit?

448. idip-paarai il-laatha (y)ae-maraa mannan,
kedupaar ilaa-nu-ng— kedum.. (ilaa-num kedum).

A king who does not have anybody to pinpoint his erring-acts then and there, will get destroyed even without an enemy, due to his inability to govern!

449. muthal- ilaar-k- ku oothiyam illai; matha-lai-yaam
saarbu- i(l)laar-k-ku, illai nhilai.

There is no profit for any person who does not invest capital. Similarly, there cannot be any stability for anybody who does not have any propping support of friends/elders/well-wishers/family-members

450. pallaar pakai koLa-lin, path-thu-adu-th-tha thee-mai-th-thae,
nha-llaar thodar-kai vidal.

Giving up friendship with good people is ten times more harmful than earning the enmity of many persons! Do not discontinue your contact with great persons!

CHAPTER- 46

AVOIDANCE OF BAD COMPANY

451. sitRinam anj-chum perumai; siRumai-thaan
sutRamaa-ch- choozh-nh-thu vidum.

Respectable persons will avoid associating with bad (mean) persons. Persons of less respectability will crowd together, claiming relationship (kinship) with one another!

452. nhi-lathth(u)- iyalpaal nheer- thiri-nh-th(u) atRaakum; maa-nh-thar-k-ku
inath-th(u) –iyal-path(u) aakum aRivu.

The quality of water will change, depending upon the quality of soil through which the water flows/permeates. The quality of human beings will depend on the type of their companionship!

453. manath-thaan-aam maa-nh-thar-k-ku uNarchchi; inath-thaan-aam
'in-naan' yena-p-padum sol.

For human beings, the intellect is revealed by the mind. The qualitative nature of persons will be revealed by the category of their companionship!

454. manathth(u) – uLathu -pO-la-k- kaatti, oruvaR-ku
inath-thuLath(u)- aakum aRivu.

Outwardly, it may appear that the wisdom of a person is revealed as it is contained in his/her mind. In reality, the wisdom of a person is what is contained in the school of thought of the companionship!

455. manam-thooy-mai, sey-vinai thooy-mai iraNdum
inam-thooy-mai thoovaa varum.

The two functions of a person, namely, purity of mind, and purity of action will be yielded, depending upon the category of companionship.

456. manam- thooyaar-k-ku yechcham nha-ndR(u)-aakum; inam-thoo-yaarkku
illai nha-ndR(u) aakaa vinai.

For those persons with purity of mind, the resulting fame will be good. For those persons whose category of companionship is good, bad effects will not occur

457. mana- nha-lam man-nuyir-kku- aakkam; ina-nhalam
(y)ellaa-p- pukazhum tharum.

For the human beings, the noble mind will yield wealth and righteousness, and the goodness of companionship will yield all fame/ reputations!

458. mana -nhalam nhan-k(u)-udaiya raa-yinum, saandRO-r-kku
ina-nhalam (y)aemaappu udai-ththu

Those persons who possess noble minds will be benefited well. Yet, the goodness of their companionship will add to their pride!

459. mana-nhala-ththin aakum, maRumai; matR(u) a-h-thum,
ina- nha-lath-thin (y)ae-maapp(u) udai-ththu.

Nobility of mind will give happiness 'during the next birth'. It will have an addition (increment) of pride due to the goodness of companionship!

(Alternatively: Nobility of mind during one's lifetime, will yield fame to that person after his/her demise! So also, the pride of companionship will give additional fame!). (Note: Fame accumulated by the ancestors will be an asset to the descendants/siblings!).

460. nhallinath-thin oong-kum thuNai- illai; thee-yinath-thin
allaR- padu-ppathoo–um il.

There cannot be a greater support /help than the goodness of companionship. At the same time, there cannot be a greater harm caused by the company of wicked persons.

CHAPTER-47

ACTION AFTER DEEP THINKING,

461. azhivathoo-um, aava-thoo-um, aaki, vazhi-payakkum
oothiyam-um soozh-nh-thu seyal.

Before starting any act, any person has to consider factors, such as, the probable gains and losses,pros and cons, and also future benefits accruing on a long term basis.

462. theri-nh-tha- inath-thodu, thaer-nh-th(u) (y)eNNi-ch- chei-vaar-k-ku,
arum-poruL yaath(u)-ondRum il.

There cannot be anything too hard to acquire, if a person decides to undertake an activity with known-person(s), and with selective thoughts!

463. aakkam karuthi muthal- izhakkum sey-vinai
ookkaar aRi-vudai yaar.

Wise persons, with a desire of enhancing additional benefits during the future, may not encourage any working method or new venture which would cause a loss to the capital itself!

464. theLivu-ila-thanai-th- thoda-ng-kaar, iLivu- (y)ennum
(y)ae-thap-paadu anj-chu- pavar.

Those wise persons who are mindful of fearing for any activity which would cause a shameful calamity, will not start any activity without clarity about the pros and cons of the proposed activity!

465. vakai-aRach- choozhaa-thu yezhu-thal, pakai-varai-p-
paaththi-p- padu-ppath(u)- O-r- aaRu.

Without surrounding the enemy as per established practices, if a king rises for war, it is like the king making his contribution to enhance the existing strength of the enemy!

466. sei-thakka alla seyak-kedum; sei-thakka,
seyyaa-mai- yaa-num—kedum.

If a person does an act which must not be done, it will bring misery to the person. If a person does not do an act which must be done immediately, it will bring misery to the person!

467. (y)eNNith thuNika karu-mam; thuNi-nh-tha-pin,
(y)eNNu-vam- (y)enbathu izhukku.

Think deeply before you decide to act. To think back after entering into action will mean blemish (blame) to the self!

468. aatRin- varu-nh-thaa- varu-th-tham, palar- nhi-ndRu,
pO-tRinum poth-thu-p- padum.

Any work, if not done by adopting proper methods and the required (preparatory) efforts, may not become successful, even with the combined efforts and support of many others who come to the rescue!

469. nhandRu- aatRal uL-Lum, thavaRu- uNdu; avar-avar,
paNb(u) aRi-nh-thu aatRaa-k- kadaiz

Even in extending beneficial help to others, errors would/ could happen, if it is not extended to suit the cultural (character- based) disposition of the recipient!

470. (y)eLLaatha (y)eNNi-ch- cheyal- vae-Ndum; tham-modu,
ko-LLaa-tha ko-LLaa-thu ulaku.

Perform any act which would not be despised/hated (not- relished) by others, because the world will not approve of anything that is not acceptable!

CHAPTER-48

KNOWING ONE'S OWN STRENGTH (APPLICABLE TO A RULER AS WELL AS A CITIZEN)

471. vinai-vali-yum, than- vali-yum, maatRaan- vali-yum,
thuNai-vali-yum, thookki-ch- cheyal.

Any act in war must be performed after weighing (analyzing) the strength required for the task, strength of the self and the strength the enemy, and the strength of the allies (on both sides).

472. ol-vathu aRi-vathu, aRi-nth(u)-athan kaN-tha-ng-ki-ch-
chelvaar-kku-ch- chellaa-tha-thu il.

For those who aim at a desired action, if they take care to acquire the required knowledge and act accordingly, with constant/ continuous/ sustained efforts, there is nothing impossible for them to achieve!.

473. udaith- tham vali-yaRi-yaar, ookkath-thin ookki,
idaik- kaN muri-nh-thaar palar!

There are many persons who started acting without knowing their own strength, out of mere courage and confidence, and got destroyed at midway, without being able to continue! (This is a lesson to others!).

474. amai-nh-thu- aang-ku ozhukaan, aLavu-aRiyaan, than-nai
viya-nh-thaan, virai-nh-thu kedum.

Any person who does not get along with others (who are involved in similar acts), and who does not know his limits of capabilities (including an analysis of income versus expenditure), and who indulges in self-flattery, will get destroyed sooner than assumed!

475. peeli-pei saakaa-dum, achchu- iRum, ap-paNdam-
saala mi-kuth-thu-p- pei-(y)in.

The axle of the cart, loaded with soft material such as feathers of peacocks (birds), will break, if the material is excessively loaded! (Note: This principle applies to physical forces and mental worries, measures of insults, etc). (Note: The bearing capacity of a strong metal such as iron and the weight of a soft material such as bird's feather are compared!).

476. nhuni-k- kombar yae-Ri-naar, a-h-thu- iRa-nh-thu- ookkin,
uyir-kku iRuthi yaaki- vidum.

Any person, climbing up a tree and reaching the top of the branch has to realize that, if he/she proceeds further beyond, it may prove to be the end of life for the climber. (Note: This concept is applicable to the limit specified for one's actions; or limit of anger etc).

477. aatRin aLav(u)-aRi-nh-thu yeeha; athu, poruL
pO-tRi vazha-ng-kum nheRi. (yeeha= yeeka).

Any person desirous of donating materialistic gifts to others, must realize the limitations of the self, being guided by the quantum of income and fixed assets! This caution is indicated in the norms for protecting one's own wealth.

478. aak(u)- aaRu aLav(u)- ittithu- aayinum, kae-du illai;
pO-ku -aaRu aka-laak- kadai.

There is no harm to any person, even if the source of income is limited, provided that the expenditures are not excessive/ expanded! (Note: Income and expenditure must be balanced!).

479. aLavu aRi-nh-thu vaazhaa-thaan vaazh-k-kai, uLa-pO-la,
illaa-ki-th thO-ndRaa-k- kedum,

The property value of a person who does not adjust (proportion/plan and execute) his/her life-style, commensurate with the limitations of income of the self, will get destroyed, although it may appear as if the wealth is 'in-tact' (not damaged)! (Latin word: intactus).

480. uLa-varai thook-kaatha oppurav(u) aaN-mai,
vaLa-varai vallai-k- kedum'

The measures of wealth of a person will soon get diminished/destroyed, if the person practices the art of giving material- help to others, without outweighing (considering) the limitation of values of his/her property in possession.

CHAPTER-49

CHOICE OF TIME FOR ACTION (APPLICABLE TO THE KING AND THE CITIZEN)

481. pakal- vellum, kookai-yai-k- kaa-kkai; ikal-vellum,
vae-nh-thar-k-ku, vae-Ndum pozhu-thu

During daytime, under broad daylight, even a Crow will win, defeating the Owl! For a king, wishing to conquer his enemy, the task of choosing the time for attack is very important!

482. paruvath-thO-du otta- -ozhukal, thiru-vi-nai-th
theeraa-mai aark-kum kayiRu.

Acting in tune with the seasons of the year is the proven rope which binds the wealth together, and prevents from diminishing! (Note: This concept of choosing time for any action can be extended to initiation of any new effort/endeavour, considering all environmental and ecological factors, including nature's settings).

483. aru-vinai yenba uLa-vO? karu-vi-yaal,
kaalam aRi-nh-thu sei(y)in?

Could there be any difficult task for anybody, if a person, who owns the necessary weapons/methods/ infrastructure, decides to act, choosing an appropriate time for commencing-the-activity?

(Note: "*karuvi*"denotes:equipment/weapons/methodology/ infrastructure/software/supporting-services/strength-of- feasibility, etc.).

484. gnaa-lam karuthi-num kai-koodum; kaalam
karuthi, idath-thaal sei(y) in.

If somebody (any person) wishes to win the entire world for himself/ herself, it will materialize, if acted upon at the right time and the right place.

485. kaa-lam karuthi, iruppar, kala-ng-kaathu;
gnaa-lam karu-thu- pavar.

Those who wish to conquer (win) the world, will wait, with out any worried-look, for the right time to come/ripen!

486. ookkam udai-yaan, odu-kkam poru-tha-kar,
thaak-kaRku-p- pae-rum thakai-th-thu.

A courageous person's hesitation (restraint) to attack the enemy (in anticipation of the right time to ripen) is similar to the strategy adopted by a fighting male-sheep taking a step backwards, in preparation for a more forceful attack! (Note: This concept helps in the business-world too! Especially in stock-market?!).

487. poLL-ena aa-ng-kae, puRam-vae-raar, kaalam- paar-th-thu,
uL-vae-r-ppar, oLLi- yavar.

Wise persons will not expose their anger outwardly (openly), when insulted (harmed) by others, on that occasion when it happens! They will wait for the right time, suppressing their anger within themselves! Their anger will be shown at the right (appropriate) time!!

(Note: This concept can be extended to the task of planning military-strategies for attacks on the enemy forces!).

488. cheRu-nharai-k kaaNin, sumakka; iRu-varai,
kaaNin, kizha-kkam thalai.

If you happen to see your enemies, do bear the excesses they cause to you, with patience, until (you sufficiently equip yourself, and) when the end comes to them, their heads could be lowered to the floor!

489. yeitha-R-ku ariyathu, iyai-nh-thakkaal, anh-nhilai-yae,
seitha-R-ku ariya seyal.

If a rare, unachievable, opportune time comes on anyone's way, the planned work must be carried out, immediately, without missing the opportunity!

490. **kokku-okka, koomb-um paruvath-thu; matRu, athan, kuththu-okka, seerth-tha idath-thu.**

Act like a Stork (fish-catching bird) while waiting quietly, without feeling any shame, waiting for the appropriate time to ripen. Act quickly when the right time is on hand, just like the same way as the Stork strikes with its beak to catch its prey. (Note: Quick action is required for acting on it, as advised in kural 466, without missing the opportune time!).

CHAPTER-50

CHOICE OF PLACE FOR ACTION

491. thodang-kaRka, yev-vinai-yum; yeLLarka, mutRum,
idam kaNda- pin-al la-thu.

A wise king must not start any act, or start insulting his enemy, until selecting a suitable place (battle-field), for besieging him, with a strong force. (Note: Selecting a battle-field is similar to selecting a site for office or industry, as the objective is success/ victory, in all cases!).

492. muraN-sae-r-nh-tha moimbi- navar-k-kum, araN-saer-nh-th(u)- aam
aakkam pala-vum tharum.

Even for those warriors with strong shoulders of might and valour, a defense-fortress (fort), if added, will yield superior gains (victory).

493. aatRaa-rum aatRi adu-ba, idan-aRinh-thu,
pO-tRaar –kaN pO-tRi-ch- chey-in.

Even persons of lesser strength can destroy the enemy forces, if they defend themselves with skill, after choosing the right- place, while facing the army of the enemy! (Note: Consolidation of the available infrastructure, and improving the efficiency of functioning are the strategies, in organizational administration!).

494. yeNNi-yaar eNNam izhappar; idan aRi-nh-thu,
thunni-yaar thunni-ch- chey-in.

Even an enemy, who, initially hoped to win the war, will lose his hope of winning, if an army chooses the right place for the battle-field, and fight vigorously with determination (resorting to fast-move) to win the war! (Note: The principle is applicable to circumventing the effort of an unreasonable enemy to initiate a war!).

495. nhedum-punal-uL vellum, muthalai; adum-punalin,
nheeng-kin athan-ai-p- piRa.

Inside deep waters, a crocodile will win the fight with any other animal! Alas! If the crocodile leaves its natural habitat of deep water, other animals only will win!!

496. kadal- Odaa, kaal -val- nhedum-thae-r! kadal-Odum
nhaa-vaay-um, O-daa nhi-lath-thu

The lofty chariot with strong wheels cannot run into the sea! So also, the large ship which is capable of traversing the sea cannot run on the land! (Note: Chariots in battlefield, and ships for foreign-trade were available in Tamil-speaking land 2000 years ago!).

497. anj-chaamai all-aal, thuNai vae-Ndaa; yenj-chaamai,
yeNNi, idath-thaal, chey-in.

No other support is needed, except fearlessness and self- confidence, for those who constantly think about the objective, without any discontinuity, and start acting after choosing the right place! (Note: This concept is applicable to situations of war and peace!).

498. siRu padai-yaan, sel-lidam sae-rin, uRu-padai-yaan
ookkam azhi-nh-thu, vidum.

A king with a small army, will be able to face a larger army, if the battlefield is familiar and favourable to him, whereas, the large army will lose its morale/courage, and may even get defeated. (Note: The morale of soldiers will be boosted up in their native -soil, if the battlefield is familiar to them!).

499. siRai-nhalanum seerum ilar-yeni-num, maa-nh-thar,
uRai- nhi-lath-thOdu ottal arithu.

It is very difficult for an enemy-king to defeat the soldiers in the battlefield located in their own native soil, even if they (the native army) do not own either the necessary strength,or a well- protected fort. (Note: There are several examples in the recorded history of the world, to prove this point!).

500. kaal-aazh- kaLaril, nhari adum; kaN-anj-chaa,
vael-aaL mukath-tha kaLiRu.

Even if a war-elephant which has faced the sleepless warriors armed with long-handled metal-pointed weapons of war, will be fearlessly attacked by a small animal like a fox, if the elephant gets into a knee-deep marshy land! (Note: The marshy land becomes a trap for a huge animal like an elephant. The surrounding environment has got relevance for the safety of any living-creature!).

CHAPTER-51

CLARITY BASED ON ANALYSIS

501. aRam, poruL, inbam, uyir-achcham, nhaan-kin
thiRam- therinh-thu, thae-Rap- padum.

There are four factors which are to be considered for judging fitness of a person for a risky managerial work, namely, i) virtuous traits, ii) freedom from greed for wealth, iii) freedom from temptations for personal pleasures, and iv) freedom from fear for risky works/challenging-undertakings/facing external threats.

502. kudi-p-piRanh-thu, kutRath-thin nheeng-ki, vadu-p-pariyum
nhaaN-udai-yaan kattae theLivu.

A person born in a good family, who is free from offensive acts, and who has got the natural shyness (determination/resolve) against doing offensive acts can be trusted with confidence for any work.

503. ariya- katRu, aasu-atRaar- kaNNum, theri-yung-kaal
inmai, arithae veLiRu.

Even in the case of those learned-scholars of faultless character, and who are thorough with advanced knowledge, if carefully examined, it is hard to find them to be totally free from some traces of ignorance! (Note: This idea tallies with the saying of Aristotle, a Greek Philosopher: 'There is no great genius without some touch of madness!': Ref:Appendix-3 A; quote 34).

504. kuNam nhaa-di, kutRam-um nhaa-di, avatRuL,
mikai nhaa-di, mikka, koLal.

In judging any person, it is fair to consider the good qualities and bad qualities, and to give importance to whichever is greater of the two, in the process of forming an opinion about that person!

505. perumai-kkum, ae-nai siRumai-kkum, thath-tham
karuma-mae kattaLai-k- kal

One's own actions will serve as the touch-stone for evaluating (judging) the greatness or meanness (shortcomings) of a person.

506. atRaarai-th- thae-Ruthal Ombu-ka; matRu, avar,
patR(u)-ilar; nhaaNaar- pazhi.

Avoid trusting those persons who do not have kith and kin (known to you), because, they may not have love for any one, and may not have any sense of shame for committing any evil act or criminal act!!

507. kaa-thanmai, kanh-thaa aRivu-aRiyaar-th- thae-Ruthal,
pae-thaimai yellaam tharum.

If an ignorant person (who is not familiar with what should be known) is, shamelessly, trusted for any important task, out of mere liking for the individual-person, it would yield all bad results characteristic of folly/stupidity/foolishness! (These results will cause harm to the person responsible for the selection!).

508. thae-raan, piRanai-th- theLin-thaan, vazhi-muRai
theeraa idumbai tharum.

If any person trusts an untried stranger and carries out all acts in accordance with the advice given by that stranger, it will cause endless miseries to the person concerned, and also to the off-springs (descendants) of that person!

509. thae-RaR-ka, yaarai-yum, thae-raathu; thae-r-nh-tha-pin,
thae-Ruka; thae-Rum poruL.

Do not trust anyone without trial. After starting to believe the person, do become clear to assign the selected task to him/her, according to the nature of the task!! (It will be good for the person who practices this policy!).

510. thae-raan theLivum, theLin-thaan-kaN ai-yu-Ravum,
theeraa idumbai tharum.

Selecting a person for a trusted responsibility without any trials, and doubting the integrity of the selected person, subsequently after the choice, will be considered erroneous (wrong), and both actions will give endless trouble.

CHAPTER-52

CHOICE OF ACTION AFTER CLARITY

511. nhanmai-yum, theemai-yum nhaa-di, nhalam-puri-nh-tha
thanmai-yaan aaLa-p- padum.

While selecting a methodology for a particular work, consider a method which will give beneficial results, and also another method which will give a harmful result or less-beneficial result. Select the methodology which will yield beneficial results. Employ a person who is well-experienced in the chosen methodology. That approach is called a good administrative skill/capability/resourcefulness.

512. vaari, perukki, vaLam-paduththu, utRavai-
aaraai-vaan seika vinai.

A person capable of i) enhancing revenue (income), ii) analyzing aspects related to enhancement of wealth and iii) examining /auditing/ appraising/comprehending the current situation must be permitted (and encouraged) to act!

513. anbu, aRivu, thae-tRam, avaa-inmai, inh-nhaan-kum,
nhan-ku (u)daiyaan kat-tae theLivu.

Clarity of action will be there with the person who has got the four essential qualities, namely, kindness, intelligence, maturity and lack of greed.

514. yenai-vakai-yaan thae-Riya-k-kaNNum, vinai-vakai-yaan
vae-R(u)- aakum maa-nh-thar palar.

After having gone through different methods of training, or after assessing the merits of methods suited for a specified action, there are some persons who do the acts differently, being guided by their own whims and fancies or discretion or choice, which they would call as 'working style'!

(Note: It may not refer to inefficient persons. It might refer to persons who introduce innovative ideas! This needs research).

515. aRinthu aatRi-ch- chei-kiR-paaRku al-laal, vinai-thaan,
siRa-nh-thaan-yendRu yae-vaR-paatRu andRu.

Work must be entrusted to a person who is familiar with the nature of work, and the methodology to be followed in order to complete it to perfection. It need not be given to any other person on the assumption of a better capability. (Note: The poet supports the authenticity of trained-personnel! Expressing fear about sustaining the productivity! This needs research).

516. sey-vaanai nhaadi, vinai-nhaadi, kaalath-thOdu,
yeitha uNar-nh-thu seyal.

For undertaking any activity, the person capable of doing the work must be chosen, the nature of work must be finalized, and the time-frame must be fixed with him/her, to get the work done to perfection. (Note: This concept relates to optimization of labour and time involved in completing the assigned-work. Earlier completion can help in financial savings! There are other benefits as well! This needs research).

517. ithanai, ithanaal, ivan- mudik-kum yendR(u)- aay-nh-thu,
athanai, avan-kaN vidal.

It must be examined as to who can do the chosen work, what are the methods to be employed, and whether the chosen person is capable of completing the work. When the decision is finalized on the choice, the responsibility of completing the work must be given entirely to the chosen person. (Note: This is a major concept which influences the success of any project. It relates to expertise!Recruitment policies!Identification of the Best Available Technology! Guideline for any Entrepreneurial idea! etc. It is like a dogma for the management science! This needs research).

518. vinaik-ku- urimai nhaa-diya pindRai, avanai-
athaRku- uriyan- aaka-ch cheyal.

After selecting a suitable person for doing the work, the entire responsibility of completing the work must be entrusted to the chosen - person!

519. vinai-k-kaN vinai-yudaiyaan kae-N-mai, vae R(u)aaka nhi-naip-paanai nheeng-kum thiru.

When a person chosen for performing a particular work, with care and devotion, if the employer raises doubt over the dedication of the worker, the employer will lose his prestige, and there will be some financial losses too! (Morale of an employee must be boosted up, and not discouraged). (Note: This relates to Industrial Management. It may have relevance to Quality Control, Productivity, Financial Management, Protection of Labour-Law, etc).

520. nhaaL-thORum nhaaduka mannan, vinai-sey-vaan kOdaa-mai-k- kOdaathu ulaku. (nhaa-dORum=nhaaL-thORum).

The king must examine the activities of his personnel, on a day-to-day basis, so that acts deviating from norms can be avoided or rectified. This caution is needed to avoid loss of morale, or for preventing abnormal things happening among the personnel or for settling disputes among the people in his country! (Note: The poet fixes the responsibility on the Top-Leader of the Establishment, urging upon the daily-monitoring of progress! This is a major policy-issue in achieving industrial prosperity/productivity!).

CHAPTER-53

LINK WITH RELATIVES

521. patRu-atRa kaNNum pazhaimai- paa raattu-thal
sutRath-thaar kaNNae uLa.

It is a customary tradition for rich families to treat (host) poor relatives: i) who were rich in the past, and ii) old relatives who have lost continuity in matrimonial links. This gesture will be considered as a cultured tradition, among relatives!

(Note: Old relatives who have switched over to ascetic-life, stand included in the list of relatives to be honoured!).

522. virupp-aRaa-ch chutRam iyai-yin, arupp(u)-aRaa
aakkam pala-vum tharum.

If a person, as the head of the family, maintains the link with relatives who show unfailing love towards that person, he deserves appreciation! Many benefits will come to him, in uninterrupted ways (without any interception)!

523. aLav(u)-aLaavu illaa-thaan vaazh-k-kai, kuLa-vaLaa-k-
kOdu- indRi nheer- nhiRai-nh-thu atRu.

The village tank, not having bunds (embankments) all around its sides, (or at least on one side) will not be able to get filled up, with water, to its full capacity, even during the rains. Similarly, the life of a person, not mingling with the relatives will become blank/ empty/dry without affection or kindness.

524. sutRath-thaal sutRap- pada- ozhu-kal, selvam-thaan
petRath-thaal petRa payan.

If the rich persons adopt the path (practice) of being surrounded by relatives in close proximity, it will be considered as the healthy benefit of acquiring the wealth!

525. koduth-thalum, in-sol-um, aatRin, adukkiya
sutRath-thaal sutRa-p- padum

A person who liberally gives to others and utters pleasant words always, will be surrounded by relatives in all ranks. (Note: The poet describes the cultural adjustments, exhibiting mutual respect for each other, irrespective of position, economic status, etc., among relatives. Relatives in all 'ranks' means, 'in different walks of life, different financial status', etc.)

526. perung-kodai-yaan, pae-Naan- vekuLi, avan-in
marung-k(u)-udaiyaar maa-nhilath-thu il.

If a person gives material help liberally to others who are in need, and if he avoids practicing anger, he will have more pleasant relatives, and friends in his fold, as a solid support. There would not be any other person, as happy as himself/herself, in this great land!

527. kaakkai karavaa karai-nh-thu uNN-um; aakkam-um
anna-nhee - raar-k-kae uLa.

The bird, crow, will not hide its food on sighting the presence of food in a particular spot. It calls all the crows in the neighbourhood, to share the food together, with them. Wealth also will be available only to those who will practice the habit of joyously sharing their food with others.

528. pothu- nhO-k-kaan vaenh-than, varisai-yaa nhO-kkin,
athu-nhO-kki, vaazh-vaar palar.

A king does not extend his regards to all alike! He does it to each category, according to the merit they deserve. There are many persons, as a group, who look forward to this kind of practice! Affection does not get affected!

529. thamar-aaki-th- than-thuRanh-thaar sutRam, amaraa-mai-k-
kaaraNam indRi varum.

If some relatives could have gone away from a person, forgetting the affectionate relationship with the self, due to some reason, they will re-unite themselves with the same person, when the reason for earlier separation gets removed!

530. uzhai-p-piri-nh-thu kaaraNath-thin vanh-thaanai, vae-nh-than izhai-thth(u)- irunh-thu, yeNNi-k- koLal.

When an old friend of the king, who left the company of the king, long back without revealing the reason, returns now to the king due to some reason, what the king could do is to wait for some time, while analyzing all details, and finally decide to accept him! May be, by satisfying his needs.

CHAPTER-54

AVOIDANCE OF FORGETFULNESS

531. iRanh-tha vekuLi-yin thee-thae, siRanh-tha
uvakai makizh-chchi-yin sOr-vu..

Forgetfulness arising out of celebrating a joyous occasion and subsequent relaxation will produce harm, more harm (carelessness) than the harm produced by excessive anger.

532. poch-chaappu-k- koll-um pukazhai; aRivinai
nhichcha nhirappu-k-kond- R(u)aangku.

Forgetfulness will destroy one's fame, similar to the constant poverty which destroys knowledge, on a daily basis!

533. poch-chaap-paar-kku illai pukazhmai; athu, ulakath-thu
yep-paal nhoolOr-k-kum thuNivu.

Fame is denied to those who are not free from forgetfulness. It is a confirmed conclusion/decision of every kind of writers and /authors of books in all disciplines (faculties) in the world! (Note: It is a citation by the poet for augmenting (strengthening) the poet's- idea).

534. ach-cham udai-yaar-kku aRaN illai; aangku-illai
poch-chaapu udai-yaar-k-ku nha-n-ku.

For those who possess fear, there is no use of any kind of fortification/ protection. Similarly,those who possess forgetfulness will not get the benefit of position or wealth!

535. munnuRa-k- kaavaa-thu izhukki-yaan, than-pizhai
pin-ooRu irang-ki- vidum.

A person who fails to arrange for preventive measures, in advance, in anticipation of an untoward incident, will have to repent for the failure of the self, after the adversity occurs! (There is no use for a late-realization).

536. izhuk-kaamai yaar- maattum, yendRum, vazhuk-kaamai
vaayin, athu –oppathu il.

If the event of forgetfulness does not happen in a person, anytime, and if it does not happen ever, that person deserves appreciation! It is a great benefit/blessing! No other benefit will be better than this!

537. ariya- yendRu aakaatha illai; poch- chavaa-k-
karuvi-yaal pO-tRi-ch che(y)yin.

There is nothing called difficult things to achieve (do), if a person attempts with dedication, on the proposed action, using the tool called 'memory' which implies freedom from forgetfulness!

538. pukazh-nh-thavai, pO-tRi-ch che(y)yal- vae-N-dum; cheyyaathu
ikazh-nh-thaar-k-ku, yezhumai-yum il.

Whatever actions have been praised by the wise-elders, must be done by all persons with dedication. For those who default, in low esteem for the elders, and miss doing that duty, there will not be any merit (credit/reward) during the seven births! (It is also interpreted that such persons will never get any benefit throughout their lifetime). (Seven births are also interpreted as seven generations). (Note: Forgetfulness includes default (failure) to carry out bounden-duties).

539. ikazh-ch-chiyin ket-taarai uLLuka; thaam-tham,
makizh-ch-chiyin mai-nh-thuRum- pO-zh-thu.

Those persons who rejoice excessively in happiness, consequently acquiring a sense of self-admiration, which in turn, gives arrogance in their minds, are needed to remember about those who got ruined due to negligence/forgetfulness/contempt for others!

540. uLLiyathu yeithal, yeLithu,man; matRum -thaan,
uLLiyathu uLLa-p- peRin.

For any person, developing a desire for achieving an objective, it must be said that it is easy to achieve it, if that person keeps on thinking about it, putting into practice whatever efforts are needed! (To keep on trying).

CHAPTER-55

RIGHTEOUS GOVERNANCE

541. Or-nh-thu- kaN Odaathu, iRai-purinh-thu, yaar-maattum,
thae-r-nh-thu–sei - va-h-thae, muRai.

Norms to be followed by any king relating to punishment for crimes are listed as follows: (i) Investigating any occurrence of crime, (ii) examining details without showing partiality (either liking or hatred), whoever it may be, and (iii) selecting a solution to render justice. This is the proper way to give punishment to offenders!

542. vaan nhO-kki vaazhum ulaku- yellaam, mannavan
kOl-nhO-kki vaazhum kudi.

People of the world look up to the sky for the mercy of the rains. Similarly, the flourishing citizens/subjects will look up to the king, for a proper/upright rule, symbolized by Scepter.

543. anh-thaNar nh-oo-Rkum aRath-thir-kum aathi-yay
nhi-ndRa-thu mannavan kO-l.

The king's Scepter, symbolizing the upright rule by the king, is considered to be more ancient than the statutes/norms for governance, which are presently being composed (formulated) by the king, with assistance from wise persons! (Note: This poem gives a historical hint: Research is needed to find out whether it could be a dissent-note recorded by the poet, against the entry of Rig-Vedic principles of four-varna system into governance. (Please see Appendix-1)..

544. kudi-thazhee-yi-k - kO-l-Ochchum maa-nhila mannan,
adi-thazhee-yi nhiRkum ulaku.

The people of the world will admire the king and remain loyal and obedient to the king of the great land, if the king renders an upright rule, taking the people along with him (by protecting the safety and welfare of the people).

545. iyalpu-uLi-k- kO-l-Ochchum mannavan nhaatta,
peyalum, viLai-yuL-um thokku.

In a country ruled by a king, who rules the land in a systematic way, as per the dictates of the Scepter, there will be good rains, and good harvest! (Note: The Nature itself will feel happy about the upright rule of the king!).

546. vae-l-andRu vendRi tharu-vathu; mannavan
kO-l; athoo-(v)um, kO-daa-thu yenin.

It is not the weapon of war which yields victory to the king! It is the Scepter!! That too, if it does not bend, implying that the style of ruling must remain impartial, righteous and upright!!!

547. iRai kaakkum; vaiyakam yellaam; avanai,
muRai kaakkum, muttaa-ch- cheyin.

The king must protect the people of the land, following the virtuous path, ensuring a system of justice, as a welfare state.The worthiness of the king will be protected by the virtuous path/force of justice. (Note: Virtue/Justice/ Righteousness being personified as a divine-force to offer protection to a duty-bound king!).

548. yeN-patha-th-thaan O-raa muRai- seyyaa mannavan
thaN-pathath-thaan thaa-nae kedum.

A king who is beyond accessibility, and who does not investigate reality, and who does not offer a proper rule in his county, will finally ruin himself, being inflicted by a sense of guilt! (Even without an enemy!).

549. kudi-puRam kaaththu- Ombi-k- kutRam kadithal,
vadu- andRu; vae-nh-than thozhil.

Any punitive (penal) action pursued by the king, in relevance to the protection of his subjects/citizens, against threats from external sources, and punishing those persons indulging in crimes within his own kingdom, does not conform to any defect/harm! It is the king's legitimate duty/work/prerogative!

550. kolai-yil- kodiyaarai vae-nh-thu oRuththal, pai-ng-koozh
kaLai-kat- ta-tha-nodu nhaer!.

The punishment ordered by the king to the cruel persons who indulge in killing others is for the purpose of protecting the people, exactly similar to destroying the weeds in the agricultural fields for the purpose of protecting the tender-seedlings/healthy crops!

CHAPTER-56

RULE-OF-TYRANNY

551. kolai-mae-R-kon -daarin kodi-thae, alai-maeR-koNdu
allavai- seithu-ozhu-kum vaenh-thu.

Any king who causes harms against virtuous path, will be understood as a cruel person, more cruel than those unruly elements who undertake the task of killing people as their work, for their own gains!

552. vae-lodu nhi-ndRaan, 'idu'-yen- dRathu- pO-lum
kO-lodu nhi-ndRaan iravu.

The king is entrusted with sovereign power, with the prestigious Scepter, to rule the people. If the king demands for tax excessively, from the people, it will look like the act of the robbers armed with weapons, forcing the innocent persons to give their wealth (to part with their wealth)!(Note: Scepter (Sceptre) is an ornamental rod carried by the king or queen on ceremonial occasions, symbolizing the sovereign authority. Scepter was very much in use in Tamil-speaking-country, 2000 years ago).

553. nhaaL-thoRum nhaadi, muRai-seyyaa mannavan
nhaaL-thoRum nhaadu kedum.

If the king does not check for crimes and resort to corrective measures every day, his kingdom will start deteriorating, day by day, (with respect to people's security, welfare and other aspects). (Note: This principle is applicable to every chief of an organization / establishment/business-house).

554. koozhum, kudi-yum, orung-ku-izhakkum, kO-l-kO-di-ch-
choozhaa-thu seyyum arasu.

A king who does not give a fair rule in his kingdom, in accordance with the norms of a righteous rule symbolized by the Scepter, will end up losing his wealth, as well as the support of his subjects (citizens)!

555. allal-pattu aatRaa-thu azhu-tha-kaN- Neer, andRae,
selvath-thai-th- thae-y-kkum padai.

The tears, shed by the people in their inability to bear the tortures/miseries inflicted upon them, will prove to be a sharp weapon (like a filing-tool), to erode the wealth and authority of the king, as powerful as an enemy force. (Wealth=Authority to rule!).

556. mannar-kku mannu-thal seng-kOnmai, ah-thu-indrae-l,
mannaa-vaam mannar-k-ku oLi.

Stability of rule is the greatness of a king, as achieved by an upright rule, symbolic of a Righteous Scepter! If the upright rule is not sustained, the royal light will be slowly quenched! The glory will be ruined!

557. thuLi-yinmai gnaa-lath-thiRku yetRu- atRae vae-nh-than,
aLi-yin-mai vaazhum uyir-k-ku.

Royal grace is to be shown towards all living creatures in the world! If it is lacking, it is similar to the failure of timely rainfall, and the consequent sufferings of the people and the sufferings of all other creatures, all forms of life, including vegetation.

558. inmai-yin innaathu- udaimai; muRai-seyyaa
mannavan kOl-keezh-p- padin.

The wealth owned by all persons will be more bothersome than suffering from poverty, if the people ever happen to come under the rule of a king who does not rule the land as per the righteous (justified, established) norms symbolized by the Scepter!

559. muRai-kOdi mannavan sey-yin, uRai-kOdi
ollaa-thu vaanam peyal.

If a king does not rule his land in a justified way, his greatness will be lost, and even the rainfall may fail, due to failure of monsoon!

560. aa-payan- kun-dRum, aRu-thozhil-Or nhool-maRappar,
kaavalan kaa-vaan (y)enin.

If the king does not protect his kingdom with care, certain bad results will be produced: i) wealth of milk will get reduced, ii) those persons, who do the endangered-professions like, art, sculpture, poetry (which could survive only with the patronage of the king), will forget the training undergone by them, as they would not have opportunities to practice what they have learned! (Ref: Sujatha Urai; Dr.KalaignarUrai; Dr.Va. Su.Pa.ManickamUrai). (Please see Appendix-1).

(Note: It is a satirical and sarcastic note against the ferocious attitude of a rude king, due to which some undesirable effects would be produced in his country. For example: A milking-cow will be afraid of such a king, thereby, being afraid of yielding milk gener ously! The cow will even be afraid of eating sufficient grass to main tain its health!).

CHAPTER-57

AVOIDANCE OF HATEFUL ACTS

561. thakkaa-ng-ku nhaadi -th- thalai-ch-chellaa vaNNath-thaal, oth-thaa-ng-ku oRuppathu vae-nh-thu.

     It is the king's duty to investigate the crimes by appropriate means and punish the criminals to such an extent that the crime will not get repeated in future by anybody else. (Punishment given to an offender in a crime must serve as a lesson to others who are likely to commit a similar crime!).

562. kadi-thu O-ch-chi, mella (y)eRi-ka, nhedi-thu aakkam nhee-ng-kaamai vaeNdu- pavar.

     A king who wishes for prolonged rule (ruling-power, not to be taken away from him), has to give punishment for crimes, in such a style, as if raising the rod very severely and forcefully, but giving the beating in a mild way (ending up with mild punishments)!

563. veru-va-nh-tha se-i-thu-ozhu-kum veng-kOlan, aa-yin, oru-va-nh-tham ollai-k- kedum.

     If a king indulges in terrorizing his subjects, his kingdom will get ruined certainly, and speedily!

564. iRai-kadi-yan (y)endRu-uraikkum innaa-ch chol, vae-nh-than, uRai-kaduki, ollai-k- kedum.

     The life (tenure) of a king will speedily get shortened, if the king is branded by the people as a cruel king who is capable of speaking out bitter and cruel words!

565. arunj-chevvi innaa mukath-thaan- perunj-chelvam pae-(ei) -kaNd(u) -anna-thu udaith-thu.

     If a king does not permit easy access to his subjects, to meet him and express their grievances, and if he shows always an angry face to others, his vast wealth will be considered as the wealth possessed by a devil which cannot be approached! (The term 'perun-j-chelvam' is also interpreted as the great blessings (opportunity) to rule the land!).

566. kadunj-chollan, kaN-(N)ilan aa-yin, nhedunj-chelvam
nheedu-indRi aa-ng-kae kedum

If a king is well-known for practicing harsh words, and showing unsympathetic attitude towards others (his subjects), his great wealth will get ruined quickly, then and there, without extension of time!

567. kadu-mozhi-yum kai-yika-nh-tha thaNdam-um, vae-nh-than
adu-muraN thae-i-kkum aram.

Harsh words and excessive punishments given for small crimes given to the subjects (involved in crimes), if practiced by a king, that defect itself, would become the tool, serving as a filing instrument, which will erode the fighting strength of a king which would otherwise be useful to him for defeating the enemy! (Note: Fighting strength of a king corresponds to the support of the warriors in his kingdom, which will be influenced by the popularity of the king among the citizens of the country). Please see Kural 388.

568. inath-th(u)-aatRi, (y)eN-Naatha vae-nh-than, sinath-thu-aatRi,
seeRin, siRukum, thiru.

A king who does not administer his wealth under constant watch, taking advice and cooperation from his ministers and other personnel, but always shows his anger to his deputies as a style of administration, will, finally find his wealth diminishing! His fame will be lost!

569. seru-va-nh-tha- pOzh-thil, siRai- sei-yaa vae-nh-than
veru-va-nh-thu, vei-thu kedum.

When enmity with a foe (enemy) is realized or anticipated, a king must do the needful to protect himself and the country, by constructing a fortress and strengthening the forces, as otherwise, he would die out of fear and sorrow!

570. kallaar-p- piNik-kum kadu-ng-kOl; athu-(v)allathu
illai, nhi-lakku-p- poRai.

There is no heavier burden to the earth than bearing the body-weight of a tyrant king who gives a terrorizing rule to his people, being influenced by the ill-advice of his illiterate-advisers!

(Note: The ideal-ruler of the land, according to the poet, is a monarch who runs the government in the style of a welfare-state, being focused on the 'protection and welfare of people', with an obliga tion to earn a good name from the people of the country, ensuring an upright rule! Research is needed to compare it with the ideology of Plato's 'Republic"!).

CHAPTER-58

COMPASSIONATE OUTLOOK

571. kaNNO-ttam (y)ennum kazhi-perum kaari-kai
uNmai-yaan uNdu-iv- (v)ulaku.

The world exists safely because of the prevalence of the most precious virtue called grace and compassion, in the minds of some good people in the world!

572. kaNNO-tta-ththu uLLathu ulakiyal; a-h-thu- ilaar,
uNmai nhi-lakku-p- poRai.

The process of life in this world, is all safe, due to the attitude of a human quality called kindness/sympathetic consideration/ compassion. The existence of persons without a sense of kind attitude/outlook is a burden to the land/ planet earth!

573. paN-yen-(n)aam, paada-Rku-iyai-b(u)- indRael; kaN-(y)enn-aam,
kaNNO-ttam illaa- tha kaN?

What is the use of a song, if it is not in tune with the harmonious melody to please the ears? Similarly, what is the use of the eyes, if a graceful outlook of kindness (grace/compassion) towards others is absent?

574. uLa-pOl mukath-thu- (y)evan sei-yum? aLa-vinaal,
kaNNO-ttam illaatha kaN?

Apart from appearing as a part of the face, what is the use of the eyes, if the required (sufficient) level of kind (gracious/compassionate) attitude (outlook) is absent, in a living person?

575. kaNNiR-ku aNi-kalam kaNNOttam; a-h-th(u)- indRael,
puN-(N)endRu uNara-p- padum.

Looks expressing kindness (grace/kind outlooks) serve as the ornament for the eyes! In the absence of such expressions, the two eyes would be considered as the sores (wounds) on the face of a person!!

576. maNNOdu iyai-nh-tha marath-th(u) -anaiyar, kaNNOdu iyai-nh-thu- kaN - NOdaa thavar.

If kindness is not revealed through the eyes in their looks, those persons are considered as human beings growing on this earth like standing- trees!

577. kaNNOttam illa-var kaN-(N)ilar; kaN-Nudai-yaar kaNNOttam in-mai-yum il.

Persons without kind (gracious/compassionate) attitude towards others are considered as blind persons, or persons without eyes! Those possessing the eyes will never be lacking the quality of kindness (grace/ compassion) towards others!

578. karumam sithai-yaamal kaNNOda- vallaar-k-ku urimai- udai-th-thu,iv-vulaku.

Those persons who are capable of showing kindness (grace/ compassion) towards others, in action, by their generous gestures, without affecting their work, can claim a right of ownership of this world (planet earth)!

579. oRuth-th(u)- aatRum paNpinaar kaNNum, kaNNOdi-p-poRuth-th(u)-aatRum paNpae thalai.

If a person shows tolerance, along with kindness (grace/ compassion) towards others who have caused insult (grief/harm) to the self, the person is said to possess a cultured attitude, which is highly admirable!

580. peya-k-kaNdum nhanju- uNdu amai-var, nhaya-th-thakka nhaakari-kam vaeNdu—pavar.

Even after having seen the poison being added to the food/ drink, for being given to the guest,, if the guest is interested to uphold the admirable culture, he/she will consume the poisoned-food, and sit in peace, suppressing the feelings of pain which could appear on the face (as a result of consuming the killing-poison), in order to ensure that the feelings of the host are not wounded!

(Note: Research is needed, whether the superior culture of idealistic tolerance, of a person (the guest)with a utopian ideology who consumes the poisoned-food, should ever give an upper hand to the poison-adding killer!

Adding poison is a punishable offence.How can it be tolerated? The guest could get killed. The host is permitted to escape?: This was the opinion expressed by '*Thanthai-Periyar*' (E.V.Ramasamy) at a public function held in the year 1956, on the occasion when a bust-level statue of Gauthama-Buddha was installed at the premises of 'Periyar Mansion Campus', at Puthur, Tiruchirapalli; in the presence of '*Mahasannidhanam Thavaththiru*' *Kundrakkudi Adigalaar!* He added an opinion that "the sociological impact of similar literature-materials must be subjected to research, as the poet himself supports rational-scrutiny in kural 355 and kural 423. Such a research must be pointed towards bringing out the difference between any 'dogma' and reality!".

(There is one example in the history of the world to take the credit of demonstrating the 'admirable-culture', as visualized by Thiruvalluvar: Greek philosopher Socrates who,knowingly, con sumed the poison, with magnanimity, to honour the verdict of the rulers of the land! Ref: 'KuRaLoviyam', 1985.p.154: by Dr.Kalaignar M. Karunanithi).

CHAPTER-59

SPYING ACTIVITIES

581. otRum, urai-saandRa nhool-um, ivai-iraNdum,
thetR(u)-enka; mannavan kaN.

Employing spies as a secret arrangement, and referring to the book of ethics/statutes (describing the norms related to governance of the land) are the two tools of a great king, to be regarded by him as important as his two eyes! (Note: The poet talks about the importance of a written-constitution relating to the governance of a country, and spying-service to maintain link with the neighbouring countries, and for spying on espionage-activities within the country, as spelled out in kural 582).

582. yellaar-k-kum yellaam nhi-kazh-pavai, ye-gn-gnaa-ndRum
val-laRithal vae-nh-than thozhil.

Gathering relevant information in his kingdom, with alertness, (by employing spies) as to whatever event happens, where it happens, when it happens, and to whom it happens, becomes the privileged work (exercise) of a king! (For the purpose of administrative convenience!).

(Note: Based on spying-report, the action to be taken on a person who is involved in espionage activities against the king is indicated in kural 895).

583. otRinaan otRi-p- poruL theri-yaa mannavan
kotRam koLa-k- kida-nh-thathu il.

There is nothing left for the king to obtain victory, if the king does not know the importance of information, brought to him by pertinent spies! (He will not earn victory).

584. vinai-sei-vaar tham-sutRam vae-Ndaa-thaar, yendRaa-ng-ku
anai-varai-yum aaraa-i-vathu otRu.

Spying arranged by a king, will include, in the analysis, all personnel in the service of the king, all persons surrounding the king (including the king's relatives), and persons opposed to the king!

585. kadaa-a- uruvodu kaN-anj-chaathu, yaaNdum
ukaa- amai valla-thae otRu.

A typical spy would be a person who has got an impressive appearance,which will not tempt others to doubt about the identity, and who will not fear the stares of others, and who will remain calm always, to withhold the contents of the mind, and who has got the sum total of all these strengths together, contained in him.

586. thuRa-nh-thaar padivath-thar- aaki, iRa-nh-thu aaraa-i-nh-thu
(y)en-seyi-num, sOrvu ila-thu otRu.

A typical spy must be a person capable of hiding in a costume of an ascetic (if necessary), doing all actions accordingly, managing to pass through every hindrance, analyzing all information gathered, and remaining determined without losing hopes, whatever be the nature of horror being inflicted upon him!

587. maRai-nh-thavai kae-tkavatRu-aaki, aRi-nh-thavai
ai-yap-paadu illa-thae otRu.

A spy must be capable of investigating what has been hidden by others, and clearing the doubts from out of the available information collected so far!

588. otRu- otRi-th tha-nh-tha poruLai-yum, matRum, Or
otRi-naal otRi-k- koLal.

It will be advisable to compare the information given by a particular spy, with that given by another spy, and decide to accept the final version, soon on the basis of comparison!

589. otR(u)-otRu uNar-aamai aaL-ka; udan- moovar
sol-thokka, - thaeRa-p- padum.

Management of spies must be done in such a way that one spy does not know the other spy. If the versions of three spies agree with each other, the content of the dispute/findings will be chosen/ inferred suitably by the king!

590. siRappu, aRiya otRin-kaN sei-yaRka; sei-yin,
puRa-p- paduth-thaan aa-kum maRai.

Public honouring for a spy must not be done, as otherwise the strategy of secret service will be leaked out!

CHAPTER-60

PERSEVERANCE AS A STRENGTH

591. udaiyar (y)ena-p- padu-vathu ookkam; a-h-thu illaar,
udaiyathu udai-yarO matRu?

A person possessing the admirable qualities of perseverance (amalgamating, traits, such-as, motivation, self-confidence, courage, characteristic-zeal, steadfastness, will-power, enthusiasm, devotion to work, and dedication to the task) is considered to possess the real asset! Other holdings (belongings) do not matter much to increase the real value of a person!

592. uLLam udaimai udaimai; poruL udaimai
nhi-llaa-thu nhee-ng-ki- vidum.

A strong mind with will-power, courage, clarity and zeal will be appreciated as the real wealth in a person. Material wealth is likely to go away, from the person, without any hesitation, or sympathy, whatsoever!

593. aakkam izha-nh-thaem- (y)endRu allaa-vaar; ookkam
oru-va-nh-tham kaith-th(u)-udai- yaar.

Those persons who possess self-confidence, will-power, and perseverance under their control, will not get distressed, even if they happen to lose their wealth!

594. aakkam athar-vinaai-ch- chellum; asaiv(u)-ilaa
ookkam udaiyaa- n-uzhai.

To a person who possesses the unshaken will-power in exercising self confidence and perseverance, without feeling exhausted, the wealth will voluntarily come to him, after enquiring the whereabouts of that person!

595. veLLath-thu- anai-ya malar-nhee-ttam; maa-nh-thar-tham
uLLath-thu anai-yathu uyarvu.

The length of the stem of a lotus flower is limited to the depth of water in the tank (water-body) in which the plant grows. Similarly, the eminence, a person can achieve, depends on the attitudes (and motivation) developed in the mind!

596. uLLuvathu yellaam uyarvu uLLal; matRu, athu,
thaLLinum thaL-Laamai nheer-th-thu.

Whatever you want to aspire for, do aspire for the best objective. That is the best way to aim at the highest. Even if it could not be achieved, it deserves a merit as if it has been achieved. Keep on trying!

597. sithaiv(u)- idaththu olkaar, ura-vOr; puthai-ambin
pattu-p-paad(u) oon-dRum kaLiRu.

A war-elephant will continue to stay in its own place, and establish its greatness, even after being wounded in the battle-field, with a shower of piercing arrows, in its body! Similarly, a person who has got a firm mind, will not be overcome by any torturing stress/shattering adversity/ruinous disaster!

598. uLLam ilaa-thavar ye-i-thaar; ulakath-thu
vaLLi-yam (y)ennum serukku.

Those persons who have perseverance and will-power in their minds will be able to earn their wealth through their hard efforts. Some of them will not be able to help others and claim that they have got the pride of performing philanthropic and charitable deeds, if they do not have sympathetic considerations in their minds towards the needy people!

599. pari-yathu koor-ng-kOtta-thu aa-yinum, yaanai
veroo-um puli-thaak- kuRin.

Although an elephant has got a huge body-weight, and sharp ivory tusks, the mighty elephant will get frightened, if a tiger encounters it (attacks it), fiercely!

600. uram - oruvaR-ku, uLLa veRukkai; a-h-thu- il-laar,
maram; makkaL aa-thalae vaeRu.

Courage (fearlessness/ boldness/ strength of mind/ zeal/ ardour/ enthusiasm) is the wealth for any person! Those who do not have it, will be considered just like trees, standing on the land! It is impossible for such persons to act like human beings!

CHAPTER-61

FREEDOM FROM LAZINESS

(Note: Laziness is not a crime; Laziness is an innocent weakness. It must be watched in children very carefully by parents. A child must be taught as to how to avoid it, to remain active and alert!).

601. kudi-(y)ennum kundRaa viLakkam, madi-(y)ennum
maasu-oora, maa-i-nh-thu kedum.

Family called eternal light will get destroyed speedily, if laziness, known as a dirt(soot) creeps in and pervades over him/ her (a member of the family). The brightness called progress will get nullified/destroyed.

602. madi-yai madi-yaa ozhukal, kudi-yai-k-
kudi-yaaka- vaeNdu pavar.

If a person desires (wants) the family to maintain its due dignity, laziness must be prevented, in the activities of the self! (This applies to every member of a family!).

603. madi- madi-k- kondu-ozhukum- pae-thai, piRa-nh-tha
kudi- madi-yum thanni-num mu-nh-thu.

If a person's way of life is affected by lazy habits, as if laziness is tied up to his body system, his family in which he is born will get destroyed, much before death occurs to him!

604. kudi- madi-nh-thu kutRam perukum; madi-madi-nh-thu
maaNda u-gna-tR- ilavar-kku.

For those persons, who, out of laziness are unable to apply the efforts for achieving dignified objectives, it must be said that the honour of their family would get destroyed, and certain crimes could multiply, (due to the combination of laziness and carelessness, which are complementary to each other)!

605. nhedu –nheer, maRavi, madi, thuyil nhaan-kum,
kedu –nheer-aar kaama-k- kalan.

Postponing of actions (procrastination), forgetfulness, laziness (lethargy), and sleepiness are the favourite ornaments (destructive jewels) worn by those persons who are destined to get destroyed or get reduced to nothing, in their lives (without their knowing that these weaknesses are harmful to them!). (Note: Procrastination = procrastinatus, (Latin word), meaning "let it be done tomorrow"!).

606. padi-yudai-yaar patRu amai-nh-tha-k-kaNNum, madi-yudai-yaar
maaN-payan (y)eithal arithu.

Those persons who possess the adverse quality of laziness will not be able to achieve any honourable benefit, for themselves,even if they have acquired the intimate contact and patronage of the king himself! (Even if the entire wealth of the king is made available to a lazy person, there would not be any benefit from it, if the laziness is continued: (as cited in Parimelazhagar Urai).

607. idi-puri-nh-thu yeLLum-sol kae-tpar, madi-puri-nh-thu
maaNda- u-gna-tRi- lavar.

Those persons who practice laziness (lethargy) and do not apply their efforts for achieving honourable objectives will be subjected to rebuke and reproach/insult/contempt/ scornful words, unnecessarily from others!

608. madimai kudimai-kkaN tha-ng-kin, than onnaar-k-ku
adimai pukuth-thi- vidum

If laziness takes shelter in a person belonging to a good family, it will create bad situations to the extent that he, ultimately, becomes a slave to the very enemy of his reputed family!

609. kudi-(y)aaNmai- yuL –va-nh-tha kutRam oruvan
madi- (y)aaNmai maa-tRa-k- kedum

When a man/woman heading the family puts away the undesirable quality of laziness, the blame (stigma/reproach/ rebuke/ shame) which had come upon the reputation of the family will disappear soon after he/she sheds down laziness and becomes smart! (madi-(y)aaNmai=negative-capacity to remain lazy! : It will not go away easily, unless special efforts are applied).

610. madi-ilaa mannavan (y)eithum adi-aLa-nh-thaan
thaa –a-yathu (y)ellaam oru-ng-ku

A king who liberates (frees) himself from laziness will gain all the lands which he had traversed through once upon a time, when he was young, and subsequently, the lands being lost to others when he started becoming lazy! (He will be able to regain his lands from his enemies who are presently owning those lands, if and only if he gets rid of his laziness!).

(Note: It is inferred that the poet is advising the king to drop out laziness to gain back his lands from other kings who are presently owning the lands!). (Another version: A king who becomes smart and active, will gain all the lands traversed by him on foot, similar to the lands won by Lord Vishnu, in one stroke!!).

Both versions describe the poet's effort to preach against laziness, covering a large spectrum of people, ranging from youngsters among ordinary people to princes and kings in the ruling-class, by 'promising' attractive-benefits, rewards and awards, for drop ping laziness from practice!).

(Note: The verse quoted from 'Silappathikaram', a Tamil-legendary-epic, insists that 'a king has to prove his valour and strength to other kings'! The inference from the viewpoint of Thirukkural, is that 'laziness' is not a desirable quality in a king. Reference cited: 'Silappathikaram', authored by Dr.S.V.Subramanian, 1998, Gangai Puthakanilayam, Chennai-600 017; 4th edition, page 163: Chapter 11: *madhurai-k-kaaNdam,kaadu- kaaN-kaathai, verse 17: "adi-yil-than-aLavu-arasar-k-ku, uNarth-thi").* This must be studied, and compared.

CHAPTER-62

FIRMNESS IN STRENUOUS ACTS

611. arumai udaith-thu- (y)endRu asaa-vaa-mai vae-Ndum;
perumai muyaR-chi tharum.

Do not hesitate to take up any work based on the fear (assumption) that the work is difficult to do. If effort is initiated, the effort itself will give the necessary (required) skills.

612. vinai-k-kaN vinai-kedal Ombal vinai-k-kuRai
theer-nh-thaa-rin theer-nh-th(u)-andRu ulaku

The world of people will abandon those who abandon their own work, and leave it incomplete! Therefore, abandoning any work, in the middle of its progress, must be avoided! It must be completed to perfection!

613. thaa-LaaNmai (y)ennum thakai-mai-k-kaN tha-ng-kitRae
vae-LaaNmai (y)ennum serukku.

The dignity (honour) of generosity will dwell only with those persons who persevere (labour hard) to produce wealth which is recognized as a pride! The wealth will enable them to help others!

614. thaa-LaaNmai illaa-thaan vae-LaaNmai pae-di-kai
vaaL- aaNmai pOla-k- kedum.

Philanthropic desires of a person will miserably fail, if he/she does not have perseverance to elevate himself/herself through hard work, and earn wealth! This failure will be similar to a strong sword becoming useless at the hands of a coward! (Note: Lack of perseverance and lack of courage are equated!).

615. inbam vizhai-yaan, vinai-vizhai-vaan, than-kae-Lir
thunbam thudai-th- thu -oondRum thooN.

A person who is not very particular about his/her personal pleasures, and at the same time, remains dedicated to work to produce wealth, will be considered as the helping-force in wiping out sufferings of family-members and relatives! Such a person is like a pillar, bearing the entire weight of the burdens of the family!

616. muyaRchi thiru-vinai aakkum; muyatRin-mai
inmai pukuth-thi vidum.

Hard work and perseverance will create wealth. Lack of hard work and perseverance will take a person into poverty (with out his/her knowledge!).

617. madi-uLaaL maa-mukadi yenba; madi- ilaan
thaaL-uLaaL thaamarai-yi- naaL.

It is said that the goddess of poverty will dwell with a person who is lazy! But the goddess of wealth will dwell with a person who is free from laziness! (Note: An individual person has got freedom to choose his acts, between the two options!).

618. poRi-(y) inmai yaar-k-kum pazhi-(y)andRu; aRivu-aRi-nh-thu
aaL-vinai inmai pazhi.

Any defect in human body is not a disgrace to any person. What is to be blamed is one's failure to initiate efforts in acquiring the required skill (capacity) to act towards an achievement! (Alternatively: Lack of good-fate cannot be blamed. What is blamed is one's failure to initiate efforts to acquire the required-skills (capacity) to act towards an achievement.

In this interpretation, the term '*poRi*' is considered as a tool, namely, the 'Fate'!).

(Note: Being born with bodily-handicaps, if assumed to be attributed due to fate, it has to be inferred that a person has to counteract all the dictates of the fate, through hard work and perseverance, as per kurals 619 & 620).

619. theivath-thaan aakaa-thu yeni-num, muyaR-chi,than
mei-varuth-tha-k- kooli tharum

Even if a task could not be achieved by the blessings of the Almighty, sustained efforts, if applied, straining the body and mind, that kind of an effort will surely yield the necessary wages/rewards! (Note: the term 'mei-varuththa' - implies 'sustained-hard work', involving physical and intellectual capabilities).

620. oozhai-yum up-pakkam kaaNpar; ulaivu-indRi-th-
thaazhaa-thu u-gna-tRu- pavar.

Persons who constantly attempt to achieve their objectives, without getting discouraged (disrupted), will be able to overtake (overcome) the destiny, to see that the fate is behind their back!

(Note: The poet is an optimist; He is a consultant who offers advice to his clients, depending upon the needs felt by the client: i) He gives encouragement to keep on trying to achieve success, vide kural 616; and ii) for those who do not meet with success in their efforts, the poet consoles them in kural 621, 628 and 629; and, iii) he continues to put some more faith in their minds to keep on trying, vide kurals 618, 619 and 620!; iv) he puts pressure on knowing more about ways and means of acquiring new capabilities in kural 472; v) he gives some new clues in kurals 483, 484 and 493; vi)He advises to consider new alternatives with regard to methodologies in kural 673; vii) he suggests for taking help (assistance) from friends in kural 651; or taking help from elders vide kural 446; vii) advises further to seek the blessings of elders in kural 443. and viii) he describes the general principle of success-formula: to remain firm in preventing disappointments; and if it occurs beyond control, to bear it with patience, until final victory is achieved, vide kural 662!(He takes this much precaution to ensure that youngsters must not be discouraged by the Fate-theories recorded in kurals 377 and 380).

CHAPTER-63

ENDURANCE AGAINST HARDSHIPS IN LIFE

621. idukkaN varu-ng-kaal nakuka; atha-nai
aduththu oorva-thu a-h-thu -oppathu il.

When trouble comes to any person, it is better to give a gentle smile, inwardly, and bear it with patience! There is no other way which will be more effective to make it move away!

622. veLLath-thu anaiya idumbai, aRivu- udaiyaan
uLLath-thil uLLa-k- kedum.

When a trouble comes to a person like a torrential flood, if a wise person continues to think about it with firmness, regarding the ways a nd me a ns of solving it, the trouble will disappear, on its own accord!

623. idumabaikku idumbai padu-ppar; idumbai-k-ku
idumbai padaa-a- thavar

Those who do not fear any trouble will remain bold, and arrange for the trouble to be in trouble, and, will finally succeed to win it over!

624. maduththa-vaai (y)ellaam pakadu- an-naan utRa
idukkaN, idarp-paadu udaith-thu.

Similar to a buffalo (bull) successfully pulling the loaded cart through a stretch of swampy land, overcoming all obstructions, a hard working person with physical strength and mental strength (will- power) will succeed in overcoming the trouble!

625. adukki varinum azhivu-il(l)aan utRa
idukkaN idukkaN padum.

When a person happens to face troubles, attacking the person in a sequence, one after another, he/she has to decide to face it with determination and will-power. In that case, the trouble itself will get into trouble, finally! (The trouble will go away!).

626. atRae-m- (y)endRu al-lal padupa-vO, petRaem-(y)endRu
Ombuthal thae-tRaa- thavar?

Why should any person ever feel the distress after losing all the wealth, saying that "I have lost it all", whereas the same person did not manage to protect the wealth with care, beforehand, at the time of getting the wealth?

627. ilakkam udampu-idumbaikku (y)endRu kalak-ka-ththai-k-
kai-yaaRaa-k- koLLaa-thaam mae-l.

Knowledgeable persons are aware of the fact that the human body is the target for physical sufferings, and do not hold it on hand (take it to heart) as a belief to worry about it! If their policy is followed, then, it would be a superior realization!

628. inbam vizhai-yaan, idumbai iya-lbu- (y)en-baan
thunbam uRuthal ilan.

A person who is not mindful of personal pleasures and who believes that getting into trouble is a natural possibility/probability, will not get into trouble! (He/she will be able to control his/her emotions, without getting upset!). Equanimity is a great strength in a person.

629. inba-th-thuL inbam vizhai-yaa-thaan, thunbath-thuL
thunbam uRu-thal, ilan.

A person who does not feel joyous and jubilant while experiencing happy events, will not feel the pain while experiencing miserable situations, showing an admirable emotional balance!

630. innaa-mai inbam -(y)ena-k-koLin, aakum-than
onnaar vizhai-yum siRappu.

If a person can face a deep trouble, taking it as a pleasing experience, the enduring capacity of the person will be appreciated and admired by all, including his/her enemies!

CHAPTER-64

IDEAL MINISTER

631. karuvi-yum kaalam-um sei-kai-yum sei-yum
aru-vinai-yum maaNdathu amai-ch-chu.

An ideal minister is a person who has got an excellent knowl edge on the following aspects:i) means of execution, ii) the apt time for action, iii) choice of the manner of execution, and iv) special nature of any difficult task to be performed!

632. van-kaN, kudi-kaaththal, katR(u) - aRithal, aaL-vinai-yOdu
ai-nh-thu-dan maaNda-thu amai-ch-chu.

A minister must possess excellence in the following five aspects: i) firmness and clarity of mind, ii) sense of commitment in offering protection to the citizens, iii) learning about norms based on virtues and justice, iv) desire to learn more and more from learned persons to enrich the wisdom of the self, and v) enthusiasm and perseverance in knowing more about issues and solutions.

633. piri-th-thalum, pae-Ni-k- koLalum, piri-nh-thaar-p-
poru-th-thalum vallathu, amai-ch-chu.

A minister must have mental ability i) to cause division among the enemies, ii) to extend an accommodating gesture in earning the friendship of the friendly team (allies), and finally, iii) to cause a merger among the divided teams/groups, in the good interest of the country!

634. theri-tha-lum, thae-r-nh-thu seyal-um, oru-thalai-yaa-ch-
chollal-um vallathu amai-ch-chu.

A minister must be capable of i) analyzing an issue with more and more details, ii) selecting an appropriate action based on available information and correlating it with precedents, and iii) uttering whatever is right to the king, without any hesitation, whatsoever!

635. aRan –aRi-nh-thu, aa-ndRu- amai-nh-tha sollaan, ye-gn- gnaa-ndRum thiRan-aRi-nh-thaan thae-r-chchi-th- thuNai.

A person who is to be chosen for assisting the king, in the role of a minister, must have the following qualifications: i) knowledge on the norms spelled out in the books of ethics/virtues/justice, ii) possessing adequate background of learning, iii) capability of ex pressing the ideas in a balanced way, using selective (apt) and humble (yet dignified) words, and iv) capacity to assess (evaluate) the strength (pros and cons) of any proposed action-plan.

636. mathi-nhu-t-pam, nhoolOdu, udai-yaar-k-ku, athi-nhu-t-pam yaa-uLa mun-nhiR-- pavai?

For a person who has got the mental ability, combined with exposure to renowned books, could there be anything which would stand in front of him/her, as an unforeseen cunning plot? Any cunning plot against such a person would not work out to his/her disadvantage!

637. seyaRkai aRi-nh-tha-k -kadai-ththum, ulakath-thu iyaRkai aRi-nh-thu seyal.

Even if unnatural (artificial/innovated/improvised) methods of performing a particular action is known through learning, it is advisable to implement (enforce) that act, after knowing (ascertain- ing) what is practicable in the world under natural settings! (Note: A pragmatic approach? Or down-to-earth approach? Or intellectually idealistic approach? Striking at a balance is still possible!).

638. aRi- kondRu, aRi-yaan (y)eninum, uRuthi uzhai-(y)iru-nh-thaan kooRal kadan.

Even if the king remains ignorant, or if he habitually enjoys rejecting wise pieces of advice, it is the bounden duty of the minister who is always present in the closer proximity of the king, to boldly and firmly express his considered-opinion! (and convince the king!).

639. pazhuthu (y)eNNum ma-nh-thiri-yin pakkath-thuL thev-vOr (y)ezhu-pathu kOdi uRum.

To have a minister who is interested in the ruin (destruction) of his own king, just by the side of the king himself, is as bad as (the king) having seven hundred million enemies in his close proximity!

(Note: Although it may sound as an exaggeration, there are evi dences in the recorded history in many countries around the world, in politics and civilian society, to prove this point).

640. muRai-p-pada-ch -choozh-nh-thum, mudivu-ilavae sei-var,
thiRap-paadu i(l)laa-a- thavar.

Those who lack executive ability will leave the work in unfinished form/ stage, even after having devised/planned the proposed- action correctly, according to the specified norms, thus causing a failure, due to his/her lack of smartness! (They may not realize their weakness! It is a pity! It is a loss for the society).

CHAPTER-65

POWER OF SPEECH

641. nhaa- nha-lam (y)ennum nhalan-udaimai, a-n(h)-nhalam
yaa-nha-lath-thu uLLa-thoo-(v)um andRu.

Eloquence, fluency, and cogency are the various skills of excellence identified with the goodness of speech, achievable by using the tongue. It is a form of wealth that can be found in a learned person. This unique characteristic of rare quality (charm) is not found in other forms of wealth!

642. aakkam-um, kae-dum- atha-naal varuthal-aal,
kaath-thu- Ombal sollin-kaN sOrvu.

Prosperity or ruin can occur to a person, as a result of the words spoken out by that person. Therefore, it becomes necessary for that person to be free from committing errors in words!

643. kae-ttaar-p- piNikkum- thakai-ya-vaai-k- kae-Laa-rum
vae-t-pa, mozhi-va-th(u)-aam sol.

The words spoken out by a person must be in such a way that whoever listened to the words remained captivated, in appreciation; and that those persons who did not have a chance to listen, would like to remain desirous of listening to those words.

644. thiRan aRi-nh-thu sollu-ka, sollai; aRa-num
poru-Lum atha-nin- oongku- il.

While speaking to others, the words must be uttered after understanding the quality of words and its impact on the listeners! This tradition is relevant to both virtuous act and beneficial use, in terms of material value and moral value!

(* Note: There is a legal hint on the topic, as indicated by the poet).

645. sollu-ka sollai-p, piRi-thu-Or-sol, ach-chollai
vellum-sol in-mai aRi-nh-thu.

Do utter a word, after making sure that any other word(from another person) cannot win the word uttered by you!

646. vae-t-path-thaam solli-p-, piRar-sol, payan-kOdal
maatchi-yin- maasu-atRaar kOL.

Uttering words which would be desired by others to hear, is the pleasant duty of those great scholars who are free from any fault in their minds. They will also be happy to enjoy and absorb the wisdom behind the words of others.

647. sol-al- vallan, sOrvu-ilan, anj-chaan, avanai,
ikal-vellal yaar-k-kum arithu.

It is very difficult for anyone (among his/her academic ri vals) to win and humiliate a person who is good in uttering appropriate words free from fault, and who remains free from fear (languor, slackness,hesitation, weariness)!

648. virai-nh-thu thozhil kae-t-kum gnaa-lam; nhira-nh—thu, inithu,
sollu-thal vallaar-p- peRin.

The people of the world will readily listen to the person and abide by his/her words, if the person is capable of arranging the ideas in a convincing way, and pleasantly speaking to the audience, with eloquence and logic. (Note: There are many evidences in the history of the world to prove this point! Example: Mark Antony's speech at Julius-Caesar's Funeral!).

649. pala -solla-k- kaamu-Ruvar, mandRa, maasu -atRa
sila-sollal thae-t-Raa- thavar

Persons who are not trained in conveying their apt ideas,cogently and briefly, using faultless and meaningful words, will only be uttering too many words to their audience (as if they are beating around the bush)!

650. iNar-oozhth-thum, nhaaRaa malar-anai-yar, katRathu
uNara- viri-th-thu- urai-yaa- thaar.

Persons who are not able to explain, to an audience, what they have learned, are comparable with the matured dense-cluster of flowers which does not have the pleasant fragrance!

CHAPTER-66

PURITY OF ACTION

651. thuNai-nhalam aakkam tha-roo-um; vinai- nha-lam
vae-Ndi-ya (y)ellaam tharum.

Good external support will yield greatness/wealth to a per son! Purity of actions of a person, will yield all things which are desired by the person! (him/her)!

652. (y)endRum oru-vu-thal vae-N-dum; puka-zho-du
nha-ndRi paya-vaa vinai.

Every person must avoid carrying out any work/act, which will not produce good benefits and fame, anytime during his/her lifetime!!

653. Oh-othal vae-N-dum; oLi-maazh-kum sei-vinai
aa-athum (y)ennu - mavar. (Oh-othal=avoiding).

Those persons who want to make steady progress in their work, to attain fame, must avoid any act which would cause damage to their reputation.

654. idukkaN -padi-num, iLi –va-nh-tha sei-yaar,
nhadu-kk(u)-atRa kaatchi—yavar.

Even during times of their sufferings, those who have got an unshaken vision/enlightenment, will not commit any act which would bring down their fame/name/reputation.

655. (y)etRu – (y)endRu, ira-ng-kuva sei-yaRka; sei-vaa-nael,
matRu, anna, sei-yaamai nha-ndRu.

Do not commit any act, about which you would repent later on, for having committed that act! If you have committed it once, it is better that it is not repeated for the second time!!

656. (y)ee-ndRaaL pasi-kaaNpaan aayi-num, sei-yaRka;
saand-ROr pazhi-k-kum vinai.

Let no person commit any act which would be condemned by virtuous persons, even when a person happens to see (witness) his mother in starvation! (thereby, being tempted to steal, in order to feed her).

657. pazhi-malai-nh-thu (y)eithi-ya aakkath-thin, saand-ROr
kazhi-nhal kura-vae thalai.

Extreme poverty of virtuous persons is far superior to mountainous heaps of wealth accumulated by evil persons who earned their wealth by carrying out evil acts!

658. kadi-nh-tha kadi-nh-thu- oraar sei-thaar-k-ku, avai-thaam,
mudi-nh-thaa-lum peezhai tharum.

Those who indulge in evil acts which are prohibited by the wise (virtuous) persons, will continue to suffer from sorrow, even if they complete doing it successfully! Evil acts will produce evil effects.

659. azha-k-koNda (y)ellaam, azha-p-pOm; izhap-pinum
piR-paya-kkum nha-Rpaa -lavai.

All the wealth obtained by making the victims shed tears of grief, will be snatched away from a person who has acted wrongly, making him cry/weep/scream. On the contrary, even if a person happens to lose the wealth which got accrued because of earning through legitimate ways (fair means), by performing good acts, it will produce good benefits later on! (Such fair wealth will come back!).

660. salath-thaal poruL–seithu, yaem-aarth-thal, pasu-maN
kalath-thuL-nheer pei-thu-iree-yi -yatRu.

The task of protecting the wealth earned by unfair/evil/foul means, becomes unattainable! Such a wealth will disappear, like the water being stored in a vessel made of wet-mud!

CHAPTER-67

EXCELLENCE IN ACTION

661. vinai-th- thitpam yenpathu oruvan manath-thitpam;
matRai-ya, (y)ellaam piRa.

Firmness in action is dominated/determined by the firmness of mind of a person. All other factors cannot be related to it.

662. ooRu - oraal, utRa-pin ol-kaamai, iv-viraNdin
aaRu-(y)enpar aa-i-nh-thavar kOL.

Wise persons who have done the analysis on firmness of action have recommended two methods, namely, i)taking preventive measures before a ruinous-result could occur, in a particular act / endeavour, and ii) remaining bold to face the trouble with firmness of mind, when it occurs as an unavoidable effect! (Note: The poet quotes the findings of other appropriate experts).

663. kadai-k-kotka-ch chei-thakka-thu aa-Nmai; idai-k-kotkin
(y)etRaa vizhumam tharum.

Revealing the details of work after it is completed successfully, corresponds to administrative excellence/manliness! Releasing the information in the middle of the work will yield non-retrievable misery!! (Note: The poet could perhaps refer to the trade-secrets, having relevance to managerial practice!). (Note: An important management strategy is explained. Maintaining the secrecy of any technical information is very important for the success of the project. In certain situations, it will assume international importance. Trade-secret is an important aspect in industrial management. It has got relevance to protection of patents, plagiarism, copyright, and other legal issues related to originality of ideas).

664. sollu-thal yaar-k-kum yeLiya; ariya-(v)aam
solli-ya- vaNNam seyal.

It is easy for anyone to preach/propagate/speak about inadvertently on any action/work! It is rather difficult to execute the action/work in accordance with what has been preached about! (Note: The poet's policy is made clear that whatever is found to be good, must be practiced by every person, vide kural 391)..

665. veeRu –yeithi maaN-daar vinai-th-thitpam vae-nh-than-kaN
ooRu-(y)eithi uLLa-p- padum.

Information relating to the perfection in work (expertise/ skill/ power of action) earned by those who attained greatness (excellence) in their work, will reach the attention of the ruler of the land, and will be remembered with honour! (Note: The poet insists that human talents must be recognized, and rewarded for encouraging good work, if it is found relevant to social welfare!).

666. (y)eNNiya, (y)eNNi-yaa-ng-ku, (y)eithu-ba, (y)eNNi-yaar
thiNNi-yar aaka-p- peRin.

Those persons who aspired for achieving a particular aim, will achieve what exactly they aspired for, provided that they remain determined with firmness in their minds to achieve it (the objective)!

667. uruvu-kaNdu (y)eLLaa-mai vae-Ndum; uruL-peru-nh-thae-r-kku a
chch(u) –aaNi annaar udaith-thu.

No person deserves (needs) to be insulted (humiliated) for having a small size of the human body, because, there are many persons of this kind, in this world, who are very valuable in their capacities, resembling the functional use of the Linch-pin of the big rolling chariot!.

668. kala-ng-kaathu kaNda vinai-k-kaN thuLa-ng-kaathu
thookkam kadi-nh-thu seyal.

Any act, chosen and finalized, needs to be carried out through hard efforts, casually without worrying about it, without sleepiness and without delay.

669. thunbam uRa -vari-num seika; thuNivu- aatRi
inbam paya-k-kum vinai.

Any action which would yield blissful benefits must be undertaken with courage, even if it involves hardships while doing it.

670. (y)enai-th- thitpam (y)eithiya-k- kaNNum, vinai-th-thitpam
vae-N-daarai vae-N-daathu ulaku.

Whatever be the various abilities and capacities a person may possess, if firmness of action and commitment to the work undertaken are absent in the person, the people of the world will not give importance to that person!

CHAPTER-68

METHODOLOGY FOR ACTION

671. soozh-ch-chi mudivu thuNivu-(y)eithal; ath-thuNivu
thaazh-ch-chiyuL tha-ng-kuthal thee-thu.

The end result of straining one's mind through deep thinking is to obtain courage to start initiating an act. If that courage is going to take shelter in delay in executing that act, it will produce harm to what was planned initially! (The delay could be caused due to some reason such as hesitation out of humility/submissiveness to external threats/ lethargy, etc.).

672. thoo-ng-ku-ka thoo-ng-ki-ch- cheyar-paala; thoo-ng-kaRka,
thoo-ng-kaa-thu sei-yum vinai.

Take your own time to execute certain works, in cases where delay helps! Do not waste time by whiling away, in carrying out certain other works which require sleepless efforts, and immediate attention.

673. ollum-vaai (y)ellaam vinai-nha-ndRae; ollaa-k-kaal,
sellum-vaai nOkki-ch cheyal.

It is advisable to perform an act immediately when the way is cleared, so that it starts giving benefits! When an act is not feasible, divert your attention towards a feasible way of getting things done! (Note: This concept talks about the necessity to consider alternatives in planning projects/schemes, instead of having a fixed idea!The idea seems to be centered towards early starting of the work, so that the capital does not remain idle!).

674. vinai, pakai, (y)endRu- iraNdin (y)ech-cham, nhi-nai-yum-kaal,
thee-(y)ech-cham pOla-th- theRum.

While carrying out a particular work, or while settling a dis pute with an enemy, you must not leave it incomplete (half-done). If it is not settled completely, then and there, it will grow like an unquenchable tongue of fire, leading to a ruinous -end/destruction!

675. poruL, karuvi, kaalam, vinai, idan-odu, ai-nh-thum,
iruL-theera (y)eNNi-ch -cheyal.

Perform an act, after contemplating without any error, in choosing the five items, namely, treasure (financial-resources), instruments, time, action and place! (The term'karuvi', referring to instruments, will stand for equipment/methodology/ software/ infrastructure, in the modern context).

676. mudivum, idai-yooRum, mutRi-yaa-ng-ku, (y)ei-thum
padu-payanum paarth-thu-ch cheyal.

While undertaking a proposed act, the following points are to be considered: i) can it be accomplished at all?, ii) will there be any hindrance? and iii) what will be the share of benefit made avail able to the self, on completion of the scheme/project!? (Note: Immediate benefits and long-term benefits are implied!).

677. sei-vinai, seivaan, seyal-muRai, av-vinai
uL-LaRi-vaan uLLam koLal.

Any person who wishes to commence doing the work has to acquire the 'technical-know-how' about the procedures for doing the work, from a person already doing the work, and to know the mind of the person already familiar with the inner details of the work/process involved. (Note: In the present context, there are consultancy services, for preparing feasibility reports for any project being proposed/contemplated!. The intention of the poet seems to give a caution to a client to avoid failures or disappointments in undertaking any new venture. Please see kurals 832; 473).

678. vinai-yaal vinai-yaakki-k- kOdal, nha-nai-kavuL
yaanai-yaal yaanai-yaath(thu) atRu.

Attempting to get one particular work done, and incidentally getting another work done in the sequence, is like using a domestically trained elephant to catch a wild elephant from the forest.

679. nhattaar-k-ku nha-lla seyal-in, virai-nh-tha-thae
ottaar-ai otti-k- koLal

For making one's own enemies to be united with the self,efforts must be pursued more urgently, than doing good things to the benefit of the existing team of friends, in order to maintain their friendship also! (Note: It is a strategic decision! Good friends will understand the situation, without misunderstanding).

680. uRai- siRiyaar uL-nha-dung-kal anj-chi-k- kuRai-peRin
koLvar periyaar-p- paNi-nh-thu.

A ruler of a small kingdom has to consider the fear which prevails in the minds of his own warriors about the powerful enemy, and decide wisely to submit himself to the mightier enemy, in a humble way, to earn the support of the superior, taking care to ensure that it is an amicable and amiable agreement/settlement! (For a small king, it is the best way to protect (retain) his kingdom, under his control, instead of being defeated or getting killed!).

CHAPTER-69

ENVOY SERVICE

681. anbu-(u)daimai, aa-ndRa kudi-p-piRath-thal, vae-nh-thu-avaa-m, paNbu-(u)daimai, thoothu-(u)raippaan paNpu.

Kindness to all, merit of birth in a respectable family, and familiarity with princely courtesies, are the qualifying requirements for an ideal envoy, in the service of a king!

682. anbu, aRivu, aaraa-i-nh-tha sol-vanmai, thoothu- urai-ppaarkku indRi (y)amai-yaatha, moondRu.

Kindness, intelligence (knowledge), capacity to choose appropriate words to be used during dialogues (instead of quick replies), and capacity to express convincingly to others (in the enemy's camp) are the three essential qualities required for an envoy (to be sent by the king)!

683. nhool-aar-uL nhool-vallan aa-kuthal, vae-laa-rul vendRi vinai (y) uraippan paNpu.

The task of visiting an enemy king, and elaborating on the victorious acts of one's own king, are the functions of an envoy. By qualification, he must have knowledge and wisdom, on par with literary experts (scholars) in the fields of governance/justice/diplomacy!

684. aRivu, uru, aa-raa-i-nh-tha kalvi,im- moo-ndRan seRivu-(u)daiyaan selka vinaikku.

A person who has got an excellent combination of three qualities, namely, a good level of general knowledge, an impressive physical appearance, and a good caliber of education can be selected for a position to be sent as an emissary to an enemy king.! (Note: Skilled diplomacy, inquisitive frame of mind, prudence,and practical wisdom are certain aspects covered in the phrase 'analytical education'= *'aa-raa-y-nh-tha-kalvi')*.

685. thokach-cholli, thoo-vaatha nhee-kki, nhaka-ch-cholli,
nhandRi payappa-th(u)-aam thoothu.

An envoy must be able to bring benevolent results to his country, by being brief in his speech, by avoiding harshness in his manners of uttering words, and by presenting facts, in a pleasant way (with a scholarly tinge of humour) in his deliberations during the delegation, in order to ensure success for the mission! (tinge= tingere, Latin word meaning flavour).

686. katRu-k- kaN- anj-chaan, sela-ch-cholli-k- kaalath-thaal
thakka-thu aRiva-th(u)-aam thoothu

Having acquired a fair knowledge of the prevailing situation, a typical envoy must feel free from fears on the eyes, and must convey points in such a language, in order that everybody understands. He must have the capacity for quickly grasping whatever is to be inferred and understood, on the occasion (at that time)!

687. kadan- aRi-nh-thu, kaalam karuthi, idan-aRi-nh-thu
(y)eNNi uraip-paan thalai.

An ideal envoy is a person who understands his duty, which warrants his careful statements to be made after careful thoughts relevant to the context, time and place, (in consideration of what information is to be gathered!).

688. thooi-mai, thuNai-mai, thuNivu-(u)daimai, im-moo-ndRin
vaai-mai vazhi-yurai-ppaan paNpu.

Truthfulness to three important characteristics, namely, i) purity of mind and action, ii) helpful attitude/loyalty towards the king who assigned the work, iii) courage and boldness of the self, are applicable to the envoy who has to speak out truthfully for evolving a solution.

689. vidu-maatRam vae-nh-tharkku uraippaan, vadu-maatRam
vaai- sOraa van-ka- Navan

The envoy assigned (sent) to meet the enemy-king, must convey his own king's message, truthfully, while standing in front of the enemy-king, with stern eyes, without any error or change, and without uttering faulty words! Firmness of mind and faultless words are important to achieve success in the mission!

690. iRuthi payap-pinum,(y)enj-chaa-thu iRai-vaR-ku
uRuthi payap-pa-th(u)aam thoothu.

An ideal envoy will bring firm benefits to his own king, without refraining from the assigned - duty. He must convey the message of his own king to the enemy-king, boldly, loyally and truth fully, even if it ends up in his own death! at the hands of the enemy- king (the fire).

CHAPTER-70

COORDINATION WITH THE KING

691. akalaa-thu aNukaa-thu, thee-k-kaay-vaar- pOl-ka
ikal-vae-nh-thar-ch- chae-r-nh-thu- ozhuku- vaar.

Those who acquaint with the king must imitate those who warm-up themselves near the fire-place, neither going too close, nor too far away, thus maintaining an optimum distance from the fire.

692. mannar vizhai-ba vizhai-yaa-mai mannar-aal
manni-ya aa-kkam tharum.

For those persons who take care not to get attracted by the things desired by the king himself, vast wealth will be coming forth to them, that too, through the king himself!

693. pOtRin ariya-vai pOtRal; kaduth-tha-pin,
thae-tRuthal yaark-kum arithu.

If those persons, closely moving with the king, want to protect themselves, they must guard themselves without committing even rare (small) errors. If once aroused on suspicion by the king, it may not be possible for anybody to console/convince/pacify the king, and save the offender!!

694. sevi-ch-chollum, sae-r-nh-tha nhakai-yum, aviththu-ozhukal,
aandRa periyaa-r -akaththu.

In the presence of the king (or elders known for their greatness of wisdom), it is recommended that a person must avoid actions such as, whispering (in the ear of a neighbour) or teasing any neighbour (or exchanging smiles with another person)!

695. (y)ep-poruLum Oraar; thodar-aar; matRu, ap-poruLai
vittak-kaal kae-tka maRai.

Those persons in the closeness of the king, must not over hear between the king and others, nor ask subsequent questions, and must prefer to listen to the king, when(any information is) revealed by the king himself, that too, courteously, without showing any eagerness to know more!

696. kuRippu-aRi-nh-thu, kaalam karuthi, veRuppu- ila
vae-Ndu- ba, vae-t-pa-ch- cholal

Understanding the signs (dispositions), and considering the appropriate time, a person in the vicinity of the king, may speak out in a pleasing manner, to the king, on any suggestion relating to things which are not displeasing to the king or things which are liked by the king!..

697. vae-t-pana solli, vinai-yila (y)e-gn-gnaa-ndRum,
kae-t-pinum, sollaa- vidal!

Whatever the king desires to hear, pleasant things may be narrated! Useless words must not be uttered, even if asked for! Just ignore it, with courtesy, if 'trapping' questions are asked!

698. iLai-yar, ina-muRai-yar, yendRu-ika-zhaar, nhi-ndRa
oLi-yOdu, ozhu-ka-p- padum.

Persons in close proximity of the king must not take liberty with the king, thinking that the king is their junior, or their relative. It will be construed as an insult! They must extend a great respect to the king in accordance with the royal courtesy that prevails!

699. 'koLap-pattae-m' -yendRu- (y)eNNi, -k- koLLaa-tha chei-yaar
thuLakk(u)- atRa kaatchi- yavar.

Those who are known for their straight forward outlooks, with a fearless vision, will not commit any act which is not agreeable to the king, although they are in the good books of the king!

700. 'pazhai-yam' (y)ena-k- karuthi, -p- paNpu-alla- chei-yum
kezhu-thakaimai kaedu tharum.

If a person assumes that he is known to the king for a long time, and therefore, he would escape from being punished by the king for any offensive act, that attitude itself will bring ruin to him!.

*(Note: This code of conduct described in this chapter gets covered under Professional Ethics, in the modern world, while interacting with senior colleagues!)

CHAPTER-71

ART OF FACIAL READING / MIND READING

701. kooRaamai nhO-kki-k- kuRippu-aRivaan ye-gn-gnaa-ndRum maaRaa-nheer vai-yakku aNi.

     Anybody who looks at a person and tells what is in the person's mind, even when the person does not utter a word, is considered as a precious expert, like an ornament (jewel) to the world surrounded by the unchanging (plentiful) sea-water.

702. ai-ya-p-padaa-athu, akath-thathu uNarvaanai,-th thei-vath-thOdu oppa-k- koLal.

     If a person is able to sense (decipher) the sense of others as to what is in the mind, such a person deserves to be considered as a divine person! (Alternatively: Such persons will be accepted as respectable and resourceful persons: Pulavar Kuzhandai-Urai).

703. kuRip-pin kuRippu- uNar- vaarai, uRuppin-uL, yaathu kodu-th-thum koLal.

     The assistance of a person who is able to sense (decipher) the feelings of others is worth having with you, even by giving any of your possessions/ even by donating an organ of your body. (Note: *'uRruppu'* is defined as a job/position in an organization/ Government: Refer to Kalaignar Urai; In the modern world, a rare expert like Mind-Reader, deserves a priority in the 'Organ –Donation- Scheme', if he/she requires it, in order to save that person, in the interest of the public / people).

704. kuRith-thathu kooRaamai-k- koLvaa-rOdu, (y)aenai uRuppu-Or - anai-yaraal, vaeRu

     Those persons who are able to read/understand what is inside our minds, sharply, without ourselves speaking out, are equal to any other persons, in respect of human body, but their mental caliber is different altogether! Differently different!!

705. kuRippin kuRippu-uNaraa- (v)aa-yin, uRuppin-uL (y)enna payath.tha-vO kaN?

What is the use of eyes as a part of the human body, if a person does not understand the neighbour's mind (being guided by the signs of the body which are being conveyed by the eyes)? (Note: The intentions of the mind are conveyed by one's eyes. The observer's eyes must be capable of reading those signals, as conveyed by the eyes of the other person!).

706. aduth-thathu kaattum paLing-ku-pOl, nhenj-cham kadu-th-thathu kaatt-um mukam.

The facial expression will reflect the anxiety/excitement of tt t t he mind, just like the reflected image of the neighbouring object being shown by a mirror (polished marble surface). (Note: A scientific hint is indicated in the polished-marble being used as a mirror! 2000-years back!).Research is needed to know whether the term '*paLingku*' could mean any artificial material used 2000 years back?

707. mukath-thin muthu-k-kuRai-nh-thathu uNdo, uvappin-um, kaayi-num, thaan-mu-nh- thuRum.

Could there be a superior wisdom than the wisdom owned by the face (of a living-person) which transmits (conveys) the signal to show the status of mind (intentions) instantaneously, whether it is cheerfulness or anger? (Note: What prevails in the mind will be revealed by facial expressions, simultaneously/concurrently).

708. mukam-nhO-kki nhi-Rka amai-yum, akam-nhO-kki utRathu, uNar-vaar-p- peRin.

If a king is able to have with him, some persons who can feel the thoughts going on in the mind of the king, it is sufficient for the king to be seated in peace, in front of those skilled persons! (A solution could possibly emerge!). (Appearance of the face of a per son is considered sufficient to know what is in his/her mind, if at all some mind-readers are there around that person to watch the fun!).

709. pakai-mai-yum kaeNmai-yum kaN-uraik-kum; kaNNin
vakai-mai uNar-vaar-p- peRin.

If there is a person who can differentiate the categories of looks on the eyes, the task of differentiating enmity from friendship will become possible, as it can be read from the eyes directly and exactly! (Note: It sounds like a convincing strategy!).

710. nhu-NNi-yam (y)enbaar, aLakkum-kOl, kaaNum-kaal,
kaN-allathu illai, piRa.

Those persons who claim that they have got sharp (fine) knowledge seem to use the "looks of the eyes" of other persons as a measuring rod, for judging the views of others! Nothing else! This is what seems to be true, if we think about it deeply!

CHAPTER-72

JUDGING THE AUDIENCE

711. avai-aRi-nh-thu, aa-raa-i-nh-thu, solluka; sollin
thokai-aRi-nh-tha thooy-mai yavar

Those persons with purity of mind who are able to judge the power of each word, must utter the words aptly, in a fitting way, after assessing the caliber of the audience!

712. idai-theri-nh-thu nha-n-ku- uNar-nh-thu solluka; sollin
nhadai-theri-nh-tha nhanmai- yavar.

Persons who have received the benefit (training) of using words appropriately, through learning, will have to utter words, taking time to explain the words, in a suitable way, after ascertaining the trends of response found among the audience!

713. avai-aRi-yaar sollal-mae-R- koL-pavar sollin
vakai-aRiyaar vallathoo-(v)um il.

Those who undertake the art of delivering a speech, without knowing the caliber of the audience, will end up being branded as those who are not familiar with the categories of words, and those who lack talent/ expertise/capacity!

714. oLiyaar -mun oLLiyar aathal; veLi-yaar-mun
vaan-chuthai vaNNam- koLal.

While interacting with wise persons, one must prove his/her excellence! While interacting with ignorant persons, one must modify the style to look like a dull person, to match with the blank/plain white colour of the slaked-lime-powder, comparable with the colour of the sky covered with white clouds!! (Note: Sky covered with cirrus cloud to indicate the intensity of white colour is a scientific hint!).

715. nhandRu -yendRa- vatRuLL-um, nhand-Rae, muthu-varuL
mu-nh-thu kiLa-vaa-ch- cheRivu.

Among all good things a person can do, as the best practice, deserving appreciation, will be the maturity of mind with which he/she avoids the desire to deliver the speech as the first person, in the gathering of elders who happen to be persons wiser than the self!

716. aatRin nhi-lai- thaLar-nh- th(u)-atRae, viyan-pulam
(y)aetRu-uNar-vaar munnar izhukku.

An error of words or concept committed by a person who is trying to deliver a speech in front of experts in the specific field of study (who have got the eminence of approving the content of the speech itself), is considered as a shameful insult to the established norms in the discipline (field of learning)! (One must be careful enough to avoid errors of words or concepts!).

717. katR(u)- aRi-nh-thaar kalvi viLa-ng-kum, kasad(u)-aRa-ch-
chol-theri-thal vallaar akath-thu.

The greatness of vast learning of the speaker will be revealed and appreciated when delivered to the audience of persons who have learned the words, free from faults, and who are strong in vocabulary

718. uNarvathu udai-yaar-mun sollal vaLar-va-than
paath-thi-yuL nheer-sori-nh- th(u)-atRu.

When a speaker delivers a speech to the audience on a subject-matter with which the audience is already familiar (to the audience having advanced knowledge), it is to be understood as a repeated exercise like sprinkling water to a growing-crop in the garden bed! (Note: The scenario described in the couplet (kural) simulates the Seminar-Speeches delivered by college-level students and attended by experts in the subject-matter (specific topic-area)).

719. pul-lavai-yuL poch-chaa-nh-thum soll-aRka, nhalla-avai-yuL
nha-n-ku sela-ch –chollu- vaar.

In the audience of learned persons, the speakers talk about good virtues, so that the message reaches the audience effectively, and they are advised not to talk about the same subject-matter to the audience of lesser-qualified persons, even by forgetfulness! (Note: It refers to the exclusive-audience of experts in the specific field of study).

720. ang-kaNath-thuL ukka amizhth(u)-atRaal, tham-kaNath-thar allaar-mun kOtti- koLal.

Speech delivered to an audience of persons who are not conversant with the knowledge of the speaker's subject-matter is considered as analogous to throwing the most precious divine food on the dirty (barren) floor!

CHAPTER-73

FREEDOM FROM STAGE FEAR

721. vakai-aRi-nh-\thu val-(l)avai vaai-sOraar, sollin
thokai aRi-nh-tha thooy-mai- yavar.

Those who are familiar with the classification of words, and who are pure in their hearts, and who are conversant with varied force of words, will not be committing errors in their speeches in the forum attended by the audience of mighty scholars/experts/persons of eminence!

722. katRaa-ruL katRaar (y)ena-p-paduvar, katRaar-mun
katRa, sela-ch- chollu- vaar.

Educated persons who are capable of narrating the subject-matter whatever they have learned so far, to the audience of the learned persons, in a satisfactory manner, will be ultimately accepted (approved) as 'learned-scholars' among the category of the learned persons. (Note: This scenario simulates the speech given by a student-candidate appearing for the viva-voce (oral) examination for the award of a degree or diploma, in front of the learned group of examiners!: It is a rhyming couplet!).

723. pakai-aka-ththu-ch- chaavaar (y)eLiyar; ariyar
avai-akath-thu anj-chaa- thavar.

Many persons are there who get killed in the battlefield while bravely fighting against their enemies! Lesser is the number of persons who are capable of talking fearlessly to the audience of learned persons!

724. katRaar-mun, katRa, sela-ch- cholli-th- thaam-katRa
mikkaa-ruL mikka-k- koLal.

In the presence of the learned audience, a person must narrate whatever he/she has learned so far, in an agreeable manner, taking care to acquire additional knowledge from the persons of higher learning, taking advantage of the opportunity to meet them! (Note: This scenario simulates

Symposiums/ Conferences conducted at National Level or International Level which help sharing of knowledge among the stake-holders, specific to any discipline of study or multi-disciplinary relevance!).

725. aatRin aLavu- aRi-nh-thu kaRka; avai-anj-chaa
maa-tRam koduth-thal poruttu.

Learn the relevant books, which would strengthen your knowledge up to the measure of defending your knowledge in any forum, without fear or hesitation! (Note: This briefing gives a clue to a student for gathering literature information for enriching his/her knowledge, in order to defend his/her scientific or professional findings in a forum of experts. This resembles the quantum of knowledge to be acquired for facing the oral examination for any degree or diploma).

726. vaaLodu-(y)en van-kaNNar allaar-kku?; nhool-odu-(y)en
nhuN-(N)avai anj-chu—pavar-k-ku?

What is the use of a sword for a coward in the battlefield? Similarly, what is the use of books to a person who is afraid of speaking to the audience (forum) of learned people?

727. pakai-aka-ththu-p- pae-di-kai oL-vaaL; avai-aka-ththu
anj-chum avan-katRa nhool.

The books that a person learns become useless, if the person is afraid of facing the audience of learned (educated) persons, just like a sharp sword becoming useless in the battlefield at the hands of a trembling-coward!

728. pallavai katRum payam-ila-rae; nhal-(l)avai-yuL
nha-n-ku sela-ch- chollaa thaar.

Although a person has learned in many schools of thought, his/her learning becomes useless if that person is unable to convey the subject very well to the ultimate effect of being accepted by the audience of the learned. (Note:The poet refers about material available to the learner, on various titles on the subject discussed in various forums (similar to the documented proceedings of deliberations in conferences held during modern times).It is a historical note on the type of literature material available to the learners, on specific subjects, during the times of the poet, some 2000 years ago!).

729. kallaa thavar-in kadai-yen-ba, katRu aRi-nh-thum,
nha-llaar avai, anjchu vaar.

A person who has acquired a good knowledge through leaning, will be considered worse than an illiterate person, if the so- called learned person is afraid of addressing a good audience! (He/she will be admired, if the fear could be overcome!).

730. uLar-(y)eninum, illaa-rodu- oppar, kaLan-anj-chi-k-
katRra, sela-ch-chollaa thaar.

Those persons who are not able to convey the subject- matter from whatever they have learned, to the audience of learned persons, in a convincing/agreeable way, will be construed (considered) as being absent in that forum, even if they are physically present! (This interpretation is different from others! A few other interpreters have interpreted that persons who cannot speak out in any forum would be considered as dead persons, although it could not have been the intention of the Poet, to disgrace them!! The poet would have marked that person 'absent' in the list of persons who attended the session!).

CHAPTER-74

IDEAL COUNTRY

731. thaLLaa viLai-yuLum, thakkaarum, thaazh-vu-ilaach-
chelvar-um, sae-r-vathu nhaadu.

A country is ideally defined as a good country where a combination of resources are available, such as i) the never-failing agricultural yields, ii) persons of reputable virtues among the subjects, and iii) rich persons of undiminished wealth; all being present together, as resources of the country!

732. perum-poruL-aal pettakka -thaaki, aru-ng-kaet-taal
aatRa viLai-vathu nhaadu.

The land must have credentials that i) it becomes desired by people because of abundant wealth, ii) it has got the capacity to overcome the harmful effects of disasters and iii) it has got the benevolence of agricultural potentials of never-failing harvests! (Note: The term '*arum-kedu*' refers to 'rare-dangers', such as, natural disasters (cyclones, floods, droughts,forest-fires, famines, pandemics for humans, diseases for cattle and vegetation, war with neighbouring countries, etc.).

733. poRai- yoru-ng-ku mael-varu-ng-kaal, thaa-ng-ki, iRaivaR-ku
iRai-oru-ng-ku nhae-r-vathu nhaadu.

An ideal country is the land which is capable of bearing the financial burden, in excess of what the country could normally bear, and is having the potential to provide the necessary resources to the king, inclusive of taxes to set right the treasury! (Note: Excessive burden may include expenses for war with a neighbouring country, or feeding the poor people (during famines), or accommodating refugees from other countries,etc.).

734. uRu-pasi-yum, Ovaa-p- piNiyum, seRu-pakai-yum,
sae-raathu iyal-vathu nhaadu.

A country's quality must be in such a way that it is free from the following drawbacks: i) an inflicting starvation, ii) never-ending diseases, and iii) severe enmity from the neighbouring countries!

(Note: The poet highlights on the need for a genuine foreign policy for promoting good relationship with the neighbouring countries! To have peace in the Land!!).

735. pal-kuzhu-vum, paazh-sei-yum ut-pakaiyum, vae-nh-thu alai-kkum
kol- kuRumbu-m, illathu nhaadu.

A country must be free from many groups working against the king, free from the disastrous evil of internal enmity, and also free from the murderous groups of savages, sometimes aiming at the very life of the king himself!(Note: The poet reiterates on the importance of internal peace and enforcement of law-and-order in the country!)

736. kaedu aRiyaa-k- ketta- (v)idaththum, vaLam-kundRaa
nhaadu-(y)enba, nhaatt-in thalai.

It is said that the best of countries in the world is the one which i) is free from any harm being caused by enemies, and ii) will recover quickly from any hardships and sufferings lasting over a short period of time, iii) will have sufficient resources which will not get depleted, even during hard times! (The term '*kaedu*' = harm, may include war, natural-disaster such as drought, famine, floods, epidemics for humans and animals, damage to crops etc).

737. iru-punalum, vaa-i-nh-tha malai-yum, varu-punalum,
val-araN-um nhaa-ttiR-ku uRuppu.

It is said that the ideal components of a country must be i) the two sources of water (rain water and spring water), ii) suitably- situated hills/ mountains (forest resources), iii) the incoming rivers (originating from the neighbouring countries), and iv) a strong Fort!

*(Note: The ideal water resources, and forest wealth of a country are described, in addition to a well-protected fort).

738. piNi-yinmai, selvam, viLaivu, inbam, (y)ae-mam,
aNi-yenba, nhaa-tti-Rku, iv- (v)ai-nh-thu.

It is said that the five ideal ornaments of a country are visualized as:i) absence of diseases, ii) abundant wealth, iii) surplus agricultural yields,

iv) happiness of people, and v) proper protection in the fortress in the country! (Note: The term '*(y)aemam*' stands for 'protection'/ 'security'!

739. nhaadu-yenba, nhaa-daa vaLath-thana; nhaa-du alla,
nhaa-da, vaLam-tharu(m) nhaadu.

It is said that an ideal country is one in which natural resources are available to produce abundant wealth. (Self-sufficiency, in resources, is the criterion). It is also said that a country is not worthy of its name, if excessive exertions of efforts are to be made to show (create) development, productivity, and prosperity! A country must not be dependent on another country for satisfying its own needs!

740. aang-ku-amaivu (y)eithi-ya-k- kaNNum, payam-(y)indRae
vee-n-thu-amaivu- illaatha nhaadu.

When all the infrastructure facilities and resources are available in a country, whereas a good king is not available to ensure fearless life for the subjects, there is no benefit of having a country at all!

CHAPTER-75

THE FORT (DEFENSE FORTIFICATION)

741. aatRu- pa-varkkum, araN- poruL; anjchi-th- thaR
pOtRu- pavar-k-kum poruL.

Fort is a defensive asset for those who perform the act of fighting against an enemy in the war! It is also, a sheltering wealth for those who want to protect themselves in fear of an enemy!

742. maNi-nheer-um, maNNum, malai-yum, aNi-nhi-zhal
kaadu-m udai-yathu araN.

A protective fort ideally comprises of i) a garland-shaped moat which serves as a clear water defensive-trench, ii) a decorative, shady forest surrounding the garland-shaped moat, iii) a vast open land, and iv) a hill. (Note: The neck portion of the garland forms the entrance to the fort! The Fort is depicted as a protected campus surrounded by a garland-shaped moat (a mini-reservoir filled with clear water) and further surrounded by a shady- forest. It corresponds to an architectural design, based on the defense-requirement to offer protection for the Fort during war-time situation). (Please see Appendix-1).

743. uyarvu, akalam, thiNmai, arumai, i-n(h)- nhaan-kin
amaivu-araN- yendRu-uraik-kum nhool.

An authoritative book on the lay-out of a fort dictates the four factors, namely, height, width (lateral dimensions of length and width), dense strength, and difficult access (not an easy access for enemies to enter), as spelled out in an authoritative book on the ideal requirements for the construction of a defense-fortress campus. The term '*arumai*' will include an 'elegant' appearance!

(Note: The term '*akalam*' represents width and length, as the two- lateral dimensions, and height '*uyarvu*' as the third (vertical) dimension. The poet refers to an authoritative book on architecture.).

744. siRu-kaapp-in pae-ri-dath-tha-thu- aaki, uRu-pakai
ookkam azhip-pathu araN.

A fort must be capable of being protected with minimum defense/force, (with compact, impressive frontage), but, must have large space in front of the fort and on the inside campus, and must ensure that guts and courage of the enemy forces are destroyed when an enemy looks at the grand (mystifying) appearance of the fort!

745. koLaRku ari-thaai-k- koNda-koozh-th-thu—aaki, akath-thaar
nhi-laikku –yeLi-thaam, nheer-athu araN.

A fort must have the appropriate provisions and components in the design to ensure the following features, namely, i) it must not be easy for the enemy to capture, ii) it must ensure adequate supply of food and other materials for those persons dwelling inside the fort, and iii) it must be ensuring easy methods for soldiers to resort to fighting from inside, and iv) it must offer safe accommodation to the occupants (inmates)!

746. (y)ella-p- poruLum udaith-thaa-i, idaththu- uthavum,
nhal-aaL udaiyathu araN.

A fort must contain all materials and supplies, and must have good defense-personnel to destroy the invading enemies, and to render assistance to the inmates, at the spot during times of crisis!

747. mutRiyum mutRaa-thu (y)eRi-nh-thum, aRai-p-paduth-thum,
patRaR-ku ari-yathu araN.

A fort must be protected in such a way that i) it is difficult for the enemy to surround the fort, ii) it becomes possible to fight from inside when the fort is surrounded all around, iii) the fort is protected to prevent the entry of enemies by plotting, or iv) it is not possible for the enemy by resorting to enter into the fort by under- ground-tunneling!

748. mutRu- aatRi, mutRi- yava-rai-yum, patRu-aatRi-p-
patRi-yaar vel-va-thu araN.

A true defense will comprise of the following: i) defeating the enemy who attempts for surrounding the fort, ii) capturing the enemy-soldiers who have already surrounded the fort, iii) releasing the own soldiers who got captured during the fight with the enemy. (Note: The merit is attributed to the design of the Fort, with all relevant features!).

749. munai-mukath-thu maa-tRalar saa-ya, vinai- mukath-thu.
veeRu- (y)eithi maaNda-thu araN.

A strong fort must be designed for ensuring the following features: (i) Destroying those enemies in front of the fort must be possible; well before the enemies could advance, (for preventing the enemies from surrounding the fort), and ii) Showing the valour of valiant warriors-in-action, in the battlefield to forcefully destroy the enemies, in coordination with the soldiers stationed inside the fort.

750. (y)enai-maatchi-th-thu aaki-ya-k- kaNNum, vinai-maatchi
illaar-kaN ill-athu araN.

Whatever be the magnificence of the fort in size and strength,if magnificence of heroic action isabsent in the cadres of personnel ofthearmy, to destroythe invading enemies and earn a meritorious victory, there is no defense for the country! Such a strong fort cannot offer defense!

CHAPTER-76

WAYS OF EARNING WEALTH

751. poruL-al- lavarai-p- poruLaa-ka-ch- cheyyum
poruL allathu illai, poruL.

It is the wealth which makes even unworthy persons as worthy (respectable) persons in the society. Therefore, there cannot be a more useful possession for a living person other than wealth (to aspire for)!

752. illaarai (y)ellaarum (y)eLLuvar; selvarai,
(y)ellaarum sey-var siRappu.

Those persons who do not have (sufficient) wealth will be despised (disliked /under-estimated) by all. All the people will ex tend special status to wealthy persons.

753. poruL (y)ennum poi-yaa- viLakkam, irul-aRukkum,
(y)eNNiya- thae-yath-thu-ch- chendRu.

Wealth, called an unfailing lamp, will cut away (remove) the darkness, and facilitate going to a foreign country, if that desire occurs in one's mind! (Note: Money carries its values even in foreign countries, including countries of enemies. This poem has got relevance to financial investments in a foreign land, by a person belonging to a particular country, in the present context of global trade).

754. aRan yee-num; inbam-um yeenum; thiRan aRi-nh-thu,
thee-thu- indRi va-nh-tha poruL.

Wealth earned through proper ways and means, without committing any evil act, will yield virtues/virtuous benefits and happiness. (It will be possible to carry out deeds which are considered to be virtuous, as those deeds would be beneficial to the needy people, thereby, bringing glory to the persons who donate!).

755. aruLodum, anb(u)-odum, vaa-raa-p- poruL-aakkam, pull-aar puraLa vidal.

Wealth not gained (earned) through routes of love and grace has to be considered as evil, and must be disowned/wasted!

756. uRu-poruLum, ulku poruLum, than, onnaar-th-theRu-poruLum, vae-nh-than poruL.

A king is eligible to have wealth from ancestors, as the legal- heir! Additionally, income through taxes from the subjects, and wealth coming from distressed enemies, would be coming to the treasury of the victorious king! (Note: These are the norms in monarchy, when personal wealth and public treasury were one and the same!).

757. aruL- (y)ennun, anbu-yeen- kuzhavi, poruL- (y)ennum- selva-ch- chevili-yaal uNdu.

For the human virtue of grace, called as the child of kindness, there is a rich foster- mother (nursing mother) called wealth, to make it possible to nourish the child, called grace! (Wealth earned by a person enables him/her to carry out philanthropic or charitable deeds!).

758. kunRu-(y)aeRi, yaanai-p-pOr kaNd(u)-atRaal, than- kaith-th(u)-ondRu uNdaa-ka-ch- cheivaan vinai.

A person who performs an act with his/her own resources of wealth can afford to get it done by employing others, safely, in a care-free style, without getting entangled in any trouble. It is as good as climbing up and ascending to the top of the hill to watch the fight of elephants down below, safely, sitting at the hill-top! (without getting entangled between the fighting-elephants!). (Note: The importance of using one's own resources as the capital for any new venture is highlighted!).

759. seika poruLai; seRu-nhar serukk(u)- aRukkum (y)e-h-ku- athan-in kooriyathu il.

Do endeavour (make an effort) to earn the wealth, because, there is no other sharper weapon which is capable of destroying the arrogance of your enemies! (Note: Making wealth means earning wealth through hard efforts in the right way and saving enough of it, to be spent on useful purposes: Kalaignar Urai).

760. oN-poruL kaazh-p-pa, iya-tRi-yaar-kku, (y)eN-poruL
(y)ae-nai ira-Ndum oru-ng-ku.

If a person endeavours and creates good wealth through honest means, abundantly, the much-desired two other forms of wealth, namely, virtue and happiness will be added together, thereby, becoming handy, to carry out good deeds! (Note: The term '*yeN- poruL*' means the other treasures such as virtuous traits and blissful experience (imparting psychological satisfaction/sense of contentment)

CHAPTER-77

EXCELLENCE OF AN ARMY,

761. uRuppu amai-nh-thu ooR(u)-anj-chaa vel-padai- vae-nh-than
veRukkai-yuL (y)ellaam thalai.

The most important wealth of a king, among other treasures, is a prestigious army, with all components of traditional outfit, with well-armed soldiers who are reputed for valour and who are capable of fearlessly fighting in the battlefield towards a meritorious victory! (The term "*uRuppu*" means various units of an army, a general term applicable to modern times as well).

762. ulaivu-idath-thu ooRu- anj-chaa, van-kaN tholaivu-idath-thu-th-
thol-padaikku al-laal arithu.

Even when the strength of an army is not adequate to fight against a strong enemy force,it becomes possible for the reputed - army which has built up its ancient record of traditional valour and heroism to fight with determination to win, in spite of obvious set-backs! It is not possible for others!!

763. olith-thak-kaal, (y)en-aam, uvari (y)eli-p-pakai?
nhaa-kam uyir-p-pa, -k- kedum!

What will happen if angry rats make huge noise resembling the noisy waves of the sea? When the king-cobra breathes with a hissing sound, the noise of the rats will die down, thereby implying that the enmity of the rats will die down! (Some interpreters have mentioned that the rats will die, on hearing the hissing sound of the snake! The rats will only run away to escape!). (Please see Appendix-1).

764. azhivu-indRu aRai-pOkaa-thu aa-ki- vazhi-va-nh-tha
van- ka Na-thu-vae padai.

The merit of a genuine army will become obvious, if it can uphold the traditional (age-old) reputation of valour and fight ferociously, thereby, avoiding destruction of soldiers, and without falling a prey to enemy's designs, and remaining loyal to the king! (This is a great blessing to the king). (Note: The king must appreciate the value of his own army. That is why the poet takes care to mention it!).

765. kootRu-udandRu mae-l-varin-um, koodi (y)ethir-nhi-Rkum
aa-tRal- athu-vae padai.

An ideal army is the one which is capable of defeating the enemy, with determination and the inborn traditional valour, even if the god of death declares a war and advances with his mighty forces in the battlefield! (Note: The terrorizing size and strength of an army is visualized as the real embodiment of death: Pulavar-Kuzhandai Urai).

766. maRam, maanam, maa-Nda vazhi-ch-chelavu, thaetRam,
(y)ena, nhaan-kae (y)ae-mam padai-kku.

The real strength of an army must have the four characteristics (virtues), namely, i) reputed valour and courage, ii) dignity/ self-respect, iii) observance of the prestigious traditions of the fore fathers, and iv) unfailing loyalty!

767. thaar-thaa-ng-ki-ch chel-vathu, thaa-nai; thalai-va-nh-tha
pOr-thaa-ng-kum thanmai aRi-nh-thu.

A brave army must be capable of advancing against the onslaught of an attack, at the same time, judging the withstanding- power of the enemy forces, and accordingly adopting the fighting-strategies (tactics), in the battlefield!

768. adal-thakai-yum, aa-tRalum, il-(y)eni-num, thaa-nai
padai-th- thakai-yaal paadu peRum.

An army will deserve merit (appreciation), if it can exhibit the splendorous nature of the army, in weaponry, by showing the skills in the flag-march (parading) elegantly, even if it lacks strength and power to destroy the enemy!!

769. siRumai-yum, sellaa-th- thuni-yum, vaRu-mai-yum,
illaa-yin, vellum padai.

If an army is free from shortage in numbers, free from poverty, and free from a sense of bitterness against the chief of army (or the king), it will surely bring victory.

(Note: Hatred against the chief of army or the king would cause miserable results, including desertion or betrayal, even at the risk of death. Three important points are highlighted: i) soldiers must be well-fed, ii) soldiers will have a high morale, if they are happy about the way in which the country is being ruled by their king, and iii) the king or army-officers must properly treat the warriors in the army during peace-time, so that their loyalty will not be at stake while fighting against an enemy in the war! In the battlefield, the morale of soldiers is important. The poet speaks on behalf of army-personnel and the people, to caution the rulers).

770. nhilai-makkaL saala udaith-thu, (y)eninum, thaanai
thalai-makkaL il, vazhi il.

Even if the brave soldiers of the native land are available in- plenty, it will not be possible to organize an army, if the leaders among the cadres are not there to lead the army!(Note: The role of a distinguished and dynamic chief of army in leading the army is highlighted).

CHAPTER-78

PRIDE OF AN ARMY

771. (y)en-ai-mun nhil-lan-min; thev-vir! palar- (y)en-ai--
mun-nhindRu, kal-nhin- dRavar!

I severely warn my dear enemies: Do not stand in front of my king to fight; Many other kings who had stood in front of my king and fought the wars, during the past years, are now standing as tomb-stones!(after being destroyed by my great king!). (Note: The term '*ai*'= leader).

772. kaana- muyal-(y)ei-tha ambin-il yaanai
pizhai-th-tha-vael (y)ae-nh-thal inithu.

It gives a more blissful pride to a warrior who holds a spear which has just missed hitting a big elephant in the battlefield, when compared to the happiness a person would enjoy in holding a dart (sharp weapon) which has successfully killed a large rabbit of the forest!

773. pae-raa-Nmai yenba, thaRu-kaN; ondRu- utRak-kaal,
ooraa-Nmai, matRu a-tha-n (y)e-h-ku.

The action of killing in the battlefield is said to be a praise- worthy manliness.The other dimension of it is to generously help the enemy who is in trouble, and if he asks for help in the battlefield! This is an additional strength to the manliness for the warrior!! (An other interpretation: Killing the enemy in the war is praised as valour! However, an enemy after being humbled, deserves mercy! Captured-enemy, or surrendering-enemy deserves to be treated with honour! This treatment extended to an enemy in the war corresponds to the most superior form of valour!). (Note: It relates to International Diplomacy relevant to prisoners of wars! Spelled out 2000 years ago!!).

774. kai-vael kaLitRodu pOkki, varu-pavan
mei-vael paRi-yaa nha-kum.

A soldier in the battlefield, who has successfully launched a flying javelin-spear at an elephant in the battlefield, feels cheerful to find a spear which has been pierced into his chest by an enemy, during his attack on the elephant, and he gives a triumphant smile, getting ready for the next battle, now that he has got an additional weapon (pulled out from his chest)!

775. vizhi-ththa- kaN vael-koNdu (y)eRiya, azhith-thu –imai-p-pin,
'ottu'-andRO van- ka Navar-k-ku?

Would it not be considered as a defeat (shame) to a valiant soldier, if he winks his eyes while showing his angry countenance (face), when an enemy throws a sharp spear towards the wide open eyes? (Note: The poet visualizes the definition of self-respect for a valiant- soldier, as the soldier himself feels!).

776. vizhu-p-puN padaa-tha-nhaaL yellaam, vazhukkin-uL
vaik-kum –than nhaa-Lai (y)eduth-thu.

Valiant heroes (soldiers) will count the number of days they have lived through, in this world, and set aside the days on which they did not have a chance to get honourably wounded in the battle field, as the days spent-in-vain, during their lifetime!

777. suzha-lum isai-vaeN-di, vaeN-daa uyir-aar
kazhal-yaappu-k- kaarikai- nheer-th-thu.

In pursuit of a revolving fame for their names, persons who wish to sacrifice their lives in the battlefield, it is appropriate that they wear the strings of tiny bells around their anklets of their legs, as a sign of heroism! The music coming from the tiny bells sings their glory, (when they move, walk around, or dance!), praising their valour! It is a motivating lyrics for them! (That will make them feel cheerful and jubilant! (Note: the term *'kazhal'* stands for the string of little bells worn around the leg as a sign of heroism! This is displayed in rural festivals in Tamil-speaking land, even during the present-times, depicting their ancestors (war-heroes), as family-gods!).

778. uRin-uyir anj-chaa maRavar iRaivan
seRi-num –seer kundRal ilar.

Those heroic soldiers, getting into the battlefield, who do not fear for their lives, will not slacken their enthusiasm, even at the time of an angry order of the king to exercise caution while advancing!(Anger of their king will not deter them from fighting ferociously,with dedication to win the war!). (Note: When the king advises the soldiers not to be very aggressive, perhaps as a strategy, and in that relevance, the king is likely to command them to be cautious,showing a tone of anger! The poet describes the nitty- gritty details of the realistic situation which could prevail in the battlefield!).

779. izhaith-thathu ika-vaamai-ch- chaa-vaarai yaa-rae
pizhaith-tha-thu oRukkiR- pavar?

When a warrior fought in the battlefield to fulfill his vow that he would die in the battlefield for the sake of victory, who else is capable of scoffing (speaking with disrespect), about his earlier defaults when he was alive! Everybody has to salute him and honour him, upholding his glory and dignity!

780. pura-nh-thaar-kaN nheer-mal-ka-ch chaakiR-pin, saa-kkaadu
ira-nh-thu-kOL thakka-thu udai-th-thu.

If a brave soldier faces death in the battlefield,while the patron(king) sheds tears in grief, that kind of death deserves to be earned, even by begging to the Almighty!

CHAPTER-79

FRIENDSHIP

781. seya-Rku -ariya yaa-vu-La, nha-t-pin? athu-pOl,
vinai-kku- ariya yaa-vuLa kaappu?

What else is there to earn, more precious than earning a good friendship? Is there any other act which can be claimed as superior than creating a good friendship which can ensure a genuine safety against one's own foes (enemies)?

782. nhiRai- nheera nheera-var kaeNmai; piRai-mathi-p-
pin-nheer-a pae-thai-yaar nha-t-pu.

Friendship with wise persons will grow,like the growth of the moon, from crescent-moon to full moon, growing day by day. Friendship with dull-headed persons will go on diminishing, from the full moon towards darkness, day by day!

783. nhavil-thoRum nhool-nha-yam pOlum, payil-thoRum,
paNpudai- yaa-Lar thodar-pu.

The more you get familiar with the contents of a book, the more is the appreciation of its content you would enjoy. Similarly, the more you move closely, with the virtuous persons, the more will be the enjoyment of your friendship with them.

784. nha-ku-thal poru-tt(u)- andRu nha-t-tal; mikuthi-k-kaN
maeR-- chendRu, idith-thal poruttu.

The purpose of making friendship is not only for enjoying humour. When a friend does something wrong, due to his/her ignorance, it is the duty of a true friend to voluntarily come forward to correct the erring- friend, with a suitable advice! If he/she does not listen, the effort can include crossing the limits, and resorting to a forceful language in giving the advice,and in making him/her get convinced!

785. puNar-ch-chi pazhaku-thal vaeNdaa; uNar-ch-chi-thaan
nha-t-pu-aam, kizha(i)mai tharum.

Meeting each other very often, or constant touch with each other, may not be the requirement of friendship.Feelings and emotions must be united in the hearts of both persons, to make a good friendship!.

786. mukam-nha-ka nhat-pathu nhat-pu-andRu; nhenj-chath-thu
akam-nhaka nhat-pathu nhatpu.

Exchanging smiles does not correspond to friendship. Unification of minds, and the pleasant feelings stored therein, corresponds to an ideal friendship!

787. azhi-vin, avai-nhee-kki, aaRu-ui-th-thu, azhi-vin-kaN
al-lal uzhap-path(u)-aam nhatpu.

True friendship has got mutual obligations to help each other, i) in keeping away from any deed which would cause trouble, ii) in encouraging to follow the virtuous path, and iii) in case of any crisis, happening to one person, the other person also deciding to join together to solve the crisis (by sharing the ordeal/trouble).

788. udukkai izha-nh-thavan kai- pOla, aa-ng-kae,
idukkaN kaLai-vathu-aam nhatpu.

True friendship comes to the rescue of a suffering-friend to take away the trouble, just like one's own hands of a person rushing forward instantly to put back, in position, the garment slipping down from the waist! (Note: This is widely cited as example of the speed and dedication with which relief measures are to be carried out during natural disasters, in offering help to the people!: A top management topic!). Ref: Gopalakrishna Gandhi (2015), "Tiruvalluvar-The Tirukkural", Aleph Book Company, New Delhi, page.xiv.

789. nhat-piRku veetRi-rukkai yaath(u-y)enil, kotp(u)-indRi
ollum-vaai- oond-Rum nhilai.

If it is asked as to what is the firm-footing of friendship, it is to be answered that it is the firmness of mind to stand together in facing any unforeseen troubles to help each other,in whatever possible ways it could be worked out, and to avoid difference of opinion on any issue!

790. 'inai-yar ivar-yemakku', 'innam-yaam', yendRu,
punai-yi-num pul-yennum nhatpu.

If one person describes the details such as i) the kind of intimacy in the friendship between the two friends, (the self and a particular friend), ii) how the two persons did come into contact with each other, iii) how deep is the intimacy or mutual obligations, etc, by fiction or real terms, then, that particular friendship will-break! Losing-its-value!

CHAPTER- 80

ASSESSMENT OF FRIENDSHIP

791. nhaa-daa-thu nhattal-in kaedu-illai; nhatta-pin,
veedu-illai nhatp(u), aaL- pavar-kku.

There cannot be more harm caused to a person, so great as making friendship, without knowing full details of any stranger, because, after making that friendship, it would be rather difficult for the person to liberate himself/herself from that unwanted friendship. It will be a pain!!

792. aa-i-nh-thu, aa-i-nh-thu, koLLaa-thaan kae-N-mai, kadai-muRai,
thaan-saam thuya-ram tharum.

If a person who does not earn a friendship, after repeated enquiry, and contemplation/deep thought, it would lead ultimately to grief, a grief which may even be leading to his/her death!

793. kuNa-num, kudi-mai-yum, ku-tRam-um, ku-ndRaa
inan-um aRi-nh-thu, yaa-kka, nhatpu.

Friendship must be made after knowing details such as the temperament of the person, in terms of virtues and weakness, details of his/her family background and the caliber of his/her companions.

794. kudi-p-piRa-nh-thu than-kaN pazhi –nhaaNu -vaan-ai-k-
kodu-th-thum koLal- vae-Ndum, nhatpu.

The friendship of a person who is born in a honourable family and who will shy away from any evil habit, is worth being earned! One must earn that kind of friendship, even by offering a gift to that person, or by doing a favour to that person, if needed! (Note: The term '*kodu-th-thum*' may mean 'by relaxing (shedding down) one's own ego'. This needs reserch).

795. azha-ch- cholli, al-lathu- idith-thu, vazha-kku-aRiya,
vallaar- nhatpu, aa-i-nh-thu koLal.

The friendship of those persons must be selectively chosen,if they are persons of well-known ability to advise others regarding the realities of worldly life! Such persons would take liberty in offering good advice, regarding what is good and what is bad, and go to the extent of making the friend shed tears, if necessary, to convince the friend who needs advice (counseling)!

796. kaet-ti-num uNdu-Or uRuthi; kiLai-gna-rai
nhee-t-ti aLa-ppath(u)-Or kOl.

Could there be a better profit than a person facing a suffering- situation in life? It helps, as a measuring rod, stretching which the responses (attitudes) of friends and relatives towards the suffering situation of the person concerned, can be measured! (It will reveal whether the cordial relationship being maintained with them, has been meaningful, or not).

797. oothi-yam yen-bathu oru-vaRku-p- pae-thai-yaar
kaeNmai oree-yi vidal.

Profit for a person is to discontinue the friendship with a senseless person.

798. uLLaR-ka uLLam-siRu-kuva; koLLaRka
allal-kaN aatRu- aRup-paar nhatpu.

Avoid thinking about anything which could make your mind to lose your courage/self-confidence. Also, discontinue the friendship of those persons who had cut off their relationship/link,with you, during your times of crisis!

799. kedu-ng-kaalai-k- kai-viduvaar- kaeNmai, adum-kaalai,
uLLi-num, uLLam sudum.

The friendship of those persons who deserted a man/woman at the time of adversity (suffering/hardship/trouble) will be painful to the heart, if he/she recollects about it, at any time, during the entire life time! More so, at the time of one's own death!

800. maru-vuka, maas(u)-atRaar kaeNmai; ondRu, yeeth-thum,
oru-vuka, opp(u)-ilaar nhatpu.

Embrace/maintain the friendship of those who are free from faults. Renounce/discontinue the friendship with those whose actions are not agreeable to the norms of the world (norms that you follow)! Renounce such friendship, even by giving a gift to them, if necessary. (Note: The term *'yeeth-thum'* has to be compared with the term *'kodu-th-thum'* in kural 794!).

CHAPTER- 81

INTIMACY IN FRIENDSHIP

801. pazhaimai yena-p-padu-vathu, yaath(u)-yenin, yaa-thum,
kizha(i)mai-yai-k- keezh-nh-thi-daa nhatpu.

What is known as intimacy in friendship, is that an act carried out by a person, needs to be (automatically) approved by the intimate friend, on whose behalf the person carried out the act! It must be construed as if the person has taken liberty with the friend, in carrying out the act (without consulting the friend, beforehand)!

802. nhat-piRk(u) uRuppu-k- kezhu-thakai-mai; matRu, athaRku,
uppu-aathal, saandROr kadan.

The right is a component /constituent of the link called friendship between two persons.Further, it is the duty of the wise persons to support/ supplement the concept!

803. pazha-kiya nhatpu -ye-van sey-yum? kezhu-thakai-mai
seith(u), aang-ku a-mai-yaak- kadai?

What is the use of a long-standing friendship of a person, if he/she does not approve an action carried out by an intimate friend, whereas, the said friend carried out the action, taking liberty of friendship with that person! (The friendship between the two persons might even break, if the act done by one intimate friend is not approved by the other person!).

804. vizhai-thakai-yaan, vaeNdi- yiruppar, kezhu-thakai-yaal
kae-Laa-thu nha-t-taar seyin.

A person of admirable nature will be pleased with his/her intimate friend, in approving whatever act the intimate friend has done, even if the person concerned has not been consulted before performing the act! (This is all possible in cases of a well-established intimacy prevailing between two intimate friends!!).

805. paethai-mai ond-RO peru-ng-kizha(i)mai (y)endRu- uNar-ka;
nhO-thakka, nha-ttaar seyin.

If a familiar (intimate) friend does something painful, it must be understood that it has been committed due to his/her foolishness or the right of friendship!

806. (y)ellai-k-kaN nhi-ndRaar, thuRa-vaar. tholai-vi-dath-thum
thollai-k-kaN nhi-ndR-aar thodarpu.

A person who stands within the boundaries of the orbit of friendship, without crossing it (without discontinuing that friendship), will not give up the link of contact with those persons who gave support during the times of crisis to the self, in facing the trouble (although some losses are being caused by them presently)!

807. azhi-va-nh-tha sei-yi-num, anbu -aRaar; anbin
vazhi- va-nh-tha kaeNmai yavar.

Friends who are drawn (attracted) through the path of kindness, will not discontinue showing kindness to a person, even if he/ she does something harmful to them!

808. kaeL-izhu-kkam kaeLaa-k- kezhu- thakai-mai, vallaar-k-ku
nhaaL – izhu-kkam, nha-t-taar seyin.

A person of admirable qualities who gives importance for intimacy of friendship will readily pardon his/her bosom-friend who has done a harmful act on a particular day, and will consider the day of occurrence of the said act as an 'unfortunate' day, and forgive that person (although many other friends have earlier complained to him/her about the harms done to them by the same individual). This would reflect the tolerance or broad-mindedness of the person who ratifies the incident.(Note: This is contrary to a normal situation, wherein, the following outlook is probable: All days of friendship will be considered regrettable, if a person does harm to a bosom- friend who never believed the fault caused, whenever others complained to him/her, about the harms done to them, by that person! Now, what has been told by others, about that particular person, has become true, in the case of self-experience, and that is why the old days of friendship with that person, must be considered regrettable! Please see Kalaignar Urai).

809. kedaa-(a)- vazhi-va-nh-tha kaeNmai-yaar, kaeNmai
vidaa-(a)r vizhai-yum ulaku.

The people of the world would very much appreciate and admire the attitude of those persons who do not discontinue their old friendships which they have been maintaining with certain families for generations together, without breaking their cordial intimacies!!

810. vizhai-yaar vizhai-yap- padu-ba, pazhai-yaar-kaN
paN-bin thalai-p-piri-yaa- thaar.

It is said that even enemies will admire the attitude of those who do not discontinue the relationship with those long-term friends, ignoring (forgetting) a few lapses on their part!

CHAPTER-82

HARMFUL FRIENDSHIP

811. paru-ku-vaar- pOli-num paNpu-ilaar kae-Nmaiperukal-in kundRal inithu.

Even if they show outwardly to relish your friendship by pouring sweet words and affectionate gestures, it is better that the friendship with those persons who lack in good qualities is to be decreased (curtailed), instead of being increased.!

812. uRin nhattu, aRin oroo-um oppi-laar kae-Nmai peRi-num, izha-p-pinum (y)en?

What is the benefit of either having or losing the friendship with those undeserving persons who maintain their friendship with you, when you remain rich, and go away from you, when you become poor?

813. uRuvathu seer thoo-k-kum nhatpum peRu-vathu koL-vaarum kaL-varum nhae-r.

Earning friendship with three categories of persons will be found useless, namely, i) those who are assessing the real value of the help received from you (perhaps expecting more), ii)those persons who never return the benefit received from you (as if they are mercenaries expecting some remuneration from you, for certain small services rendered to you), and iii) the real thieves?! (Note: This interpretation needs a debate! Other interpreters have cited the hired-women as 'the persons who receive anything given to them'. This may be re-examined, as the heading of the Chapter is: 'Harmful Friendship'. Hired- women cannot be included in the category of friends).

814. amar-akath-thu, aa-tRu- aRu-kkum kallaa-maa an-naar,
thamar-in, thani-mai thalai.

It is better to be all alone, than acquiring friendship of an unreliable person who is like a horse (brought up and groomed over even before war, by the warrior, and yet) running away in the battle-field, after toppling down the rider-warrior, cutting away from the chosen path!

815. seithu-(y)ae-mam saa-raa-ch, chiRi-yavar pun-kaeNmai
yei-thal-in yei-thaa-mai nhandRu.

If you create friendship with those mean-persons who can not (do not) offer you protection, at the time of troubles happening to you, it is better to avoid that kind of friendship than continuing with it!

816. paethai perung-kezhee-yi nhat-pin aRi-v(u)-udai-yaar
(y)aeth(u) inmai kOdi uRum

Remaining as a stranger to wise persons (inability to acquire the acquaintance with wise persons) is ten million times worthier than having friendship with foolish persons!

(Note: Although acquaintance with wise persons is yet to be earned, there would not be any immediate benefit. However, if acquaintance can be earned, with them, there could be some benefit, to the individual who earns that acquaintance. In the case of friendship with foolish persons, there is no benefit at all, anytime during the tenure of friendship! Therefore, these two cases are compared!).

817. nha-kai-vakai-yar aaki-ya, nhat-pin, pakai-var-aal,
pathth(u)-aduth-tha kOdi uRum.

The harms caused by one's own enemies are more worthier,to the tune of tens of ten million times, compared to the benefits arising out of the friendship with those persons who pretend to be humorous, and who are being induced by their own designs for the purpose of earning personal benefits for themselves, from out of friendship with you!

(Note: This needs a debate. Humorous-friends (merry-making-friends) and enemies are compared. Humour without intimacy and depth (dedication) of friendship may yield some harmful effects, if the 'pretending' friends happen to be spies employed by enemies!

That is why the two cases are compared! Suspicion on the intentions of such folks could be justified in kural 821).

818. ollum- karu-mam udatRu- pavar -kaeNmai,
sol-laa-daar, sOra vidal.

Silently and slowly, discontinue the friendship with those persons who are capable of doing an act which can help you, (in your favour), and yet, they avoid taking it up.

819. kana-vinum innaa-thu, mannO? vinai-vaeRu-
sol-vaeRu- pattaar thodar-pu.

The friendship with those persons whose words are different from their actions will cause harmful effects even during (your) dreams.

820. yenai-th-thum kuRu-ku-thal Ombal, manai-k-kezhee-yi
mand-Ril pazhi-p-paar thodar-pu.

If persons who make friends with you, when you are in the house,whereas they find pleasure in indulging in the habit of despising (insulting) you, or talking ill about you, in your absence in public places, in front of an audience, then it is time that you decide to keep away from such folks.

CHAPTER-83

FORBIDDEN – FRIENDSHIP

821. seer-idam kaaNin, yeRi-thaR-ku-p patta-dai
nhae-raa nhi-ra-nh-th-avar nhatpu.

The friendships of persons who are not united by heart with you, and who are pretending as friends, until the opportune time ripens for them to strike you down, is similar to an anvil used for breaking a steel plate into two pieces! (Your enemies may be behind them!)

822. inam-pO-ndRu, inam-allaar- kaeNmai, maka-Lir
manam-pOla vaeRu padum.

Your friendship with those persons who pretend to belong to your caliber, will not remain steady, as they do not belong to your calibre, by words, thoughts and deeds! That kind of friendship will be like the wavering mind of hired-women who are not steady in their thinking-style!

823. pala nhalla katRa-k- kadai-th-thum, manam-nhallar
aaku-thal, maa-Naar-k-k(u) arithu.

It is very hard for a bad (malicious/cunning) person who develops inimical (oppugnant, hostile, antagonistic, opposing) attitude towards others, to become good-hearted and 'soft-natured', although he/she might have learned many good books, thoroughly without errors!!

(Note: Many persons, by nature, may have hesitation to have friendship with others, unless they belong to the same alignment by calibre (human qualities), viz., 'the bad matching with the bad', and, 'the good matching with the good'! This relates to persons who have got fixed-ideas in their minds, thereby, refusing to develop a refined-attitude, utilizing the benefit of earning education, and being (having been) exposed to a broader contact with the outside-world! Oppugnancy=Latin word, oppugnantia,

.... meaning 'opposing', or 'antagonistic').

824. mukath-thin ini-ya nha-kaa-a- akath-th(u)-innaa
vanj-charai anj-chap- padum.

One must cautiously fear the actions of a deceitful person who appears with a sweet smile on the face, and yet with harmful feelings in the mind!

825. manath-thin amai-yaa-thavarai, yenai-th-thu – ondRum
sol-li-naal thae-RaR-paatR(u) andRu

Unless a person is friendly with you,in the heart of hearts, you must not take his/her words for granted, on any issue! Swinging into action based on his/her words (of advice!) must be avoided!

826. nhatt-aar-pOl nhalla-vai solli-num, ottaar-sol
ollai uNara-p- padum.

Words coming from the enemies will be (must be) readily felt, then and there, even if they use good words to make it appear, as if the words are coming from your bosom friends!

827. sol-vaNa-kkam onnaar-kaN koLLaR-ka, vil-vaNakkam
thee-ng-ku kuRi-th-thamai- yaan

Bow is curved in shape, indicating enmity. Similarly, humility in words must not be taken for granted, in the case of enemies, as it may produce harm! (One must have sufficient smartness to understand it).

828. thozhutha-kai- uLLum, padai odu-ng-kum; on-naar
azhutha- kaN- Nee-rum, anai-th-thu.

Within the folded hands to worship a person, it is possible to hide a killing-weapon, within the palms. The tears of an enemy, pretending to cry is similar in nature. The tears of enemies could hide vengeance! (Note: This is a great prophecy, revealed 2000- years back! Many political assassinations have been caused, in this style, in many parts of the world, including the assassination of Julius Caesar! A great hero!!).

829. mika-ch cheithu, tham-yeLLu- vaarai, nhaka-ch-cheithu
nhatpin-uL saa-p-pullal- paatRu.

Friendship with those persons who praise you beyond limits outwardly,while they may despise you within their hearts, needs to be reviewed!You must extend the same treatment to them, by making them smile, at the same time, resolving to let the friendship with such folks, slowly to dissipate, and finally to discontinue!!

830. pakai –nhatp(u)-aam kaalam varu-ng-kaal, muka(m)-nhattu,
aka(m)-nhatpu oree-yi vidal.

If a person gets a chance to make friends with the erstwhile-enemies, he/she will be advised to encourage that friendship by exchanging smiles to start with, and drop that friendship subsequently, in due course of time!

CHAPTER-84

CARELESSNESS-OUT-OF-FOOLISHNESS

831. pae-thai-mai (y)enpathu-ondRu yaath(u)-(y)enin, yae-tham-koNdu,
oothi-yam pOka vidal.

Foolishness is one which makes a person to accept the loss due to distorted understanding, and consequently let (permit) the gain go away from the self!

832. paethai-mai-yuL (y)ellaam paethai-mai, kaa-than-mai
kai-yalla than-kaN seyal.

The worst stupidity among all the stupidities, is one's desire to do what the person is not capable of doing, when the required technical know-how to do the work is not known to him/her! (Note: This refers to persons who do not take help from those who possess the specific-knowledge which is required for carrying out a particular task, in order to earn success. In the modern-era, there is ample opportunities for correcting the situation, by preferring to go in for outsourcing, in order to earn success. However, if there is no willingness on the part of the individual-person, to investigate and find out the gate-to-success, the prospects will still remain closed. Please refer to kural 517).

833. nhaa-Naa-mai, nhaa-daamai, nhaar-inmai, yaath(u)-ondRum,
pae-Naa-mai pae-thai thozhil.

The characteristics (zeal) of a foolish person could be: i)failure to feel ashamed of doing bad/evil acts, ii) failure to develop a desire to do good things, iii) failure to develop sympathy towards others, and, iv) failure to take care of the interest of the self!

(Note: Self-denial goes unnoticed by the self! Nobody realizes it, until irreversible damage occurs to a person. The poet cautions about it, sufficiently, to make a person become aware of it!).

834. Othi uNar-nh-thum, piRar-kk(u)- urai-th-thum, thaan- ada-ng-kaa-p-pae-thai-yin pae-thai-yaar il.

If a person reads and understands thoroughly the contents of a concept (principle/belief), and preaches, all about it, to others, and yet does not abide by what is being taught to others, such a person is a greater fool among all other fools. (Note: This idea is reiterated in kural 664; and also in kural 391).

835. orumai-ch- cheyal- aatRum pae-thai, yezhu-mai-yum thaan-pukk(u) azhu-nh-thum aLaRu.

A foolish person is capable of enacting an evil act (or a series of evil acts), during the tenure of one birth (lifetime) itself, which would make him/her eligible to suffer during all the seven births, consecutively, if he/she remains careless!

(Note: This is a new idea about multiple offence (crimes/faults/evil-acts), each of which is eligible for punishment, in the real world, or after death. It ascertains that a person, escaping punishment in the real world, has to undergo punishment in the hell).

836. poy-padum ondRO; punai-pooNum, kai-yaRiyaa-p-pae-thai vinai - maeR- koLin.

If a foolish person undertakes an act without knowing the methods of doing it, it may end up in a failure and loss of wealth! Legal implications may entail him in punishable offence, if he at- tempts doing a work about which he does not possess any prior knowledge, in which case, it becomes a trap!! (Note: These are probabilities!). **(Example: Entering into business is appreciated. But selling contraband (prohibited) items will entrap him/her in a punishable offence!)**

837. (y)ae-thilaar aara-th, thamar-pasip-par, pae-thai perum-selvam utRa-k- kadai.

Foolish person who has created wealth will extend feasts/ dinners to others who are not at all related to him/her, by hosting dinners in his/her own place, in addition to extending other benefits to them, while his kith and kin (relatives) of that person (who brought him/her up from childhood) are starving, without food, in their places! (Note: These are often unfortunate realities in the world, about which the poet wants to record his displeasure!).

838. mai-yal oruvan kaLith-that-Raal, pae-thai, than
kai-yo-ndRu udai-mai peRin.

If a foolish person gets the wealth on hand, he will behave to others in such a way that it resembles the act of a mad person intoxicated with liquor! (by non-coherent responses!).

839. perithu, inithu, pae-thai-yaar kaeNmai; piri-vin-kaN
peezhai- tharu-vathu- ondRu, il.

More pleasant is the friendship with foolish persons, be cause, on parting with each other, there would not be any end result, in producing unhappiness/regret/distress! (Note: A joke/Satire!?).

840. kazhaa-ak-kaal paLLi-yul vai-th-th(u)-atRaal, saandROr
kuzhaa-a-ththu-p- pae-thai pukal.

If a foolish person enters into the gathering of wise persons, they may not relish the company! He may not relish it also. It (his entry) is like placing the unwashed-foot on to the cot (bedding/mattress)in the bedroom!

CHAPTER-85

LACK OF KNOWLEDGE

841. aRiv(u)-inmai, inmai-yuL inmai; piRi-thu-inmai
inmai-yaa vaiyaa-thu ulaku.

Shortage of knowledge (ignorance) in a person is considered as the worst form of shortage! The people of the world will not blame a person for any other kind of shortages (except ignorance)!

842. aRiv(u)-ilaan nhenj-chu –uva-nh-thu (y)eethal, piRithu-yaa-thum
illai; peRu-vaan thavam!

If a foolish/senseless person cheerfully gives something as a gift to any other person, it is due to 'nothing- but- the- good -luck' (good fortune) of the person who receives it! (A joke!).

843. aRiv(u)-ilaar, thaam, tham-mai-p- peezhi-k-kum peezhai
cheRu-vaar-k-kum, sei-thal ari-thu.

Senseless persons are capable of causing harm to themselves to such an extent which would be difficult to be caused even by their enemies.

844. veNmai yena-p-paduvathu, yaathu-yenin, oNmai
'udai-yam-yaam'-(y)ennum serukku.

Lack of sense in a person is what is called a senseless false-pride, which makes him believe that he possesses excellence in knowledge!

845. kallaa-tha mae-R-koNdu ozhukal, kasadu-aRa-
vallathoo-(v)um ai-yam tharum.

If foolish persons pretend to possess knowledge in a sub ject-matter which they have not learned, the deficiency will be noticed by others, from their talk, easily. It will create a suspicion about their knowledge in the subject-matter which they have learned thoroughly!

846. atRam maRaith-thalO pul-laRivu; tham-vayin,
kutRam maRai-yaa vazhi.

If a person does not take care to erase the fault, which he has got within himself, the practice of covering the body with dress will reveal his senselessness!

(Note: The poet refers to moral weaknesses which are not physically visible; and which cannot be hidden by covering with costumes!).

847. aru-maRai sO-rum; aRivu-ilaan sei-yum
perum-iRai thaa-nae thana-kku.

(i) If a foolish person who cannot practice good acts which are prescribed in books of ethics/righteousness/virtues, it will bring upon himself/herself great miseries!(Another version: (ii). Foolish person who lets out a guarded-secret, which must be protected with care, will be bringing on himself/herself a great harm,due to negligence/ignorance!). (Note: The term '*aru-maRai*' means i) 'holy' principles of righteousness/ethics, and

ii) 'guarded' secrets. Hence the difference in two different interpretations).

848. (y)ae-va-vum sei-ka-laan; thaan-thae-Raan; av-vuyir
pO-(o)m- aLavum-Or nhOy.. (pO-(o)m= pOkum).

If a foolish person does not start acting (on good deeds), even after being advised by others who take interest in him, and if he does not decide by himself to start acting (on doing good deeds) by his own decision, it will reveal his foolishness. This kind of dis ease will continue throughout his life, up to point of his death. (It is a botheration to others! Although, others sympathize with him for his weakness!).

849. kaaNaa-thaan kaatu-vaan; thaan kaaNaan; kaaNaa-thaan,
kaNdaan-aam, thaan- kaNda- vaaRu.

A person who has not seen an object wants to show the object 'seen by him' to another person; He is not able to show it (the object) to that person. Realizing the fact that he has not succeeded, in his efforts to show the object to another person, (whereas he has never seen the object at all), he continues to believe that he has seen the object! He is satisfied with his level of understanding (wisdom) that the object exists exactly as he has seen it!

(Note: The key-statement for the analysis is the phrase used by the poet: '*thaan-kaaNaan*", meaning that "the person has not seen the object". Yet, he wants to show the object to another person. Please see Appendix-1. It is a rhyming couplet!).

850. ulakath-thaar uNdu-(y)enpathu, il-(y)enpaan, vaiyath-thu
'alakai'-yaa vaik-kap- padum.

When all the people of the world testify the existence of an object, if a person says that the object does not exist, then the person is a bitter person, similar to the wild shrub, Aloe (*katRaazhai*) which is bitter by taste, and is thorny by touch, in the assessment by the people!

In case of the majority of people believing in superstitions, the man who does not believe in that superstition qualifies for being called as the 'Aloe', *katRaazhai*, a herbal plant which offers cure for the illness. (Please see Appendix-1).

CHAPTER-86

HATEFUL ATTITUDE

This Chapter is on Hatred/Animosity/Dislike/Hostility. This is a dangerous human quality.It must be corrected from childhood.Parents, teachers, well-wishers of the family do have a role to play, in this task.A correct attitude towards tolerance of a fellow-being will have to be developed in each person, so as to ensure orderliness in human interactions. One's own emotional and psychological equilibrium is involved in the issue! Human qualities such as lack of patience, lack of self-confidence, practice of back-biting, jealousy, using harsh words, desire to pick up bad habits, etc., must be carefully and silently watched in behavioral response of the child,so that it becomes possible to correct it when the signal shows emerging! Please see kural 879.

851. ikal-(y)enba (y)ella uyir-k-kum, pakal-(y)ennum
paN-p(u)-in-mai paa-rik-kum nhOy.

According to the wisdom of learned persons, hatred (discordance) is considered as a disease which spreads sense of disunion/enmity, by eroding tolerance among all people. This promotes uncultured response among the living-persons!

852. pakal karuthi-p- patRaa seyi-num, ikal-karuthi
innaa - sei- yaa-mai thalai.

If a stranger (who is neither a friend nor a foe) does harm to a person,dueto some inexplicable reason, or conflicting interest, to prevent others from coming closer to him/her, it will be appreciated, if the affected person does not develop hatred (animosity), nor retaliate in doing harm to that offender!

853. ikal (y)ennum (y)evva-nhoy nheekkin, thaval- illaa-th-
thaa-vil viLakkam tharum.

If it is possible for a person to get rid of a disease called 'hatred'(discordance - based - animosity), such an action would give that person the faultless fame which would shine for ever!

854. inbath-thuL inbam payak-kum, ikal- (y)ennum,
thunbath-thuL thunbam kedin.

If it is possible to get rid of hatred (animosity) towards others, a beneficial effect will be produced, which is called a blissful-bliss/delightful - delight!! Discordance is known as distress within distress. Everyone must liberate himself/herself from that weakness!

855. ikal-(y)ethir saai-nh-thu ozhuka- vallaa-rai, yaa-rae
mikal-ookkum thanmai- yavar?

If a person adopts a policy of avoiding hatred(animosity) towards anybody, in words and deeds, is it possible for anybody to conquer such a person? It is not possible! Victory will always be with him/her!

856. ikal-in mikal-inith(u- y) enbavan vaazh-k-kai
thavalum kedalum nha-Nith-thu.

If a person believes that excessive hatred (animosity), if practiced, will be good to his/her benefit, the life of such a person will soon experience poverty and suffering/distress/even death!

857. mikal-mae-val mei-p-poruL kaaNaar, ikal-mae-val
innaa aRivi- navar.

Those who believe in hatred (animosity) being applied in excess, will not know its bad effects, which would be produced on the self, and others! They will not know the conquering strength of truth! They are being guided by evil-doing desires! Truthfulness to virtues will bring victory to those who practice virtuous actions!

858. ikaliR-ku (y)ethir- saai-thal aa-kkam; athanai,
mikal-ookkin ookkum-aam, kae-du.

Taking a path opposed to hatred (discordance) will bring wealth/strength. Instead, if hatred is encouraged more and more, the faster will be the rate at which distress will approach the person who promotes hatred!

859. ikal-kaaNaan aakkam –varum-kaal, athanai
mikal-kaaNum, kaedu tharaR-ku.

When wealth comes to a person, he/she will not desire for hatred (animosity)! If a person wants to have destruction for the self, such a person will opt for showing excessive hatred!

(Note: Avoidance of hatred towards others will give you peace of mind, which will promote personal progress and prosperity! Others will not come against you, during your advancement!Even if they do not help you in your efforts, it will be a great help from them, if they do not cause any trouble to you!).

860. ikalaan-aam innaatha (y)ellaam, nha-kalaan -aam
nhal-nhayam (y)ennum serukku.

Developing hatred (animosity) towards others will bring only miseries to the self! Friendly relationship with others will bring cheer and hospitality, ensuring pride for all the persons concerned!

CHAPTER-87

STRENGTH OF AN ENEMY

861. vali-yaar-k-ku maaRu-yaetRal Ombuka; Ombaa,
meli-yaar-mael maeka pakai.

You can agree to any offer of reconciliation from a mightier enemy. But you can easily avoid the enmity with weak persons, so that your kind attitude is exhibited!(Please See Appendix-1).

862. anbu-ilan, aa-ndRa thuNai-ilan, thaan-thuv-vaan,
(y)en-pariyum (y)aeth(u)-ilaan thuppu?

How would it be possible for a king, to overcome the might of an enemy in the war, if he does not have kindness (to earn the sympathy of others), and does not earn a reliable force of support for help, and does not have sufficient strength of the self?

(Note: Whatever applies to a king is applicable to an individual citizen, as a moral!)

863. anj-chum aRiyaan, amai-vu ilan, yee-ka-laan
thanj-cham (y)eLiyan pakai-k-ku.

It is easy for an enemy to win a person i) who has got fear in the mind, ii) who does not have adequate knowledge, iii) who does not get along with others, and iv) who does not give anything to others, by way of help, at the hour of need (to earn their support)!

864. nh-eeng-kaan vekuLi, nhiRai-ilan, (y)e-gn-gnaa-ndRum,
yaa-ng-ka-Num, yaar-k-kum,(y)eLithu.

It is easy for anybody, always and at any place, to win a person who does not control his anger, and who does not have charitable attitude and virtuous calibre, in his/her mind! (If he/she helps others when they are in need, they will come to his/her help, when trouble comes to that person!).

865. vazhi- nhO-k-kaan, vaai-p-pana sei-yaan, pazhi-nhO-kkaan, paNbu-ilan patRaar-k-ku ini-thu.

A king i) who does not foresee the consequences, ii) who does not carry out preparatory arrangements for enhancing victory which would have been otherwise possible, iii) who does not take care to avoid doing any act which would earn absolute blame from others, and iv) who does not have any virtue worth-mentioning, will be considered as a pleasing object for attack by his enemies.

866. kaaNaa-ch- chinath-thaan, kazhi-peru-ng- kaamath-thaan, pae-Naa-mai paeNa-p- padum.

If a person indulges in actions of lust, and shows excessive anger without being able to see reasons behind any of his acts, and is unable to arrange for his protection and security, then, in that case, the enmity of such a person will be enjoyed by his enemies! (It will bring misery to such a king!).

867. koduth-thum koLal-vaeNdum, mandRa, aduth-thu-iru-nh-thu maaNaa-tha sei-vaan pakai.

It is advisable to the king to earn the enmity (hatred) of a person, outwardly, even by giving a gift, if the person is suspected to be capable of preventing the victory of the king, (as the king suspects that the person is helping the enemy), whereas the person is always present near the king, pretending to be loyal to the king!

(Note: It is not clear whether the gift has to be given to the inimical person, or to anybody else (outsider) who will be instrumental in truncating the link between the helpless king and the offender! Even if it costs some money, it should be done at any cost, to break the harmful link! and save the king!! The poet might have meant to pay him profusely in order to get rid of his services. Ref: kural 794 and 800).

868. kuNan-ilanaa-i-k- kutRam pala-(v)aayin, maatRaa-r-kku inan-ilan-aam, (y)ae-maappu udaith-thu.

If a king does not have any virtues, and happens to indulge in bad deeds. and does not have any allies to come to his rescue, he will be considered as a helpless person! He will be a good prey to his enemies!(His weaknesses will add strength to his enemies).

869. cheRuvaar-k-ku-ch chaeN-ika-vaa inbam, aRivu-ilaa
anj-chum pakaivar-p- peRin.

The enemies will feel excessively happy, if they find a per son who remains senseless and who is always afraid of others!

870. kallaan vekuLum siRu- poruL, (y)e-gn-gnaa-ndRum
ollaa-nai- ollaathu oLi.

Pride and fame will not be available, any time, to any person who does not come forward to condemn (oppose, nullify) the vengeful act (evil act) caused to others, by an uneducated (uncultured) person! (Please see Appendix-1).

CHAPTER-88

APPRAISAL OF ENEMY'S STRENGTH

871. pakai-(y)ennum paNbu ila-thanai, oruvan
nha-kai-yae-yum vae-NdaR-paatRu andRu

Enmity is a meritless human quality, and therefore, it must not be entertained even for fun, with anybody, any time, in the life of a good person!

872. vil(l)-ae-r uzhavar pakai koLin-um, koLLa-Rka,
sol(l)-ae-r uzhavar pakai.

Even if you end up earning the enmity of those who handle the weapons of war, you must not earn the enmity of those who handle words as weapons of war, such as wise persons, poets, scholars, etc.!

(Note: This is an advice to kings. In the present context, the Government machinery must not earn the enmity of the media, namely, the Press, Broadcasting media, Telecasting media, Social media, Writers, Social Activists, etc).

873. (y)ae-mut- Ravari-num, (y)ae-zhai thami-yanaa-y-p-
pallaar pakai- koL- pavan

A person who earns the enmity of many persons, who stands alone, all by himself, (without any support from anybody else), will be considered as a person who enjoys less intelligence than a mad man! (Note: He has to reconsider his attitude for self-correction).

874. pakai-nhatpaa-k koNd(u)-ozhu-kum paNbu- (u)dai yaa-Lan
thakai-mai-k-kaN tha-ng-kitRu ulaku.

The world will feel comfortable with a magnanimous person, who is capable of conducting himself, with courtesy, in such a way as to treat enmity on par with friendship! (The world of people will support the activities of such a person!).

(Note: Extending courtesy to friends and enemies in equal measures (?!) sounds like a strategy, if executed with caution!).

875. than-thuNai indRaal, pakai iraNdaal, thaan,oruvan-
in-thuNai-yaa-k- koLka-(a)vatRin ondRu.

Any helpless person, having two enemies, must choose one of the two persons as a trustworthy friend for himself/herself, so that he/she is not left alone!

(Note: This amounts to putting 'that person' on observation? Shall we call it on 'probation'?).

876. thae-Rinum, thae-Raa -vidinum, azhi-vin-kaN
thae-Raan, pakaa-an vidal.

The act of clarifying whether a particular person is a friend or foe, for you, cannot be decided at the time of danger coming to you! It is better to keep the person aloof, and watch, without worrying \about it! (Note: This amounts to the act of putting him under observation. Shall we call it 'on probation'?).

877. nhO-vaR-ka, nho-nh-thathu aRi-yaar-k-ku; mae-vaRka
men-mai pakaivar akath-thu.

Do not narrate your sufferings to those friends who are not aware of it. Do not reveal your weakness to your enemies or to anybody else (as otherwise, it is likely to reach your enemies)!

878. vakai-aRi-nh-thu, thaR-chei-thu, thaR-kaappa, maa-yum
pakaivar-kaN patta serukku.

If a person understands the methods of handling attacks from enemies, and arranges for self-protection, by taking steps appropriately, the vengeful pride (acrimonious joy) of the enemy will get destroyed!

879. iLai-th(u)- aaka, muL-maram kol-ka; kaLai-yu-nhar,
kai-kollum, kaazh-th-tha- (v)idaththu.

A thorny tree must be destroyed when it is young. If it gets fully grown, it will cause injuries to the hands of the person who cuts it to remove it.

(Note: It applies to small illness, personal desires for bad acts, bad habits, feelings of enmity, etc., which are to be curbed when it just emerges; well before it could attain maturity!)

880. uyir-p-pa uLar-allar; mandRa, seyir-p-pavar
semmal sithai-k-kalaa thaar.

Those who do not have the guts/glory to smash the arrogance of a ferocious enemy (who cannot be 'tamed'), would be considered as inefficient persons. Although they are breathing to stay alive, they will not to be considered to exist, at all!(Do not give time for the 'confirmed' enemy who is beyond being 'tamed' to become stronger, by delaying your attack(Please refer to kural 879).

(Note: This is a different policy of the poet. He advocates peace, normally, for avoiding enmity, in kural 250. The poet advises to enter into a peace-agreement with a mightier enemy, if an offer of peace-agreement sounds feasible, in kural 861. In case, if doors are closed for entering into peace with another king, such a king can be termed as an enemy who cannot be 'tamed'; In such a case, the poet advises the capable-king to avoid delay, in entering into war! This kural 880 talks about such a situation. There are other cases also, related to the foreign-policy(!), if we can call it that way!! If the king strengthens himself, suitably to resist or defeat any known- enemy, without fail, as stated in kural 878, it is considered satisfac tory; he can afford to keep quiet, and stay calm, after building up the necessary strength. When the strength of the army is not sufficient to defeat an enemy, it is unwise to declare a war against an enemy, as stated in kural 465. If a king feels that the strength of his army is not adequate to enter into war with a mightier king, the advice of the poet is that the king can work out a peaceful settlement, with the stronger enemy, by being polite in the approach, intelligently saving his kingdom from the war, and saving his authority to rule his own kingdom, in which case, it is termed as a honourable defeat, although he has to share some portion of the revenue of his kingdom with the enemy-king who has become his superior! vide kural 680).

Note: In the present situation of arms-race, during the twenty- first century, every country in the world is following the policy of strengthening the war-weapon potentials, in accordance with financial affordability,as stipulated in kural 878, day by day, to remain strong enough; and simultaneously collecting the up-to-date information on the fighting-strength of an enemy of its choice!

Thiruvalluvar retains his relevance! He encourages defense build- up vide kural 878, permitting everybody to remain strong. How ever, nobody must initiate the war, so that the world remains safe! That describes the balance of power!In kural 990, the poet entrusts the safety of the world to the wisdom of elders in the society! Perhaps, the poet expects the virtuous persons to intervene, if the ruler of the land goes wrong, to impress upon ruler to give an upright rule, and to prevent a war! In the modern context, the responsibility rests with the United Nations Organisation (UNO)!

CHAPTER-89

INTERNAL ENMITY

881. nhizhal- nheerum, innaa-tha- innaa; thamar-nheerum,
innaa-(v)aam, innaa se(i)-yin.

Shadow, or water is considered to be beneficial for a person normally. If the quality is bad, each will be harmful to a person. Similarly, if the quality of one's relative is not good, it will bring harm to a person. (although it is generally believed that that the relatives will only be helpful to a person).

882. vaaL-pOl pakai-varai anj-chaRka; anjchu-ka,
kaeL-pOl pakai-var thodar-pu.

Do not be afraid of enemies who are visible like sharp sword. Be afraid of those relatives who might have link with the enemies. (Yet, they will be pretending to be friendly).

883. ut-pakai anj-chi-th,-thaR- kaa-kka; ulaiv(u)-idath-thu
maN-pakai-yin maaNath- theRum. (mat-pakai=maN-pakai).

You must guard yourself against internal enmity! If you remain slackened, it will certainly destroy you, similar to a pot-maker's act of slicing the clay of the defective-products, using a sharp cuttingtool!

(Note: An industrial process of mud pot-making is mentioned. When the specimen develops a small defect, such as a crack, or deformed shape, the finished-specimen is destroyed to recover the wet mud paste, by cutting the specimen with a sharp weapon! That example is quoted by the poet! To impress upon the end-result of internal enmity, it is clearly stated that it will be a forceful and merciless- killing)!

884. mana(m)-maaNaa ut-pakai thOndRin, ina(m)-maaNaa
(y)ae-tham palavum tharum

If internal enmity remains without a total refinement of mind in a person, it may end up in losing the relationship of all the persons with whom he/she may have got links, thus, yielding severe harms to all the relatives concerned!

885. uRal-muRai-yaan ut-pakai thOndRin, iRal-muRai-yaan
(y)aetham palavum tharum.

If internal enmity erupts, within the internal structure of the family unit, there will be several harms which would result, as severe as total destruction! Fatal destruction!

886. ondRaa-mai ondRi-yaar kaN-padin, (y)e-gn-gnaa-ndRum,
pon-dRaa-mai ond-Ral arithu.

If internal enmity erupts among relatives, even death may prove to be difficult to be avoided!

887. seppin puNar-ch-chi-pOl, koodin-um koodaa-thae,
ut-pakai utRa kudi.

A family, inflicted with internal enmity, will not get united in minds, always remaining separated with a gap, just like the gap between a copper-vessel (pot) and the lid placed on the top!

888. aram-porutha pon-pOla-th- thae-yum, uram-poruthu
ut-pakai utRa kudi.

A family subjected to internal enmity will lose its strength, similar to the way in which a material made of gold gets eroded, when a filing tool (made of iron) moves to and fro against it, repeat edly!

(Note: The poem helps to know the use of an ornament made of gold, and file made out of iron which were in use 2000 years ago, during the lifetime of Thiruvalluvar in Tamil nadu, India).

889. (y)eL-pakavu anna siRu-mai-th-thae aa-yinum,
ut-pakai uLLa-thaam kaedu.

Although internal enmity is a small factor, as small as a split in the sesame-seed, between the nut and the skin, it is capable of causing a great harm!

(Note: Sesame-seed is an oil-producing seed. Seasamum (Latin); Seasamon (Greek).

890. udam-baadu ilaa-thavar vaazh-k-kaai, kuda-ng-kar-uL
paam-bOdu udan-uRai-nh- th(u)-atRu.

If there is no mutual understanding between the two persons living together in the same place, then, their life will be as miserable as living with a poisonous snake inside a small hut! (It may apply to a married couple who have got 'no-affection', on a mutual basis!).. (One person may function as a snake, causing death to the other person)!

CHAPTER-90

AVOIDANCE OF HARM TO WISE PERSONS

891. aa-tRuvaar aa-tRal (y)ikazhaa-mai; pO-tRu-vaar
pOt-Ral-uL (y)ellam thalai.

Causing insult to the good work done by eminent persons,must be avoided, with care, by every person. That action will deserve appreciation by others, above all virtues! It is a kind of self-protection recommended for any living- person.

(Also interpreted as: Among all other virtues, the most desirable virtue for a living person is to avoid causing insult to eminent persons).

892. periyaarai-p- pae-Naathu ozhukin, periyaar-aal,
pae-raa idumbai tharum.

If a person leads a life without respecting the words of wise persons in the society, it will bring perpetual harm (insurmountable miseries) to the person concerned!

893. kedal-vaeNdin, kae-Laathu seika; adal- vaeN-din
aatRu pavar-kaN izhukku.

If a king wants to harm himself, let him decide to act on his own idea, without listening to the advice of his able advisors! If the king wants to ruin himself, let him cause insult to those who can achieve victory for the king/ or to those who would extend benevolent gestures to the king! (Note: These are certain acts which must be avoided! Whatever advice applies to the king, is valid for the common man, as a moral).

894. kootRa-th-thai-k- kai-yaal viLi-th-th(u)-atR-aal, aa-tRu-vaar-k-ku,
aat-Raathaar innaa seyal.

If a weak person does harm to a strong person, it amounts to summoning (inviting) death to come, in advance, stretching one's own arms wholeheartedly, to welcome it, toward self-destruction!

895. yaaNdu-ch-chendRu, yaaNdum, uLar-aa-kaar, ve-nh-thup-pin, vae-nh-thu seRap-pat- tavar.

Any person, after having involved in espionage-activities against a king, and for that reason, having earned t he violent fury of the king, (based on severe-spying report about the activities of t hat person), cannot survive anywhere (in the world), wherever that person may go! (Please See Appendix-1).

896. (y)eri-yaal sudap-padinum, ui-vu-uNdaam; ui-yaar, periyaar-p- pizhai-th-thu ozhuku -vaar.

Even after getting burnt by fire, a person may survive and get back to normal life. Those individuals, whose way of life is to despise (insult) the wise (noble) persons, will never flourish in life!

897. vakai-maaNda vaazhkkai-yum, vaan- poruLum, (y)enn-aam, thakai-maaNda thakkaar seRin?

"What is the benefit of a person having a luxurious life-style, with the backing of a huge wealth, if a great man blessed with virtuous qualities shows the fury towards that person? Some harm would happen to that person. His backings and wealth will be of no use! (Note: This can be taken as a general advice to all people to avoid inviting the wrath of wise-elders! However, the fault on the part of the person facing the wrath of the wise-man has not been explicitly mentioned, in this couplet! This needs a debate.

We assumed that there should have been some genuine reason for the anger of the great man, without which the wise-man would not have shown his fury (This, we did, in order to justify his anger)!The reason for the fury of the wise-man has not been stated in the couplet!

(We added a phrase, as a trial, "If anybody commits a fault to earn the fury of a great man blessed with virtuous traits (characteristics), some harm would occur to the offender!" Then, it makes sense! Without this phrase, the 'judgement on the punishment' will be in error! Please see kurals 896 & 898, in which cases, the fault of the offender is specifically mentioned, in both couplets). Please see Appendix - 1.

898. kundRu- annaar, kundRa mathip-pin, kudi-yodu,
nhi-ndRa-n-naar maai-var nhi-laththu.

If a person, having a stronghold on the land (a person of local reputation), happens to insult a great man of mountainous fame, the offender will get ruined with family!. (Please see kural 896).

899. (y)aenh-thiya koLkai-yaar seeRin, idai-muri-nh-thu,
vae-nh-than-um, vae-nh- thu kedum.

If great persons who uphold lofty principles, aimed at the welfare of the people of the world, happen to show violent anger, even the king would happen to lose his kingdom, and get ruined! (Note: The fault committed by the king has not been mentioned, in this couplet! As a trial, we added a phrase: "Out of displeasure over the evil-doing by the persons-in- power",... if great persons who uphold lofty principles, aimed at the welfare of the people of the world, happen to show violent anger, even the king would happen to lose his kingdom, and get ruined. In that case, it makes sense! (Please see kurals 896 and 898, wherein, the faults of the offender have been specifically mentioned). Please see Appendix-1.

900. iRanthu-amai-nh-tha saarpu-(u)daiyar aa-yinum, ui-yaar
siRa-nh-thu- amai-nh-tha seer-aar seRin.

However much a person may enjoy the backing of wealth, external support,and facilities, the person may not flourish in life, if a great person blessed with noble qualities happens to develop anger towards him!

(Note: The fault caused by that person earning the anger of the elderly wise-man is not mentioned in the couplet. Here, we decided to add the words: "due to some irksome response from the person concerned!" Then it makes sense!. (This needs further research. The poet firmly believes that the wise-men will not develop anger on unreasonable grounds. If they become angry on any occasion, they will quickly decide to control it, vide kural 29, in sympathy for the person likely to be affected by the horrifying effects of such an anger! This assumption, however, can be even considered arbitrary. (Please see kural 896 and 898, wherein, there is a valid mention of an offence which causes the anger (wrath) of the great man, correlating it with the sufferings of the offender).

The interpretations of kural-couplets 897, 899 and 900 are to be read/ explained in the light of kural-couplets 896, 898 and 29. Please see Appendix-1.

CHAPTER-91

MAN-BEING-GUIDED-BY-A-WOMAN(HENPECKED HUSBAND)

901. manai-vizhai-vaar, maaN-payan (y)ei-thaar, vinai-vizhai-vaar
vaeNdaa-pp poruLum athu.

A man who listens always to the commands of his wife, as her husband, on every decision-making occasion, cannot attain nobler gains in his life! His attitude, in this respect, is something unnecessary and unbecoming of those who are mindful of carrying out actions of perfection (related to the targets being aimed at).(This depends on the time allotted for other duties undertaken by him).

(Note: This does not prevent a man from consulting his wife on major policy-issues).

902. paeNaa-thu peN-vizhai-vaan aa-kkam, peri-ya-thOr
nhaaN-aa-ka nhaaNu-th tharum.

A person who does not take care of his commitment to duties/development/creativity/wealth-management, will be subjected to shame, if he gives priority to his spending more time with a woman, in admiration for her beauty! (please see kural 909).

(Note: This kural seems to refer to those who do not devote sufficient time for external duties, other than devoting time for sensual pleasures! In *Silappathikaaram*, a Tamil epic, the hero-'Kovalan', a multi-millionaire, by heredity, loses all his wealth as is described in Chapter 9, verse-70, describing his regret that he lost mountainous quantum of wealth by his non-attentiveness to his reputed family-trade of imports and exports! The verse is: '*kulam-tharu-vaan-poruL-kundRam-tholai-nh- tha-ilampaadu-nhaaNu-th-tharum-(y)enakku!*': meaning, 'I have lost my ancestral wealth of mountainous- quantum, due to my carelessness:I feel ashamed'!).

(Ref: *'Silappathikaaram'*, Dr.S.V.Subramanian, 1996, Gangai Puththaka nhilayam, Chennai, p.70)

903. illaaL-kaN thaazh-nh-tha iyalbu-inmai, (y)e-gn-gnaa-ndRum
nha-llaar-uL nhaa-Nuth- tharum.

The absence of independent nature of a husband (in a person) who bows down to the dictates of his wife will produce a sense of shame in that person always, which he will feel, more especially, in the presence (company) of other men who are free from this weakness!

904. manai-yaaLai anj-chum maRumai-yi laa-Lan
vinai-yaaNmai veeRu-(y)ei-thal indRu.

A husband who is afraid of his wife will not be able to prove his proficiency in his achievements /undertakings. He is deemed to have been entrapped in a situation for which there is no alternate arrangement (for freedom) in his entrapment!

(Alternatively: There will not be any good benefit in the're-birth' of a man who fears his wife, and fails to perform benevolent deeds of excellence!). (Note: The trend in literature 2000 years ago, seemed to emphasize on acquiring certain virtues, during one's own lifetime, showing enthusiasm towards qualifying for better prospects during rebirths,or liberation from rebirth itself!"

905. illaa-Lai anj-chuvaan anjchum; matRu, (y)egn-gnaa-ndRum
nhallaar-k-ku nhalla seyal.

A man who is afraid of his wife will never be able to do good things to good persons, ever in his lifetime!

906. imai-yaar-in vaazhi-num, paadu-ila-rae, il-laaL
amai-aar-thOL anj-chu- pavar.

There are men who are afraid of their wives, out of admiration (appreciation) of her beauty of the attractive bamboo-like shapely-shoulders. Such men will not be respected in the outside world, even if they live luxuriously, on par with the luxuries enjoyed by those who live in heaven!

907. peN-(y)ae-val sei-thu-ozhukum aa-Nmai-yin nhaa-N-udai-p-
peN-Nae perumai udaith-thu.

Womanhood, of a wife, practicing shyness and modesty deserves more merit /appreciation/admiration, compared to the manhood of a husband who always obediently carries out the command of his wife (without ever having a freedom to incorporate his corrective suggestions, if any) in all his activities!

908. nha-ttaar kuRai-mudiyaar, nhandR(u)-aatRaar, nhan-nhu-thal-aaL
pett-aang-ku ozhuku- pavar.

Any man who acts according to the wishes (whims and fan cies) of his wife, being attracted by her beautiful (fascinating) forehead, will not be able to carry out the requests of his intimate friends, or, to carry out any other good acts of virtues which would fetch him benefits of fame!

909. aRa-vinai-yum aan-dRa poruLum, piRa-vinai-yum,
peN-(y)aeval sei-vaar-kaN il.

For a man who is asked to carry out the orders of his wife, it will not be possible to carry out any act for a noble cause, or for earning good wealth, or for any other act intended for a praise worthy purpose!

910. (y)eN-saer-nh-tha nhenj-chath- thidan-udai-yaar-k-ku, (y)e-gn- gnaa-ndRum,
peN-saer-nh-thu-aam pae-thaimai il.

Men who are capable of thinking freely, with an analytical mind, having clarity in their thoughts, will not be susceptible to be dominated by their wives (They will consult their wives on major policy-issues!).

CHAPTER-92

WANTON WOMEN

911. anbin vizhai-yaar, poruL -vizhaiyum aay-thodi-yaar
in-sol izhukku-th- tharum.

The sweet words of a hired-woman, wearing beautiful bangles in her tender forearms, will bring shame to a man, as she does not like the man out of real kindness, but she artificially likes the man only for his wealth!

912. payan-thookki-p- paNbu-uraikkum paNb(u)-il makaLir,
nhayan-thookki nhaLLaa vidal.

It is advisable to curtail the acquaintance of any hired-woman, in the interest of one's own welfare, as these characterless women are capable of showing affection, only in consideration of the quantum of monetary benefits they would get, in- return for their affection being shown!

913. porut-peNdir poy-m-mai muyakkam, irutt(u)-aRai-yil,
yae-thil- piNam- thazhee-yi- yatRu.

For any person, the false pleasure enjoyed with a hired- woman, is similar to embracing a dead-body of an unrelated per son, in a dark room.

914. porut-poruLaar pun-nhalam thO-yaar, arut-poruL
aayum aRivi- navar.

Those wise persons who are in the pursuit of earning the wealth of divine grace will not lower their status by stooping down to develop a desire for the false pleasure with any hired-woman who is prepared to lose the most precious honour of her womanhood, for material gains!

915. pothu-nhalath-thaar, pun-nhalam thO-yaar, mathi-nha-lath-thin
maaNda aRivi- navar.

Persons who have got excellent refinement of mind will not be interested in the false pleasure offered by any hired-woman as the same woman extends her pleasure to many others, among the general public, to whoever offers material benefits!

916. than--nhalam paarip-paar, thO-yaar, thakai-serukki-p-
pun-nhalam paarip-paar thOL.

Those persons who want to safeguard their own welfare and self-respect will not develop a desire for embracing the shoulders of a hired-woman who has deviated from the normal qualities of a woman, by the (self-assumed) arrogance of knowing other skills, and whose interest is for promoting the sale of her false enjoyments!

917. nhiRai-nhenj-cham illa-var thOi-var, piRa -nhenj-chil
paeNi-p- puNar-pavar thOL.

Those persons who do not have got a satisfied-mind, or persons having a weak mindset, are probable to develop a desire for embracing the shoulders of a hired-woman, who is in the habit of entertaining other thoughts about other men in her heart, pretending to enjoy the union with the present patron!

918. aayum aRivinar - allaar-k-ku aNang-ku yenba
maa-ya makaLir muyakku

If a person, with insufficient knowledge to search the truth, happens to be attracted towards the embrace of a hired-woman, it is said that it is due to the act of a devil in the form of a tempting (fascinating) hired-woman!

919. varaivu-ilaa maaN-izhai-yaar men-thOL, purai-yilaa-p-
poori-yar-kaL aazhum aLaRu.

The tender/soft shoulders of hired-women who wear clothes of luxurious fibers and attractive ornaments who have the bad reputation of mating with any person, whether good or bad, are considered as slush into which worthless men of low calibre and criminals are immersed. It is as bad as an experience in the Hell!

920. iru-mana-p- peNdirum, kaLLum, kavaRum
thiru-nhee-kka-p- pattaar tho-darpu.

Any person will become poor (being separated from wealth), if he develops any one of the following three links, namely, i) link with a hired-woman of two hearts (one real and the other false), ii) addiction to intoxicating liquor, or iii) participation in any gambling activities.

CHAPTER-93

AVOIDANCE OF CONSUMING LIQUOR

921. utka-p- padaa-ar oLi-yizhap-par, (y)e-gn-gnaa-ndRum
kaL-kaathal koNdu-ozhuku- vaar.

Those persons who consume liquor will lose their reputa tion in the society, and their enemies will lose fear for them, forever. (Enemies will give them trouble).

922. uNNaR-ka kaLLai; uNil-uNka; saandRO-raal
(y)eN-Na-p- pada- vaeNdaa- thaar.

Do not drink liquor, if you want to remain respected. If you cannot stop drinking liquor, drink it, if you do not want to be remembered/respected by the wise persons!

923. (y)een-dRaaL mukath-thae-yum innaa-thaal, (y)en-matRu,
saandROr mukath-thu-k- kaLi?

If drunken intoxication of a son produces unpleasant expressions on the face of his mother, what could be the expressions which could be expected from the faces of the respectable wise persons (who could be outsiders, not related to the family at all)?

924. nhaaN-(y)ennum nhal-laaL puRam-kodukkum, kaL-(y)ennum
pae-Naaa-p- peru-ng-kutRath- thaarkku.

For those who do not have the control over the habit of drunkenness, by consuming liquor, the pleasant lady called Modesty will turn her back, in protest, on seeing the faces of intoxicated persons! (Also interpreted as: The benefit-yielding goddess called Modesty will go away from the drunkard!).

925. kai-yaRi- yaamai- yudaith-thae, poruL –kodu-ththu
mei-aRi- yaa-mai koLal.

It is the deliberate ignorance of using the hands to give money (wealth), to get a material which would make you to lose the conscience of your mind/intellect/ body-system!

926. thunj-chinaar seth-thaarin- vae-Ru-allar, (y)e-gn-gnaa-ndRum
nhanj-chu- uNpaar, kaL-uN- pavar

The facial appearances of those who sleep are not different from those who are dead! Always, it must be remembered that those who consume liquor and sleep are not different from those who consume a killing-poison!

927. uL-(L)otRi, uL-Loor nha-kap-paduvar, (y)e-gn-gnaa-ndRum
kaL-(L)otRi-k- kaN-saai- pavar.

Those who consume liquor and droop in drowsiness, hanging down their eyes in privacy, will be found out by their neighbours, by detecting, and they will be insulted by those neighbours (who are living in the same village)!

928. 'kaLi-th-thu –aRi-yaen'(y)enba-thu kai-viduka; nhenj-chath-thu
oLith-tha-thoo-(v)um aa-ng-kae mikum.

Stop saying that you would not develop drunkenness after consuming liquor! Whatever you have hidden in your heart will be exposed, in the trance (in subconscious state)!

929. kaLith-thaanai-k- kaaraNam- kaattu-thal, keezh-nheer-k-
kuLi-th-thaanai-th- thee-th-thuree-yi yatRu!

Effort of explaining the reasons to a person intoxicated with liquor, as to why should he stop the habit of doing it, will become useless. Such an effort will be similar to searching for locating a drowned-person, below the deep water, by holding a torch of open- flame! (Open- flame immersed inside water, will get extinguished. It will not be possible, at all, to locate the person inside the water!).

930. kaL-uNNaa-p- pOzh-thil kaLith-thaanai-k- kaa-Nu-ng-kaal
uLLaan-kol, uNda-than sOrvu.

When a person is not drunk, if he happens to see another person who is fully intoxicated after consuming liquor, will he understand the condition of the disgrace which would be experienced by a drunkard? (If he is a sensible person, he will understand the insult that one could bring upon himself, when drunk). (Note: The poet longs to see, like a worried-mother, a change of mind in a person (so n) habituated to drinking habits).

CHAPTER-94

GAMBLING

931. vae-Nda-Rka vendRi-di-num sooth(u)-inai, vendRa-thoo-(v)um
thooNdil-pon meen-vizhu-ng-ki yatRu.

Even if a person is able to win, he must not develop a desire to participate in gambling. After winning, whatever gain has been won, is likely to be re-invested in a bait which gets swallowed by the Fish along with the hook! (Note: Bait along with the fishing- hook is depicted as golden (valuable) bait as swallowed by the fish).

932. ondRu- (y)eithi, nhooRu- izhakkum soothar-k-kum uN-daam-kol
nha-ndRu- (y)eithi vaazh-vath(u)-Or aaRu? (poet's wish)

For a gambler who wins one game and loses one-hundred games subsequently, could there be a better way of life for that person to get benefited? (Note: The poet laments! With care. To find an alternate rehabilitation scheme for the gamblers!).

933. uruL –aayam, O-vaathu kooRin, poruL-aayam
pO-oy-p- puRa-mae padum.

If a person plays a gambling game of rolling-dice, without giving himself a break, all resources of his wealth will go away from him, to reach the opponent's hands! He will be the loser!

934. siRumai- pala-sei-thu, seer-azhikkum- sooth(uv)-in
vaRumai tharu-vathu –ondRu, il.

There cannot be any other act of a person, which will bring poverty to him, more surely than the act of gambling which brings many belittling-miseries, to the person, thus, destroying one's reputation completely!

935. kavaRum, kazhakam-um, kai-yum- tharukki,
i(v)-aRiyaar; il-laaki- yaar.

A person who does not give up the habit of gambling, will become a very poor person (a bankrupt/insolvent)!

(Note: He has to forget all about gambling place/ gambling tools/ gambling skills, altogether, abruptly, all at the same time! If he wants to get transformed! Such a realization in the mind of a gambler is not likely to occur! That becomes a disappointment of a well-wisher, as spelled out in kural 932).

936. akad(u)-aaraar, allal uzhap-par, soothu- (y)ennum
mukadi-yaal moo-da-p-pat- taar.

Those persons covered (embraced) by the goddess of poverty, called gambling, will suffer in distress, without having food on- time, being unable to satisfy their hunger and thirst!

(Note: It amounts to self-denial of bodily-needs, in respect of physical, moral and emotional aspects).

937. pazhakiya selvam-um, paNbum, kedukkum,
kazhaka-th-thu-k- kaalai pukin.

If a person spends all the time in the gambling place, the old inherited wealth of the family will get destroyed along with the honour, dignity, self-respect, character, and all virtuous qualities, altogether, in total (in toto!).

938. poruL- keduth-thu,-p- poi-mael koLee-yi, aruL-keduth-thu,
al-lal uzhppi-kkum soothu.

Gambling habit will make the person destroy his wealth, by making him to tell lies, in making him lose his characteristic courteous behavior and all good virtues, and finally entangling him in utter poverty!

939. udai, selvam, ooN, oLi, kalvi, yendR(u) ai-nh-thum
adai-yaa-vaam, aayam koLin.

If a person gets into the habit of gambling, he will lose all the five- forms of blessings, namely, prestigious dress, wealth, nutritious food, fame for the self and the benefit of wisdom earned through education!

940. izhath-thoRoo-um, kaathali-kkum soo-thae- pOl, thun-bam
uzhath-thoRoo-um, kaathatR(u) uyir.

The more the gambler loses, the more will be the desire of the gambler to continue with the game (gambling), similar to a person's desire to stay alive, when the body develops struggling- distress, while fighting against death!

CHAPTER-95

MEDICINE AND EATING HABITS

941. mikinum kuRai-yinum nhOy-sei-yum nh-oolOr
vaLi-mutha-laa (y)eNNiya moondRu

Disease will be caused in a human body, if one of the three aspects becomes excessive, or deficient, namely, gas, bile or phlegm, as indicated by authors of books in the discipline of medicine.

942. maru-nh-thu-(y)ena vaeNdaa-vaam, yaak-kai-k-ku, arunh-thi-yathu
atRa-thu- pOtRi uNin.

It is believed that medicines are not required for a person, if food is taken in, after making sure that the food eaten already has been digested fully. (Note: Medicine and Eating Habits are correlated)

943. atRaal aLavu-aRi-nh-thu uNka; a-h-thu, (u)dambu
petRaan nhe-dithu- ui-kkum aaRu.

When you feel hungry, eat your food, after knowing your limit. That is the way for any person having a human body, wishing to increase the life-time/longevity.

944. atRathu aRi-nh-thu kadai-p-pidi-ththu, maaR(u)-alla
thui-kka, thu-vara-p- pasi-th-thu.

After knowing that the food eaten before has been digested and when hunger is more, eat the food, strictly following the restrictions relating to food whichever is not agreeable (likely to cause allergic symptoms). (The term *'thuiikka'* means (conveys) the idea: "Eat slowly, and chew your food!" (Note: The concept of allergic food is introduced).

945. maaRu-paadu il-laa-tha uNdi maRu-th-thu - uN-Nin,
ooRu-paadu illai, uyir-k-ku.

There will not be any harm to life, if food which is not disagreeable to the body-system is eaten (consumed). (Note: The concept of allergic food is given importance).

946. izhivu-aRi-nh-thu uN-paan-kaN inbam-pOl, nhi-Rkum
kazhi-pae-r -irai-yaan-kaN nhOy

Similar to the happiness dwelling (prevailing) with a person who eats food in a measure which is a bit less than the permitted level, the disease will cheerfully dwell in the person who eats food in excessive measures, overlooking (violating) the permitted levels.

947. thee-(y)aLav(u) andRi-th theri-yaan, peri-thu-uNNin,
nhOy-aLav(u) indRi, -p- padum.

To a person who eats food excessively, without knowing the limits of his hunger, disease will also be inflicting upon him/her excessively!

948. nhOy-nhaa-di, nhOy-muthal nhaa-di, athu-thaNik-kum
vaai-nhaa-di, vaa-y-ppa-ch- cheyal.

The duties of a medical practitioner can be indicated in the following steps: i) to investigate the nature of illness, ii) to investigate the cause of illness, iii) to determine a method of suitable treatment which is capable of offering relief and iv) doing the need ful to make the relief viable. (Note: Step-by-step procedures are indicated for the attention of the physician attending on the patient, touching upon the cause of illness, identification of the causative agent (the source of infection), diagnosis and the subsequent method of treatment (therapeutics).The phrase *"nhOi-nhaadi"* relates to the study of the nature of illness, *"nhOi-mudhal-nhaadi"*, covers the investigation part of the disease-causing pathogen (micro- organisms,including viruses, molds, fungus,etc), or chemical agent, or radiation-factors, etc; *"athu-thaNikkum-vaai-nhaadi"* covers host- response data on trials of anti-bacterial/anti-viral drugs; and *"vaaippa- seyal"* refers to diagnosis and treatment, by selecting and administering a therapeutic medicine. This sequence is indicated 2000 years ago, by the poet).

949. utRaan aLavum, piNi-aLavum, kaalam-um,
katRaan karuthi-ch- cheyal.

The various aspects to be considered by the doctor who is qualified in the field of medicine are: i) the details of the patient (relating to clinical symptoms, the natural-resistance of the patient (immunity), allergies, etc), ii) details relating to the nature of illness, iii) its present stage, and iv) the duration of time required for treatment to obtain a cure!

(Note: The concept of natural immunity is hidden in the term "*utRaan-aLavum*'.

950. utRavan, theer-p-paan, maru-nh-thu,uzhai-ch- chelvaan–(y)endRu, appaal-nhaaR- kootRae maru-nh-thu.

The process of offering treatment to illness essentially com prises of four major divisions, namely, i) the patient who is getting the treatment, ii) the doctor who is giving treatment to the patient, iii) medicine which is appropriately chosen, and iv) an attendant who takes care of the suffering-patient! (Note: This broadly specifies the infrastructure needed for an ideal health-care establishment!). Nursing care is included as the fourth aspect.

CHAPTER-96

GOOD-FAMILY-BACKGROUND

951. il-piRa-nh-thaar - kaN-allathu, illai; iyal-baa-ka-ch-
cheppam-um nhaa-Num oru-ng-ku.

It is hard to find the following qualities in persons born in ordinary families: i) inborn/ consistent qualities of fairness and neutrality (in mind, words and deeds), and ii) modesty/determination to keep away from evil acts. (These qualities (traits) will be found in members of good families).

952. ozhukkam-um, vaai-mai-yum, nhaa-Num, im- moondRum,
izhuk-kaar, kudi-p- piRa-nh- thaar.

Persons having been born in respectable families will not deviate from the three qualities, such as i) good conduct, ii) truthful ness and iii) modesty(shying away from crimes).

953. nhakai, yeekai, in-sol, ika-zhaa-mai, nhaan-kum
vakai-(y)enba; vaai-mai-k- kudikku.

It is said that the four praiseworthy qualities will be found (imbibed) in persons born in good (well-known) families reputed for truthfulness, namely, i) cheerfulness(when they interact with others), ii) showing interest in giving moral and material help to the needy, iii) uttering pleasant words, and iv) avoidance of extending insult to others.

954. adukkiya- kOdi peRi-num, kudi-p-piRa-nh-thaar
kundRu-va- sei-thal ilar.

Persons born in good families will not lower their standards by doing things which are below their dignity, even if the wealth (stacked in tens of millions worth) is offered!

(Note: The quantum of wealth is expressed in conceptional or notional or abstract or ideational values, instead of indicating in terms of currency of a particular country).

955. vazha-ng-ku-vathu uL-veezh-nh-tha-k- kaNNum, pazha-ng-kudi paNpil thalai-p-piri-thal indRu.

Ancient families will not discontinue the tradition of giving material help to others, even if those families fall down in wealth! They will not do any thing detrimental to their dignity.

956. salam-patRi-ch- chaalbu-ila sei-yaar; maasu- atRa kulam-patRi vaazh-thum-(y)en- paar.

Those families who have taken a vow that they will stick close to each other as a flawless group, will not commit any act which lacks honour, and which involves deceit or detriment to what they believe in, even when they become poor!

957. kudi-p-piRa-nh-thaar- kaN-viLa-ng-kum kutRam, visum-pin mathi-k-kaN 'maRu'-p-pOl uyar-nh-thu.

The fault prevailing in persons born in reputed families, will be clearly known to others predominantly as a dark spot seen on the surface of the full-moon! Therefore, they will take care to see that no such blemish occurs! (Note: The term 'Kulam' refers to reputed families by their dignified actions. Ref: Kural 958).

958. nha-lath-thin-kaN nhaar-inmai thOndRin, avanai-k- kulath-thi-kaN ai-yap- padum.

If the attitude of sympathy/affection/decency is lacking in a person, hailing from a respectable family, the genuineness of his/her ancestry will be doubted!

959. nhi-lath-thil kida-nh-thamai kaal-kaattum; kaattum kulath-thil piRa-nh-thaar-vaai-ch- chol.

The evidence of richness of crops, in growing, in the soil, will be revealed by the bottom-stem of the crop (stubble) which remains in the soil, after harvest is carried out! The culture of the family in which a person is born will be revealed by the words coming from his/her mouth!

960. nha-lam-vaeNdin nhaa-N-udaimai vaeNdum; kulam-vaeNdin,
vaeNdum yaar-k-kum paNivu.

If a person wants happiness, shyness against evil acts must be practiced. (It is also called modesty). If the pride of the family is to be given prominence, a person must practice humility to reveal the greatness of the family-background!

CHAPTER-97

PERSONAL HONOUR / SELF - RESPECT

961. indRi amai-yaa-ch chiRappina (v) aa-yi-num,
kun-dRa varu-ba, vidal.

Keep away from doing or participating in any evil act which would bring bad name to your reputed family, even if you are made to believe that a particular act, if carried out, would bring benefit to meet your immediate requirement of the family!

962. seeri-num seer-alla, sei-yaa-rae, seer-odu
pae-raaNmai vae-Ndu pavar.

Great persons who want to maintain their magnanimity and genuine fame will not resort to do anything dishonourable even, for increasing their popularity!

963. peruk-kath-thu vae-Ndum, paNithal; siRiya
suruk-kath-thu vae-Ndum uyar-vu!

Humility is needed when a person is growing in prosperity. Dignity (and self-respect) must be maintained even in poverty/adversity.

964. thalai-yin izhi-nh-tha mayir-anaiyar, maa-nh-thar
nhi-lai-yin (y)izhi-nh-tha-k- kadai.

If human beings,who were erstwhile in good status, (yet) happen to fall down to low status, due to their own bad actions, they will lose their values (dignity), similar to the hair falling down from the head, losing its value!

965. kundRin anai-yaar-um kundRu-var; kundRuva
kundRi- anai-ya se(i)yin.

Persons of great fame of mountainous magnitudes (measures) will be brought low in public esteem, if they happen to commit an act of low caliber, even in a small measure, as small as the red seed of crab's eye (rosary pea, *kuNdumaNi, kundRimaNi*)!

966. pukazh-indR-aal; puth-thaeL-nhaa-t-tu ui-yaa-thaal; (y)en-matRu, (y)ikazh-vaar-pin sendRu nhilai?

If a person goes to stand behind those persons who insult him, with a scornful outlook/attitude, there will not be any fame for him, and heavenly bliss will be denied to him. What else is there for him to gain? (He loses the prestige of the family).

967. ottaar-pin sendRu-oruvan vaazh-thalin, a-nh-nhilai-yae 'kettaan' ena-p-padu-thal nha-ndRu.

If a good person decides to go behind some bad people, for the purpose of earning his livelihood, whereas he cannot mix/ mingle with them, due to difference in calibers/qualities, it will be viewed /judged that it is worthwhile for him to die in honour, in poverty, than continuing in the same helpless situation!

968. maru-nh-thO-matRu oon-Ombum vaazhkkai; peru-nh-thakai-mai peed(u)-azhi-ya va-nh-tha idath-thu?

When the great honour of the family has reached a stage of losing its prestigious past-glory(excellence/eminence), due to some bad deeds, it is a painful experience to live in unhappiness, like consuming medicine to prolong-maintaining the body and soul together! Even 'death' could not be a medicine (remedy) to recover the honour! Continuance of routine life, to safeguard the body (devoid of soul?) is a painful experience, which might be gone through! (Note: Bad deed leading to the loss of honour for the family could have been avoided!).

969. mayir-nheep-pin vaa-zhaa-k kavari-maa annaar, uyir-nheep-par maa-nam varin.

The '*Kavarimaa*' Yak species has got the instinct to die, when it loses its hair from its body! There are similar persons among the human beings, who will die, if they lose their honour, thinking that death could recover their honour!! (Note: *Kavarimaa* is an animal (Yak–species) living in the upper Himalayas-region which will die when its hair is removed from its body, undergoing mental and physical agony! It becomes a poetic similarity to men who end their lives when they happen to lose their honour for some reason, thinking that death would recover their prestigious self-respect!).

970. (y)iLi-varin vaazhaa-tha maa-nam udai-yaar
oLi-thozhu-thu (y)ae-th-thum ulaku

If any disgrace is inflicted upon the dignity of great persons,they will immediately prefer to die, to restore their honour! The world will uphold the fame of such persons, by worshiping them, with lights lit in honour of the departed souls!

CHAPTER-98

GREATNESS OF PERSONS

971. oLi-oru-vaRku uLLa veRukkai; iLi-oru-vaRku
a-h-thu–iRa-nh-thu vaazh-thum yenal.

Fame is considered as a wealth in abundance which gives courage and confidence for a person. It is an insult for any person to live after the fame is lost.

972. piRappu ok-kum, (y)ellaa uyir-k-kum; siRappu, ov-vaa
sei-thozhil vae-tRu-mai- yaan.

All human beings are equal to one another, on birth. The importance/ dignity assigned to each of them varies, depending on the difference in the quality-characteristic of their actions/activities!

(Note': There are differences in the interpretations, comparing "work" versus "deeds". i) In the case of work, dignity of labour is the criterion. ii) In the case of deeds, virtue becomes the criterion. It becomes a debatable topic. Refer to kural 973. Please see Appendix-1).

Rajaji (Sri C.Rajagopalachari) was of the opinion that there is a provision for adding supplement to the ideology of Rig-Veda, vide verse 1-89-1 which states: "Let noble thoughts come to us from every side". Perhaps, he might have wanted to give a liberal interpretation of the verses relating to the 4-varna ideology of Rig Veda! Please see Appendix 9).

973. mae-l –iru-nh-thum, mae-la-llaar, mae-l-allar; keezh-iru-nh-thum
keezh-allaar keezh-al- lavar.

Even if some persons are placed in high status, if the actions of those persons are not good, they will not be considered by others to belong to high status. Even if some other persons are placed in low status, if their actions are good, they will be considered to deserve a higher dignity! (Please refer to Kalaignar Urai).

974. orumai makali-rae pOla-p- peru-mai-yum
thannai-th-thaan koNdu-ozhu-kin uNdu.

Like a woman getting dedicated to a single man, thereby earning greatness for her qualities, it is possible for a man to qualify for the same greatness, by guarding himself in the virtuous path, in respect of personal morality! (Comparable with kural 54).

975. perumai udai-ya-var, aatRu-vaar; aatRin
arumai udai-ya seyal.

Great persons reputed for their benevolent acts, in the past, will be able to carry out rare deeds which are normally difficult for others to do! They will always observe established rules and norms in their actions.

976. siRi-yaar uNarch-chi-yuL illai; 'periyaa-rai-p-
paeNi-k-koL vaem'-yennum nhO-kku.

It is rare to see small persons with their attitude in favour of appreciating and protecting the wise-persons who are well-known for their services to the society! Small persons will get benefited, if they take care of wise-persons (in availing their advice and guidance required for the current undertakings of the youngsters!).

977. iRap-pae puri-nh-tha thozhi-tR(u)-aam; siRappum-thaan
seer-al- lavar-kaN padin.

If any special empowerment (related to material resources /position / power) is made available to any undeserving (unworthy)person, it will be helpful only to enhance the arrogance of the per son beyond the limits, and the consequent excesses/outrages (atrocities), in action!. (It will be difficult for anybody to circumvent it).

978. paNiyum-aam, (y)endRum perumai; siRumai
aNi-yum-aam than-nai viya-nh-thu.

Great persons will not exhibit their pride while interacting with others, taking care to practice humility, on all occasions.On the contrary, mean-minded persons will decorate themselves in self- flattery, all the time. (They will not extend courtesy to others).

979. perumai peru-mitham inmai; siRumai
peru-mitham oor-nh-thu vidal.

Famous persons with real greatness will not have arrogance. Mean persons, on the contrary, will exhibit extreme arrogance beyond limits, and will not practice courtesy while interacting with others!

980. atRam maRaik-kum perumai; siRumai-thaan
kutRa-mae kooRi vidum.

Great persons will have the magnanimity not to highlight the shortcomings of others, and prefer to hide them in their minds, whereas mean persons will always take pleasure in repeatedly mag- nifying the shortcomings (faults) of others, and extending insult to them.

CHAPTER-99

RIGHTEOUS PERSONS /PERFECTION IN RIGHTEOUSNESS

981. kadan (y)enba, nha-llavai- (y)ellaam; kadan aRi-nh-thu
saandRaaN-mai maeR-koL- pavar-k-ku.

It is said that those good persons who undertake the virtuous path do have the conviction (belief) that it is their duty to perform all good works to the benefit of the society.

982. kuNa –nhalam saandROr nhalan-ae; piRa-nhalam
(y)e-nh-nha-lath-thu uLLathoo-um andRu.

For virtuous persons, perfection in human qualities is the best asset. Other assets do not have that glory and merit. The virtuous qualities have to be learned from them!(Alternatively: The magnificence of virtuous qualities in great persons becomes exemplary, to be considered as a hallmark which is worth being followed in practice. This greatness cannot be found in other traits).

983. anbu, nhaa-N, oppu-ravu, kaNNO-ttam, vaai-mai-yodu
ai-nh-thu –saalbu oondRi-ya thooN.

The five tracts considered as solid pillars bearing the weight of virtues are: i) kindness, ii) shyness to keep away from offensive actions, iii) helping others in their genuine needs, iv) showing sympathy towards the sufferings of others and v) truthfulness.

984. kollaa nha-lath-tha-thu nhOn-mai; piRar-theemai
sollaa nha-lath-tha-thu saal-bu.

Penance is related to goodness in not killing any living creature in this world! It is admired!! Similarly, avoidance of highlighting the faults of others is also considered as a good virtue in good persons!

985. aa-tRu-vaar aa-tRal paNithal; athu- saandROr
maa-tRaa-rai maa-tRum padai

The very strength of those who can perform good things is the quality of humility. It is the most forceful weapon to change the attitude of enemies/ others.

986. saal-biRku-k- kattaLai yaath(u)-(y)enil, thOlvi
thulai-yallaar kaNNum koLal.

The touch-stone of the perfection in virtues is what is called magnanimity/ generosity/tolerance to admit the defeat of the self in a fight (competitions, sports) with a person of lesser strength (status- wise; achievements - wise). It reflects a good culture.

987. innaa -sei- thaar-k-kum ini-ya-vae sei-yaa-k-kaal
(y)enna payath-tha-vO saal-bu?

What is the use of one's perfection in virtues, if it is not possible to extend a pleasing-benefit even to a person who had done something harmful to the self.

988. inmai oruvaRku iLivu – andRu; saalbu –(y)ennum
thiNmai-uN- daaka-p- peRin

Poverty is not a shame on any person, if the moral strength of goodness in virtues is created (embedded) in that person!. (That person will feel it, if he/she watches the response from others who will greatly admire his/ her good qualities). The person will remain good in his/her activities. The society will continue to show respect to him/her, as usual.(Please see kurals 1010, 659).

989. oozhi peyari-num, thaam –peya-raar; saandRaa-Nmai-k-ku
aazhi (y)ena-p- padu- vaar.

Great persons of virtues, who are eminently referred to as the ocean of virtues, will not even change in their views (attitudes) and actions, even if the most calamitous overturning of the water- bodies (oceans) occur, implying the destruction of the world!

990. saandRavar saandRaa-Nmai kundRin, iru-nhilam-thaan
thaa-ng-kaathu, mannO, poRai.

If the perfection of virtues in virtuous persons slackens (gets reduced), the ever-living world will not be able to bear the burden of instability (imbalance), with patience.

(Note: The poet feels that it is the last hope of the earth to expect good persons to stand firm in protecting the norms for maintaining human virtues! If they ever go astray, it will affect all the people in the world. Social order and justice will be in danger! There will be no other force to protect the people. This kind of situation, if created, will earn the fury of the planet-earth, namely, the force of Nature! In kural 731, virtuous persons are categorized as one of the resources of an ideal country. Therefore, the poet fixes the responsibility on good persons to show interest in the welfare of the people in the country. Perhaps, the poet expects the virtuous persons to intervene, if the ruler of the land goes wrong, to impress upon the ruler to give an upright rule, in the light of reasons explained in kurals 445, 446, 447, 448, 555, 556, 880, 989, 996). The role of elders in this relevance can be understood as the role of the United Nations Organisation (UNO)!

CHAPTER-100

CULTURAL COURTEOUSNESS

991. yeN-patha-th-thaal (y)eithal (y)eLithu- (y)enba; yaar-maattum, paNpu- udaimai (y)ennum vazhakku.

It is said a person will deserve the respect of all the people, if he/she is easily accessible to others and is showing unassuming modesty, thereby acquiring virtuous greatness (in the traditional practice of courtesy)!

992. anbu-udaimai, aa-ndRa kudi-p-piRath-thal iv-viraNdum, paNpu-udai-mai (y)ennum vazhakku.

Kindness and the benefit of having been born in a honourable family are the two factors related to the traditional practice of courteous attitude!

993. uRuppu-oth-thal makkaL-oppu an-dRaal; veRuth-thakka paNpu-oththal oppath(u)-aam, oppu.

Similarity in physical size of the body is not considered important among the human beings. The richness in similarities of courteous attitude (cultured behaviour) is the only admirable similarity.

994. nhaya-nodu nhandRi puri-nh-tha payan-udaiyaar paNpu-paa- raa-ttum, ulaku.

Those benevolent persons who help others in their hour of need in their justified ways, will be admired (appreciated) by the people of the world for their courteous gestures. Their commitment to moral values and righteousness will be admired!

995. nhakai-yuLLum innaa-thu, ika-zh-ch-chi; pakai-yuLLum, paNpu-uLa, paadu-aRivaar maattu.

Even while interacting with each other in a humorous way, the practice of extending insult to any person is harmful. Even among enemies, this courteous tradition is being entertained, by virtuous persons who are capable of understanding the probable feelings of the insulted persons.

996. paNpu-udai-yaar-p- patt(u)-uNdu, ulakam; athu-(y)ind-Rael,
maN-pukku maai-vathu man!

The world flourishes, being benefited by the virtuous persons, and their courtesies! Without it, it is probable that this orderly fame (glory/majesty/magnificence) of the world-order will get destroyed, being buried deep into the mud! (Please see kural 990).

997. aram-pOlum koor-mai-ya- rae-num, maram-pOl-var
makka-t- paNpu illaa- thavar.

Those persons, lacking in human virtues and courtesies, are similar to the trees standing on land, although their mind could be as sharp as a filing-tool! They will be categorized as irrational people!

998. nhaNbu-aatRaa-r-aaki, nha-yam-ila sei-vaar-k-kum
paNbu-aatRaar aa-thal kadai

It will bring bad reputation to a virtuous person (courteous person), if he/she does not show courteous attitude towards those who do not extend friendship, and to those who do cause harm to the self! (Tolerance to bad people must be practiced on the basis of forgiveness).

999. nha-kal-vallar al-laar-k-ku, maa-yiru gnaa-lam
pakalum-paaR- patt(u)-andRu, iruL.

For those melancholic (gloomy/moody/preoccupied) persons who cannot maintain themselves in joyful (joyous/cheerful) mood, in response to friendly persons in this world, even daytime filled with bright sunlight will appear to them, as nighttime filled with utter darkness! (They deserve our mercy).

1000. paNpu-ilaan petRa perunj-chelvam, nhan-paal,
kalam-thee-mai- yaal-thiri-nh-th(u)- atRu.

The great wealth acquired by those persons who are lacking in virtues and courtesies will become useless, similar to the good milk kept in contaminated container (vessel) getting spoiled!

CHAPTER-101

WORTHLESS WEALTH

1001. vaith-thaan-vaai saan-dRa perum-poruL, a-h-thu-uNNaan
seth-thaan, seyak-kida-nh-thathu il.

What is the benefit of the wealth to him, if a person accumulates wealth abundantly, overflowing in the house, but does not enjoy the fruits of it sufficiently, due to his miserable attitude of miserliness, and dies abruptly. It is a pity that he did not know how to enjoy the pleasure of helping others, with the wealth which he earned through great efforts!

1002. poruL-aan-aam (y)ellaam-(y)endRu yee-yaa-thu iva-Rum
maru-Laan-aam maaNaa-p- piRappu.

A rich person who believes that anything can be achieved by wealth, who is never in the habit of giving anything to others, by way of help, and who remains confused (perplexed) in the intensive desire of wealth, is considered as a person of meritless birth!

1003. yeettam ivaRi isai-vae-N-daa aadavar
thOtRam nhi-lakku-p- poRai.

The very birth of men, who practice intensive desire for earning wealth and who do not have a desire for acquiring fame through their good deeds, will be considered as a burden to the mother- earth.

1004. yech-cham-yendRu (y)en-(y)eNNum- kollO, oru-varaal
nha-ch-chap- padaa-a- thavan?

What kind of fame a person could expect to get after his/ her death, if he/ she is not liked by any other living person in this world, during the entire life-time? (Every person must do a good deed during his/her lifetime, which is worth being remembered after his/her death!).

1005. kodup-pa-thoo-(v)um, thui-p-pathoo-(v)um, illaar-k-ku, adukki-ya kOdi- uN- daa-yi-num il.

For those who are not taking pleasure in helping others, and themselves not at all showing interest in enjoying their hard- earned wealth, generously, there is no benefit for them, even if properties get accumulated to the tune of millions and millions of worth! They only remain poor (in their minds)!

1006. (y)ae-tham perunj-chelvam thaan-thuv-vaan, thak-kaar-k-ku – ondRu
yeethal iyal-b(u) -ilaa- thaan.

Great wealth itself becomes harmful (as a disease) to a person who owns it, if he/she does not enjoy it to the best satisfaction of the self, or if he/ she does not have a tendency to give even a small portion of it to the deserving (needy) persons, as a graceful help.

1007. atRaar-k-ku -ondRu aa-tRaa-thaan selvam mika-nhalam
petRaaL thami-yaL-mooth-th(u)- atRu.

The wealth of a rich person who does not give any help to others is similar to a beautiful woman, with all virtues, getting older without a happy marriage!The wealth becomes purposeless and useless. It is pathetic in both cases.

1008. nha-ch-chap- padaa-thavan selvam, nhadu-ooruL
nha -ch-chu maram-pazhuth- thatRu,

The wealth of a person who is not liked by any one, (because of the fact that he is not helpful to others), is similar to a poisonous tree, bearing ripe-fruits, right in the middle of the village! (Nobody else will get benefited). As a matter of fact, both will produce harm to others!

1009. anbu-oree-yi-th than-setRu, aRam-nhO-kkaa-thu yeetti-ya
oN-poruL koL-vaar piRar.

Merciless strangers (thieves) will swallow the wealth accumulated by a person who earned it through hard labour(efforts), without observing virtuous norms and without showing kindness to others, while earning, and who did not use it either for personal comforts, or for good charity purposes!

1010. seeru-dai-ch- chelvar siRu-thuni maari
vaRam-koor-nh-th(u)- anai-yathu, udaith-thu.

If a family of virtuous and reputed rich persons happens to suffer from poverty over a short period of time, it is similar to the most benevolent cloud remaining dry for a short duration of time.

(Situation will give relief to them, shortly thereafter!). Please see kural 659; Wealth of virtuous people will come back to them, even if lost once!).

CHAPTER-102

SHYNESS AGAINST EVIL ACTS

1011. karumath-thaal nhaa-Nuthal nhaa-Nuth- thiru-nhuthal
nhal-lavar nhaaNu-p- piRa.

Shyness of a person from committing a wrong deed means the avoidance of evil deeds. This is applicable to all living persons, relevant to a policy on self-control, related to public safety and welfare/social orderliness. The shyness of a young woman who has got the grandness of appearance of eye-brows, experiencing a respectable blushing while looking at others, is quite different (related to personal calibre and emotional integrity)! (Note: Two meanings of the Tamil - term: *'nhaaN'!*

1012. ooN-udai yech-cham uyirk-k(u)-(y)ellaam, vaeR(u)-alla,
nhaaN-udai-mai maa-nh-thar siRappu.

Food, clothing, and other needs are said to be required for all living human beings. But there is one more need, namely,the virtue of shyness towards committing any offensive actions. This is of a special significance to be acquired by all persons of admirable caliber. This has got relevance to yardstick on virtues!

1013. oonai-k- kuRith-tha uyir-(y)ellaam nhaaN –(y)ennum
nhan-mai- kuRith-tha-thu saal-bu.

All forms of life are having the structure of the body as a general feature. The human quality called excellence of virtues accommodates a substantive/genuine ingredient called shyness to keep away from evil actions. That virtue relates to excellence in human qualities.

1014. aNi-andRO nhaaN-udai-mai saandROr-k-ku; a-h-thu-indRael
piNi-andRO, peedu nhadai?

Shyness towards faulty actions is considered as an ornament for the virtuous persons, without which, the majestic manner of walking like a stylish lion will be misunderstood as the symptom of a disease! In which case, it will not be admired as elegance!

1015. piRar-pazhi-yum, tham-pazhi-yum, nhaaNu-vaar, nhaa-Nu-k-ku
uRai-pathi (y)ennum ulaku.

Those virtuous persons who feel shy about the blame-worthy acts of others, as if it were their own act of offence, in addition to their own determination not to commit any crime, will be appreciated by the people, as the protectors for the shyness against blame- worthy acts. (If a person takes responsibility for the offence done by others, it becomes a source of strength for the society in protecting the victims affected by any evil act. It protects the poor people (weaker sections) in society; and that is why, the honour is being given by the society to that great person who takes up the responsibility).

1016. nhaaN-vae-li koL- Laa-thu, mannO, viyan-gnaa-lam
pae-Na-lar mae-laa- yavar.

Virtuous and great persons will consider shyness against evil act as a fence (defense) for protecting their status (honour), rather than any other device of protection, in this wide world (Ref; KalaignarUrai).

1017. nhaa-Naal uyi-rai-th- thuRap-par, uyir-p-porut-taal
nhaaN-thuRavaar, nhaaN-aaL- pavar.

Those who serve as protectors for the virtue of shyness against faulty (blame-worthy) acts, will not abandon their virtue of shyness for the sake of saving their lives, and will prefer to die to save their pride of proclaiming shyness against non-virtuous acts! (Nobody can threaten them to commit non-virtuous acts, by compulsion!).

1018. piRar-nhaaNa-th- thakka-thu, thaan-nhaaNaan aa-yin
aRam-nhaaNa-th- thakkathu udaith-thu.

If a person commits a blame-worthy/criminal act, from which all others shy away, then the force of virtue will shy away (keep away) from that person! (Such a person will be branded as non- virtuous; the protective force of virtue will not come forward to protect him: He will be exposed to danger!).

1019. kulam-sudum, koLkai pizhaip-pin; nha-lam-sudum
nhaaN-inmai nhi-ndRa-k- kadai.

If a person violates the good principles of life, it will destroy the good name of the family in which the person is born! If a person commits blame-worthy acts, without observing shyness against it, all the benefits, likely to come to him/her,normally, will be prevented! The benefits being enjoyed presently will be disturbed (being taken away from him)!

1020. nhaaN-akath-thu il-laar (y)iya-kkam, mara-p-paavai
nhaa-Naal uyi-r-marutti- yatRu,

The style of functioning of those persons who do not have shyness against committing crime (blame-worthy acts), is similar to the lifeless act of wooden doll which is being made to move around, by a human operator, with the help of a rope, to make it appear, as if the doll is alive!

(Note: Thepoet considers that persons committing offensive crimes will not use their mind before doing the evil acts. They will lack conscience, as if they are being operated by merciless forces!). (Note: The term '*nhaa-Naal*' in the second line of the couplet = with the help of a rope).

CHAPTER-103

PROMOTING FAMILY WELFARE

1021. karumam se(i)ya-oruvan 'kai-thoo- vaen'-(y)ennum
perumai-yin peedu-udai-yathu il.

There cannot be a greater pride for a person, if he/she decides that he/she will not stop the efforts for upbringing the family to a prosperous level. (It is a commitment and duty to be carried out with dedication, by a member of the family!).

1022. aaL-vinai-yum, aa-ndRa aRi-vum, (y)ena-iraNdin
nheeL-vinai-yaal nhee-Lum kudi.

Enthusiasm (perseverance) to work and matured wisdom are the two aspects, the continued application of which will support the family and ensure prosperity! The benefits will be yielded for a longer period of time.

1023. kudi-sei-val (y)ennum oru-vaRku-th- thei-vam
madi-thatRu-th thaan-mu-nh- thu-Rum

If a person decides to uplift the family, the deity called the force of nature, will come forward to help that person, tightening the clothes around its waist!

1024. soozhaa-mal thaa-nae mudiv(u)-(y)eithum, tham-kudi-yai-th
thaa-zhaa-thu u-gna-tRu- pavar-k-ku.

If any person wants to uplift his/her family through constant efforts, in a vigorous way, it will work out successfully, without interruption/intervention from others!

1025. kutRam ilan-aai-k- kudi-sei-thu vaazh-vaanai-ch-
chu-tRumaa-ch- chut-Rum ulaku.

If a person performs all necessary acts without committing any fault in upbringing the family, such person's friendship (kinship) will be admired (and desired) by all the people, in the world!

1026. nhal-aaNmai (y)enpathu oruvaR-ku –th- thaan-piRa-nh-tha
il-laa-Nmai aa-kki-k- koLal.

The admirable domestic management of the family in which a person is born will be glorified as his/her overall capacity in governance and leadership!

1027. amar-akath-thu van-kaNNar pOla-th- thamar-akath-thum
aa-tRu-vaar mae-t-Rae poRai.

In the battle-field, the responsibility to fight and win the war is given to persons of valour and will-power. Similarly, the responsibility of bearing the burden of domestic management falls on the shoulders of the person who can do it very well!

1028. kudi-sei-vaar-k-ku illai, paruvam; madi-sei-thu
maa-nam karutha-k- kedum.

For those who want to raise the family, in a prosperous way, it is not necessary to wait for the so-called 'appropriate time' or 'auspicious time'. It is not necessary to postpone things due to laziness, or false pride! If it is delayed, (due to reasons, such as, hesitation, unwillingness, insults from others, threats from others,ill- advice from others, etc), the benevolent results will be affected

1029. idumbai-k-kae koL-kalam kollO, kudum-bath-thai-k-
kutRam maRai-p-paan udambu?

When a single person, as a member of the family comes forward to withstand all the shortcomings/troubles/accusations coming to various other members of the family, it becomes too much for a single person to bear it, as if he/she is a holding-vessel for all troubles! Is it not?

1030. idukkaN-kaal kondRida, veezhum; aduth-thu-oondRum
nhal-aaL ilaa-tha kudi.

Any family will collapse due to the attack of the powerful axe of distress (harm/evil/misfortune), if the family does not have an 'able-person' to re-establish (re-construct) the family!

CHAPTER-104

FARMING / AGRICULTURE

1031. suzha-ndRum-(y)aer-p- pinnathu ulakam; atha-naal
uzha-nh-thum uzha-vae thalai.

Although the people of the world revolve around many other works, all those works are dependent on the farming-work (agriculture), for satisfying the requirement of food. It is the best work, although several hardships are involved in doing it.

* Note: The poem mentions the fact that the world 'revolves'/rotates. Research is needed to claim that Thiruvalluvar was the first person to talk about the rotation/revolving of the globe/the planet-earth! The poet seems to mock at the greatness of the globe, as if the power of revolving around itself gives pride for the planet. Still, it suffers from one weakness,namely, it remains fully dependent on the hard work of farmers to feed its people! (Ref: en.m.wikipedia.org>wiki>Earth's Rotation. This needs research.

1032. uzhuvaar ulakath-thaar-kku aaNi; a-h-thu aa-tRaa-thu
(y)ezhu-vaarai- (y)ellam poRu-ththu.

The farmers are like the linchpins of wheels supporting the world, as they provide food to all the people, including those whoever refused to work in the field, fearing the pains involved in doing the farming-work!

1033. uzhuthu-uNdu vaazhvaa-rae vaazh-vaar; matRu (y)ellaam
thozhuthu-uNdu pin-sel pavar.

Those who undertake the work of tilling the soil, using the plough, to produce food, thereby, supporting themselves, deserve the merit of living their own lives with freedom! All others, engaged in other works go behind their masters, praising them for the support (patronage) for their very survival!

1034. pala-kudai nhee-zhalum tham –kudai-k-keezh-k- kaaNbar
alaku-udai nhee-zha- lavar.

The farmers, having the benevolence of unlimited measures of the most abundant grains (wealth), do have the capacity of earning the popularity for their grains from among the citizens of their own kingdom, and also among the citizens of other (different) kingdoms, and thereby bringing them, under their own umbrella of influence, thus bringing fame to their own king!

1035. iravaar, ira-ppaar-kku-ondRu (y)eevar; kara-vaathu
kai-sei-thu-ooN maa-lai yavar.

The farmers will not resort to begging from others. They will eat the food which they themselves produce (which is a praiseworthy privilege, for them)! They will give help to others without hiding or murmuring! They deserve a great admiration!

1036. uzhavi-naar kai-m-mada-ng-kin illai 'vizhai-vath-oo-(v)um
vittaem'-(y)en paar-k-kum nhilai.

If the farmers fold their hands and do not do the farming - work, there is no support for those ascetics/saints who had declared that they had abandoned the desires of the world, and yet, are dependent on the patronage from the farmers, for their food requirements!

1037. thodi-p-puzhuthi ka-h-saa uNakkin, pidi-ththu-(y)eru-vum
vae-Ndaa-thu saala-p- padum.

If ploughing (tilling the soil with plough) is done to break the soil mud-balls to quarter (smaller) size, and if it can be dried, the growth of crops will be plentiful / healthy, without even a handful of cow-dung being needed to be applied as a manure!

(*Note: Fineness of the soil is highlighted as a technical clue for the benefit of agriculturists, to increase the yield!). Mud-balls are bro ken from large lumps to finer size so that surface area of particles increases per unit weight of soil. Permeation of water through the soil will become enabled with ease, during irrigation to the field. It is a scientific hint, related to water absorption by soil, and transfer of water to the root-zone of crops).

1038. ae-rinum nha-ndRaal eru-(v)iduthal; katta-pin
nhee-ri-num nha-ndRu-athan kaa-ppu.

For healthier crops, application of manure is done, which is more important than ploughing itself. After the removal of weeds, watering is done! More important than watering, is the protection of crops! (Note: All activities are sequentially indicated as farming procedure).

1039. sellaan kizha-van iruppin, nhi-lam pula-nh-thu
il-laaL-in oodi vidum!

If the farmer who owns the land does not visit the land often, it (the land) will feel upset about it, and will show anger and displeasure, more than the wife of that farmer! (Note: It is the poet's imagination that the land responds to the attitude of the farmer like a human being, showing interest (concern) in the welfare of the farmer himself! Please see kural 1040).

1040. ilam- endRu asai-yi irup-paarai-k- kaaNin
nhi-lam-(y)ennum nhal-laaL nha-kum!

The good lady (woman) called land will laugh mildly and unpleasantly at the attitude of the farmer who owns the land, and who keeps himself idle, without doing any work, putting the blame on his poverty, as an excuse!

CHAPTER-105

POVERTY

1041. inmai-yin innaa-tha-thu yaathu –(y)enin, inmai-yin
inmai-yae in-naa tha-thu!

What is more painful than poverty,if it is asked as a question, the answer will be that poverty itself will be more painful than poverty!

1042. immai (y)ena-oru paavi, maRu-mai-yum
immai-yum indRi varum.

There is a cruel person called poverty, who will attack people during this birth and the next birth, without differentiating between the two, to make them feel miserable!(Another version: If poverty attacks a person ever, at initial stage of one's life time, it is capable of affecting him both in the beginning of his life as well as during the later part of his lifetime!). (Note: The poet expresses concern about poverty affecting certain sections of the society, for generations together, without break!).

1043. thol-vara-vum thO-lum kedukkum, thokai-yaaka
nhal-kuravu (y)ennum nha-sai.

If a person gets into hankering-poverty, known as a pathetic situation, leading to ridicule (mockery/insults), he/she will be driven to carry out certain acts which will bring damage to his/her family-prestige and ancient fame! (Hankering poverty means a situ ation which will make a person to long for (crave for) actions, good and bad, in order to get rid of poverty, due to which actions, the prestige and ancient fame of his/her family would go away!).

1044. iR-piRa-nh-thaar kaNNeyum in-mai iLi-va-nh-tha
soR-piRa-kkum sOrvu tharum (iR=il); (soR=sol).

Even in persons born in good families, if poverty comes in, it will create some situations leading to the utterance of bad words, with a tendency to develop hopelessness/weariness!

1045. nha-l-kuravu (y)ennum idumbai-yuL pal-kurai-th
thun-bang-kaL sendRu padum.

Poverty is not alone! Within poverty itself, a variety of sufferings are contained! A sequence of miseries, (each with its own painful effects) will occur.

1046. nhaR-poruL nha-nku-(u)Nar-nh-thu solli-num, nhal- koor-nh-thaar
soR-poruL sOrvu padum (nhaR= nal). (soR= sol).

If a poor person speaks out words of well-conceived thoughts of wisdom, the contents of his/her ideas will not be accepted by others! (What a pity, it is!!). (Note: The poet regrets for the non-appreciative attitude of privileged persons towards intelligent folks among the poor! The poet insists that everyone must be exposed to education, to eradicate such insults!).

1047. aRam-saaraa nhal-kuravu yeendRa-thaa(i)- yaa-num
piRan-pOla nhO-kkap- padum

A person who has deviated from virtuous path and ended up with poverty will be treated like an alien (stranger), by everyone, including the own mother of that person! (Mother would never want her child to act in the wrong path to fight against poverty!). (Note: If a rich person becomes poor after having involved himself in non-virtuous activities, prohibited-activities, illegal- business,gambling, etc., he will not deserve sympathy from any body in the family, including (from) his mother. (Please see Kural 939).

1048. indRum varu-vathu kollO, nhe-ru-nha-lum
kondRathu pOlum nhi-rappu?

A person affected by acute poverty asks a question to him self: “The poverty tortured me like death, yesterday. I am deeply worried whether it would come today too?” (The pathos contin- ues!).

1049. nhe-rup-pinuL thunj-chalum aa-kum; nhira-ppinuL
yaa-th(u)-ondRum kaN-paadu ari-thu.

It may even be possible to sleep in the middle of a burning- flame (fire). But, it is impossible to sleep at all, in the midst of poverty!

1050. thuppu-ravu illaar, thuva-rath- thuRa-vaa-mai
uppiR-kum kaadi-k-kum koo-tRu.

Poor persons, not having any resources to support themselves, and who do not decide to become ascetics (by renouncing the desires of worldly life) will be destined to become dependent on others, to consume ordinary food such as fermented-gruel and salt (that too, to be given by others)!

CHAPTER-106

BEGGING

1051. irakka irath-thakkaar-k- kaaNin; karappin
avar-pazhi, tham-pazhi andRu.

A beggar can beg from a sympathizing-person who will give with pleasure. If the probable giver hides what he/she is likely to give, then, the blame will not fall u p on the person who begs, whereas, the blame will fall upon the person who fails to give!

1052. inbam oruvaR-ku irath-thal iranh-thavai
thunbam uRaa-a- varin.

Begging could bring happiness to a beggar, provided that the material is coming forth without causing any trouble, either to the giver (or to the receiver)!

1053. karapp(u)-ila nhenj-chin kadan-aRivaar mun-nhi-ndRu
irappum - Or yae-yer udai-th-thu.

If a person stands before a donor who understands the situation, and becomes considerate in his/her heart, and comes forward to readily help, it can be said that 'even the act of begging becomes pleasant/honourable/blissful'!

1054. irath-thalum yeetha-lae pOlum! karath-thal
kana-vilum thaetRa-thaar maattu.

If the donor does not contemplate hiding the materials which are in his/her possession, even during his/her dreams, it can be said that begging is as honourable as donating!

1055. karap-pilaar vaiya-kaththu uNmai-yaal kaN-nhindRu
irap-pavar maeR-koL vathu.

Only because of the fact that there are people who readily give material help to those who beg for help, without hiding what ever they could afford to give, it is happening that there are another set of people to stand in front of the donors and ask for help, without feeling a n y delicacy!

1056. karappu- idumbai illaarai-k-kaaNin, nhirappu idumbai
yellaam oru-ng-ku kedum.

The moment of spotting a donor who does not have the habit of hiding the material that is possessed by him/her, the fear about acute poverty would get erased in the mind of the person who came for begging

1057. ikazh-nh-thu (y)eLLaathu, yeevaa-rai-k- kaaNin, makizh-nh- thu – uLLam
uL-LuL uva-p-pathu udai-ththu

Those who receive help will rejoice in their hearts, and feel cheerful, when they happen to see the donors who give happily, without extending ill-treatment or scolding or teasing!

1058. irappaarai illaa-yin yeer-ng-kaN-maa gnaa-lam
marap-paavai sendRu-va-nh-th(u)- atRu.

If there are no beggars, the human activities of the cool wide world will be limited to an uninteresting scenario, resembling the coming-and-going of the wooden dolls!

1059. yeevaar-kaN (y)en-uNdaam thOtram ira-nh-thu-kOL
mae-vaar ilaa-ak- kadai?

If there is nobody to beg for the desired help, the bright reputation (prestige/proud privilege) of giving to the needy people, will not shine forth for the privileged (rich) persons! (Note: There are people in this world who find pleasure in helping others!).

1060. irappaan veku-Laa- mai vaeNdum; nhi-rapp(u)-idumbai
thaa-nae-yum saalum kari.

Anger must be avoided by a beggar! The person who was unable to give could be another poor person (like the beggar himself/herself) affected with poverty! This reason could be easily guessed by the beggar, from his/ her own suffering-experience! (Note: This is a real, pragmatic opinion!)..

CHAPTER-107

SHYNESS FOR BEGGING

1061. karavaathu uva-nh-th(u) –(y)eeyum kaN-(N)annaar kaNNum
iravaa-mai kOdi yuRum. (Poet's advice!).

It is worth for ten-millions of value, in terms of honour, if a person getting pushed into the situation of begging, could avoid receiving any help from a donor who happily gives, without hiding! (*Note: If begging is to be avoided even from willing donor, it means that begging must not be practiced at all! This is the ideal situation which will be pleasing to the poet! No poverty! No begging! Please see kural 1062).

1062. ira-nh-thum uyir-vaazh-thal vaeNdin, para-nh-thu
keduka ulaku iyatRi- yaan. (Poet's anger).

If some people are necessitated to live on-begging for the sake of keeping themselves alive, it is worthwhile to cry-out: "Let the Creator of the world get destroyed, fast, after loitering around, as the helpless beggars do!" (Another version: "Let the ruler of the land, who decides on the distribution of wealth in his country, take up the responsibility for the pitiable situations of beggars! Let it be a curse on the ruler: "Let the king himself loiter around, like the beg gars, in poverty, and get destroyed speedily!").

1063. 'inmai idumbai ira-nh-thu –theer v(u)-aam'-(y)ennum
vanmai-yin van-paatta-thu il. (Poet's satire).

It is a cruel decision that those persons inflicted (affected) with acute poverty decide and resort to solve their sufferings through the method of begging from others! It is a cruel mentality at the cost of self-respect!

1064. idam-(y)ellaam koLLaa-th- thakai-th-thae idam-illaa-k-
kaalum irav(u)-ollaa-ch- chaal-bu. (Poet's idealism).

The glory of a person who does not go for begging, even when there is no place for him/her to reside(shelter), is greater than the huge space available in the entire world! That glory is larger than the sizeofthe universe!

1065. theL-nheer adu-puRkai (y)aayi-num, thaaL-tha-nh-tha-thu
uNNa-lin oong-k(u)-ini-yathu il. (theNNeer=theL-nheer).

The food that you have earned through your hard labour, although tasting bland like clear water, boiled with gruel, is tastier than any other food! There could be no other food superior to it!

1066. aavi-Rku nheer-(y)endRu irap-pinum, nhaa-vi-Rku
iravin iLi – va-nh-tha-thu il.

The act of begging for water to feed the thirsty-cow(treating her as good as a mother) brings shame to the tongue of the person who asked for water! (*Note: Begging, under any circumstance destroys one's honour! Refer.kural 656).

1067. 'irappan irap-paarai (y)ellaam irappin,
kara-ppaar iravan-min'— yendRu! (Poet's appeal).

Advice from Thiruvalluvar!: "I beg for a favour from all those persons who have resorted to begging, in order to support themselves: My prayer is that: "Do not beg from those who hide the materials which they have got, whereas they could have given to you, with ease, without hiding!" (Note: The poet feels that the self-respect of the beggar is injured when the donor refuses to give!).

1068. iravu-(y)ennum yae-maapp(u)- il thONi, karavu –(y)ennum
paar-thaa-kka-p- pakku vidum.

The practice of begging is like a boat which does not have protection. It will be broken by the rock (submerged) below the water, called "hiding of materials"! (paar = soft rock),

1069. irav(u)-uLLa uLLam uru-kum; karav(u)-uLLa
uLLa-thoo-um indRi-k- kedum.

The mind of beggars will melt at the thought of their plight of being necessitated to beg from others! When they further think about some people hiding the material which could have been generously given to them, their mind loses further hope, with a broken heart!

1070. karappa-var-k-ku yaa-ng-ku-oLikkum kollO, irappa-var
sollaa-da-p- pO-om uyir? (Poet's sympathy).

When a beggar begs from a person who hides the material/object which could have been given to the beggar, the beggar being disappointed, on hearing the word "No", feels that his soul is flying away from his body. A question arises as to where exactly the soul of the donor could have been mercilessly hiding at that time?

(Note: The various forms of human sufferings, on the economic conditions of the society, namely, poverty and begging, continues for the past 2000 years. The sympathetic thoughts which bothered the peace of mind in the poet's considerations remain valid even during the 21st Century!).

It implies that human efforts are needed to resolve the problem of distribution of wealth, in the light of kural 1062, accepting the interpretation that the rulers of the lands must take up the responsibility for a rational distribution of wealth among the ever-increasing population of the world! That will convince the great poet Thiruvalluvar who expressed so much of a concern for the suffering masses, on the economic front!

CHAPTER-108

MEANNESS

1071. makka-Lae pOlvar kayavar; avar-anna
oppaar(i) yaam-kaNda-thu il! (poet's observation).

The evil persons look like the normal human beings! The resemblance is exact! We have not seen any other better resemblance!! (*Note: It is a satire that the calibers are different between the two categories of persons, namely, normal human beings versus unscrupulous persons!).

1072. nha-ndru- aRi- vaa-rin, kayavar thiru-udai-yar;
nhe-nj-chath-thu avalam ilar.

Evil persons do have more wealth than those wise persons who have got more worldly knowledge, due to the fact that the evil persons do not have a natural sympathy in their minds, to help others! (The unscrupulous persons will never have worries in their minds, nor sympathy for others!).

1073. thae-var anai-yar kayavar, avarum-thaam
mae-vana seith(u)-ozhu-ka- laan

Evil persons are like heavenly persons, as they can afford to act as they like, ignoring the obligations to social justice (value- system/ normal human virtues)!

(Note: It is a satire that the unscrupulous persons behave like celestial persons, although they have a need to obey the law of the land applicable to all people (human beings) living on the land!).

1074. akap-patti aavaarai-k- kaaNin, avar-in,
mikap-pattu-ch- chem.-maakkum keezh.

Evil persons will feel superior to those who are lesser than them, and develop a false pride in their mind, thereby, enhancing their arrogance!

1075. ach-cha-mae keezh-kaLa-thu aa-chaa-ram;(y)ech-cham
avaa-uNdael uNdaam siRi-thu

Fear is the regulating factor for the people of low caliber, in their efforts to behave better, and to play it safe! Additional reason could be their desire for gains!

1076. aRai-paRai annar kayavar, thaam kae-tta
maRai-piRar-k-ku ui-th-thu-uraikka - laan!

Whatever is being heard by the evil persons, as secret information, will be revealed to others, by them, as if beating a drum and communicating the matter to all, knowingly, out of ignorance! (Please see KalaignerUrai).

1077. yeer-ng-kai vithi-raar kayavar; kodi-Ru-udai-k-kum
koon-kai-yar al-laa- thavar-k-ku!

The evil persons will not even shake their wet hands after eating food, fearing that the food particles would fall down to feed the ants. They will not give food to others except to those who are capable of hitting their faces(jaws) with folded (clinched) fists forcibly.

1078. solla-p- payan-paduvar saan-dROr; karumbu-pOl
kolla-p- payan-padum keezh.

Virtuous persons will render help voluntarily, if they are just informed about the need! Persons of low caliber will give help, only if they are pressurized to give, just like the way by which the sugarcane is subjected to crushing to take out the juice of it!

(Note: Crushing ofsugarcane, asan industrialunit, is indicated in the ancient era! In Tamil Nadu,India, some 2000 years ago!).

1079. udup-pathoo-(v)um uN-pathoo-(v)um kaa-Nin, piRar-mae-l
vadu-k-kaaNa vatRaa-kum keezh.

If persons of low calibre (mind/attitude) happen to see the decent costumes (dresses) and good food availed (enjoyed) by others, they will find fault with those poor persons, and pour out complaints, even to implicate them in offensive acts (which could be false allegations!).

1080. (y)etRi-R-ku uri-yar kayavar-ondRu utRa-k-kaal
vitRa-R-ku uri-yar virai-nh-thu.

What is the use of persons whose human quality is low? They will speedily sell themselves in order to protect themselves, if any trouble comes to them, without being mind

PART - III

PERSONAL LIFE:
Notes on Family Life
(Love-Life / Blissful Love / Desire for Pleasure)

CHAPTER-109

ADMIRATION OF BEAUTY

1081. aNang–ku–kol aa–i–mayil kollO? kana–ng–kuzhai\
maathar–kol? maa–lum, (y)en nhenj-chu!

He feels: "I admire the beauty of this young woman with attractive jewels! At the same time, I wonder whether she could be a young female (angel) from the heaven, or a fascinating/gorgeous attractive human being! She resembles a stylish and elegant peacock"!!

(He feels/thinks:..... treated as dramatic monologue: soliloquy!).

1082. nhO–k–ki–naaL, nhOk–ke–thir nhOkku–thal, thaakku–aNa–ng–ku
thaanai–k–koN danna–thu udai–th–thu!

He feels: It appears as if a celestial damsel wages war against me, with her powerful army of piercing eyes to contend (fight)! When this attractive woman, whom I admire, returns my inquisitive look, with her powerful eyes, I feel captivated!

1083. paNdu –aRi–yaen, kootRu–(y)en patha–nai; ini–aRi–nh–thaen
peN–thakai–yaal paer–amar–k– kattu!

He feels: I never have known what could be the effect of confronting with a killing-agent! Now I have learned it. It is the fascinating feminine grace of the look coming from the battling eyes of this woman whom I have seen just now!

1084. kaNdaar uyir–uNNum thO–tRath–thaal peN–thakai–p–
pae–thai–k–ku amarth–thana kaN

He feels: The eyes of a woman is designed in such a way that a person who looks at those eyes will face a life-taking onslaught! Is it for protecting the feminine grace? How come, she appears to be so innocent?

1085. 1085. kootRa–mO, kaNNO, piNai–yO mada–varal
nhOkkam–im moondRum udaith–thu!

He feels: The eyes of this attractive woman are capable of representing three looks: i) the fierce look of a death-causing enemy. ii) the look of a normal / friendly partner, and iii) the graceful look of an innocent female deer.

1086. kodum–puruvam kOdaa maRaip–pin nha–du–ng–ku –a–gna–r
sei–yala, man, ivaL kaN.

He feels: Her fascinating eyes are so impressive, in appealing to my desires! I will feel a lot safer, if at all, her long eye-lids could move a little bit, to give a protecting-coverage, so as to block the direct view!

1087. kadaa–ak kaLitRin–mael kat-padaam maathar
padaa–a mulai–mael thukil!

He feels: I watched with admiration the gigantic appearance of an aggressive/restless elephant with an ornamental cloth covering and adoring its impressive face! So impressive is the soft decorative silk cloth covering the firm bosoms (breasts) of this beautiful woman whom I admire!

1088. oL–nhu–thaR– ku–Oh!0h! udai–nh–tha–thae! gnaa–t–pinuL
nha–NNaa–rum utkum –(y)en peedu!

He feels: My valourous strength which I could prove to my enemies in the battlefield is almost succumbing when I look at the shining (elegant) forehead of this attractive woman! I am amazed!!

(Note: Oh! oh!! = expression of wonder; is it so? could it be? probably?)

1089. piNai- (y)aer, mada - nhO-k-kum, nhaaNum udai-yaa-t-ku
aNi-(y)evanO, (y)ae-thila tha-nh-thu?

He feels:"What kind of additional beauty the artificial jewels can give to a young woman who is naturally beautiful, with an elegant/inquisitive look, resembling the captivating stare of a female deer, and above all, with the communicative/innocent shyness"!

1090. uNdaar–kaN al–lathu adu–nhaRaa–k– kaamam–pOl,
kaNdaar makizh–sei–thal indRu

He feels: Happiness out of intoxication will be available to a person when he consumes distilled (processed) liquor. It is not as enjoyable as the captivating happiness the lovers will enjoy, on just seeing each other! (Nobody gets intoxicated on just seeing the liquor!).

CHAPTER-110

ASCERTAINING FEELINGS

1091. iru-nhOkku ivaL-uN-kaN uLLathu; oru-nhOkku
nhOy-nhOkku, ondRu, a-n(h)-nhOy maru-nh-thu.

He feels: My woman-in love has got two kinds of looks inside her attractive (captivating) eyes; one look to make me sick; and the other look to cure (heal) my sickness!

(Note: The term '*uN-kanN*'-refers to 'absorbing - look').

1092. kaN–kaLavu koLLum siRu–nhOkkam kaamath–thil
sem– paakam andRu; perithu.

He feels: Her affectionate looks pointed at me,which she manages to steal on seeing me at closer proximity, (in the presence of others) means more than half-of-confirming her loving- desire, for me! Yes, for sure!

1093. nhOkkinaaL; nhOkki iRai–nj–chinaaL; a–h–thu –avaL
yaappinuL attiya nheer.

He feels: She looked at me sharply! Affection and her longing desire were hidden behind that lightning-look! That signifies her effort of spraying water for a growing plant, namely, the budding love between the two of us!

1094. yaan nhOkkum kaalai nhilan–nhOkkum; nhOkkaa–k–kaal
thaan–nhOkki, mella nha–kum.

He feels: "When I look at her, she avoids looking at me, and prefers to look at the floor! When I do not look at her, she steals a glance at me, and smiles within herself, softly, with a hidden blushing"!

***

(CHAPTER-110 : this line to be placed before kural 1091)

1095. kuRi–k–koNdu nhOkkaa–mai al–laal, oru–kaN
siRak–kaNith–thaaR pOla nha–kum.

He feels: She does not look straight on me. But she takes pleasure to steal a glance at me, as if with a squint eye, and smiles to herself, without others watching it! (It is a fun! However, it means something pleasant, as a favourable signal to me!).

1096. uRa–a– thavar–pOl so(l)li–num, seRaa–ar–sol
ollai uNara–p– padum.

He feels; Her words may sound as unfriendly as if uttered to an unrelated person; but, it can be easily realized sooner that a loving-kindness was hidden behind the harsh words!

1097. seRaa–ach– chiRu sollum, setRaar–pOl nhOkkum
uRaa–ar–pO–ndru utRaar kuRippu.

He thinks: Sometimes, it happens that persons who have natural (mutual) affection for each other might behave in public as if they are not known to each other, (playfully) uttering unkind words and outwardly exchanging unfriendly looks! (It applies to lovers with a good understanding!).

1098. asai–yi–y aRku uNdu– aaNdu–Or (y)ae–(y)er–yaan nhOkka–p–
pasai–yi–naL pai–ya nhakum

He feels: Not being discouraged by the circumstances, I gave a pleading glance at the woman I admire! In response, she gave a warm /gentle smile! I am sure that it is a comforting sign for me! I understand her to be a gentle and kind person!

1099. (y)ae–thi–laar pOla–p– pothu–nhOkku nhOkkuthal
kaa–tha–laar kaNNae uLa.

He wonders: Exchanging indifferent glances at each other, in the style of strangers, is a common occurrence, only between young lovers, when they happen to meet in public places!

1100. kaNNodu kaNN–iNai nhOkku–okkin, vaa–i–ch–choRkaL
(y)enna paya–num ila.

She feels: "When the eyes of lovers are exchanging their looks with communicative union of minds,what could be the use of mere words? Does it mean that words become redundant?

CHAPTER-111

REJOICING ON UNION

1101. kaNdu–kae–ttu, uNdu–uyir–th–thu, utRu–aRi–yum a–i–m–pula–num
oN–thodi kaN–Nae uLa.

He feels: Seeing with eyes, hearing with ears, smelling with nose, tasting with the tongue, touching with fingers are the benefits of five senses which are available in one person, "my woman" who is wearing many pairs of glittering bangles! (Note: Similar admiration, about him, will prevail in the mind of "his woman")!

1102. piNikku maru–nh–thu piRa–man; aNi–yizhai
than–nhO–y–kku–th– thaa–nae maru–nh–thu.

He feels: For any human sickness, medicines are made from various other materials. For the sickness caused in me due to the craving desires for my beautiful woman-in-love, she herself proves to be the medicine!

(Note: The term 'jewelled woman' stands for describing the beauty, consisting of natural beauty and artificial beauty. The term "Izhai" stands for 'young woman';The term 'aNi-izhai' could mean the woman who is an embodiment of beauty; similar to the word 'aai- izhai", meaning a woman of 'selected-virtues'! She herself imbibes (inculcates) good virtues in her,learning the clue from her role-model, ...perhaps her mother!).

1103. thaam–veezh–vaar men–thOL thu–yi–lin ini–thu–kol
thaa–marai–k– kaN–Naan ulaku?

He feels: It is more blissful to sleep by embracing the soft shoulders of my woman-in-love, than dwelling in the heaven presided over by Lord Vishnu (who has got Lotus-flower-like eyes)! Is it not?

(Note: The woman is described to have got soft/attractive shoulders).

****

1104. nhee–ng–kin theRoo–um; kuRukum–kaal thaN, (y)ennum–
thee, yaa–Ndu–p– petRaaL ivaL?

He wonders: Where-from did my woman-in-love get the source of fire (energy) in her body? which gives a cooling effect to my body when I approach her, whereas it gives a heating effect to my body when I go away from her? (Note: This is opposed to the 'natural' law of heat-transfer described in kural 691!).

1105. vae–tta pozhu–thin avai–avai pOlu–mae
thOttaar kathu–p–pi–naaL thOL.

He feels: Every time when I desire for some blissful experience, to keep me cheerful, it is made possible only when I get my woman-in-love with me to embrace her elegant shoulders, further beautified by the plait of hair attached to which are the sweet- smelling fragrant flowers! Whatever I desire for, I am able to derive it, from that embrace!

1106. uRu–thORu uyir–thaLir–p–pa–th– thee–Nda–laal, pae–thai–k–ku
amizh–thin iyan–dRana thOL.

He feels: Whenever I embrace the attractive shoulders of my woman-in love, I feel that I have absorbed new energy of life! I infer that her shoulders could have been made from nectar/ambro- sia!

(Note: Ambrosia is the food for gods and goddesses, according to Greek mythology. Nectar is a sugar-rich liquid produced by plants in glands called nectaries or nectarines, within the flowers with which it attracts pollinating animals (ants, bats, bees, beetles, birds, butterflies, flies, moths,,etc....Ref: https://en.m.wikipedia.org>wiki> Nectar)..

1107. tham–mil iru–nh–thu, tha–mathu–paath–thu, uNda–tRaal
am–maa arivai muya–kku.

He feels: I will get a pleasant satisfaction by earning wealth through my own efforts, and sharing my food with all others. Similar contentment in my mind can be attained by me, only by embracing my beloved woman- in-love!

(Note: The poet compares moral happiness and sensual happiness, as the two components of contentment in a healthy mind!)

1108. veezhum iruvar–k–ku ini–thae vaLi–idai -p-
pOzha–p– padaa–a– muya–kku.

He feels: If the lovers embrace each other so tightly that even a small mass of air (breeze) cannot pass through the grip, it could provide them the ecstatic/wholesome/fulfilling joy.

1109. oodalal, uNar–thal, puNar–thal, ivai–kaamam
koodi–yaar petRa payan.

He wonders: The benefit of love will be realized best between a man and woman united by mutual affection through certain factors, such as, entering into false-quarrel, ii) realizing the interruption in happiness due to the false-quarrel, and iii) settling the quarrel by improved understanding (reconciliation) by their own efforts, and iv) getting united through a blissful embrace.

1110. aRi–thORu aRi–yaamai kaNd(u)–atRaal, kaamam
seRi–thORum sae–yi–zhai maattu.

He feels: The blissful experience of embracing my woman- in-love who has got a child-like innocence in love-making, and who happens to give a different experience during each time of the union, as both of us feel, as if new levels of ignorance are revealed on every occasion, enjoying unexplored levels of blissful experiences!

(Note: Some authors have interpreted "*sae-izhai*" as red-coloured woman or woman wearing red-coloured jewels. This is modified as "*saey + izhai*", meaning a woman having a child-like innocence! The term: "child-like innocence" is more appropriate for the context, from psychological viewpoint. This needs further research! This aspect has got more sensitive implications on mutual attraction between a man and a woman. The colour of the woman or the jewels of the woman, is not given importance in the present theme of the couplet! It is the alignment of the mindset, mutual admiration, emotional-craving, etc., which are important!).

CHAPTER-112

PRAISING-HER-QUALITIES

1111. nhal–nheerai, vaazhi anich–cha–mae! nhin–ni–num,
mel–nhee–raL yaam –veezh– pa–vaL!

He speaks: "Oh! My dear Anicham flower! Greetings! Long live your beauty! You are well-known for your softness and tenderness! It is my pleasure to tell you that my woman, whom I adore and love is softer than you! Tenderer in feelings too"! (Note: The softness of Anicham flower is mentioned in Sanskrit literature by Poet Kalidasa (4th-5th Century CE): "The arms of Paarvathi are imagined to be softer than even the Sirisam- flower"... Kumarasambhava 1:41; (Note: Paarvathi is the wife of Lord Shivaa).

"The body of Sudarsana is said to as tender as the delicate Sirisam-flower! Raghuvamsa 18:45.(Ref: https:// tamilandvedas.com>sirisam:

Srisam and Anicham flowers in Tamil and Sanskrit literatures, vide Post no.3599, by London Swaminathan, dated 2nd February 2017).

1112. malar–kaa–Nin mai–yaa–th–thi nhenj–chae, ivaL–kaN
palar–kaaNum poo–vo–kkum yendRu.

He feels: The eyes of my woman-in-love are as attractive as fresh flowers growing in the garden! I feel elated/jubilant, whenever I happen to see the flowers growing on the land! How ever, I feel the shame for my ignorance also! The flowers seen by all people in the world are attractive due to their appearance and freshness only! The eyes of my woman-in-love are superior as they are attached to her mind which exhibits her emotions, as well. I underestimated the real value!

1113. muRi–maeni, muththam, muRuval, veRi–nhaa–tRam
vael–uN–kaN vae–y–th–thOL avatku.

He feels: Let me tell you something about my woman-in- love with whom I happen to have fallen in love! Her complexion is like a tender leaf, her shoulders are like soft bamboo stems, her teeth as white as pearls(capable of giving pleasant smiles), her breath having a good fragrance, her painted eyes capable of shooting looks like a war-weapon (spear) which could carry a message along with it! (Note: please see kural 1091: The term '*uN-kaN*' may refer to "absorbing look"; '*uN*'- means swallowing or eating: Kurals 1091; 1172; 1174; 1212; 1271).

1114. kaa–Nin kuva–Lai kavizh–nh–thu nhi–lan–nhO–kkum
maaN–izhai kaN–ov–vaem (y)endRu.

He wonders: The natural modesty makes my honourable woman-in-love to bow down her eyes staring at the ground always, in front of any male- visitor. The blue-lotus flowers will feel that they cannot compete with the charm of the eyes of this woman, and accepting their defeat, the flowers are lowering their petals towards the ground in shame of the defeat!

(Note: The petals of Blue-lotus flowers will always be found pointing towards the ground, as if the heads of the plant are brought down in shame! The plant as such will be standing upright!! Only the flowers feel shy, in shame of the defeat!! A poetic description of a natural scenario!). Please refer to Kalaignar Urai.

1115. anich–cha–p–poo–k– kaal–kaLai–yaaL, pei–thaaL, nhusu–p–piRku
nhalla padaa–a– paRai.

He wonders: "She was wearing the soft Anichcham flower on the back of her head (adoring her plaited hair), without removing the stalk (stem-portion). She ended up falling down to the floor due to excessive weight of the stalk of the flower. It brought pains to her waist. The beating of the Parai- drum* corresponded to a saddening blare instead of a merry-making music, signifying this (unpleasant) incident"! (Please refer to Kalaignar Urai). (Note: This is the feeling of a lover!).

(Note: * The drum refers to the ancient musical drum (Parai) for which citations are available in ancient Tamil Literature: (i) *Parai(isaikkaruvi)*:History: Wikipedia (tn.m.wikipedia.org); (ii) Home

Music: "Secular and Sacred", The Hindu. 3 January 2013. Retrieved 11 September 2016.(Dr.Raama Kausalya explains through ancient literature and *Tyagaraja*: article by Suganthy Krishnamachari:.... Some evidence also indicated in the reference, relating to the ancient instrument to have been used as an accompaniment for the occasion of Siva-Uma cosmic dance! "*Parai* and Conch were used in auspicious functions such as wed dings: Kurunthogai). The '*kombu*' (Bugle, or Horn) is a usual accompanying musical instrument used in public reception to the king, in massive congregations, when the merry-making tunes of '*parai-drum*'-beatings, termed as '*kottu*' or '*muzhakku*', '*kottu-yezhuppu*' are played. The '*kombu*' makes a noise resembling the trumpeting voice of a war-elephant, symbolizing royal elegance, dignity and valour. The importance of *parai-drum* used in various occasions of social life, in the ancient history of the Tamil-speaking regions is elaborated in detail in: https://en.m.wikipedia.org/wiki/Parai.

(Note: The sound of *Yaazh, Kombu*,Conch Shell (*valampuri sanghu*), Horn, etc, can be heard in 'You Tube'- versions).

(Ref: It is claimed that about 35 different tunes are played in the ancient-Parai-drum (a percussion type of instrument) to suit various occasions of merry-making, festive occasions, royal functions, war- victories, sports, as well as mourning-salutes, according to Dr.Zoe C.Sherinian, Professor of Ethnomusicology, University of Oklahoma, U.S.A.).

Ancient Tamil music is the historical predecessor of the Carnatic music, during the Sangam-period which spanned from 500 BCE to 200 BCE. *Tholkappiyam* makes a mention about '*yaazh*', a melodic instrument, and '*parai*', a percussion instrument, while correlating a particular mood of the poem to be synchronized with the corresponding musical mood (*paN*) pertaining to each of the five landscapes *(thiNai)*. Ref: en.m.wikipedia.og>wiki>Ancient Tamil Music. (Note-2: Adoring the hairstyle with flowers: http://in.pinterest.com>rakshanaz).

1116. mathi–yum mada–nh–thai mukan–um aRi–yaa
pathi–yin kala–ng–kiya meen.

He wonders: The various stars in the sky remain confused in differentiating the degrees of brightness between the beautiful countenance (face) of my woman and the face of the moon, the stars are changing their positions often, being unable to solve the puzzle!

(Note: A scientific hint is conveyed about the constant motion of stars. The term "*pathy-in* = without sticking to its position!).

(Note: 1)."As the Earth rotates with an axis that is pointed in the direction of the North Star, stars appear to move from east to west in theSky"—Jeff-Mangum,..6-years-ago: (https://public.nrao.edu>ask>why). Article: Why Do Stars Appear To Move in the Night-Sky?

2) Understanding-Astronomy:Motion of Stars: (https:// physics.weber.edu>starmotion). (It takes a little less than an hour for the stars to move by 15 degrees, and therefore, it taskes a little less than 24 hours for the stars to complete an entire circle.In fact, it takes just 23 hours and 56 minutes (4-minutes less than the full day)! During those last 4-minutes, the stars will move by an additional degree. So in exactly 24 hours,the stars actually move by 361 degrees, not 360 degrees".

1117. aRu–vaa–i nhiRai–nh–tha avir–mathi–kku–p– pOla
maRu–uNdO maa–thar mukath–thu?

He wonders: The moon grows from small size to greater size, giving the most pleasant lunar-light. However, there are black spots on the face of the moon.There are no such black-spots on the bright face of my woman-in-love!

(Note: Almost 17% of moon's surface are covered by dark spots called "maria", meaning "sea" in Latin language, because the Astronomers thought that it could be lunar-seas! They are actually, volcanic plains, as per NASA-report. www.washingtonpost.com news: Feb., 9, 2015). "NASA gives us an amazing look at the 'dark-side' of the moon", by Abby Ohlheiser. Science. The Washington post).

1118. maa–thar mukam–pOL oLi–vida vallai–yael,
kaa–thalai vaazhi mathi!

He speaks: Oh, my dear moon! Long live! If you can release light on your face as bright as my woman-in-love can do, I will become your admirer, and propose love to you!

(Note: The intensity of moonlight varies from 0.05 lux illumination to 0.10 lux illumination, depending on the lunar phase! When a full moon appearing as "super-moon", in certain geographical locations of the tropics, the illumination can go up to 0.32 lux). Ref: https://en.m.wikipedia.org >wiki> Moonlight).

1119. malar–anna kaN–NaaL mukam–oth–thi– yaa-yin
palar–kaaNa–th– thOn–dRal mathi!

He speaks:Oh,Moon! If you ever wish to appear on the sky, with your face as bright as the bright face of my woman-in- love, who has got very attractive bright eyes comparable with fresh natural flowers, please do not show up at all, to the public! (Duller appearance is permitted! I do not want you to be a competitor for my woman-in-love!

1120. anich–cha–mum, anna–th–thin thoovi–yum, maa–thar
adikku nhe–ru–nj–chi–p– pazham!

He feels: "The delicate foot-palms of my woman are so soft, that even the naturally blossoming *Anichcham* flower (supposed to have the softest petals) or the soft feathers of the Swan-bird, will prove to be as hurtful as a thorny fruit called '*nherunchi*', when she walks over those soft materials spread on the floor"! (Please see kural 1111).

CHAPTER-113

EXCELLENCE OF LOVE

1121. paa–lodu thae–n kala–nh–th(u)– atRae, paNi–mozhi
vaal–(y)eyi–Ru ooRi–ya nheer!

He feels: The water emerging betwixt the pearly white teeth of my woman-in-love, who is a soft-spoken person, does taste like a mixture of milk and honey!

1122. udambodu uyir–idai (y)enna–matRu, anna
mada–nh–thai–yodu yem–midai nha–t–pu.

He feels: "I feel that my relationship with my life-partner and me is just similar to the linkage between the human body and the soul; the two cannot be separated"!.

(Note: Similar feelings will be prevalent in the mind of "his life-partner"!).

1123. karu–maNi–yil paa–vaa–i, nhee, pOthaa–i; yaam veezhum
thiru–nhu–thaRku illai idam.

He feels: I wish to accommodate my woman-in-love (who is having attractive eye-brows) within my eyes! I request the pupil of my eye to vacate its presently recorded image, and create a space for her to occupy that space!

(Note: The man-in-love wants her to be with him all the time! It is understandable! This is another symptom of love-sickness, as inferred by his desire to accommodate her in his eyes! He is unable to think about practical realities. He has to come up with a practical solution! Somebody has to take the message to him/her, if we want to help this couple!If she is accommodated within his eyes, he won't be able to see her at all!).

1124. vaazh–thal uyir–kk(u)–annaL aa–yizhai; saathal
athaRk(u) –annaL nhee–ng–kum idath–thu.

He feels: My woman-in-love is the real embodiment of the most precious good qualities selectively chosen by her, and when she is with me, I feel like living purposefully, with body and soul, combined together! When she leaves, I feel that it means death to me (I am gone!)

(Note: The term '*aai-izhai*' means a young woman who has earned (imbibed in her) all virtuous(good) qualities, selectively chosen by her, in order to be a good person!).

1125. uLLuvan man, yaan maRappin; maRapp(u)–aRi–yaen
oL(L)–amar–k– kaN–NaaL kuNam.

He feels: How can I recollect about the good virtues of my woman-in-love,who has got bright battling eyes and praise-wor thy qualities! How can I recollect? I do not forget it all! Recollecting becomes necessary only if I forget! (Note: The hero reacts, sharply, answering the complaint of an intimate friend who advised the hero to think (visualize) about the pathetic situation of the heroine who lives in her home-town, far away from her husband's place, being separated by the decision of her husband to move out of town, for work!). (Note: The intimate friend came forward to advise his bosom-friend, taking liberty, on the strength of kural 784).To the friend, the hero explains that he is thinking about her all the time! He does not forget her! He cannot afford to forget! For him, she is the very soul of his life! The friend understands that the physical separation of a couple could prove to be an unbearable ordeal! (However, the friend realizes that they have to wait until the right time comes up, for re-uniting the couple!). As a fellow-man, the friend understands.

1126. kaN–uLLin pOkaar; imai–ppin paru–va–raar;
nhuNNi–yar, (y)e–ng– kaatha lavar.

She feels: My man-in love is a fine gentleman! He will not go away from my eyes. He will not get upset even if I blink my eyes! He is such a fine person!

(When she told this to her maid, the maid looked at her sharply. After a pause, she advised the heroine that she should send a message to the young man as to how much his absence is being felt!).

1127. kaN–uLLaar kaatha– lava–raa–ka–k– kaNNum
(y)ezhu–thaem, kara–p–paakku aRi–nh–thu.

She feels: I do not paint my eyes! My man-in-love is inside my eyes! If I ever try to paint my eyes, my man-in-love will go away (during the time of painting the eyes!). I cannot bear the pain of his absence!

(When she told this to her maid, she assured that she will talk to the parents of the heroine, all about it, and do something to resolve the matter about expediting the marriage-proposal!).

1128. nhenj–chath–thaar kaatha– lavar–aaka vei–thu–uNdal
anj–chu–thum, vae–paakku aRi–nh–thu.

She feels: I do not eat hot food, as I fear that my man- in-love who is inside my heart would feel the heat and pain! (Note: She told this to her maid. She encouraged the heroine that she would prove to be a dedicated partner for that lucky-boy!).

1129. imai–p–pin karap–paakku aRi–val, anai–th–thiR–kae
(y)aethilar (y)ennum–iv voor.

She speaks: I do not wink my eyes, fearing that my man- in-love will go away! But the people of this village will blame him only, for making me sleepless (being unkind)!

(When she told her maid about her feelings as to how she felt the absence of her husband, the maid felt that it has become a social problem, and that responsible persons like elders must take efforts to improve the employment opportunities in local areas, so that the young couples will be able to work and reside in the same town!).

1130. uva–nh–thu–uRaivar, uLLa–ththuL (y)endRum; ika–nh–thu – uRaivar
(y)aethi–lar (y)ennum–iv voor.

She speaks: My man-in-love and myself live together in the heart of hearts, though physically separated! Still, the people of this village have started blaming that we remain separated, and that he is responsible for the separation! (When she told this to her maid, she replied that the heroine must inform her husband, requesting him to pay frequent visits, if at all possible!).

CHAPTER-114

SHEDDING THE SENSE OF SHYNESS

1131. kaamam uzha–nh–thu varu–nh–thinaar–kku (y)ae–mam
madal–allathu illai vali.

He analyses: A man feels the agony of being separated from his woman-in love and prefers to publicly make it (the love) known to others, seeking the intervention of elders! There is no other alter- native strength of support for him! except riding on a Palmyra-horse!*

(Note: * riding in a Palmyra–horse is a symbolic demonstration of a man who has fallen in love with a woman of his choice, when the woman and man are unable to meet each other. Riding a Palmyra-horse is termed as "riding a Madal;", where the hero is accompanied by his friends, who walk along the streets of the village, as if it is a joyous procession, to make the matter known to the elders of the village! So that the elders would request both parents of the couple to get the two youngsters married, sooner, in a family- function).

1132. nhO–naa uda–mbum uyi–rum madal–(y)ae–Rum
nhaa–Ninai nhee–kki nhi–Ruth–thu.

He starts thinking: I have decided to set my sense of shame at a distance away from me, and ride on the Palmyra-horse, in order to save myself from the sufferings of my body and soul, as these sufferings have been caused by the separation of my woman-in-love! (I must find a solution for it!).

1133. nhaa–Nodu, nhal(l)–aaNmai paNdu–udai–yaen indRu –udai–yaen
kaa–mutRaar (y)ae–Rum madal.

He determines: During the past, I used to care for the norms meant for a man's honour, namely, shyness and controlling power on manliness with pride. Today is different! I am deciding to ride on a Palmyra-horse, meant for those unsuccessful men who are in love!

1134. kaa–maa–k– kadum–punal ui–kku–mae, nhaa–Nodu
nhal(l)–aaNmai (y)ennum puNai.

He wonders: The torrential flood of passion for love will wash away the helpless boats called shyness and manly pride!

1135. thodalai–k– kuRu–nh–thodi tha–nh–thaaL, madal–odu
maalai uzha–kkum thuyar.

He feels: My woman who wears attractive girdle-ornament around her slender waist, and glittering bangles around her beautiful fore-arms has given me two gifts, namely, i) painful eve- nings craving for happiness, and ii) the painful experience of riding on a Palmyra-horse!

1136. madal–oor–thal yaa–math–thum uLLu–vaen, mandRa,
padal–ollaa pae–thai–kku–(y)en kaN.

He feels: My eyes are refusing to sleep; as my mind is always thinking about that young woman whom I love: I am left with no other option at midnight, except to be pondering over myself, riding a Palmyra-horse! (Why not? I am not ashamed!).

1137. kadal–anna, kaamam uzha–nh–thum, madal–yae–Raa–p–
pe–NN–in peru–nh–thakka–thu il.

She feels: A woman has got the unparalleled honour to her credit in self- control of personal human desire, as she cannot come forward to tell the world about her abundant desire (as huge as the size of a sea) for love-making, by drawing the attention of the public by exercises such as riding a Palmyra-horse (which is open for a man only)!,

(Note: The challenge for a woman is to withstand her natural desires and keep them under control. Please see kurals 54 and 57. Kural 54 describes the pride of chastity. Kural 57 describes that it is the great burden of protecting one's own feminine-chastity with self control and determination. The god-given feminine shyness comes to the rescue, offering protection. The poet makes a diplomatic and gentle reference about feminine shyness in kural 1011, while insisting on "Shyness against Evil Acts". That much caution and vigil is to be exercised by an individual person to 'remain-good', in these two challenges! Both topics are relevant to self-control and self-care!! Feminine shyness is for protecting honour and dignity of the self. Similarly, shyness against evil acts, applicable to both genders, is meant for the imbibing a virtuous trait/character/ righteous ness/ethical strength/moral excellence! (Virtue=Virtus (Latin).

1138. nhi–Rai–ariyar, man–aLiyar, (y)ennaa–thu, kaamam
maRai–iRa–nh–thu, mandRu padum.

The maid feels: A woman may be a virtuous person with all dignities, worthy of being shown respect and sympathy. But, if she develops a love- making desire, it will be exposed mercilessly to the outside world! It will not be a secret any more!

(Note: The poet feels that a woman has to be more careful in suppressing her feelings and in exercising self-control, as he believes that the people around her will not be in a position to properly understand her feelings in the proper light!).

1139. aRi–ki–laar (y)ellaar–um (y)en–dRae, (y)en kaamam
maRukin, maRu–kum, maruNdu.

She feels:My love-affair, with a man whom I love, thinks that it is not known to anybody other than the two of us! But, it (the news of my love- affair) is wandering all around the streets of this village! (It is made to be known to everyone in the village, by my own looks, body-language,and the way I move around and express myself, while talking to others!).

1140. yaa–ng–kaNNiR, kaaNa nhaku–ba, aRiv(u)–illaar
yaam–patta, thaam–padaa vaaRu

He and She (together) feel: "Many persons might not have undergone through the agony behind love-making! Such persons would laugh at us, when they happen to see us (without showing sympathy"!

CHAPTER-115

CAUTIONING ABOUT RUMOURS

1141. alar–(y)ezha, aa–ruyir nhiR–kum, atha–nai–p–
palar aRi–yaar paak–ki–yath– thaal

She feels; I feel confident that my marriage with my man whom I love will become a reality, due to the rumour graciously spread by the people of this village. That is why I am alive! Fortu nately, many people do not know that!s

1142. malar –anna kaNNaaL arumai aRi–yaa–thu
alar–(y)emakku, yee–nh–thathu–iv voor.

He regrets: Instead of appreciating the worthiness of this beautiful girl with lotus-flower-like eyes, the rumour-mongers of this village spread gossips, which have indirectly helped me to get her, as my own! (I have to thank them, instead of being angry with them"!).

1143. uRaa–athO oor–aRi–nh– tha kav–vai? atha–nai–p–
peRaa–athu petR(u)–anna nhee–rth–thu.

He thinks: Would it not be possible for the gossiping group of the village to spread the rumour in a clamorous way, regarding my love with my woman-in-love (the matter being known to them already)? Only then, my marriage which would otherwise would not become feasible, would surely become a reality! (The rumours help the couple!)

1144. kavvai–yaal kav–vithu kaamam; athu indRael
tha–v–vennum than–mai izha–nh–thu.

He thinks: Love between a man and woman gets pro moted through gossips and rumours, (like the seed thrown into the soil, getting sprouted as a plant), as otherwise the love will get withered away!

1145. kaLith-thoRum kaL-(L)uNdal vae-tta-tRaal, kaamam veLi-p-padu- nh thORum, inithu.

He feels: The sense of craving for happiness increases in a person (who is accustomed to drinking) as the liquor starts reach ing his throat! Similarly, in a lover's mind, happiness increases when gossip and rumour start spreading about the love-affair between him and his woman-in-love!

1146. kaN–dathu, mannum, oru–nhaaL alar–mannum thing–kaLai–p– paambu–koN–d(u)– atRu.

He wonders: "I met my woman-in-love only once! But I am surprised to know that the rumours about the event has spread all around us, like the story behind the lunar-eclipse, wherein the snake swallows the moon in full"!

1147. ooravar kavvai yeru–(v)aaka, annai–sol nheer–aaka, nhee–Lum in(h)– nhOy.

She contemplates: When a man falls in love with a woman, the gossip and rumours about the lovers serve as the manuring (fertiliz ing) agent, and the mother's words of concern (and care) serve as watering, for the budding plant of love to grow!

1148. nhe–y–yaal yeri–nhuthu–p–paem (y)endR(u)–atRaal, kavvai–yaal kaamam nhu–thup–paem yenal.

He realizes: Extinguishing of the burning-fire by pouring ghee (derivative of butter) will not be possible to put down (quench) the fire! Similarly, the process of love-making (uniting the two hearts of a man and a woman) cannot be stopped by listening to gossips and rumours!

1149. alar–nhaaNa ol–vathO, anj–chal–Ombu (y)endRaar palar–nhaaNa, nhee–th–tha-k- kadai

She feels: When I parted with my man-in-love, he asked me not to worry about parting; He made that promise in the presence of many others to their dismay! I believe that assurance. Then, why should I worry about the gossips and rumours? Why should he worr y about it? (She seeks the help of her maid to send a message to him, to expedite his arrival).

1150. thaam vae–Ndin, nha–lkuvar kaathalar; yaam–vaeNdum
kavvai, ye–dukkum–iv voor

She speaks to her man-in-love: We both planned to get married, as man and woman. That is why they are spreading rumours about our love-affair, in order to help us! They will be supporting us if we decide to get married!

(Note: Some interpreters have stated that it could be an elopement)

CHAPTER-116

ENDURING PAINS OF PARTING

1151. sel–laa–mai uN–dael (y)enakku, urai; matRu–nhin
val–vara–vu, vaazh–vaar–k-ku, urai.

She speaks to her husband going abroad: "Tell me anything whatever you want to say to me, if you are not going to part with me for ever! If you are going to tell me about your date of return after your prolonged stay abroad, I may not have the patience to stay alive until then, bearing the pains of parting! You may have to talk to any other 'person' who would stay alive until you would return home! Not to me!!"

1152. in–kaN udaith–thavar paarval; piri–vu anj–chum
pun–kaN udaith–thaal puNarvu.

She feels: In those days, it was a fulfilling experience for me to have a look at him and communicate through my eyes; but, now I am deeply worried about the horrors of parting with each other, even while I am able to enjoy embracing him!

1153. ari–tharO thae–tRam aRivu–udai–yaar kaNNum
pirivu–Or idath–thu–uNmai yaan.

She stands confused: My husband is a knowledgeable person who knows the painful experiences I may have to go through in his absence! Knowing all that, if he wants to part with me (for an assignment in a far-away place), I do not know as to how could I take his words of promise to be true,the promise to return soon? Will there be any disappointment? How much of an affection truly he has got for me?(She expresses her fear and doubts to her maid, who advised her to bear the burden of parting, with patience and hope! As there is no other way!).

1154. aLith–thu–anj–chal (y)endRu–avar nhee–p–pin theLi–th–tha–sol
thae–Ri–yaar–k– ku uNdO thavaRu?

Wife says after sending her husband abroad: “He poured affection to me and promised that he would not leave me; but he has departed. Is there anything wrong with me in believing his words of promise sprayed on to me? Yes; It is my fault. I should not have believed him at all”!

1155. Ombin amai–nh–thaar piri–vu–Ombal; matRa–var
nhee–ng kin ari–thaal puNarvu.

She cries: My husband is the only person who can protect my life; If he departs from me, I may not survive. Realizing his duty, he has to avoid the separation. If parting happens, unavoidably, I may not be able to see him and embrace him at all! (When she told this to her maid, she replied to the heroine that the parents and other elders in the family would impress upon the young man to return soon to rejoin the family!).

1156. piri–vu–uraik–kum van–kaNNar aa–yin, ari–thu, avar
nhal–kuvar (y)en–num nhasai.

She feels: If my husband is cruel enough to say that he would return very soon to rejoin me, after his trip abroad, then I would conclude that he may not show me affection even after his coming back!(When she told this to her maid, she suggested that her parents must talk to the young man all about the plan in detail, so that the heroine would develop more courage to bear the ordeal!).

1157. thuRaivan thuRa–nh–tha–mai thootRaa kol, mun–kai
iRai–iRavaa nhi–ndRa vaLai.

She speaks: If my husband goes away from me to a far off land, I would lose weight, and my bangles would slide down, all away from my forearms, making my agony known to the outside world, and leave it to their ridicule!

(When she told this to her maid, she looked at her face sharply. After giving a friendly smile, the maid started advising the heroine, that she should learn one thing in particular: i) that the opinion of others must not be given any importance whatsoever, by a young couple, that too, in the early part of their life! and ii) that ‘Life’ itself is an experiment,wherein, success has to be worked out with patience and courage, combined with hardwork and perseverance! She, further said, it is the woman who has to raise the family, by having the patience, and helping the husband in all his endeavours, thereby, building up a prosperous future for the children! A man and woman, together have got a role to play in building up an ideal fam ily. Many such families make a decent society. Many such good societies will make a strong nation. That is how, I imagine that the young generation must plan building up their future, in the beaten- track of our forefathers, with love and kindness to all, and malice towards none! Every good family is a miniature unit of the global society. So,young lady, be bold! Courage and Confidence are the first capitals in human life! Good Luck!).

1158. in-naathu inan-il oor vaazh-thal; atha-ni-num
innaa–thu, ini–yaar–p– piri–vu.

She feels the pain: It will be a painful experience for me to live in a place where there are no kith and kin (relatives) who will offer me moral support! More painful, it will be, for me to live in a place, in the absence of my beloved husband!

1159. thodin–chudin allathu kaama–nhOy– pOla,
vidin–sudal aa–tRu–mO thee?

She wonders: Fire has a property that it will hurt a person who touches it! But love-sickness hurts when the man and his woman are located in far off places, being separated. Why should the fire cause harm to distant objects, unlike nature?! (please see Kural 1104).

1160. arithu–aatRi, allal–nhOy nheekki–p– pirivu–aatRi–p–
pin–iru–nh–thu, vaazh–vaar palar.

She compares: There are many women in this world who give consent to their husbands who go away from them on assignment (for earning income), enduring the pains of parting, and yet surviving! (Why don't I have that strength, patience and endurance?).

(Note: Many men go to far off places in connection with their business. A wife does not accompany him. She has to live with ei ther her parents,or with the parents of her husband. In a joint-family system, a wife, as a woman, is exposed to several hardships. The poet is describing the sentiments of one such a young woman. Please read kural 1205.).

CHAPTER-117

LOSING HEALTH ON PARTING

1161. maRai–p–paen–man yaan, i–h–thO nhO–y–ai; iRai–ppa–var–k–ku,
ootRu –nheer pOla mikum.

She speaks out: "I would like to suppress my love-sickness and hide it from others! But I find that it is flowing out like the water coming out of an aquifer-spring to the benefit of those interested in baling out (drawing out) water and spraying it to the sky!! (helping those who wish to spread the rumour"!).

1162. karath–thalum aa–tR–aen, in(h)– nhO–yai, nhOy sei–thaar–k-ku
uraith–thalum nhaa–Nu–th tharum.

She speaks: I am not able to hide the love-sickness which I have acquired due to my parting with my man-in-love; I feel shy to even inform him about it, although I feel that he must take up the responsibility of causing it!

(She tells her maid, who replies that the feelings of the wife must be communicated to the husband, so that he is aware of it! Nothing should be hidden from a husband. He should be told about all problems for which he is responsible, so that he would take steps to remove the causes for such problems. Shyness is bad in this respect. Shyness between a husband and wife must not hinder the intimacy between the two of them!).(Note: The maid seems to be a knowledgeable person!).

1163. kaa–mam–um, nhaa–Num, uyir–kaa–vaa–th thoong–kum, yen
nhO–naa udambin akath–thu.

She speaks: Not being able to withstand the pains of parting from my man-in-love, I feel that my slender body is carrying my very soul as a shoulder-pole of "kaavadi" to which my unbound desire for his nearness is attached at one-end, and my inborn shyness is attached to the other-end! The burden of pain due to the separation of my man-in-love is too much to bear, for me!! (She tells the maid who is trying to console her).

(Note: "*Kaavadi*", also spelt as "*kavadi*", is a shoulder-pole to which gift-materials for the family-god are attached at both ends, to be carried by the pious person, from home to the shrine of the the family-god, for earning a favour of personal choice!). Here, the prayer is that her man-in-love must soon return to his home from abroad to rejoin her!

1164. kaa–ma–k– kadal, mannum, uNdae; athu, nhee–nh–thum
(y)ae–ma–p puNai, mannum, il.

She speaks: Love-sickness is pervading in me like a vast sea. I do not have a raft (boat, catamaran) using which I can cross the sea! (She tells the maid, pleading that the message must reach her man-in-love).

1165. thu–ppin yevan –aavar, man–kol, thuyar–vara–vu
nha–t–pin–uL aa–tRu– pavar.

She speaks: When I am showing affection and friendship with him, my man-in-love causes miseries/pains to me, by his prolonged absence from me! I have a need to find out as to how he would behave in future? Will he be a reliable person at all? I am wondering as to how he would behave, in case of developing suspicion about my unconditional love! What will happen, if he develops some hatred or inimical attitude towards me?

(She shares the doubt with her maid. The maid, as a friend and self-assumed guardian of the girl, feels the pain involved in the statements of the heroine about her husband. She believes that 'the pleasure of showing love must be mutual, and reciprocal.' Once the wife develops a sense of insecurity, and when it reaches a third- party (including the maid), the issue gets complicated. She advises the young woman to avoid suspicion that her husband would ever suspect her of infidelity, (or breach of loyalty, if the word needs to be understood that way!). The only thing is that any husband must make it a point, not to be tricked or misguided by any outsider, in matters prevailing between the husband and wife. The maid assured that the husband of her heroine did not belong to that category of husbands who would doubt the integrity of 'his own wife'! She advised the young woman not to indulge in such kind of thinking by doubting the care and love of her husband who is away from home, who will be undergoing the same kind of pains caused by love- sickness!!)

(Note: This couplet simulates a situation which prevailed between the doubting-Othello and the innocent Desdemona, in the Shakespearean-play: "Othello". Desdemona's statement is worth being recollected here: "His unkindness may defeat my life; But never taint my love"... said Desdemona....(Act IV, Scene 2). As a man falling a prey to the plot designed by an unscrupulous villain, Othello, the great warrior, got defeated in life, who finally lamented: "I kissed thee ere I killed thee - No way but this, Killing myself to die upon a kiss"...William Shakespeare, in Othello,Act 5, Sc.2).

(Note: This needs further research based on psychological fac tors!).

1166. inbam kadal–matRu–k– kaamam; a–h–thu, adum–kaal,
thun–bam atha–nin peri–thu.

She wonders: The blissful happiness in love-making is so large as the sea! Still greater will be the pain, if parting between the man and woman occurs (or if parting is necessitated)!(She is answering to the maid who was saying that happiness and suffering are common in love-life!).

1167. kaamak kadum punal nhee–nh–thi–k– karai–kaa–Naen;
yaa–math–thum yaa–nae, u–Lae–n

She says: I am experiencing a torrential flood of desires of craving for the blissful company of my man-in-love; I am unable to swim across the current to reach the shore (to find a solution)! There is no one to help me at midnight excepting myself!

(She is narrating her plight to her maid who remains helpless in giving a suitable reply. The maid gives only a meaningful nod. The heroine feels happy that she could at least share her thoughts of pain with her affectionate maid! The maid felt that it could offer a temporary relief in her heroine's mind!).

1168. mannuyir– (y)ellaam thuyi–tRi aLith–thu, iraa;
(y)en–alla–thu illai, thuNai.

She feels: This 'nighttime hours' deserves my sympa thies, as it has helped all other forms of life to sleep with comfort. But, it does not have any company except myself. I am all alone without my partner; so does the 'nighttime hours', being left alone! (Poetic imagination: 'nighttime hours' being treated as a person!).

1169. kodi–yaar kodumai–yin, thaam –kodiya in(h)–nhaaL
nhe–diya kazhi–yum iraa.

She speaks: More cruel is this longest night-time period, than the cruelty of the absence of my man-in-love who doesn't have any concern (sympathy) for me! (She describes her agony to her maid).

1170. uLLam–pO–ndRu uL–vazhi–ch– chel–kiR–pin veLLa–nheer
nheenh–thala, mannO, yen kaN.

She says out, thinking about her husband living abroad: 'My thoughts about him can travel very fast to reach the place where he has gone to! If at all, it is really made possible for me to travel fast like my thoughts, I need not swim across this flowing flood of tears pouring out from my eyes"!!

(Note: The speed of 'thought' strikes a scientific flavour of imagination! Speed of thought is conceptualized, in contrast to travel time required to reach the distant destination, by other modes of travel: The travel time required to reach the destination, irrespective of distance, adopting the 'speed of thought', is zero days, zero hours, zero minutes and zero seconds (instantaneous)! Such a travel-mode has not yet been invented, by the scientific world!).

CHAPTER-118

EAGERNESS TO SEE

(The heroine describes the agony experienced by her eyes which are craving for seeing her man-in-love, in person!)

1171. kaN–thaam,kalu–zh–vathu yevan–kolO? thaN–daa–nhOy
thaam–kaa–tta, yaam–kaN– dathu.

She wonders: "This love-sickness which I am experiencing now is the result of my seeing him on that day, when I saw him first! The same eyes which showed him to me at that time, are crying now to me, to show him to them"!!

1172. theri–nh–thu –uNaraa nhO–kkiya– uN–kaN, pari–nh–thu– uNa–raa–p–
pai–thal uzha–ppathu yevan?

She speaks: My beautiful painted eyes were anxiously looking at him (my man-in-love) when we met, for the first time, (sometime back), with happiness, and joy! They (my eyes) did not foresee the probability that there would be subsequent occasions of disappointment in not being able to see him again! My poor eyes feel the pain now, without feeling bad about their own fault? (Note: Perhaps, this is the description of her sufferings as expressed to her maid. It is a fun in the mono-drama! When she treats her eyes to be different from her own self!). ('uN-kaN': Kurals 1091; 1113; 1174; 1212; 1271).

1173. kathum–ena–th– thaam–nhOkki–th– thaa–mae kalu–zhum;
ithu, nha–kath– thakka–thu, udaith–thu.

She speaks: My innocent eyes were over-enthusiastic to see my man-in-love, when we had a chance to see each other, for the first time! Now, my eyes start crying (weeping) as they are un- able to see him. Is it not funny? (This is a reply given to her maid who requested her not to cry! The maid admires the poetic imagination of the heroine!).

1174. peyal–aatRaa nheer–ula–nh–tha uN–kaN uyal–aatRaa
uyvu–il–nhOy yen–kaN nhiRuth–thu.

She speaks: My beautiful painted eyes, after having introduced my man-in-love to me, have actually caused a major harm to me, in initiating an incurable disease of love-sickness in me!! My eyes have gone dry, as they have exhausted themselves in crying,and they cannot cry any more!(This is her reply to the maid who advised her to remain calm)..

1175. padal–aatRaa paithal uzha–k–kum kadal–aatRaa–k
– kaama–nhOy sei–tha–(y)en–kaN.

She speaks: Recently, my eyes have been responsible in introducing my man-in-love to me and causing love-sickness in huge magnitude which cannot be even borne (withstood) by a sea (in spite of it having a higher mass)! Now, my eyes are suffering due to sleeplessness (insomnia)! (She replies to her maid who requested her to control her emotions!).

1176. Oh!oh!, ini–thae, (y)emakku–in–nhOy sei–tha kaN
thaa–am, ithaR–pat– tathu!

She speaks: My foolish eyes were responsible for entrapping me in love-sickness by introducing my man-in-love to me, and made me suffer terribly, during the present times. They are undergoing the pains similar to me. I am delighted about it! They really deserve to suffer!(This is her reply to her maid who asked her to stop crying). (Note: Oh! oh!: Kural 1204).

1177. uzha–nh–thu, uzha–nh–thu, uL–nheer aRuka, vizhai–nh–thu,
izhai–nh–thu
vaeNdi– yavar–k–kaNda kaN!

She speaks: My attractive eyes which gazed (looked steadfastly) at him(my man-in-love), with a desirous willingness and enthusiasm to earn his love, sometime back, are now undergoing distress of sleeplessness, repeatedly. I am afraid that my eyes may even go dry, disabling them from crying!Any way, my eyes deserve that punishment! (She replied to her maid who told her that a relief from worries is nearing!).

1178. pae–Naa–thu pettaar, uLar–mannO, matRu–avar–k–\
kaa–Naa–thu, amai–vila, kaN.

She speaks: I have a feeling that my man-in-love seems to love me, using sweet words, and not by heart! This is bothering me! But the pity is that my eyes become restless; they want to see him! (She expresses a doubt, she is right now having in her mind. Her maid asked her to give him some more time, instead of coming to rash conclusions!).

1179. vaaraa–k–kaal thunj–chaa; varin–thunj–chaa; aa–yidai,
aa–ra–gna–r utRa–na kaN.

She speaks: My eyes are friendly to me! They do not sleep when my man- in-love does not visit me, as they are anxiously waiting for his arrival. Once he is with me, my eyes are always awake, fearing that he would depart soon! Thus, both-ways, they are being subjected to suffering only, but not rejoicing! (She replies to her maid who is trying to make her sleep!).

1180. maRai–peRal ooraar–k–ku arithu andRaal, yem–pOl,
aRai–paRai kaN–Naar– aka–th–thu.

She feels: As a beaten-drum makes noise and helps people hear the noise, my sorrow-stricken eyes enable (help) the people to read my worries from my eyes. My worries, related to love-sickness, are no more a secret!

(She answers her maid who asked her whether it is hard to sup press the worries, so that her sleeplessness is not revealed to oth ers!).

CHAPTER-119

WEAKNESS DUE TO PARTING

(This section deals with health symptoms of a woman being inflicted with love-sickness, whose symptoms can have a variety, such as malnutrition, colour change in skin, insomnia, mental depression, etc).

1181. nhaya–nh–tha–varkku nhal–kaamai nhae–r–nh–thae–n, pasa–nh– tha– (y)en
paN–bi–yaar–kku urai–kkO piRa?

She talks to herself: My husband wanted to go on an assignment to a far-off place, leaving me alone.At that time, I gave permission for it. To whom could I complain about the after-effects of this terrible separation? My skin colour is becoming pale. I have to bear with it!(She is talking to herself, regretting for her decision in permitting him to leave!).

1182. avar, tha–nh–thaar, (y)ennum thakai–yaal,ivar–thanh–thu, (y)en mae–ni–mae–l, oorum pasa–p–pu!

She is getting agitated: The fading of my skin (paleness) thinks that it is a gift from my man-in-love, and assumes its own- freedom to spread all over my body! I am helpless!

1183. saa–yalum, nhaa–Num, avar–koN–daar; kai–m–maaRa, nhO–yum, pasalai–yum, tha–nh–thu.

She speaks: My husband, while going out on an assignment in a far off place, has taken away my beauty and delicate modesty, and has given me, in turn, this distressing love-sickness and the fading-skin (sallow-skin, sickly complexion) attributable to love-sickness! (She tells her maid, who is listening to her, with sympathy, and admiration for her sense of humour!).

1184. uLLuvan man,yaan; urai–p–pathu, avar–thiRa–maal,
kaLLam piRa–vO pasa–p–pu?

She says (thinking about her husband who is away): "I have been all the time thinking about the good qualities of my partner-in- life!; and all the time praising his fame!! It is as good as myself feeling that 'he is always with me'! Why, then, the symptoms of love-sickness should occur to me? Is it deceptive or what?

1185. uvakkaaN, (y)em kaa–thalar sel–vaar; iva–k–kaaN,(y)en
mae–ni pasa–ppu, oor– vathu.

She wonders: My husband parted with me, for an assignment at a far off place, only a short while ago! How come, the symptom of love-sickness, such as fading of skin starts appearing, immediately after his departure?

1186. viLakku–atRam paar–kkum iruLae–pOl, koN–kan
muyakku–atRam- paar–k–kum, pasa–ppu.

She speaks: Darkness sets in when lights become dim (less bright). Similarly, the first symptom of love-sickness (fading-skin) starts showing up in my body immediately when the hold of my husband's embrace is slackened? It is too much of a symptom to appear! (She tells her husband, not to leave her alone, on any lame- excuse!).

1187. pulli–k kida–nh–thaen, pudai–peyar–nh–thaen; av–vaLa–vil,
aLLi–k–koL- vat–Rae, pasa–ppu.

She speaks: I was in bed, embracing my husband. When I rolled away from him, the symptom of fading-skin started showing up! (She tells her husband, who laughs, enjoying the joke!).

1188. 'pasa–nh–thaaL, ivaL'–(y)en–pathu al–laal,'ivaLai–th–
thuRa–nh–thaar avar'–(y)en–baar, il!

She speaks: Everybody blames me for developing symptom of fading-skin (paleness) in my body! They do not blame my husband for parting with me and leaving me alone! It is unfair to ignore (excuse) the cause, and blame the effect.

(She tells her maid who mocks at her for the 'discovery' of the concept of 'cause' and the 'effect'!).

1189. pasa–kka–man paat–taa–ng–ku,(y)en maeni, nha–ya–p–pith–thaar
nhal–nhilaiyar aavar (y)enin.

She feels: Let the symptoms of love-sickness intensify in my body, if it is going to enhance the welfare of my man-in-love who convinced me while seeking my permission for his departure on his assignment abroad! I will gladly endure the ordeal, if my sufferings are going to offer prosperity for him; because, I live for him! Let him become a person of stable footing, status-wise!!

(Note: It is a good example for a dramatic irony! The heroine challenges his wisdom in prolonging the stay outside of his home-town!).

1190. pasa–ppu–(y)ena–p– paer–peRu–thal nha–ndRae; nhayap–pith–thaar
nhal–kaamai thoo–tRaar, (y)enin.

She feels: I do not worry about my sufferings from the symptoms of love- sickness. I will be happy, if others do not blame my man-in-love, saying that he does not have mercy towards me, while seeking my permission to be away from me for his assign ment abroad! (She tells her maid who admires the wisdom behind the statement).

CHAPTER-120

FEELING THE LONELINESS

(This is a section wherein the heroine assumes that her affectiontowards him is more than his affection available to her from him).

1191. thaam–veezh–vaar tham–veezha–p– pet–Ravar pet–Raarae kaama–th–thu–k– kaazh–il kani.

The maid speaks: If a woman falls in love with a man who falls in love with her, they will be a very successful couple, indeed, as they will enjoy their life blissfully even during old age, without a feeling of getting old! (like a fruit which does not become over-ripe ever!)

(Alternate interpretation: If a woman falls in love with a man who loves her, in turn, and if they get married, such a couple will enjoy their life very happily, as if they have got a precious seedless fruit!).

(Note: The concept of seedless fruit (in the sense in which it is understood in the present context) needs further research, with its relevance 2000 years ago! The poet could have referred to fleshy- fruits such as Mango-fruit, Papaya-fruit, Plantain-fruit,which are comfortable, in the mouth, while munching!).

1192. vaazh–vaar–kku vaa–nam paya–nh–thatRaal, veezh–vaar–kku veezhvaar aLi–kkum aLi.

The maid says: To all those who live in this world, the sky gives a benevolence of the rains. Similarly, love and kindness are being shared mutually between the pair (man and woman) who have fallen in love! Showering affection on each other!!

The maid speaks (another version): A man and woman, as lovers, have to meet and share their kindness mutually, as often as possible! It is like the timely rains made available by Nature, to support all forms of life living in the world!).

1193. veezhu–nhar veezha–p– padu–vaar–k-ku amai–yu–mae
"vaazhu–nham', (y)ennum serukku.

The maid speaks: If a woman loves a man who loves her, such a couple, if married, will have the pride of leading an ideal life, with a sense of togetherness in body and soul! That is a pride and privilege for them!

1194. veezha–p– padu–vaar kezhee–yi–yilar, thaam–veezh–vaar
veezha–p– padaa–ar, (y)enin.

The maid speaks: A man who is respected (esteemed) by all persons around him, except his wife, will be missing the essence of his life; A woman respected (esteemed) by all persons around her, except her hus band, will be missing the essence of her life! (Note: It is a statement applicable to both genders!).

1195. nhaam–kaathal koN–daar nha–makku–(y)evan sei–ba–vO
thaam kaathal koL–Laa–k– kadai?

She speaks: If I show affection and love towards a man, I will be happy, only if he shows the same measure of affection and love towards me. If he does not reciprocate, there will be no benefit from him to me! Nor any benefit from me to him! (We will become typical strangers, that way!).

(She tells this to her maid who advises her to exercise caution while selecting a partner for her life!).

1196. oru–thalaai–yaan innaa–thu kaamam–kaap– pOla
iru–thalai– yaa–num, ini–thu.

He speaks: Love towards each other will bring happiness to the couple. One-sided love will bring misery in life. It is said that the weight placed on one side of the shoulder-pole must be equal to the weight placed on the other side of the shoulder-pole, so that it will be in balance! Mutual affection will ensure happiness in married-life!

(The hero tells his friend who agrees with him that it must be a principle to be followed by any young man or woman while selecting a life-partner for himself/herself!).

1197. paru–varalum pai–thalum kaaNaan–kol, kaaman
oruvar–kaN nhi–ndRu–ozhuku vaan?

She speaks: Cupid, also called the god of love, must exert the influence equally on me and my man-in-love! If he (Cupid) attacks me more, I am subjected to love-sickness, excessively thereby, suffering from health symptoms, as my man-in-love is far away from me! This is not at all fair!

(She narrates her sufferings to her maid who is unable to pacify her! The maid spreads her hands saying that she is not aware of the concept of Cupid!).

(Note: In classical mythology, Cupid is the God of Desire, Erotic Love, Attraction and Affection! He is portrayed as the son of Venus (the goddess of Love) and Mars (the god of war), as cited in Latin literature. The symbol is Bow and Arrow! The Greek counterpart is Eros! (Ref:https:// en.m.wikipedia.org>wiki>Cupid). The Indian mythology identifies *Kamadeva* (male-god), and his life-partner is *Rati*(female). The weapon of *Kamadeva* is also Bow and Arrow. There seems to be a similarity between Latin Literature and Sanskrit Literature, in this relevance).Ref: https:// en.n.wikipedia.org>wiki>Kamadeva).

1198. veezh–vaarin in–sol peRaa–athu ulakath–thu
vaazh–vaarin van–kaNaar, il.

She speaks:There cannot b e any other woman in the world, so hard-hearted and insensitive except the one woman who is capable of surviving without even receiving kind words or letters or any sort of communication from her husband who is living far away from her, making her to suffer in pains caused by love-sickness!

(She laments, narrating her own plight, to her maid, who finds it difficult to console her! The heroine abuses herself as a hard-hearted person, for her pathetic situation of not being able to receive any communication from her husband who is residing far away from her.)

(Please see the Notes below kural 1205, for knowing the reasons of separation between husband and wife, during the husband's business-trips).

1199. nha–sai–i–yaar nhal–kaar (y)eni–num avar–maattu
isai–yum ini–ya, sevi–k–ku.

She feels: I will be willing to be satisfied to receive words of praise about him, always with happiness, although my dear husband (loved and chosen by me) may not be showing affection towards me nowadays! (As he is far away from me, I have to be sympathetic towards him).

1200. uRaa–ar–kku uRu–nhOy urai–p–paai! kada–lai–ch
- cheraa–a–ai!! vaazhiya nhenj–chu!!!.

She clarifies: "Long live, my dear conscience! You have to convey the mental agonies which I have been going through, to my man-in-love who has not responded to my love! Do not show your anger to the sea, as it is preoccupied with its own noises of waves!! Perhaps his situation is like the noisy sea! He could have been preoccupied with other thoughts! Don't be angry with him. Keep on trying, to tell him about my love, please"!!

(Note: Other interpreters have concluded as if the woman asks her conscience to stop the effort of communicating her longing-desires of love to the non-responsive lover!).(Please see Appendix-1).

CHAPTER-121

RESTLESS LONGINGS

(This section describes the memory of past events being remem bered).

1201. uLL–inum thee–raa–p– peru–makizh sei–tha–laal
kaL–Linum kaamam, ini–thu.

He speaks: When I am far away from my wife, I recollect with pleasure the grand old days when the two of us enjoyed together the sweet experiences with unlimited affection and love! When I recollect the old memories, it gives me a more fulfilling (rapturous) delight than getting intoxicated with liquor! Liquor has to be consumed to have a sense of delight. But the very thought of sweet-old memories gives a matchless happiness! (When he tells this to his friend, he replies that the pain of separation between the husband and wife has to be endured with determination and will-power, in the interest of the family-unit! The friend advises that a mention of liquor itself is to be avoided, while comparing family-pleasures and emotional experiences!).

1202. (y)enaith–thu, ondRu ini–thae–kaaN kaamam–thaam; veezh–vaar
nhi–nai–ppa varu–vathu–ondRu, il.

She feels: Always, I am thinking of my husband who is far away from home. It brings me my old memories of sweet mo ments we had enjoyed, in those good old days! I am not even both ered about my present sufferings in the absence of my man-in-love! Every time I think about the old memories, it gives me limitless delight, without bounds! It keeps me cheerful, without any feeling of sufferings.

(Note: This couplet is applicable to the husband who remembers his wife all the time while being located far away from home! It is a reciprocation in the sufferings too!).

1203. nhinai–p– pavar pOndRu, nhinai–yaar–kol, thum–mal, sinai–p–pathu pOndRu, kedum.

She gets confused: I feel like sneezing; but it stops! May be, my husband who is far away from home, thinks about me? Why did then the sneezing stop? I know what it is! He stopped thinking about me! How sad! (Note: This couplet also is reversible! It is applicable to him exactly as it is applicable to her!),

1204. yaam–um uLae–m–kol, avar–nhenj–chath–thu?(y)em–nhenj–chath–thu
Oh!oh!! uLa–rae avar!

She feels: "He is always present in my heart, always! Am I there in his heart? I am yet to know"! (Note: Oh, oh = expression of wonder; meaning, is it so? could it be?... probably!)

1205. tham–nhenj–chath–thu,(y)emmai–k–kadi–koN–daar;nhaa–Naar–kol
(y)em –nhenj–chath–thu Ovaa varal?

She speaks: He does not give a place in his heart for me! He is closing the entry tightly! But he does not feel shy to enter into my heart and stay therein! Very frequently, he does that! He doesn't have any shame in doing that!

(She narrates this to her maid, elaborating on the details of how her man- in-love behaves! She seems to seek an advice from the maid! The maid tells the heroine; "As a man,working in a far-off place, he will have his own duties to perform. During leisure hours, definitely, any husband will be remembering his wife! What else he could do in a far-off land, being separated from the family. It is the wife, therefore, who is to visualize this situation and console herself, instead of getting confused! Next time when he visits here, I am going to tell him that he has to take his wife along with him, to wherever he goes, ignoring the social-taboo which the superstitious society has imposed, banning the travel of women across the sea!). (Note: The customary (traditional) belief of the ancient people did not encourage women travelling with their husbands when the husbands go abroad, for the purpose of earning wealth. The poem from "Tholkaappiyam" appears in '*poRul.-*

athikaram. verse 980' - which reads as *"mun - nheer vazha - k - kam maka-doo - u ....vhO- dillai.."*

(Ref:: 'THOLKAAPPIYAM,, authored by Dr. S.V.Subramanian,, 1998, published by Manivasagar Pathippagam, Chennai, page. 364).

(This indicates a historical note, that women do not accompany their husbands when they go on business trips during which the husbands stay away from home for many years. The plight of women becomes miserable as well as that of men! This separation between a husband and a wife exerts a sociological impact, in the sense that the family-growth (the privilege of having children) is arrested (curtailed) during the period of their separation. The reason for men departing alone on outside assignments to far off places, leaving their wives at the custody of the elders of their families, is based on economical compulsions. Other reasons cited for not taking their wives along with them can be narrated as follows: i) fear about the safety of the family in the unknown land to wherever they go for earning wealth; ii) affordability of family maintenance in an unknown (foreign) land; and iii) religious faith prohibiting the travel of women from crossing the sea to reach a foreign land).

Research is needed to verify whether traders from foreign countries such as Egypt, Greece, Arabian countries, China, etc., brought their wives to Tamil Nadu, 2000 years ago, when they travelled to Tamil Nadu which had got established trade links with those countries, by land-route and sea route!

1206. matRu–yaan (y)en–uLae–n, mannO, ava–rodu–yaan
utRa–nhaaL, uLLa, uLae–n.

She speaks: Being parted with my husband who is far away from home, I am alive still! The old memories of my happy days when I enjoyed my blissful experiences with him come to my mind, and give me new energy to keep me alive! (She describes her thoughts to her maid who told her that the troubles of loneliness must be overcome by self-determination! At any cost!! Thinking about old-sweet memories will give a healing effect, the maid said).

1207. maRa–ppin (y)evan–aavan maR–kol? maRappu–aRi–yaen uLLinum uLLam sudum!

She feels: When I think about his going to a far off place, my heart burns. I quickly recollect the happy days I spent joyously with my beloved husband. Being unable to bear the pains of sepa- ration, I recollect my old sweet memories, to bring me back to life! If I ever forget to recollect these memories, I cannot imagine what would happen to me! Probably, I will go mad, burning my heart! (Ref: kural 1270)..

1208. (y)enai–th–thu nhi–nai–ppinum kaa–yaar, anai–th–thu, andRO kaa–thalar sei–yum siRappu!

She speaks: So many times I think about him with plea sure, in his absence. Whatsoever I think about him, he does not get angry about it! He does not think that it is a botheration to him. Is it not a special privilege he gives me in his absence? (She tells her maid that her husband tolerates her unpleasant/irrelevant words also, without getting angry! The maid gives a pleasant smile!)

1209. viLi–yum–(y)en in–nuyir 'vaeR(u)–allam', (y)enbaar, aLi–(y)inmai aa–tRa nhi–nai–nh–thu.

She speaks: My husband used to say that his soul and mine is one and the same! But, it appears to me that he does not show sympathy towards me! I doubt whether he has got any concern for me,at all? I am not able to control my emotions when I think all about it! I feel as if my life is slowly sagging! (She reveals her mental agony to her maid who asks her to have some more patience, and endurance in the heart!).

1210. vidaa–athu sen–dRaa–rai–k– kaNNi–naal kaaNa–p– padaa–athi– vaazhi mathi!

She speaks: "Long live, my dear moon! My man-in-love halfheartedly went away, parting with me, just now, although, he wanted to stay back with me longer! I wish to spot out as to where exactly, he is now! Do not disappear! Continue shining!!Please!!"

CHAPTER-122

REVEALING THE DREAMS

1211. kaathalar thoo–thodu va–nh–tha 'kana–vi–nukku'
yaathu–sei vaen,kol, viru–nh–thu?

She imagines: "A dream brought a message from my man-in- love! How do I host a dinner to that dream? When? Where? I am perplexed!"!

1212. kayal–uN–kaN yaan –ira–ppa–th– thunj–chin kala–nh–thaar–k-ku
uyal–uNmai saa–tRu–vaen man.

She feels: I requested my beloved painted eyes (which resemble the beautiful carp-fish) to sleep! If my eyes agree to sleep, I will have a dream. My dream will give me a chance to tell my husband (who is away from me) that I manage to keep myself alive, in spite of my sufferings, during his absence from me!

(Note: The carp-fish, Cyprinus carpio, (known as '*kayal-meen*' in Tamil), is well-known for its stylish elegance while swimming! (Note: In Tamil literature, poets take pleasure (fancy) in describing the eyes of a woman as '*kayal-vizhi*', meaning a woman having attractive eyes, resembling the carp fish whose gliding movement in the water is stylish!).

1213. nha–na–vi–naal nha–l–kaa– thavarai–k– kana–vinaal
kaa–Ndal–in uNdu,(y)en uyir!

She consoles herself: My husband is far away from home! I am able to see him only in my dream, and that privilege keeps me alive, although I am not able to see him in person! I will inform him that I am all safe here.

1214. kanavi–naal uNdaakum kaa–mam nha–na–vi–naal
nhal–kaarai nhaadi–th– thara–Rku!

She speaks: My husband is far away from home! My dream brings him to me! I am able to have physical interaction with him, deriving immense pleasure in my dream! Although, in reality, when I am awake, he does not come to me at all! I am getting a blissful pleasure only in my dreams! Does it mean that dreaming is an alter native provision for balancing the emotions?

(She tells her maid, as if she is happy.The maid gives a meaningful smile to encourage her cheerful feelings which can offer solace to the mind!)

1215. nhana–vi–naal kaNda–thoo–(v)um, aa–ng–kae, kanavum–thaan kaNda pozhu–thae, ini–thu!

She clarifies: In those days, when I was with my husband,we used to share our affection through physical contact, and enjoy the blissful happiness!The same happiness, I am able to derive from my satisfying-dreams, when I am able to see him in my dream! However, it is only a momentary happiness!

1216. nhanavu–yena ondR(u)–illai; aayin, kanavi–naal kaathalar nhee–ng–kalar, man.

She speaks: My husband lives at a location far away from me! I was having good fun with my husband in my dream, talking, joking, laughing, and feeling joyously cheerful! Suddenly, I woke up! I could not see my husband's handsome face; the scene ended abruptly! If I did not wake up, I could have continued to be with my husband; he would not have departed at all! It is greatly disappointing to me!(She tells her maid about this dream. The maid feels happy that the girl is able to console herself!).

1217. nhana–vinaal nhal–kaa–k– kodi–yaar, kana–vinaal (y)en–(y)emmai–p– peezhi–p– pathu?

She speaks: My husband is far away from home. He does not come to me in person to take care of me! Shall I call him a cruel person? But he appears in my dreams very often, to pacify me. But, a dream can give happiness only partially; it becomes a torture, when I wake up and feel the reality! Why should he come in my dream to torture me, whereas he does not decide to come in person? (When she tells this to her maid, the maid tries to convince her that dreaming brings solace to the mind, when the painful feelings of separation could torture the mind! It offers a psychological relief!).

1218. thunj–chum –kaal thOL–maelar aaki, vizhi–k–kum–kaal
nhenj–chath–thar aavar virai–nh–thu!

She imagines: My husband is living at a place far away from our home, leaving me alone! In my dream, he embraces me, resting on my shoulders! When I suddenly wake up, I look for him, anxiously, and find that he has migrated to my soul, speedily, and is hiding there!!(She tells this to her maid who feels that the girl needs a lot of counseling!).

1219. nhanavi–naal nhal–kaa–rai nhOvar, kanavi–naal
kaathalar–k– kaaNaa– thavar.

The maid says to the heroine: A woman-in-love will be angry with her man-in-love, on the complaint that he does not come in person to cheer her up, only if she could not see him and interact with him in her dreams! (This is applicable to the man-in-love also, just to withhold (suppress/ control) the emotions and anxieties; al though temporarily!).

1220. nhanavi–naal nham–nhee–th–thaar (y)enbar, kanavi–naal
kaaNaar–kol, iv–(v)oo– ravar?

She consoles herself: "In real life, the people of my village believe that my man-in-love has deserted me (abandoned me)! Don't they see that he comes to see me, always, in my dreams, every night"?

CHAPTER-123

CHEERLESS EVENINGS

1221. maa–lai–yO? allai, maNa–nh–thaar uyir–uNNum–
vaelai, nhee! vaazhi pozhu–thu!!

She speaks: "Long live, my dear evening-hours! For bringing the twilight to me! As a young woman, living far away from my husband's place, I see you as a sharp weapon which can give me a torture (life-killing experience), in the absence of my beloved man! Yet, I convey my Best Wishes to you"!

1222. pun–kaNNai vaazhi, maruL–maa–lai, (y)em–kaeL–pOl,
van–kaNNa– thO, nhin–thuNai?

She speaks: (The heroine personifies (visualizes) the 'evening-hours' as another human person (female) who has been separated from her life's partner,and asks kindly): "Oh, my dear 'evening-hours'! My greetings! Are you also sobbing, in bewilderment, like me, thinking about your lover for deserting you mercilessly, just like 'my-man' did? in keeping himself in a far off place, without thinking about me? especially during these pleasant hours?"

1223. pani–arumbi–p– paithal–koL maa–lai, thuni–arumbi–th–
thunbam vaLara varum!

She feels: The evening hours, fast approaches, marked by a misty dew-fall, causing unpleasant chillness, to slowly aggravate my symptoms of love-sickness, initiating a bit of hatred for my plight, thus increasing my distress. (The evening-hours used to be pleasant only in the company of my man-in-love; not when I am away from him!).

1224. kaathalar il–vazhi maa–lai,kolai–k–kaLath–thu,
(y)ae–thilar pOla varum!

She feels: When my man-in-love is far away from me, and when I am all alone, the evening- hours will approach me like a merciless stranger, with a plan to kill (torture) me, at the very site of slaughtering (the place of execution, the field of massacre)!

1225. kaa–lai–kku –ch– chey–tha, nha–ndRu, yen–kol? yevan–kol,yaan
maalai–kku–ch – chey–tha pakai?

She wonders: I have not done anything beneficial to the 'morning-hours'; and I have not done anything harmful to the 'evening-hours', to make a difference, in their response to me! (Still, the 'evening-hours' are hostile (unfriendly) to me. It is all due to the absence of my man-in-love who lives at a distant location, far away from me! I used to appreciate the 'evening-hours', (welcoming it, in anticipation), only when my husband was available near me!).

1226. maa–lai–nhOy sei–thal maNa–nh–thaar aka–laa–tha
kaa–lai aRi–nh–tha–thu il–ae–n.

She feels: I never experienced unhappy moments during the 'evening-hours', to make a difference,in my happiness, during the days when my husband did not part with me for taking up an assignment in a far-off place! Now, in his absence, I feel that the'evening-hours' are capable of bringing a sickening experience to me!

1227. kaa–lai arumbi–p– pakal–(y)ellaam pOthu–aaki,
maa–lai mala–rum –in(h)–nhOy!

She feels: "This love-sickness starts sprouting in the early- morning-twilight hours, before dawn, gets growing during the day- time hours, and blossoms as a flower in the evening-twilight hours, exhibiting its torturous-symptoms in me, in full-bloom. What a wonder to see and admire! But, it gives me pain. It is an illness which I have to endure, all by myself"! (Note: Civil Twilight from 6:9 - 6:30 (Morning); 18:15 - 18:36 (Evening).

1228. azhal–pOlum maa–lai–k-ku–th– thoo–thu–aaki,
a a y a n kuzhal–pO–lum, ko–l-lum padai!

She tal ks to her se lf: A shepherd's flute in the late afternoon sounds like an alarm, announcing the arrival of evening-hours which, to me, sounds like the arrival of a killing-army! But it sounds like a pleasant music to others! (All because of the fact that I am living far away from my husband! The pleasant music of flute makes me feel more about his absence, and end up experiencing more harmful effects of love-sickness!).

1229. pathi – maruNdu, paithal uzhakkum, mathi–maruNdu
maalai padar–tharum pO–zh–thu!

The maid gets worried: When a woman feels upset about the absence of her husband, excessively straining her mind, and feels the pain during evening-hours to the extent of developing mental depression, the entire village gets worried, and comes forward to advise her to bear it in silence! (Note: The entire village shares the distress!).

1230. poruL–maa–lai– yaa–La–rai uLLi, maruL–maalai
maa–yum, (y)en maa–yaa uyir!

She deplores: My husband went away from me on a business trip to earn wealth. I have been bearing the burden of loneliness with patience! My life which I have preserved carefully all these long years, is perhaps going to be lost, during this bewildering night, at the very thought of him who is more particular about earning his wealth than caring about me!

(Please see the Notes below kural 1205, for knowing the reasons of separation between husband and wife, during the husband's business-trips. The term *'maa-yaa-uyir'* means her frustration that 'her life refuses to face death', on the delicate hope that he would return home very soon, all safe! Please read kural 1270!).

CHAPTER-124

HEALTH ISSUES

1231. siRu–mai nha–maakku–ozhiya–ch– chaeN–sen–dRaar, uLLi, nha–Ru–malar nhaa–Nina kaN.

Heroine's maid (well-wisher) speaks: "Your husband has gone to a far-off place for earning wealth; leaving you alone to suffer from the pains of parting! You shed tears, all the time, thinking about him. Your eyes have become dry, losing their usual lustre (glow)! Your attractive eyes, now feel shy, even to look at the fresh flowers, in defeat, in the competition for freshness and brightness! How pathetic, oh! my dear!! I feel upset about it.(The maid impressed upon the heroine to remain bold and patient until the right time emerges!).

1232. nhaya– nh–thavar nhal–kaamai sollu–va pOlum,
pasa–nh–thu pani–vaarum kaN.

She believes: Symptoms of love-sickness,indicated by my pale complexion and watery eyes will only betray the lack of love from my beloved lover! I believe so!

(She shares her worries with her maid, who corrects her, saying, that he will be equally worried, and therefore, the situation must be endured by both partners in life!).

1233. thaNa–nh–thamai saala aRi–vippa pOlum,
maNa–nh–tha –nhaaL vee–ng–kiya thOL.

The maid says: My dear young lady!Your shoulders bulged(swelled, putting weight) out of happiness and emotional contentment, immediately after your marriage! Now that your husband has gone to afar off place, you have become weak, and the shoulders have become very thin! Is it to announce to the outside world that your husband is away from you?

(The heroine replies that the maid must console her, instead of inducing the heroine to develop self-pity! The maid feels happy about the correction, and praises the intelligence of the heroine!).

1234. paNai–nhee–ng–ki–p– pai–nh–thodi sOrum, thuNai–nhee–ng–ki–th–
thol–kavin vaa–diya thOL

The maid says: My dear young lady, Do you feel the absence of your husband very much? After your husband's departure, you have lost weight, so much, that your beautiful shoulders have lost the natural elegance, and your artistically-made, decorative bangles are sliding down from your tender forearms! (I am really worried! Take care!!). (The heroine feels happy about the concern expressed by the maid, who, at times, pours out a motherly advice along with an enduring affection!).

1235. kodi–yaar kodu–mai urai–kkum thodi–yodu
thol–kavin vaa–diya thOL.

The maid says: I notice some symptoms of love-sickness in you: you are losing the natural beauty of your elegant shoulders; your attractive fore- arms have become thinner, making the ornamental (artistically-made) bangles slide away from your attractive forearms! For all these outcomes, your husband must be blamed, calling him a cruel person!

(The maid adds: My dear lady, do not get upset for my blaming him! I know that you will never blame him, or nor let him down when others blame him!! The heroine smiled, feeling happy about the compliments of the maid).

1236. thodi–yodu thOL–nhe–kizha, nhO–val avarai–k–
'kodi–yar' (y)ena–k–kooRal nho–nh–thu.

She deplores: Looking at me with concern, people say that I have lost weight, my shoulders have thinned down, and my bangles are sliding down from my forearms which have become very thin, losing weight! They say that my husband could be a cruel man! I feel bad!

(It is true that he is far away from home on an assignment! He is not at fault. I crave for his company! The fault is with me too!).

1237. paadu peRu–thi–yO nhenj–chae! kodi–yaar–k–ku, (y)en
vaa–du– thOL poosal, urai–th–thu?

She speaks to her heart: My dear heart! Why can't you take the credit by narrating my sufferings to my merciless husband about my hardships and distress which I am undergoing in his absence, highlighting the thinning down of my glamorous shoulders, and the fading elegant beauty which he used to admire!

1238. muya–ng–kiya kai–kaLai, ookka–p– pasa–nh–tha–thu
pai–nh–thodi–p– pae–thai nhu–thal

The husband feels: When I used to loosen my air-tight grip during the blissful embrace, she used to feel unhappy; as if her forearms had become thinner to make the ornamental bangles slide away from her forearms, and as if, her bright forehead suddenly becomes pale! Now that I am far away from her, I do not know how miserably she will fight out the torturous love-sickness? I miss enjoying her innocence! I miss her beauty of forearms decorated with ornamental bangles of artistic designs!.

(While he pities for the helpless situation of his wife, he himself is undergoing the pains of separation! They are a resourceful couple, separated due to economic compulsions!)

1239. muya–kku–idai–th– thaN–vaLi pOzha–p– pasappu–utRa
pae–thai peru–mazhai–k– kaN!

The husband gets worried: When I was holding her tight with my strong arms during the embrace, and when I loosened the grip, she could not tolerate a cool breeze passing through the gap between the two of us, and she felt bad, as if I am parting with her! Her long cool eyes started fading, as if in love-sickness, in quite a contrast to her lovely freshness, glowing in the eyes!! (The husband is contemplating on the present scenario of his wife's pitiable condition! Shall we call it self-pity? If so, nobody can help. He has to go home: Refer kural 1270).

1240. kaN–Nin pasappO? paru–varal (y)ei–thindRae,
oN–Nuthal se–i–tha–thu kaNdu.

The maid speaks: Oh, my dear young lady! You are always thinking about your husband who is far away from your home! Your love-sickness has caused a sallow complexion on your beautifully- bright forehead! In sympathy for it, your eyes have started fading in freshness! I am deeply worried! (Send word to him, she adds!).

CHAPTER-125

TALKING TO THE HEART

(This section describes the heroine communicating with her heart as to how her mind gets disturbed when she lives away from her husband who has gone out to a far off location for earning wealth)

1241. nhinai–th–thu, ondRu sol–laa–yO, nhenj–chae! (y)enai–th–thu–ondRum,
(y)ev–va–nhOy theer–k–kum maru–nh–thu?

She speaks: "Oh my dear heart! Think deeply to suggest a medicine to cure my incurable disease called love-sickness! This medicine that you suggest can be of any nature! (excepting perhaps a poison!)".

1242. kaathal avar–ilar, aaka– nhee nhO–vathu,
paethai–mai, vaazhi–(y)en nhenj–chu!

She speaks: Oh, my dear heart! The man whom you love is not caring for you! After having understood that signal, is it not foolish to think about him, or worry about it all the time?Any way, my best wishes to you! I bless you to live long happily!

1243. irunh–thu–uLLi (y)en, parithal nhenj–chae! pari–nh–th(u)–uLLal
pai–thal– nhOy, sei–thaar–kaN il!

She speaks: Oh, my dear heart! My husband who lives away from me, in his place of work, who is responsible for causing this horrible love- sickness to me, does not seem to show any sym- pathetic gesture towards me, to solve the crisis. But, you seem to be thinking about him night and day! What is the use! How is it justi fied!! Tell me!!!

1244. kaN–Num koLa–ch–chaeRi nhenj–chae! ivai–(y)ennai–th–thin–num, avar–k–kaaNal utRu.

She speaks: Oh, my dear heart! When you plan to go to see my husband who lives in his place of work, located in a far off place, better take my eyes along with you! My eyes are torturing me, to show my-man to them as otherwise, they will swallow me, if you do not do that!!

1245. setRaar (y)ena– k–kai vidal uNdO, nhenj–chae–yaam, utRaal, uRaa–a– thavar?

She speaks: Oh, my dear heart! I cannot abandon (ignore/ discard/ discontinue/forsake) my love for him, although he refuses to show affection towards me! I am unable to conclude that he hates me!

(The maid who heard these words from the heroine feels that the heroine's apprehension about her husband's lack of love for her may not be real. Lack of communication could be the reason for her frustration!).

1246. kala–nh–thu, uNar–th–thum,kaa–thalar–k– kaNdaal, pula–nh–thu - uNaraa–i,
poi–k–kaa–y–vu, kaa–i–thi, (y)en nhenj–chu!

She speaks: Oh,my dear heart! When I see my husband, with a false anger, he pacifies me in a joyous embrace! Whenever you see him, you will not feel like developing a false anger at all! You will voluntarily surrender to him! What is wrong with you now? You seem to exhibit a really strong false anger now? Taking advantage of his usual response to your false anger, do you plan to have a blissful embrace with him?

(Her heart and mind are the same in so far as her desires are concerned, in the case of her husband!).

1247. kaa–mam vidu–ondRO, nhaa–N–vidu, nhal–nhenj–chae! yaanO, poRaen, iv–(v)– iraNdu!

She speaks: Oh, my dear heart! Please understand one thing very clearly! You can give prominence to your desire for a man, in which case shyness is lost! If you can give prominence to shyness, there is no room for a personal desire for a man! You have freedom to choose anyone of the two! As far as I am concerned, I cannot decide between the two, as they are exclusive of each other! The choice is tricky!!

(The heroine cries in frustration and despair, in the presence of her maid). (The Maid says that the puzzle can be solved, when a woman decides in favour of a life's companion on mutual confirmation to be united through marriage!).

1248. pari–nh–thu–avar nha–l–kaar–(y)endRu, (y)aeng–ki–p– piri–nh–thavar
pin–selvaa–i, pae–thai,(y)en nhenj–chu!

She speaks; Oh, my dear heart! My man-in-love has given me a hint that he may not show his kindness towards me, and has departed! But still, you want to go behind him, even while regretting that craving for his kindness is of no use!You are foolish!

(When she tells this to her maid, she replies:This may represent a changing (wavering)-mind! But, he will come back to you. He will be missing you, in his thoughts. There is still hope for the best results. Time is the cure!).

1249. uL–Lath–thaar, kaatha– lavar–aaka, uLLi, nhee
yaar–uzhai–ch– chaeRi,(y)en nhenj–chu?

She talks: "Oh my dear heart! My man-in-love resides in my mind (all the time near you, as a companion)! While this is so, whom do you want to see and enquire about his whereabouts?".

1250. thu–nnaa–th– thuRa–nh–thaa–rai, nhenj–chaththu udai–yae–maa
in–num, izhath–thum kavin!.

She speaks:To be thinking of a person who has not shown any intention of coming nearer me (befriending me), seems to be foolish. I guess that he has deserted me, ultimately leaving me alone!It will make me end up losing my prestige as well as my heal thand beauty, I think! (The maid responds: "This sounds like a temporary anger of the heroine! Let us wait for some more time! She knows that he has got more affection for her than what she has understood").

CHAPTER-126

FEMININE MODESTY

(This section describes the outspoken desires of the heroine)

1251. kaama–k– kaNi–ch–chi udai–kkum nhiRai – yennum
nhaaNu–th–thaazh vee–zh–th–tha katha–vu.

She contemplates: The intensive desire for sexual pleasure between a man and woman is capable of being used as an an axe to break the prestigious chastity of a woman, which is protected by the bolt called shyness! (The maid says that it is the responsibility of a woman to protect her chastity, the most prestigious virtue in a woman, with the help of natural shyness, which she has to maintain with a strong will-power! Please see kurals 54; 57).

1252. kaamam (y)ena, ondRO, kaN–NindRu,ye(n) nhenj–chath–thai
yaa–math–thum aa–Lum thozhil!

The maid speaks: The desire for sexual pleasure is a weakness in me, as I am a woman! It controls the mind even during midnight, without rational thinking! I remain blind to any sensible thinking! It is a cruel experience!

(The maid advises the heroine to control emotions and desires,in order to keep up the prestigious honour of the self! Mutual dedication to each other must be confirmed before confirming the love!).

1253. maRai–p–paen–man kaama–th–thai yaa–nO; kuRi–ppu–indRi–th–
thummal–pOl thO–ndRi vidum!

She feels: I am trying to suppress my sexual feelings within my mind under control. Involuntarily, it explodes like a sneeze, out of control. (The maid cautions that one's self- respect and honour need to be protected with stern determination and will-power, whether it is a man or woman! Please see kural 974).

1254. nhiRai–udai–yaen (y)en–paen, man, yaa–nO, (y)en kaa–mam
maRai–(y)iRa–nh–thu, mandRu padum.

She speaks: I was thinking that I am having my feminine desires under control so far! But today, I feel that my weakness of this kind of desires has reached the attention of the public, breaking the barriers of secrecy. I do not know how!

(The maid listens to the words of the heroine and advises her to be careful in words, courtesies and body-language, in order to maintain caution in public, so as to safeguard one's own self-respect! Feminine desires are to be controlled with determination and will- power, without revealing it out, either by words or moves (gestures)!). (Please see Kural 1137).

1255. setRaar–pin sel–laa–p– peru–nh–thakai–mai, kaama–nhOy
utRaar aRi–vathu ondRu, andRu..

She speaks: Theoretically speaking, a woman's thought must not go behind the man who does not show his affection to wards her! But it does not happen in every case. A woman afflicted with extreme affection for the man-in-love, does not want to follow this honourable policy, although she is aware of it! Her mind will be going after him. (However, she must exercise control over it)!

(She tells this to her maid about her inability to forget him! The maid advises her to keep on trying to pursue his love with patience, as advised in kural 1200, in addition to applying self-control and e xe rc is ing ca u t i on!

1256. setRavar pin–sae–Ral vaeNdi aLith–tharO
yetRu,(y)ennai utRa thuyar.

She thinks: I decided to go behind my man-in- love, to rejoin him, on my own initiative! It can be attributed to my shameless love-sickness or blind-affection! My experience is painful. It needs to be analyzed on sympathetic considerations! I wonder whether it could be the trapping nature of love-sickness?

(Another interpretation: My efforts of pursuing my love towards my man-in-love, although he was a bit hesitant, have yielded me good results! I would describe it as a love earned on sympathetic gestures to suit my whims and fancies!) That kind of love-sickness is painful, so to say! (She tells her maid about her painful experience! The maid replies that it is due to a natural affection. A lot of talking will help to confirm the mutual commitment!)

1257. nhaaN, (y)ena ondRO, aRiya–lam, kaama–th–thaal
paeNi–yaar petpa se(i)y–in.

She speaks: I will not be mindful of observing modesty, if my beloved man-in-love returns after a period of separation, and embraces me to give me happiness, to fulfill my desires! I need not have a sense of shame with him! (She tells her maid happily, instead of complaining about her agonies and sufferings to her all the time! The maid feels happy about it).

1258. pan–maaya–k– kaLvan paNi–mozhi andRO, nha–m
peNmai udai–kkum padai?

She speaks: My man-in love uses enticing (charming, alluring, flowery, tempting) words, in a cheerful way, so politely, and so pleasingly, while making love with me, which makes me lose all my feminine firmness! (She happily tells her maid who mocks at her, saying that all men use this as an art of love-making technique, to break the feminine modesty!).

1259. pula–p–pal (y)ena–ch–chendRaen; pulli–nae–n, nhenj–cham
kalath–thal uRu–vathu kaNdu!

She speaks: "I thought of starting a love-quarrel (by my showing my silent anger) with him, when I went to see him in his place. However, on seeing him, the scene changed: my mind started ignoring my feelings and merged with (his) emotions. Due to the betrayal of my mind, I ended up embracing him!" (When her maid heard this, she commented, "clever girl"!).

1260. nhi–Nam thee–yil,itt(u)–anna, nhenj–inaar–k–ku,uNdO
puNar–nh–thu, oodi nhiR–paem (y)enal.?

She speaks: My tender heart melts like a fatty substance melting in fire, when my husband embraces me, after returning from a far off place, and gives me the happiness I could imagine! While this is so, would I dare to start a love-quarrel to irritate him? (She tells this to her maid who replies that this is the exact maturity of mind in a woman which keeps the couple in the right track!).

CHAPTER-127

MUTUAL DESIRE TO MEET

1261. vaaL–atRu–p– puR–kendRa kaNNum; avar, sendRa
nhaaL, otRi–th– thae–y–nh–tha viral

She feels: I touch and read my markings on the wall about the date of his departure from home, every day, to count how many days have passed since his departure, and my fingers have become worn out! I look for him in the direction towards which he proceeded while going from home, anxiously awaiting his arrival, every day, focusing my anxiously searching-eyes, at frequent intervals of time, and my sharp eyes have begun to lose the lustre, becoming dull and dim, out of disappointment each time!

(She tells her maid about her painful experience, fluctuating between eagerness and disappointment, in waiting for arrival of her beloved husband from abroad! She told these details to the maid who congratulated her for her knowledge of counting the number of days, from the markings on the wall!).

(Note: This couplet indicates that the women were educated and well-informed about calendars and counting the number of days! This needs research to find out whether opportunity for learning (education) was made available to women in Tamil-nadu, 2000 years back?)

1262. ila–ng–kizhaa–i! indRu maRa–ppin (y)en thOL–mael
kalam, kazhi–yum, kaa–rikai nhee–th–thu.

She speaks addressing her maid: Oh, my dear maid! You are looking beautiful today, as I can see from your glittering ornaments! I am very much upset today! Even if I make an attempt to forget about the pains of parting with my husband, who is far away from home, my shoulders are losing their structural beauty and strength, and my stylish bangles are sliding down my ever-resilient forearms!

(The pains of parting with him remains unchanged whether I think about it or forget about it!. The maid feels happy about the normal mood with which the heroine has made a reference about the jewels of the maid! That means that the heroine is slowly recovering from her worries about her husband!).

1263. uran–nha–sai–yi, uLLam–thuNai–yaaka–ch– chendRaar
varal–nhasai–yi, in–num uL–aen!

She speaks: "Without being particular about family pleasures, my husband has gone to a far off place, in search of victory and fame, with his will-power as the only companion for his support! It is fair on my part to keep myself alive and fit, anticipating his safe return to rejoin me! I decided to remain alive until he comes back home"! (Her maid feels happy that the heroine has decided to bear the sufferings of separation between the husband and wife, remembering the duty of a wife, ideally suited to an aspiring (ambitious) young man!).

1264. koodiya kaamam piri–nh–thaar varavu–uLLi–k
- kOdu–kodu (y)ae–Rum, (y)en nhenj–chu.

She speaks: On knowing that my husband is coming home to re-join me and to have fun with me, after a period of long absence, my mind is jumping in happiness and joy, similar to a monkey jumping from one branch of a tree to another branch of tree, and finally reaching the top of the tree to have a glance at the in- coming guest! (The maid is happy that the heroine is in an elated mood! The more the merrier is the heroine, the more happier is maid!!).

1265. kaa–Nka, man, koN–kanai–k– kaN(N)aara; kaNda–pin
nhee–ng–kum, (y)en men–thOL pasappu.

She feels: I am going to see my beloved husband who is coming home to re-join me! Let me see him with my own eyes to relieve their pain! When he joins me, and gives me the first hug, all the symptoms of my love-sickness will disappear, including the faded skin on my slender shoulders!

1266. varuka,man, koN–kan oru–nhaaL; paru–kuvan
paithal–nhO-y (y)ellaam keda.

She hopes: On a happy day, my husband will return from his far- off land! On that day, I will quench all my thirsts, in his benign company, so that all the symptoms of love-sickness could fly away!

1267. pulap–paen–kol; pullu–vaen kollO; kalap–paen –kol
kaN, anna kae–Lir varin?

She wonders: When my husband, (whom I consider to be as precious as my own eyes to me), returns to home today. I am wondering what I would do to celebrate the joy! Would I start a love-quarrel, taking up the topic of his prolonged stay outside the home, leaving me to suffer in loneliness? Or would I embrace him with all affection and love? Or would I do both these actions to enjoy the fun? I do not know it, at all!

(She tells the maid about it, with joy. The maid feels contended and happy. It is a great relief for the maid).

1268. vinai–kala–nh–thu, vendR(u)–yeeka vae–nh–than;manai–kala–nh–thu
maa–lai ayar–kam viru–nh–thu.

He speaks: As a soldier in the battlefield, I am fighting in the war to bring victory to my king! When all of us return to our homes,with a victorious flag, I will celebrate the victory-dinner at home,with my beloved wife in the most pleasant evening, along with the beloved members of the family!

(Note: This is the first example of a man going on an assignment of war, instead of going on business trip, or for earning wages to far off places! In this particular couplet: The soldier in the battlefield considers that the duty is the 'first' priority, and the 'second' is only personal pleasure! Of course, he is anxious to reach home all safe,earning victory in the war! Recollecting the memory of his beloved wife, he wishes to have a sumptuous dinner at home, sharing happiness joyously with his wife, and family! He calls it a dinner in honour of the king! That reflects his patriotism!).

(Inference: When the king is in the battlefield, no celebration will be entertained among the citizens. Merchants, poets, scholars and other citizens, young and old, will wait for the king to return home, with victory! Every citizen will have a victory-dinner in his home, sharing the happiness, with all family members! It will be like a celebration with all festivities! It could imply that the husband and wife, among the civilians, would avoid embraces during war time. It is like a penance (and prayers)! Dinners at home only after the victorious king returns to his palace!Voluntarily undertaken as a penance during wartime, or socially observed as a custom, the citizens do pray for the victory of their country! It makes sense, in a disciplined society!). This viewpoint needs research!

1269. oru–nhaaL (y)ezhu–nhaaL–pOl sellum; chae–N sendRaar
varu–nhaaL– vaith–thu (y)ae–ng–ku pavar–k–ku!

The maid speaks: "Passing of one day appears is as painful as seven long days, for a wife who is anxiously waiting for her husband to return from a far off place! It will be a similar feeling for her husband too"!!

(Note: "Sometimes, patience is forcibly thrust on some people)". She murmurs!).

1270. peRin–(y)en–naam, pet–Rakkaal –(y)en–naam, uRin–(y)en–naam,
uL–Lam udai–nh–thu ukka–k– kaal?

He speaks: "What would happen, if my woman-in-love can not bear the pain of parting with me (as her rightful man-in-love) over a long period of time, and happens to get affected with mental depression? She will not be in her senses! I would not be of any use to her; she would not be of any use to me; and, even if we embrace each other, there would not be any use, for both!

(Let me hasten to reach there, wherever she is now!so that I can see her in person, and save her from a total ruin, to restore the happiness of me and my beloved wife!").

(Note: Some interpreters have described the pathetic part of the story, and left it there, in which case, it is categorized as a tragedy, in the Shakespearean sense! However, *Manakkudavar Urai* has made it a Comedy, as it is described that it is a story of a worried-husband, blabbering about his wife's plight affected by their long separation! When the husband decides to return home speedily, it becomes a Comedy, as it is established that the wife is all safe!! This story forms an 'anti-climax' in the art of drama!). (Please see Ap pendix-1).

CHAPTER-128

MUTUAL FEELINGS

(This sections describes the improvement in understanding between persons unified by love).

1271. karappi–num kai–yi–ka–nh–thu, ol–laa–nhin uN–kaN
urai–kkal uRu–vathu–ondRu uNdu.

He speaks to her: "My dear young lady, You seem to con ceal (hide) your feelings, without telling me what it is! Beyond your control, your painted attractive eyes do convey to me, a special message which I have clearly understood, with pleasure! (I will tell you later, what it is! Not now!!)".

(Note: a historical hint is revealed regarding the painting of Eyes, for beautifying the appearance, being practiced by some privileged young women in Tamilnadu, 2000 years ago!)

1272. kaN–nhi–Rai–nh –tha kaari–kai–k– kaambu–(y)aer–thOL paethai–kku–p–
peN–nhi–Rai–nh–tha nheer–mai peri–thu!

He feels proud: The woman I admire is a beautiful person to look at, enchanting my eyes with a graceful appearance, gorgeously - elegant shoulders resembling the bamboo-like combination of shape and shining-softness, and her quality-characteristics imbibed with a pleasing feminine charm and modesty in her womanhood!

1273. maNi–yil thi–kazh–tharu nhool–pOl, mada–nh–thai
aNi–yil thi–kazh–vathu–ondRu uNdu.

He admires: I am admiring the beauty of my woman-in- love! Her charm has got some special significance which cannot be immediately read out, similar to the invisible thread which holds together the precious gems, in the ornament made to resemble a garland (or necklace)!

1274. mukai–mokkuL uL–Lathu nhaa–tRam–pOl, pae–thai
nha–kai–mokkuL uL–Lathu–ondRu uNdu.

He admires: I am able to visualize some aspect (a message?) which is hidden behind the captivating smile of this young woman, like the good-smelling fragrance hidden behind the buds, just before blossoming of the flower!

1275. seRi–thodi sei–th(u)–iRa–nh–tha kaLLam uRu–thuyar
theer–k–kum maru–nh–thu– ondRu udai–th–thu.

He wonders: I have just now acquired a love-sickness on seeing this beautiful young woman who seems to have left signal which sounds like a remedy for my sickness! That signal seems to be hidden behind the crowded bangles which she is wearing!

1276. perithu–aatRi–p– petpa–k– kala–ththal, arithu–aatRi
anbu–inmai soozh–vathu udai–th–thu.

She doubts: Presently, I am happy that my man-in-love has come and shown his affection for me, showering his love; but I am afraid that it gives a signal to me, about the probability of his leaving me, to be separated by his another venture of a business-trip! It is a frightening thought!

1277. thaN–(N)am thuRai–van thaNa–nh–thamai, nha–m–minum
mun–nam uNar–nh–tha vaLai.

She speaks: I am presently going to have nice time with my husband, who has just now returned from abroad! He belongs to this sea-shore area! (A busy person!). Fearing that he could have a plan to leave me soon, my intelligent bangles show me a signal by sliding down my forearms, warning me that he would part with me abruptly, after this meeting! How clever my bangles are!!

(She tells this to her maid, who, in-turn, pleads that she can bring it to the notice of her husband, so that he would plan staying with the heroine, for many more days at home! As a busy person, he would have his own compulsion of duties! The maid is an intelligent person. She believes that a man must devote sufficient time to earn wealth, sacrificing some personal pleasure, if necessary, as other wise some undesirable effect could result as indicated in kural 902).

1278. snhe–ru–nha–tRu–ch– chend–Raar,(y)em kaa–thalar (y)aam-um (y)ezhu–nhaaL–ae–m, mae–ni pasa–nh–thu.

She speaks: My husband left me only yesterday, for a trip to a far off place, on an assignment! But I could sense this seven days earlier, as my skin started producing a faded complexion!

(She told this to to her maid who consoled her that her husband will come back soon!).

1279. thodi–nhOkki, men–thOL–um nhOkki, adi–nhOkki, a–h–thu, aaNdu,avaL, sei– tha–thu!

The maid speaks:In the presence of her husband, a heroine looked at her rolling bangles in the forearms; she managed to stare at her shoulders; and finally, she looked at her attractive feet; to indicate the various parts of her beautiful body that would record the symptoms of 'love- sickness', which would occur to her, if her husband parted with her, on an assignment abroad! This is what all she did! She meant that her husband must take her along with him to wherever he goes, so that she would not suffer from the treacherous symptoms of love-sickness! (She was looking at the face of her husband, anticipating a response!).

(Note: This is a story told by a maid to her heroine).

(The maid must have felt: If the husband has been intelligent enough, he would have known the mind of his wife, and, would have decided to take her, along with him, to wherever he goes!).

(The story told by the maid is the solution for offering freedom to women who suffer from the most-cruel separation of 'husbands and wives'! The maid is a reformist who did not believe in the ban imposed by the society, prohibiting the travel of women across the sea, to reach the far-off land!!). (Please see the details of the ban on foreign travel by women in the notes below kural 1205).

1280. peNNi–naal peNmai udai–th–thu, (y)en–ba, kaN–Ni–naal kaama–nhO–y, solli, iravu.

The maid says to the heroine: My dear young lady! Do you know that the womanhood gets a greater charm, if you make it known to your man-in-love, through your attractive eyes about your longing- desire for embracing him, as if you are begging!

(Note: The maid plays an intelligent role in solving several tough and sensitive issues about which many men and women, among the youth, remain generally ignorant.She offers advice on 'home-making!').

CHAPTER-129

EAGERNESS TO EMBRACE

(This section relates to the desire of lovers to meet and embrace eachother).

1281. uLLa–k– kaLith–thal–um, kaaNa makizh–thal–um,
kaLLu–k–ku, il; kaama–th–thiRku uNdu.

He analyzes: A man will be happy when he thinks about his woman-in-love (or seeing her in his dream); so also when he is able to see her in person! It is not similar to the happiness of those who consume liquor, because, they have to consume the liquor to feel happy! They cannot derive pleasure on thinking about liquor (in imagination or in a dream) or on just seeing liquor in front of them!

1282. thinai–th– thuNai–yum oodaa–mai vae–Ndum; panai–th–thuNai–yum
kaa–mam nhi–Rai–ya vari–n.

She speaks: When a woman has got a desire to have union with her husband, she should not enter into a love-quarrel at all! If she gets a desire for it, in measures as huge as a Palmyra seed, she should not have any trace of feeling in her mind to develop a love- quarrel as tiny as the size of a millet-seed!

(The heroine tells this generalized principle to the maid who raised a question 'about timing of love-quarrel to be initiated by a wife, with her husband'! The maid feels happy about the 'intelligent-idea' be hind this practical policy, as described by the heroine!!),

(Note: Millet-seed and the seed of Palmyra tree are compared; ie., seed versus seed. The size of a palm-tree-seed is (more than) several hundred times larger than the size of a millet-seed).

1283. paeNaa–thu petpa–vae sei–yi–num, koNkan–ai–k–
kaaNaa–thu amai–yala kaN.

She speaks: Even if my husband does not take care about me, remaining negligent to me,preferring to do whatever he likes, my eyes will not remain peaceful without seeing him! That is my kindness towards him!

(When she told these words to the maid, she pacified the heroine to have some more patience, and that the situation would improve in due course of time! Generally, a man observes a lot, before he exposes his mind. However, it varies from person to person.Perhaps, 'your-man' may be a 'time-taker'. So, said the maid, to her heroine! To make her understand!!).

1284. oodaR–kaN sendRae–n,man, thOzhi,athu–maRa–nh–thu
koodaR–kaN sendRa–thu,(y)en nhenj–chu!

She speaks: My dear maid! I wanted to start a love-quarrel with my husband yesterday! But, when I saw him in person, my heart started developing a desire to embrace him! (What can I do when my heart betrays my earlier decision?).That is how I ended up embracing him. (The maid was delighted to hear these words!).

1285. (y)ezhu–thum–kaal kOl–kaaNaa–k– kaN–Nae–pOl, koNkan
pazhi, kaaNae–n, kaNda idath–thu.

She speaks to her maid (Personal Confidante): "When I paint my eyes, I do not see the brush-stem of the rod, using which I do the painting for my eyes! So also, when I look at the face of my man-in- love, while I see him in person, I do not see (remember) his follies(faults/ shortcomings)"!

1286. kaa–Num–kaal, kaaNae–n, thava–Raaya; kaaNaa–k–kaal
kaaNae–n, thavaR(u)–al–lavai.

She wonders about her husband: "When I see him in person, face to face, his faults do not come to my mind! When I am all alone, in his absence, I see only his faults (ignoring all his virtues and good qualities)".

1287. ui–ththal aRi–nh–thu punal–paa–i–– pava–rae–pOl,
poi–th–thal aRi–nh–thu,(y)en pula–nh–thu.

She speaks: If a person jumps into the river, knowing fully well that the flood will carry the person away, it is bad! But, if there is somebody to save the person, he can confidently jump into the river! Similarly, if the wife starts a love-quarrel, the husband will end it, giving her an embrace! Does it not mean that starting a love- quarrel is a beneficial act, just like jumping into the river when there is a person to come to the rescue?(When she tells this to the maid, the intelligent maid answers: "She, who starts the love-quarrel, will not be left out, 'un-cared' for!). Is it a waste-move to start a love - quarrel? Not at all!"

1288. iLith–thakka innaa se(i)–yi–num, kaLith–thaar–k–ku–k–
kaL–(L)atrae, kaLva, nhi–n maar–bu!

She speaks to her husband, in their pleasant moments: The liquor causes shameful harms to the modesty of persons whoever consume it! Still, to those who are accustomed to drink liquor, the experience becomes enjoyable! Similarly, I get intoxicated by embracing your broad-bosom-chest; I do not feel the shame, as you have stolen my heart!

1289. mala–rin–um mel–lithu kaamam; silar, athan
sev–vi thalai–p– padu– vaar.

He speaks: The pleasure derived from love-making is softer than a flower! Only a few persons will understand the value of it!(He tells the maid of the heroine, so that she will convey the message to the heroine, about his soft approach!).

1290. kaN–Nin thuni–th–thae kala–ng–kinaaL, pullu–thal
(y)enni–num thaan–vithup(pu) utRu.

He feels happy: She was showing signs of feigned-dislike when we saw each other in close proximity. When I passionately looked at her. she rushed forward to embrace me with boundless affection. (She could not carry out the feigned-dislike, as she initially pro posed to do!)

CHAPTER-130

INTERACTION WITH THE MIND

(This section describes the ideas in the minds of the loving- man and loving-woman)

1291. avar–nhenj–chu avar–k–ku, aathal kaNdum,(y)evan–nhenj–chae nhee, (y)emakku aakaa tha–thu?

She speaks: Oh, my dear heart! You know that the heart of my man-in- love does not care for me, but it is true to him (he being selfish). Knowing all that fully well, you are not sincere to me, but you are sincere to him! What is the reason?

1292. uRaa–a– thavar–k–kaNda kaN–Num, ava–rai–ch–cheRaa–ar–yena–ch– chaeRi,(y)en nhenj–chu!

She speaks: Oh, my dear heart! You know that my man-in- love does not have affection for me! But yet, you seem to go behind him, assuming that he will not get angry with me! Is it not your ignorance?

1293. kettaar–kku nha–ttaar–il (y)en–bathO, nhenj–chae, nhee pettaa–ng–ku avar–pin selal?

She speaks: Oh, my dear heart! You are going behind my man-in-love, without even consulting me! Do you think that there is nobody to come to the rescue of a person (a woman) let down by a man? To stand as a solid support behind a person who faced disappointments in life, you have to be with me! Understand?

1294. ini–anna nhin–nodu soozh–vaar,yaar, nhenj–chae, thuni–sei–thu, thuv–vaai, kaaN matRu?

She speaks: Oh, my dear heart! You do not believe in start ing a love-quarrel, so that it could end in a compromise, and the resulting embrace; for which you are not agreeable! Who else will be willing to talk about it to you, anymore? I don't want to do that!! (Please see Kurals 1284; 1324).

1295. pe–Raa–a–mai anj–chum; peRin, piri–vu anj–chum;
aRaa–a– idumbai–th–thu,(y)en nhenj–chu!

She speaks: "Before I got him, my mind used to worry whether I could get him or not! After I got him within my hold (fold), my mind would worry whether he would go away from me! Thus, my mind stands worried all the time"!!!

1296. thani–yae iru–nh–thu, nhi–nai–th–thak–kaal, (y)ennai–th–
thi–ni–ya iru–nh–thathu, (y)en nhenj–chu!

She feels: I live all alone by myself. My husband lives in a far-off land. When I think of my beloved husband in my loneliness, I feel the pain when I think about the tyranny being caused by his separation, as if my own heart is eating me up! I cannot bear it any more!

(She tells this to her maid who has brought a message from the husband of the heroine! She consoles the heroine, assuring that the message will be conveyed back to him!).

1297. nhaa–Num maRa–nh–thae–n; avar–maRak– kallaa, (y)en
maaNaa mada, nhenj–chil pattu!

She feels : My heart is not able to forget my man-in-love! My heart does not want any dignity, it looks like! By being friendly with my heart, it has made me lose my valuable modesty!

1298. (y)eL–Lin iLi–vaam, (y)endRu (y)eNNi, avar–thi–Ram
uL–Lum uyir–k–kaa–thal nhenj–chu!

She speaks: My husband has a little bit of misunderstanding with me. He lives alone. I live in a separate place. To say something ill about him, will mean insulting my own self! That is what my dear heart thinks, all the time! Thinking about his abilities, capabilities, and achievements is better appreciated. Whatever my heart thinks is going to be good for me!

(When sshe tells this to her maid, the maid replies that the lack of communication from her husband must not be misunderstood that it is due to some misunderstanding between the husband and wife! He might be busy with his work in an unknown land. As a matter of fact,he needs sympathy! Poor man, what kind of daily-routines he would be having, we do not know! So, the option for a wife being separated from her husband is to pray for his success and well- being in a far-off place, so that he returns home safely!).

1299. **thun–bath–thiRku yaa–rae thuNai– yaavaar, thaam–udai–ya nhenj-cham thuNai-(y)al vazhi?**

She feels : "Oh my dear heart! I *am asking a question to you!* When I get some distress(trouble), would you come forward to help me? If you do not come to my rescue, who else will do it"?

1300. **than–jam thamar–allar (y)ae–th(u)–ilaar, thaam–udai–ya nhenj–cham thamar, al vazhi!**

She thinks: One's own heart is sometimes likely to act like a stranger to the self! Then, how can we expect strangers to behave like kith and kin? (Please see Kural 1284).

(She complains to her maid that her heart does not co-operate with herself, when she starts a love-quarrel with her husband, alleging that her heart betrays her and rushes to make peace with her husband! The maid gives a gentle smile and feels happy about the fun!).

CHAPTER-131

LOVE-QUARREL

(Love-quarrel is an occasional occurrence, between a husband and wife. Each of them has got equal responsibility to solve it! It is also, nowadays, believed that the man has got a higher responsibility to resolve it).

(A 'third-party involvement', sometimes, helps; some-other times,it hurts producing an unpleasant harm!).

1301. pullaa–thu iraa–ap– pulath– thai avar–uRum
allal–nhO–y kaaN–ka–m, siRi–thu!

She says to herself: Let me not try to embrace my man- in-love! Let me start a false-anger (love-quarrel) with him! I want to enjoy the fun, in watching how he responds to his-suffering, at least for a while!

1302. uppu–amai–nh– thatRaal pulavi; athu,siRi–thu
mik–katRaal nhee–La vidal.

The maid analyzes: Love-quarrel (false-dislike) must be apportioned in small measures like the salt being added to food, so that the food remains tasty! Prolonged love-quarrel is not desirable, like adding excessive salt to food!!

1303. ala–nh–thaarai al–lal–nhO–y sei–thatRaal tham–mai–p–
pula–nh–thaa–rai–p– pullaa vidal.

The maid speaks to the heroine's man-in-love: Dear gentle man, greetings. It is generally believed that it is a fair honour for the man to pacify a woman who enters into a love-quarrel with her man-in-love, for some valid reason or unfair reason! If it is not done, it will amount to extending grief to an already-grieved person! Don't you think so? I think that it is a man's prerogative to resolve the problem.

(Note: It is generally said that a man and woman engaged in feigned dislike (love-quarrel) must not permit it to last for a long period of time!

If they themselves do not resolve it, some others in the family must intervene and end the crisis! Otherwise, this unfortunate failure will correspond to a cruel act like cutting a withered creeper plant at its very root! (Please see Kural 1304).

1304. oodi ya–varai uNa–raa–mai vaadiya
vaLLi mu–thal–ari–nh–thatRu

The maid analyzes: If the persons involved in the love-quarrel (feigned dislike) are not pacified to restore normalcy, the result will be branded as cruel, just like cutting the roots of a tender creeper-plant which has already withered! (Note: Who will come forward for restoring peace? It all depends on the moods of the individuals concerned! Husband must take up the initiation, in the modern trend!)

1305. nhala–th–thakai nhal–la–var–k–ku (y)ae–(y)er pulath–thakai
poo–anna kaN–Naar akath–thu.

He feels within himself: The feigned dislike (love-quarrel) enacted by a beautiful woman with flower-like fresh and bright attractive-eyes, will be admired and appreciated by a cultured young man with good virtues, as it adds pride and privilege to him! (as it leads to enhanced love and intimacy between the man and woman!).

1306. thuni–yum pulavi–yum illaa–yin, kaa–mam
kani–yum karu–k–kaa–yum atRu.

Tha maid analyzes: Small love-quarrel which prevails for a short period of time, and big love-quarrel prevailing for a longer period of time, essentially promote enhanced affection between a man and woman bounded by love! Love-life without these two enjoyable moments will be dull, and not enjoyable like eating either over-ripe fruit or eating unripe fruit!

1307. ooda–lin uNdu–aa–ng–ku–Or thunbam; pu–Nar–vathu
nhee–du–vathu andRu,kol, (y)endRu.

He Thinks: There is one disadvantage in love-quarrel, in the sense that there will be a displeasure when doubt is raised in one partner's mind whether the duration of blissful embrace will continue for a longer period of time or whether another love-quarrel will set in sooner! (Note: Ref. Kural 1258).

1308. nhO–thal (y)evan,matRu nho–nh–thaar–(y)endRu, a-h-thu a-Riyum kaatha–lar illaa vazhi?

She feels: If the husband does not sympathize with his wife's sufferings and fails to take appropriate measures to remove the difficulties, by showering affection, what could be the benefit expected from worrying about it?

(Another interpretation: If the wife does not sympathize with her husband's sufferings and fails to take appropriate measures to re move the difficulties,by showering affection, what could be the benefit expected from worrying about it?) (Note: This is one of the couplets applicable to both genders).

(Note: When the heroine makes a mention about her worries to the maid, the intelligent maid says that there should not be any egoistic feeling between the husband and wife. Therefore, initiating a dialogue on any topic related to domestic management will be a good idea to break the stalemate! It is always the woman who must start the dialogue, as recommended in kural 51,which empowers a woman as the head of the portfolio of home-management!).

1309. nheerum nhi–zhal–athu, ini–thae, pula–vi–yum
vee–zhu–nhar kaN–Nae ini–thu.

The maid tells the heroine: Water contained under the shade of a tree is supposed to be tastier! Similarly, love-quarrel will be pleasant only between the two persons united by mutual kindness, affection and love.

(Note: Taste of water 'under then shade' relates to a scientific hint. It must be researched!). It talks about the shade of a tree and the taste of water contained below (under) the shade, in a natural setting. Has got any relevance to water-quality concerning minerals and enzymes?

1310. oodal uNa–ng–ka vidu–vaa–rOdu, (y)en–nhenj–cham
'koo–du–vaem' (y)en–pathu avaa!

She speaks: As a result of love-quarrel between me and my beloved husband, his silence prevails for a longer period of time! He does not care about my losing weight, and becoming paler! I have a desire in my heart to resolve the matter! It is out of my affection for him which makes me think so! Nothing else!

(She tells her decision (resolve) to her maid, who appreciates her magnanimity in shedding down the egoistic attitude! After all, the husband and wife do not live for themselves alone! The life has got a greater purpose: to generate a dynasty of good off-springs! That will be their contribution to the world! Ref: kural 60).

CHAPTER-132

INTIMACY

(This section describes the tendency of the woman to create a reason for starting a love-quarrel, either for fun, or for testing his affection for her)

1311. peN–(N)iya–laar (y)ellaa–rum, kaN–Nin pothu uNpar
nhaN–Nae–n para–th–tha –nhi–n maar–bu.

She speaks: My dear husband! You have a reputation of relishing the pleasure with hired-women! Whoever has got feminine features would be willing to share pleasure with you, as those 'sweet- natured-beautiies' will be yearning for your blissful embrace! I will never embrace your chest, hereafter!

1312. oodi irun–th–thae–maa–th– thu–mmi–naar yaam–tham–mai
'nheedu–vaazh–ka' (y)en–paakku aRi–nh–thu!

She speaks: When I was having a love-quarrel with my husband, I was not in talking-terms with my husband! My intelligent husband started sneezing, thinking that I will sing the chorus "Live Long for a Hundred Years", as the custom dictates! Only, I murmured those words to satisfy my conscience! Not to please him! Anyway, I got defeated in my game of love-quarrel!

(She narrated the incident to her maid, who replied: "That is a good girl"!).

1313. kOttu–p–poo–ch – choo–dinum, kaa–yum, 'oruth–thi–yai–k-
kaatti–ya, choo–dineer' (y)endRu.

He speaks: Out of happiness, or for imitating my country- cousins (who are males), I used to wear flowers from wild-bushes, other than flowers from agricultural (Marutham) lands.My beloved wife will become wild, abusing me that I wanted to please some other woman who could be my concubine! I do not get wounded, because I have got her confidence! She was just mocking (kid- ding) at me, out of admiration and my affection for her, appreciating my handsomeness in the rural setting! Perhaps, feeling happy about my manliness! Who knows?

1314. 'yaari–num kaa–tha–lam' yen–drae–naa, oodinaaL
'yaari–num yaari–num' (y)endRu.

He speaks: I told my beloved wife that I loved her more than anybody else! She started weeping! She asked for an explanation: "With whom did youcompare me?", meaning, "with how many women?" She started the love- quarrel! I had a tough time to convince her!

1315. "immai–p– piRa–p–pil piri–yalam', (y)end–Rae–naa,
kaN–nhiRai nheer, koN– danaL.

He speaks out: I told her that I will not part with her during this birth in our lives. She starts sobbing (gently crying)! Tears poured out! She is worried that I would desert her during the next birth!

1316. 'uLLi–nae–n', (y)endRae–n, matRu, '(y)en–maRa–nh–theer'? – (y) edR(u)– (y)ennai–p–
pull–aaL, pulath–thak– kanaL

He speaks: I told her that I always remembered her when I was out of town. She started crying! She asked me: "To remember me, you have to forget me! Why did you forget me, first of all, to remember me the second time?" She pulled her hands away, from my embrace! She started sulking!!

1317. vazhu–th–thinaaL, thummi–nae– naa–ka, azhi–th–thu, azhu–thaaL
'yaar,uLLi–th– thum–mi–neer?'– (y)endRu.

He speaks: I felt like sneezing. When I sneezed, she narrated the chorus "Live long for a Hundred Years". After that, she asked "Which woman thought about you to cause you sneezing?". Before I could give an answer, she started sulking!

1318. thummu–ch– cheRuppa, azhu–thaaL,'nhu–mar–uLLal,
yem–mai maRaith–thirO?'–(y)endRu.

He speaks: Fearing her usual remarks, I suppressed my sneezing sensation. She asked me, "which woman thinks about you fearing whom you are suppressing your sneeze, and hiding it from me?" And, before I could ever think about an answer, she started her sulking!

1319. thannai uNar–th–thinum kaa–yum,'piRar–kku,nheer
in(h)–nhee–rar aaku–thir', (y)endRu.

He speaks: When my wife starts sulking, I make an effort to solve the crisis by using soft language and pleasing words; she asks me back, "are you using this technique of uttering polite words to pacify your (other) female friends?". I am at a loss, as to how to manage such a situation which she creates!

1320. nhi–naith–thu, irun–nh–thu, nhOk–ki–num, kaa–yum;'anaith–thu, nheer
yaa–r–uLLi– nhOk–ki–neer?'– (y)endRu.

He speaks: When I look at her constantly, admiring her beauty, she shoots a question to me: "With which of your female-friends you are comparing my physical beauty?". I feel terribly up- set! She starts sulking! (I think, I have to spend a lot of time patiently with her, to set things right! Hoping for an obvious benefit, I may have to perform this duty!).

CHAPTER-133

HAPPINESS OF LOVE QUARREL (JOY OF SULKING)

1321. illai thavaRu, avar–k–ku, aa–yinum, oodu–thal
val–lathu, avar aLikku maa–Ru!

She says: "Even if there is no fault on his side, I wish to start a love -quarrel (feigned -dislike), as a loving life-partner! It enhances love, affection and bondage, That is why"!! (When she told this to her maid, she called her "a naughty-girl!").

1322. oodal–in thOn–dRum siRu–thuni nhal–aLi
vaa–di–num paadu peRum.

She feels: "Although the love-quarrel (feigned-dislike) causes a bit of displeasure and consequent 'fading-effect' in his kindness, persisting over a short period of time, it helps to increase the love and affection which deserves appreciation and delight!(ultimately when the quarrel is all over!)."

1323. pula–th–thal–in puth–thaeL–nhaadu uNdO? nhilath–thodu
nheer– iyai–nh– tha–nnaar aka–th–thu!

He admires: Could there be a better celestial (heavenly) land which would ensure a more satisfying bliss when compared to the pleasure felt by a man and woman experiencing the blissful- pleasure of feigned-dislike and the subsequent embrace, resembling the hugging of the sea and sky at the horizon in the earth- planet?

1324. pulli– vidaa, ap– pula–vi–yuL thO–nd–Rum, (y)en,
uL–Lam udai–k–kum padai.

She speaks: When we embrace each other immediately when my love quarrel reaches a compromise, I am unable to loosen the grip, as my husband goes on using his flowery words and captivating language which becomes a powerful weapon to break my soul. My anger is gone, at the very touch of my partner. The minds are unified! We forget all about the world!

(She tells this to her maid who asked about the fate of the sulking behaviour of the heroine! The maid knows that a man is clever enough to lighten the mood of the sulking partner, and bring back warmth and affection back into the relationship! It is not a technique! Perhaps, it is derived from the instinct?! An admirable human response! Aimed at fulfilling the very purpose of human life!).

1325. thava–R(u)–ilar aa–yi–num, thaam –veezh–vaar, men–thOL
akaRal–in,aa–ng–ku, ondRu udai–th–thu.

He recollects: Any man who is free from any defect, may, sometimes, happen to be misunderstood by his wife who starts a love- quarrel! As a result, he will have to suffer from loneliness! He will feel pleased by such loneliness at the very remembrance of having embraced the soft shoulders of his dear partner! (Situation will improve very soon).

(Note: Very soon, the love-quarrel will get resolved! Therefore, his experience is mentioned as blissful!)

1326. uNal–i–num uNda–thu aRal, ini–thu; kaa–mam
puNar–thal–in oodal ini–thu.

She admires: Eating food is enjoyable! More enjoyable is the time needed for digestion of food! Similarly, the time spent during love-quarrel seems to be more enjoyable, than the act of embracing, in order to enhance more affection!

1327. oodalil thO–tRa–var ven–dRaar! athu,mannum,
kooda–lil kaaNa–p– padum.

The maid tells her heroine: In the game of love-quarrel (feigned-dislike), whoever is the loser becomes the winner (between the two of them)! That logic will be realized best, when the feigned-dislike comes to an end, and when the blissful-embrace commences!

1328. oodi–p– peRu–kuvam,kollO,nhu–thal–veyar–p–pa–(k) - koo–da–lil thO–ndRiya uppu?

He contemplates: I look forward to let her start a love-quarrel with me, so that it will lead to another occasion when I can have a long-lasting, blissful-pleasure with her, similar to last time, when my love -making embrace made her forehead perspire!

1329. ooduka, mannO, oLi–(y) izhai, yaam–irappa, nhee–duka, mannO, iraa!

He feels: I will be happy if my dear wife (whose beauty is enhanced by her natural brightness on the face) starts a love- quarrel. It will give me a chance to make the night prolonged, so that I will enjoy the pleasure of speaking out flowery words, with the pleasure of selectively choosing appropriate words of pleading and imploring, in a poetic style, to slowly change her mood, and bring her back to the refreshing romantic grandeur! False anger adds delight between a husband and wife! More blissful experience becomes possible after embracing each other, marking the end of the false-anger!

1330. ooduthal kaa–math–thiR–ku, inbam! athaRku, inbam, koodi muya–ng–ka–p– peRin!!

He glorifies feigned-dislike: False anger adds a fabulous delight between a husband and wife! More blissful experience becomes possible, after embracing each other, thus, marking the end of the false-anger!

(The End)

APPENDIX-1

MY FINDINGS

AUTHOR'S FINDINGS

In my humble efforts to understand the ideas of Thiruvalluvar, I am listing a few highlights in which I have found new interpretations (different from that of others), as detailed below:

1. kural.8: aRa-aazhi anh-thaNan thaaL- saernh-thaarkku al-laal piRa- aazhi nheenh-thal arithu.

   The Almighty is like the deep ocean of virtues. It is possible to swim across the sea of the present life (full of miseries and testing times), for those who follow the virtuous path, in imitation of the path taken by the Almighty; For others who live in this world, and yet, do not follow the virtuous path of the Almighty, it is not possible to swim across the sea of life, containing sufferings and tribulations! (Also, interpreted as 'sea of rebirths'). (Note: God, the Almighty, is depicted as the 'sea of virtues/ righteousness/ethics'.

   a. Kural 30 declares: "An ascetic (saintly person) is considered to be an embodiment of virtues, as the requirement is to show, in action, a noble attitude(universal kindness) towards all forms of life, living in this world. Such a person will be designated as an "*anh-tha- Nar*"*!* (The term "*anh-tha-Nar*" becomes meaningful, based on the excellence in human qualities, and not by any other consideration).

      The term '*anh-tha-Nar*'is found in Buddhistic literature, as detailed below:

      i. Santanu, an advisor to the Enlightened Emperor Ashoka, said "He alone is a Brahmin, who, by purity of thought, words, and deeds has liberated himself from all evil, and who, through his compassion and understanding, strives towards the sacred and divine! (page

237 in "Ashoka The Great", authored by WytzeKeuning, translatedby J.E.Steur, 2011, Published by Rupa& Co, New Delhi, India)..

ii. In the words of Emperor Ashoka, "...That recognition of human value (the deepest part of his soul being good, regardless of ' *varna*' or sect) is Dharma (Dhammam)", cited in page 761, in "Ashoka The Great", authored by WytzeKeuning. By inference, the term "*anh-tha-Nar*" applies to a person of any '*varna*' by thevirtue of superiority in quality of purity in thoughts, words and deeds, and kindness and compassion towards all forms of life!

b. The term '*anh-tha-Nar*' is often being confused with '*paar-p-paan*= brahmin) which is found in kural 134, in describing a brahmin-priest, which reads as: "If a priest, born in a Brahmin-family, loses the memory of the holy scriptures, it is possible to learn it again! If the priest does not practice good conduct, he will lose the benefit of his birth in a good family". The exact word used by the poet is: "paar-p-paan",referring to a person belonging to a Brahmin community, as defined in Tamil Dictionary (*Tholkaappiyam), Porul-athikaram* poem 1453 which states: 'All people will listen to the words of *paar-p-paar* and *aRivaar*'! (Note: *aRivaar*=those who possess wisdom). The inference is that '*anh-tha-Nar and 'paar-p-paan*' are the two separate words used by the poet: Thiruvalluvar).

Please refer to:i).WIKIPEDIA; tn.m.wikipedia.org/wiki/%EO, 'anh-tha-Nar', and ii). Tholkappiyam-Thelivurai, S.V.Subramanian. 1998; Manivasagar Pathippagam, Chennai, pp.568-569).'*thol-kaa-p-pi-yam'; (**'poruL'**): poem 1453.*

2. Kural.37: aRaththu-aaRu ithu yena- vaeNdaa; sivikai poRuth-thaan-Odu oornh-thaan idai.

Describing the details of 'benefits of following the virtuous path' becomes unnecessary, to the persons carrying the palanquin, or the person(s) riding inside it! (Any preaching by others does not convince them, on virtues, as violation of virtues and human rights have already occurred, in their actions).The privileged person (the rider) will be too proud to listen to preaching on virtues!. Those who carry the palanquin will be afraid of listening to any such preaching! This needs research! Some of the interpreters were 'too kind' to comment that the benefits earned during the 'previous births' have been instrumental to their present 'sufferings- versus-comforts', respectively, in the case of those who carry the palanquin, versus the rider(s) inside the palanquin!

3. Kural 68: thammin tham-makkaL aRivudaimai, maa-nhi-laththu man-nu-yirkku yellaam inithu

   The knowledge earned by the children is more useful to others, living in this wide world, than the measures of happiness felt by the parents themselves. (Another version: The intelligence of the next generation (off-springs) will be higher than the intelligence of the parents. It is a positive benefit for the society). Parents will be benefited; as well as others!. (Ref: https:// en.m.wikipedia.org>wiki>The Flynn Effect-Wikipedia: Young generations performing better than older generations. This is claimed due to two factors: I) better schooling, and ii) better nutrition!).

4. Kural 205. ilan - yendRu theeya-vai seiyaRka; sei-yin, ilan-aakum; matRum peyarth-thu.

   Do not do any harm to a person, thinking that the recipient is a poor person who cannot retaliate. If you do, you yourself will become a poor person, in return for what you did! Your position will 'revert itself from richness (wealth,riches) to poverty'!!) (This interpretation needs further research). (Please refer to Kural 204).

   (Points for consideration in the research:i). Kural 1079 describes the animosity possessed by a privileged person against the under-privileged people: "If persons of low calibre (mind/attitude) happen to see the decent costumes (dresses) and good food availed (enjoyed) by others, they will feel jealous about it, and find fault with those poor persons, and pour out complaints, even to implicate them in offensive crimes, which could be false allegations".

   Thiruvalluvar takes up the initiative to caution such mightier persons with muscle-power, advising them not to cause harm to the poor people, 'warning' them that they would get affected, if they violate the norms of justice, vide kural 204.

   Thiruvalluvar has understood that some unscrupulous persons are capable of doing anything they like, without caring for any elders in the society!

Please see kural 1073 which reads as "The evil persons look like heavenly beings, as they can afford to act as they like, ignoring the obligations to social justice (value-system, normal human virtues)". It is a satire that the unscrupulous persons, possessing meanness in their attitude, do behave like 'celestial persons', by assuming freedom to do whatever they like to do, without caring for public opinion, although, as human beings, they have a need to obey the law of the land which is equally applicable to all human beings living on the land. The poet has understood them, in the way described in kural 1075 which reads as "Fear is the regulating factor for the people of low calibre, in their efforts to behave better, to play it safe! Additional reason could be their desire for gains". Therefore, the poet, after understanding well that 'Fear' is the only language to which the mean-minded people would listen, preferred to caution them in kural 1018 that no act which is disagreeable to others, must be done by those unscrupulous persons. This is reiterated clearly in kural 204, cautioning them that the force of virtues will cause poverty in them, if they ever do harm to the poor persons, thus, cursing that they would be driven to poverty, if they ever attempt doing the offence of causing harm to the helpless (poor) people!! This is similar to bringing them under the ambit of the force of 'Virtue/Righteousness/ Ethics', acting as a force, as described in kural 1018: "If a person commits a blame- worthy/criminal act, from which all others shy away, then the force of virtue will keep away from that offender, withdrawing a probable protection!" The inference is that the force of Nature (the Almighty) will not extend protection to the offender, when he/she happens to suffer! (This is similar to writing a judgement in kural 205, by invoking a proviso contained in kurals 1018 and 204!)

5. Kural 236. thO-ndRin pukazhodu thO-ndRuka; ah- thu-ilaar thO-ndRalin thO-ndRaamai nha-ndRu.

   The entry of any person, born in this world, to any disci pline of study, will be better appreciated, if some contribution is going to be made by that person to the benefit of the discipline, so that the person may deserve a fame! In the case of others who are not capable of generating a similar fame for themselves, their existence in this world may not produce any significance! (Note: Contribution of knowledge by an individual person to the field of his/her own profession is considered important to the development of the specific field).

6. Kural 346.'yaan'-' yenathu'- yennum serukku-aRuppaan, vaanO-r-kku uyar-nh-tha ulakam pukum.

   (Note: The words '*uganhtha- ulakam pukum*': considered).

   A person who eradicates(erases/wipes out) from his mind, the various human qualities of vanity, such as the false-pride which would make a person utter words like "I", and "Me", "My belongings", will be elevated to the status, deserving entry into the 'higher world', on par with the heavenly beings. (This is the benefit of earning freedom from human desires, by an ascetic person).

   (Note: An abode superior to heaven ('higher world'), is being indicated into which an ascetic person becomes eligible to enter! The term '*vaanOrkku-uyar-nh-tha-ulagam*' refers to 'another heaven' higher than (superior to) the heaven occupied by the heavenly beings). IT MUST BE ASCERTAINED WHETHER THIS IS THE EXPECTATION OF THE POET.

   The phrase must be revised as "*vaanOrkku-uganhtha- ulagam*" meaning 'the heaven meant for heavenly-dwellers', in which case, it becomes valid for the present knowledge about the heaven! The heaven is meant for heavenly persons, whereas, "Higher world above the heavenly beings" isa new concept.

   If the phrase "*vaanOr-kku-uyarnh-tha-ulagam*" is accepted, it would mean the 'upper-house of the heaven'. There is no such entity. Here comes a confusion. Heaven is the most superior abode. There is no other house superior to heaven. This needs research. The poet believes that human-persons in the ascetic order do have the eligibility to enter into the heaven, if they erase the feelings of self-pride, by shedding the sense of attachment, such as "I" "Me", "My belongings" from their minds. The poet's intention could not have been to place them in a status superior to heavenly-dwellers; but in equal status on par with them. *Parimelazhagar*, the most popular interpreter(commentator) of Thirukkural describes that: 'the heaven which is not attainable for heavenly persons, will be made available to those human persons in the ascetic order who shed down the feelings of vanity, such as "I", "me", "my belongings", etc, from their minds'. This interpretation needs to be re- viewed whetherit would convince the common logic. The heavenly persons are alreadythere. It (the heaven) is legitimately meant for them. There is nothing called "heaven not being attainable by heavenly persons". Heaven is their home. Therefore, the compromising interpretation could be "the heaven which is 'exclusively meant for heavenly-persons' (vaanOrkku-uganhtha-ulagam),will be kept open for those ascetics who shed their vanity-qualities, such as "I", "me", "My belongings", from their minds andact accordingly"! This needs further research. The error in the 'word' could have occurred while copying the text of the poet from palmyra- leaf (palm-leaf) recordings, comparing the words '*uga-nh-tha-ulagam*',versus, '*uyar-nh-tha- ulagam*'.

In most of the religions, the 'Heaven' is understood as a common religious cosmological or transcendent (supernatural) place where 'beings' such as gods, angels, spirits, saints, or venerated- ancestors are said to originate from, or be enthroned in, or reside in (Refer: Wikipedia: Heaven).This helps to understand the concept of heaven, into which every living-person wants to 'enter', after the life ends in this earthly-world! It needs a careful study in order to understand the policy of Thiruvalluvar, the author of Thirukkural, with reference to eligibility-criteria for the humans to enter into the heaven, vide kural 50 and 58 (for family-persons resorting to domestic-life), and kural 346 (for persons resorting to ascetic-life!

7. **Kural 543.** anh-thaNar nh-oo-Rkum aRath-thir-kum aathi-yay
nhi-ndRa-thu mannavan kO-l.

The king's upright rule, symbolized by the Scepter, is considered to be more ancient than the statutes (norms for governance), which are presently being formulated by the ruler of the land, with assistance from wise persons (learned-saints, namely, 'anh-tha-Nars'), 'during the life-time of Thiruvalluvar'!

(Note: The poet expresses a fear that ideas which are alien to the ancient Tamil culture/ traditions could find entry into the 'proposed' new administrative norms, if they are made without accommodating the general (Scepter-) principles of governance based on the beaten-track which were in vogue for the 'past' thousands of years in the Tamil-speaking land. The poet's apprehension could have been based on the fear that the new statutes (proposed by the king) could be influenced by the Rig-vedic principles of 4-varuna-categorization of the society! (Because of the involvement of learned-scholars ('*anh-tha-Nars*') belonging to a sanskrit-influenced school of thought, in the task of making new statutes for governance of the land).

In kural 503, the probability of some traces of ignorance being seen to be prevalent in highly qualified wise men, is indicated. If such persons are involved in law-making process, their ignorance and their distorted attitudes, could contribute harmful sociological ideology to be embedded in the statutes, due to which some perennial hardships could occur to the society, in the way that the people would be governed by the king! This is where a collective-wisdom is warranted, in such an important task of framing new statutes for governance!! (This is why collective wisdom of many persons is considered to be better than a singular opinion of a learned person). This needs research, to verify whether it could be a dissent note expressed by the poet, against the introduction of the the Rig-Veda- based-principles of the 4-Varuna categorization of the human society, which could have been done with the patronage of the king?(Please see Appendix-9).

(Thiruvalluvar's suspicion about the unbiased attitude of learned-persons tallies with the saying of Aristotle:

"There is no great genius without some touch of madness".... Aristotle, Greek philosopher (384-324 BC)........(tallying with kural 503: in the chapter dealing with 'Clarity based on analysis').

Time period when Thirukkural was composed: Dr.M.Rajamanickanaar estimated that the great poet Thiruvalluvar could have lived in Tamil-country between the 3rd Century BC, and 1st Century BC (vide "History of Tamil language and Literature, p.123; as cited in "Thiruvalluvar" by Justice S.Maharajan, SakityaAkademi Publication, 2017). Many other authors have agreed with this estimate of time.

If it is assumed that 'the knowledge (data-base) available from the old scriptures of ancient philosophies (representing Brah-manism, now being identified with Hinduism), Buddhistic philosophies, and Jainism-philosophies, could have been referred to by Thiruvalluvar. He could have compared it with the traditions and beliefs of ancient Tamil-culture which is claimed to have originated a few thousands of years ago, earlier to

Thiruvalluvar. He seems to have disagreed with many concepts, coming from vedic ideologies. Some other ideologies could have coincided or conflicted with Tamil culture. But the major truth is that the couplets relating to norms of virtues/righteousness/ethics are significantly unique, as devised by Thiruvalluvar,… unique, in the sense that i) the relationship between god and man describes a new order; ii) the god is depicted as an embodiment of virtues; iii) humans are equal to each other by birth; gambling is prohibited; v) drinking liquor is prohibited; vi)extra-marital-relationship by man or woman is prohibited; vii) prostitution is prohibited;viii) charity is supported; ix) heaven is kept open for virtuous persons, both,for males,females, and righteous ascetics; x) king must not terrorize people;xi) he must offer an upright rule, as otherwise, he will be uprooted; xii) no discrimination in ordering punishment for the same crime;xiii) duties are prescribed uniformly for all human beings, without showing any difference in social status, etc., using the term 'aRam'.

It-is-a-unique-literature,in-which-justice-without-bias-is-demanded!The poet insists that a person sitting in judgement of any offense committed by an individual person must be free from faults or biases (Please see kural 436). Discipline/ Truthfulness/ Grace/ Compassion/ Kindness/ Neutrality, etc are being highlighted in human-life!! Non-killing and Non-Violence are highlighted! Sympathy for the poor is insisted! The right to education is fixed on the individual person's persuasion!Elevated status, sympathy and appreciation are granted for farmers who feed the world-population! Friendship,mutual help, avoidance of laziness, avoidance of hatred, insistence on high-calibre of human qualities, for establishing a new social order, etc, have been spelled out! Management principles are elaborated! Medicine and eating habits are correlated, in addition to indicating a good infrastructure for healthcare facility! Elders and wise persons are upheld! All features for a harmonious and peaceful society have been incorporated! It is a genuinely original work; and not an imitation!

That is why, Thiruvalluvar is considered as the last Indian philosopher to create his own version of scriptures, worth being admired by the people of the world!

In the book by Justice S.Maharajan (2017), the following points were highlighted:

i. Indigenous religions and ritualistic practices, such as worship of local gods prevailed in the Tamil-speaking country, at the time when the Buddhism, Jainism, and Vedic Brahmanism migrated from North of India towards South.(Justice S.Maharajan, 2017, "Thiruvalluvar", Sakitya Akademy Publication, pp.12-13).

ii. "At that period of time, a policy not-adopted by Buddhists orJainism-promoters, was adopted by the promoters of Vedic Brah- manism, in giving new names to gods worshiped by the Tamil People, namely, *Kandan (Murugan)*, *"SaeyOne"*, the god of *kuRinjchi*- land was made "*Skandan, Subramanian*"), and "*MaayOh-ne*", the god of '*Mullai*-land was made as "*VishNu*". When Tamil people started believing in these ideologies, protest-notes were recorded by Tamil- poets, in '*PuRa-nhaa-nooRu*', poem 335", "*kuRunthogai*,poem 156", and "*kaliththogai*, poem 65", etc.(Ref: Is It Tamil or Sanskrit?, under the caption: "*Thamizhaa? Samaskrithamaa*?', authored by Dr.Kannapiraan, 'KRS', Thadagam Publications, 2021, pp.27-33. (Note: Saivism *, and Vaishnavism** referred above can be understood in this historical setting).

People in the Tamil-speaking lands were mainly worshipers of 'ancestors', especially 'war-heroes', different local gods, and the rural masses were worshipers of Nature! Sun-god being remembered in spirit, not necessarily in the form of idols, but by remembering the cooperation of the Nature in their profession of cultivation (such as timely rainfalls, and conducive seasonal weather- patterns), with gratitude, in celebrating 'Pongal Festival', as a symbolic gesture of showing their gratitude to the Nature, immediately after the harvest! The land had its own traditional culture during the days of Thiruvalluvar!.

It is, therefore, reasonable to assume that the society-dedi cated poet Thiruvalluvar could have devoted time, to come up with his own- 'veda', namely, 'ThirukkuRaL' in which he prescribed uniform codes for "*ARam*", equality among human beings (in kural 972), equality before law (in kurals-436, 541, 549), upright-rule in land-adminstration (kurals 542, 544, 555, 551, 552), avoidance of killing, avoidance of gambling, practice of kindness-compassion- love-charity, avoidance of back- biting, respecting and protecting the elders, exercising caution against the wicked, recognition of domestic life as phase of 'aRam', whereas the family-man is burdened with many responsibilities, namely, helping the poor and ascetics (without expecting anything in return), practicing domestic hospitality,etc.

The poet took care to assure them that divine status would be granted to those persons who lead a perfect-life (in kural 50), in the domestic order, the heaven being kept open for those women who lead a virtuous life (in kural 58)!

The good king being regarded as the Divine Power (in kural 388)! He showed how to lead a domestic life with a loving-woman, how to how affection, how to bring forth good children so that the society will feel the blissful experience from the wisdom of those children in kural 68, etc. He glorified the role of woman as the good- wife and good-mother of the family (in kural 60). He insisted that morality of a man must be in the same order as that of a woman, in kural 974, on par with the chastity insisted upon for a woman in kural 54. He described the entire spectrum of human life, including the need for earning wealth in accordance with the virtuous norms, (kurals 754 &755), need to spend on others who are in need by way of charity in Kural 221, how to take care of health, how to exercise self-control, how to make friends, how to manage enemies, how to bring up the family towards progress, how to do business, how to start your own establishment, how to do management of men and materials, where to observe endurance without getting depressed, when and where to change strategies in doing work, how to put your faith on endeavours, how to overcome the dictates of fate, how to avoid bad thoughts, how to avoid bad words, etc. In brief, the poet described the ways for leading a meaningful life, from childhood up to the time of completing the journey of life, without hurting others, and to leave behind a good reputation, as an eligibility-criterion for reaching the heaven (as cited in kural 50)!

i. He continues to be your consultant, if you accept him as your guide! He lives with us! (Though Thiruvalluvar lived around2000 years ago, it does not seem he is dead! (Ref: Justice S.Maharajan, "Thiruvalluvar", SahityaAkademi Publication, 2017 ,p.7).

ii. In kural 972, the poet has formulated a new theory "All are created equal by birth". This can be claimed as an amendment to Rig-Vedic provision of the four-varna system of the Hindu-society. There is provision for such a new ideology, in Rig-Veda, vide sloka I-89-1, which reads as "Let noble thoughts come to us from every side!", as cited by Sri C.Rajagoplachari, in the first page of his book "KURAL: The Great Book of TIRU-VALLUVAR, 1965". This will remove the differences between Thirukkural and Manu Smriti (MS), in slokas 1:100, 8:270; 2:31; 1:103; 1:99; 4:80 which were considered to be in conflict with kural 972. (Please refer to Navalar Urai, page xv; "*ThirukkuralTheLivurai, 1991*", authored by Dr.Navalar R.Nedunchezhian).

iii. It is worthwhile to remember the famous quote from Kamil Zvelebil, a Czech-scholar who carried out extensive research on Indian-Languages: "...Tamil culture is independent, and not derived!..not imitative! It is 'pre-Sanskrit'! And from this point of view, Tamil alone stands apart, when compared to major languages and literature of India". (ht tps:// karkanirka.org> uniquenessoftamil_dr_ Zvelbil's_ quotes_from_Smile_ Of_Murugan).

iv. ***'thamizh-naattu-th-thei-vang-kaL'*: (Gods of the Thamizh- people): *"maa-yO-n mae-ya kaadu-uRai- ulakam-um,***

sae-yOn- mae-ya mai-varai- ulakam-um, vae-nh-than mae-ya theem- punal ulakam-um, varu.Na-n mae-ya peru-maNal ulakam-um, mullai, kuRi-nj-chi.maru-tham,nhe-i-thal yena,solli-ya muRai-yaal solla-vum padoo-mae!".... (cited from thol-kaa-p-piyam, po.aka.5)

v. ***'thamizh-makka-Lin- marabu-kaL': (Traditions of the Thamizh-people): "thei-vam, uNaa-vae, maa, maram, puL, paRai, sei-thi, yaa-zhin pa-ku-thi-yodu, thokai, yi,***

***av-vakai piRa-vum, 'karu'-vena mozhi-ba!...(cited from thol-kaa-p- piyam, po.aka.*180).**

(Ref: "*thol-kaa-p-piya-th thamizhar*", authored by 'saami-

Chidambara-naar', August 2002, New Century Book House, (P) Ltd, Chennai).

(The lifestyle of the people who lived in Tamil-country has to be understood, in order to appreciate the social commitment of the poet Thiruvalluvar who wanted to fulfill through his ideology. It is the belief of many Tamil-scholars that Thiruvalluvar who wanted the people to educate themselves, and lead a purposeful life, by adopting the virtues of love and kindness, to create an orderly society, free from crimes! He condemns gambling. He wants people to exercise caution against liquor. What is good for the self must be done to others! What is harmful to the self would be harmful to others also, and hence, it must not be extended to others by any person! Good friendship is a wealth, worthy of being earned by any person! He describes the relationship between God and man as a personal relationship. No intermediaries are described. Every bad act will bring bad results to the person the same day! The poet cautions people to remain vigilant against bad elements in the society.Earning of wealth must be pursued through righteous, virtuous and legitimate ways. The poet cautions the society against those who resort to cheating and fraud! He wants people to think rationally, without believing in whatever is being told to them.

He believes that the people's welfare is the supreme concern for the ruler of the land.He cautions the king that a tyrannical rule would lead to a collapse of the kingdom itself, making the king to lose the crown. He believes that the tears of the suffering masses would bring destruction to the ruler of the land. He promises to them that every living human being will become eligible to live in the heaven, if he/she leads a virtuous life! He seems to be a ferocious lover of humanity, showing the righteous path of life. He sympathizes with poor people who are driven to an acute poverty, forcing them to resort to begging. He appeals to them, not to willfully select the practice of begging, as it corresponds to the most cruel way of thinking. He preaches that a person must earn a living by hard work, so that he would enjoy his own food which comes through his hard labour! He gives freedom to people to be angry with the king, if the king's actions are bad. He advises the king to endure the scoldings of the people, and to redress their grievances, so that he will be regarded as their god in human form. The concept of democracy is being taught by the poet, in the style of monarchy!

He wants every person to avoid laziness, lethargy,and procrastination. He gives ideas on business management, financial management, home-management, governance, justice, healthcare, charity, and every human (genuine) need. His wisdom was absolute, wholesome and deep. His method of expressing dissent about certain social evils was so gentle and diplomatic that it took about mare than 2000 years to get ready to understand him properly! He is one of the great men who lived some 2000 years ago, in this world, who cared very much that people must live happily, with all human comforts, with mutual love, kindness and compassion.

He wanted every king to be ready for war, any time, and, cautioned that he should avoid initiating a war with anybody, with either a weak enemy or a stronger enemy, in kural 861! It becomes a policy of peace, recommended for being adopted, in today's world scenario!

The knowledge on religious philosophies of Jainism, Buddhism, and the Cult of Vedas was available to the poet, in the background of the ancient Tamil beliefs and practices, for the purpose of reference. The poet had freedom to compare them, in the light of Tamil- traditions and beliefs, prevailing in the land, while composing Thirukkural. He has made it as a world document! To deserve the treatise being hailed as the "Universal Scriptures"! The future researchers may consider the historical background under which the poet could have arrived at such a compromising document in the contents of THIRUKKURAL

8. **Kural 560.** aa-payan- kundRum, aRu-thozhil-Or nhool-maRappar, kaavalan kaavaan yenin.

   If the king does not protect his kingdom with care, certain bad results will be produced: i) wealth of milk will get reduced, ii) those persons who do the endangered professions like, art, sculpture, poetry (which could survive only with the patronage of the king), will forget the training undergone by them, as they would not have opportunities to practice whatever they have learnt! (Ref: Sujatha Urai; Dr.KalaignarUrai; Dr.Va. Su.Pa.ManickamUrai). (Note: It is a satirical and sarcastic note against the ferocious attitude of a rude-king to conclude that a milking-cow will be afraid of such a king, thereby, being afraid of yielding milk generously! The cow will even be afraid of eating sufficient grass to maintain its health!).

   (In Tholkappiyam, Porul athikaram, verse 74, as cited above, in Tamil, indicates some 6-duties for Brahmanas, 5-duties for Kshatriyas, and

6-duties for Vaishyas! However, Parimelazhagar, the popular interpreter of Thirukkural assumed that the six duties of Brahmanas will 'only' be affected adversely by the tyrannical rule of a king! This needs to be researched!).

9. **Kural 742. maNi-nheerum, maNNum,malaiyum,aNi-nhi- zhal kaadum udaiyathu araN!**

   A protective fort ideally comprises of i) a garland-shaped moat which serves as a clear water defensive trench (mini-reservoir), constructed all around the fort, ii) a shady forest surrounding the garland-shaped moat,

   iii) a vast open land, and iv) a hill. (Note: The neck portion of the garland forms the entrance to the fort! The 'Fort' is depicted as a protected campus surrounded by a garland- shaped moat, and further surrounded by a shady forest. It corresponds to an architectural design, based on the defense-requirement for protecting the fort, during war-time situation). (Ref: moat- Wikipedia: https://en.m.wikipedia.org>wiki).

10. **Kural 763.** olith-thak-kaal, yen-aam, uvari yeli-p-pakai?
    nhaa-kam uyir-p-pa, -k- kedum.

    The interpretation of kural 763 is slightly modified: "What will happen, if angry rats, as a group, make noisy sounds resembling the sound of the noisy-waves of the sea? When a King- Cobra breathes, with a 'hissing' sound, the noise of the rats will die down, and the enmity of the rats will get destroyed." (Note: Some interpreters have stated that the rats will be destroyed on hearing the hissing sound of the King-Cobra! It is the interpreters who have killed the rats, and not the poet! (It is to be taken in a lighter vein!). Thiruvalluvar is an ecologist who believed that the rats and snakes have to co-exist, in spite of their enmity! Therefore, he preferred to state that the enmity between the rats and snake got lost, on hearing the hissing noise of the King-Cobra, thus, helping the rats to run away!).

    (Note: This couplet signifies the enmity between unequal enemies! Perhaps, highlighting the lack of unity among the weaker-party in the fight!).

11. Kural 849. kaaNaa-thaan kaatu-vaan; thaan kaaNaan; kaaNaathaan, kaNdaan-aam, thaan- kaNda- vaaRu.

    A person, who has not seen a particular object, wants to show the object 'seen by him' to another person; He is not able to show it (the object) to that person. Realizing the fact that he has not succeeded in showing the object to the other person, he continues to believe that he has seen the object! He is satisfied with his level of understanding (wisdom) that the object exists exactly as he has seen it! (Note: He has not realized that he has not seen the object. He does not reveal the fact to others. That is a wilful-falsehood on his part). (It sounds like a satire to the acts of bad- persons who claim that they have acquired new wisdom, and exploit the ignorance of others, similar to the cheating styles of those depicted in kurals 274 and 278). Kural 278 states that there are bad persons in the world, “with dirt in their minds, pretending as honourable persons, but doing tricks of disappearing along the river-water in a specific location in the river, to claim a show of strength, and yet, practicing a hideous conduct in the background, in real life”! In kural 274, the poet refers to a person who hides himself in the outward appearance of an ascetic/saint, whereas he indulges in sinful activities, and his actions can be considered similar to the action of a hunter who hides himself behind the bushes before striking at a bird to catch his prey!”. The fact of the matter is that ignorant (fraudulent) persons try to show that they can impart knowledge to others, without themselves acquiring sufficient knowledge to qualify themselves, in order to become eligible to show the way to others! (Note: Heraclitus of Ephasus, an ancient Greek philosopher (6th century BC), as cited in Fragments, states: “Many fail to grasp what they have seen, and cannot judge what they have learned, although they tell themselves: ‘they know’....” This observation tallies with kural 849!).(Some interpreters elaborate on the ignorance of the second person who was unable to see the object shown by the first (fraudulent) man who was trying to show the object which he has never seen before!).

12. **Kural 850. ulakaththaar 'uNdu' yenbapthu, 'il'-yenpaan vaiyath-thu**
'alakai'-yaa vai-k-kap- padum!

When all the people of the world testify the ‘existence’ of an object, if a person says that the object ‘does not exist’, then the person is branded as a bitter person (and a thorny person too!), similar to the wild shrub, Aloe (katRaazhai) which is bitter by taste, and is thorny by touch. In case of superstition widely believed-in by majority of the people, a person who does not believe in superstitions, is considered as valuable as ‘katRaazhai’ which has got a herbal (curing) value!(Note: The term Aloe (kaRRalai, katRaazhai) is used as a mocking-word (teasing-word, kidding-word), like calling a useless-person as "padhar" which means a chaffy-stuff, or "pannaade" (panna-tie), referring to a fibrous cloth-like web around the leaf-stack of a palmyra tree or coconut tree (referring to a person of limited use/knowledge); or calling somebody as "piNNaakku", puNNaakku ('poda-puNNaakku'), while referring to a brainless per son!

(*puNNaakku* is nothing but oil-cake, which remains as a waste- material, after extracting oil from any oil-seeds, such as sesame seeds, or coconut, groundnut (peanuts)!).

(katRaazhai, also spelt as "kaRRalai" referring to: Cacti ethinocereus; Acanthocereus tetragonus; cactus; Prickly pear cactus (Opentiaechios), etc. (https://tamil.samayam.com>health>aloe.vera); OR, aloe vera, health benefits From tamil.samayam.com).

(Ref; Digital Dictionaries of South Asia University of Madras Tamil Lexicon, p.143). There are two 'competitive'- meanings (among the many other meanings) for the word (ALAGAI) used by Thiruvalluvar: namely, i) KatRaazhai or ii) Ghost, vide Madras University Tamil Lexicon! Other interpreters have selected the meaning: Ghost!)(Note: All other interpreters stated that such a person is similar to a ghost!) (If the interpretation revealed in this book (katRaazhai) is accepted, persons who had been branded as 'ghosts' would be liberated as 'human-beings', after having been referred to as ghosts for the past 2000-years!!). It is confidently believed that this new interpretation would be valid in the light of the freedom of thinking permitted and insisted upon, by the great poet Thiruvalluvar, in Kurals 355, 423 and 140, as described below:

a. Kural355: "Whatever be the substance, whatever be the nature of the substance, it can be ascertained as wisdom in a person, if the true nature of it can be reliably assessed/seen/evaluated!';

b. Kural 423: "Whatever is being heard, from whomsoever it may be, the truth behind whatever is being heard must be ascer tained by an individual person. This is called wisdom!";

c. Kural 140: Those who do not learn to live with other people of the world, in agreement with the prescribed-norms of the society, are *considered as illiterate/ignorant persons who lack worldly-wisdom,* even if they have learned many things! (In the light of these ideas clarified in kurals 355, 423 and 140, it is inferred that, it could not have been the intention of Thiruvalluvar to 'curse' a person as a 'ghost', for a difference of opinion or faith, in not agreeing with themasses). Such a person can be called as an ignorant person, but not as a ghost.

13. **Kural 861.** vali-yaar-k-ku maaRu-yaetRal Ombuka; Ombaa, meli-yaar-mael maeka pakai.

    You can agree to any offer of reconciliation from a mightier enemy. But you can easily avoid the enmity with weak persons, so that your kind attitude is exhibited, (and you will have peace of mind!).

    (Note: This seems to be the policy recommended by the poet for those who do not want to have any enmity, with either a stronger enemy or a weaker enemy! This tallies with the idea conveyed in kural 250 which reads as "Any man should remember and contemplate, at the time of rushing upon a person, who is weaker than himself, as to how he would tremble (get terrified), if persons mightier than himself ever come upon him?!" This would help a person who wants to claim that he practices kindness and compassion).

    (Note: THIS CONCEPT, IF PRACTICED, WILL PREVENT WAR, AND EBNABLE WORLD-PEACE!).

14. **Kural 870.** kallaan vekuLum siRu- poruL, ye-gn-gnaa- ndRum ollaan-ai ollaathu oLi.

    Pride and fame will not be available, at any time, to any person who does not come forward to condemn/nullify the atrocious act(evil act) caused to others, by an uneducated (uncultured) person (brute)!

    (Note: The poet fixes the responsibility on virtuous persons for condemning or counteracting against the wrongful act of an unruly person who attacks the helpless people, as expected of them in kural 244 (according to which: "For a person who takes care of all forms of life on earth, and administers (shows) compassion and kindness, there is no necessity for any act(burden) of worrying about the life(safety) of the self!" Such persons will come forward to defend the poor! It becomes the social responsibility to defend the poor and the weak, in a cultured-society, so that the 'good-doer' (*nallathu- sei-pavar*) will win the fame!! (Note: The term 'uneducated' person ('*kallaan*') refers to a person who is not aware of virtuous norms of interacting with the fellow-men!). The probability of 'un- educated' person attacking the poor people is indicated in kural 1079 which states: "If persons of low caliber (mind/attitude) happen to see the decent clothes(dresses) and good food enjoyed by others(who are poorer than themselves), they would find fault with those poor persons (out of jealousy) and pour out complaints, even to implicate them in offensive acts which could correspond to false allegations. Who is there to help the poor? That is the purpose for which this couplet is composed by the poet!). Other interpreters have stated that fame and reputation will not reach a king who does not wage a war against an 'uneducated' king to defeat him, although the earnings gained in defeating the 'small' king may be 'small' and meagre! However, this kind of interpretation would be 'considered' as opposed to the policy of Thiruvalluvar as stated in kural 250, which states that "any person must remember, at the time of rushing upon a weaker person (than himself), as to how he would tremble (get- terrified) if mightier persons, ever, come upon him!". (That is how, he becomes eligible to be regarded as a kind and compassionate person!). The poet is a peace-maker! Not a poet who encourages the strong person to attack a small person to crush him, just be cause the small person (*kallaan)* has not received education!

15. **Kural 895.** yaaNdu-ch-chendRu, yaaNdum, uLar-aakaar, venh- thup-pin,
    vae-nh-thu seRap-pat- tavar.

    A person, having involved in espionage activities, and for that reason, having earned the violent fury of the king, cannot survive anywhere (in the world), to wherever the person may go!

    (Thiruvalluvar has used a word "*venh-thuppin*", which means, "based on severe spying report". This has got relevance to spying or espionage activities by the accused - person! (The term "thuppu" means secret investigation and the subsequent information on evidence (proof), in this context, whereas the other meaning of the same term (*thuppu*) refers to resources, consumption, strength, etc)! Collecting information by the king through officially- employed spies is encouraged in kural-couplets 581, 582, 583 & 584. Spying will cover everybody, including the king's relatives).

16. Kural 897. vakai-maaNda vaazhkkai-yum, vaan- poruLum, yenn-aam, thakai-maaNda thakkaar seRin?

    "What is the benefit of a person having a luxurious life-style, with the backing of a huge wealth, if a great man blessed with virtuous qualities shows the fury towards that person? Some harm would happen to that person. His backings and wealth will be of no use! (Note: This is a general advice to all people to avoid inviting the wrath of wise-elders! However, the fault on the part of the per son facing the wrath of the wise-man has not been explicitly mentioned! This needs a debate.

    We assumed that there should have been some genuine reason for the anger of the great man, without which the wise-man would not have shown his fury (This, we did, in order to justify his anger)! The reason for the fury of the wise-man has not been stated in the couplet 897!

    (We added a phrase, as a trial, "If anybody commits a fault to earn the fury of a great man blessed with virtuous traits (characteristics), some serious harm would occur to the offender!" Then, it makes sense! Without this phrase, the 'judgement on the punishment' will be in error! Please see kural 896 & 898, in which cases, the fault of the offender is specifically mentioned, in both couplets)..

17. **Kural** 899. yaenh-thiya koLkai-yaar seeRin, idai- murinh-thu, vae-nh-than-um, vae-nh- thu kedum.

    If great persons who uphold lofty principles, aimed at the welfare of the people of the world, happen to show violent anger, even the king would happen to lose his kingdom, and get ruined! (Note: The fault committed by the king has not been mentioned. As a trial, we added a phrase: "out of displeasure over the evil-doing by the person-in-power, even the king would happen to lose his kingdom, and get ruined". In that case, it makes sense! (Please see kurals 896 and 898, wherein, the faults of the offender have been specifically mentioned).

18. **Kural 900.** iRanthu-amainh-tha saarpu-(u)daiyar aayinum, uyyaar, siRanh-thu- amainh-tha seeraar seRin.

    However much a person may enjoy the backing of wealth, external support,and facilities, the person may not flourish in life, if great persons blessed with noble qualities happen to develop anger towards him. ('due to some irksome response from that person concerned!').

(Note: The fault caused by that person earning the anger of the elders is not mentioned,in the couplet-900).

Here, we decided to add the words: "due to some irksome response from the person concerned!". (This needs further research, as the harm done by offender to cause the anger of the great person has not been spelled out in the couplet).

The poet firmly believes that the wise-men will not develop anger on unreasonable grounds. If a wise-man becomes angry on any occasion, he will quickly decide to control it, vide kural 29, in sympathy for the person who is likely to be affected by the horrifying effects of such an anger! (Please see kural 896 and 898, where there is a valid mention of an offence which causes the anger (wrath) of the great man, correlating it with the sufferings of the offender). Could there be some reason for not- mentioning the fault of the offender in kurals 897.899 and 900?

G.U.Pope analyzed the case from the view-point of 'puranic' stories, as detailed below:

G.U.Pope has given a commentary as follows: under the heading: 'Offending Kings and Saints: "Thiruvallvar, in the Tamil Veda Tirukkural says: (i) If those wise-men of rigorous penance become enraged, even 'Indra' will crash from power and position (kural 899). ('Nahusan' – 'Agastya' episode mentioned by both Valluvar and 'Manu'). (ii) Should they, who stand as high as the hills, look with disfavour, even men of firm standing in the world (would) perish with all their race (kural 898). Manu in his Manava Dharma Shastra says: (i) 7-39: Let him, though he may already be modest, constantly learn modesty from them; for a king who is modest never perishes; (ii) 7-40 Through a want of modesty, many kings have perished, together with their belongings; through modesty, even hermits in the forest have gained kingdoms; (iii)7-41. Through a want of humility, 'Vena' perished; likewise, king 'Nahusha', 'Sudas', the son of 'Pigavana', 'Samukha', and 'Nemi'". (Ref: Manu in Tirukkural: More couplets compared by G.U. Pope (post No. 4467).

(Note: These details necessitate a detailed research to find out whether kural couplets number 897, 899 and 900 could be considered as 'insertions' from others, at a later period of time?, because, Thiruvalluvar will not justify any punishment on others, without specifying the crime committed by the offender. These couplets make a mention about the anger of these wise-men, without describing the offence committed by the person who gets perished or punished; thereby, lacking the usual logic, characteristic of Thiruvalluvar! Those who undertake this research have to remember the command given by Thiruvalluvar in kurals 355; 423; and, in the light of duties spelled out by the poet as 'bounden-duties of the land-ruler', in kurals 549; 558; 542; 561).

(Note: This could imply the egoistic issue between a ruler of the land and a saint, often referred to in 'puranic' stories, arising out of difference of opinion between the ruler and the saint (who, some- times. happens to be referred as Raja-Guru "Teacher for the King"), in matters related to settling disputes or punishing crimes.

If kurals 897, 899 and 900 are assumed to be composed by Thiruvalluvar, such couplets can be construed as 'advice' given to the ruler (by the poet) to avoid a controversy, with the poet's magnanimous intention to save the ruler of the land, from the fury of the wise-man who remained more popular with innocent people! As a peace-making move, adopted by the poet, a direct-clash between the poet and the saint is avoided! In this relevance, this could be the friendly advice of the poet who sympathizes with the helpless situation of the king, in situations of the people being set-against the king, by the plot devised by the intelligent saint (who could have had the madness referred to by the Greek philosopher Aristotle: who said: "There is no great genius without some touch of madness"! (This danger to the ruler of the land has to be visualized in the light of kural 639 which could happen to the king, being caused by one of his personal-staff, in the rank of a bad minister, with a hidden-enmity!).

Kurals 897, 899 and 900 remain a mystery, in so far as the situation under which they were composed. The poet would not have let down his 'neutral'–stand, on any account.

Any compromise sounds improbable, in view of kural 118. which states: "A weighing balance decides the true weight of an object by balancing the two pans, with reference to a neutral mark. Similarly, wise persons do maintain a fair stand, without deviating from neutrality!".

There are some theoretical conflicts, too, in the matter! In kural 388, the poet declares: "A king who rules the land upholding the virtuous path, and protecting the people with care, will be remembered in the hearts of the people, as God Himself, in human- form!".Such a status could not save the king from the 'fury' of a saint! It is a pity! This ideological conflict needs research!

Thiruvalluvar could have lived in a confused society, excessively, overpowered by religious leaders, compared to the rulers of the land! He mentions about good kings and bad kings, good saints and cheating-saints,virtuous persons and unscrupulous persons, good ministers and bad ministers, farmers and other professionals, poor people, illiterates, beggars,scholars, etc, thus covering a large spec trum of people. He highlights the probability that a king would get ruined, if he does not ensure an adequately upright-rule, thereby, earning the wrath of the people (kurals 555, 560, 551, 552, 553, 554, 566, 567). The poet feels that a king is answerable to the people, and not necessarily to the saint, who comes into the scene in the advisory role (perhaps chosen by the king, as advised in kurals 446 and 447).

The queries raised by G.U.Pope on Kurals like 897, 899 and 900 must be studied further, considering the socio-political situations which prevailed in Tamil-country, during the lifetime of Poet Thiruvalluvar!

19. **Kural 972. piRappu okkom (y)ellaa uyirkkum; siRappu, ov-vaa, sei-thozhil vaetRumai- yaan**

All human beings are equal to one another, on birth. The importance (dignity) assigned to each of them varies, depending on the difference in the quality-characteristic of their actions/activities! (The term 'thozhil' is used in kural-couplets 394; 428; 549; 582; 833; 1252: They can be studied for research purposes).

(Note': There are differences in the interpretations, comparing "work" versus "deeds". i) In the case of work, dignity of labour is the criterion. ii) In the case of deeds, virtue becomes the criterion. It becomes a debatable topic. (Refer to kural 973). Please see Appendix-9).

Inequality by birth, of a child, described in Rig Veda (book 10; hymn 90:12) is moderated/amended in this kural-couplet, as an alternative to the four-varna system of social segregation. As Thirukkural is accepted as the Fifth-Veda in the oldest Indian religion, this aspect elevates the status of Thirukkural as Universal Scriptures, agreeing with the major philosophies of many other religions in the world, in so far as the equality among the humans is concerned! The status of women enshrined in Thirukkural (vide kural 54, 60, 974, 58) makes it all the more universally- acceptable (Please see Appendix-8, item 's').

The fundamental logic for this kural-couplet could have emerged from the scientific reality that all babies are born to mothers, and, hence, all the babies born to mothers are equal to one another. This logic behind kural 972 could be considered as a modification to the concept of babies being born from various parts of a male- god. According to Thiruvalluvar, the poet, the Almighty is impartial, not having likes and dislikes, vide kural 4.Therefore, the Almighty cannot afford to exercise partiality among his children! This is how, it could be considered as an amendment to Rig Vedic verses which describe the origin of 'Varna' among the humans.

(Note: Kural 972: "*piRappu okkum (y)ellaa uyirkkum*" is identified as an iconic reference with Tamil Literature, along with puRanhaanooRu poem: "*yaadhum oorae, yaavarum kaeLir*".

20. Kural 1200. uRaa-ar-kku uRu-nhoy urai-p-paai! kada-lai-ch
cheRaa-a-ai!! vaazhiya, nhenj-chu!!!

She speaks: Long live, my dear conscience! You have to convey the mental agonies which I have been going through, to my man-in-love who has not responded to my love! Do not show your anger to the sea, as it is preoccupied with its own noises of waves!! Perhaps, his situation is like the noisy sea! He could have been preoccupied with other thoughts! Don't be angry with him. Keep on trying, to tell him about my love, please!! (Note: Other interpreters have concluded, as if the woman asks her conscience to stop the effort of communicating her longing-desires of love to the non-responsive lover!).

21. **Kural 1270. peRin-(y)en-naam?, pet-Rakkaal (y)ennaam?, uRin (y) ennaam?**
    uLLam udai-nh-thu ukka-k-kaal?

    He speaks: What would happen, if my woman-in-love cannot bear the pain of parting with me?... as her rightful man-in- love has been separated from her, over a long period of time, due to which,. if she happens to get affected by mental depression?

    In that case, she would not be in her senses! I would not be of any use to her, when we happen to meet?... She would not be of any use to me?... and, even if we embrace each other, there would not be any use, for both! (Therefore. let me hasten to reach there, wherever she is now!.so that I can see her in person,.and save her from a total ruin, to restore the happiness of me and my beloved wife!).

    (Note: Some interpreters have described the pathetic part of the story, and left it there, in which case, it is categorized as a tragedy, in the Shakespearean sense! However, *ManakkudavarUrai* has made it a Comedy, as it was described that it was a story of a worried- husband, blabbering about his wife's plight affected by the separation of the couple, for a long time! When the man decides to return home speedily, it becomes a Comedy, as it is established that the wife is all safe!! This story is an example of an 'anti-climax' in the art of drama!).

APPENDIX-2

TRIBUTES TO THIRUVALLUVAR, THE POET

(Ref: https://en.m.wikipedia.org,wiki): Impact of the Tirukkural)

1. "Sage Thiruvalluvar, priest of thy lowly clan*, No tongue repeats, no speech reveals thy name, Yet, all things changing, dieth not thy fame, For thou art bard of universal man!. While lands far off have heard

   with strange surprise, Faint echoes of thy song! Though all the earth. Men hail thee brother, seer of spotless soul" — (G.U.Pope, 1820-1908). (en.m.wikipedia.org).

   (Note: Publicity for Kural was missing for Thiruvalluvar's Thirukkural, during the days of G.U.Pope, as revealed by his poem! Dr.G.U.Pope is one of the persons responsible for the propagation of Thirukkural around the world! Thank God! 'The faint echoes' referred to, in his poem, has now become a 'vibrant-echo' around the world during 2021!).

2. Thirukkural is "A text book of indispensable authority on moral life"....

   ...."The maxims of (Thiru) Valluvar have touched my soul. There is none who has given such a treasure of wisdom like him" (Mahatma Gandhi, 1869-1948).

3. "Thirukkural gives the knowledge of the simple and clear truth which finds place in every soul that is not stupefied by religious and scientific superstitions—the truth that, for our life, one law is valid—the law of love, which brings the highest happiness to every individual, as well as to all mankind!" (Leo Tolstoy, 1828-1910).

4. Avvaiyaar, a Tamil Poet, claimed to be a contemporary poet during the lifetime of Thiruvalluvar (the author of Thirukkural), pays a tribute that "One Kural couplet consisting of two lines can be considered as a capsule which has compressed the energy-equivalent to what would be released

by breaking an atom, the energy being as huge as what would be required to overturn the seven seas of the world!". (Note: It is a thought-provoking concept of 'breaking an atom', and correlating it with a release of huge quantum of energy being known to a female poet of Tamil Literature who lived 2000 years ago! This needs further research!).

5. "The master piece of Tamil Literature—one of the highest and purest expressions of human thought. That which, above all, is wonderful in the 'Kural' ..." M.Ariel, French Translator of Thirukkural (in Journal Asiatique (November-December, 1848: Monsieur Ariel (E.S.Ariel), or M.Ariel, 'Kural de Thiruvalluvar').

6. "The ideas of great Saint Thiruvalluvar will apply not only to India, but the whole world!"(Rabindranath Tagore, 1861-1941).

7. "It is the gospel of Love, and a code of soul-luminous life!" (C.Rajagopalachari, 1878-1972, Freedom-Fighter for Independence of India, A scholar in Tamil and Sanskrit, Former Governor General of India).

8. "Thirukkural is gnomic poetry, the greatest in planned conception and force of execution ever written in this kind", Sir Aurobindo, (1872-1950), Indian Nationalist, Philosopher,Yogi, and Poet.

9. "Thiruvalluvar was one of the greatest products of Indian culture. The saint's idealism, his philosophy, humane practical sense and cultural ethical code had mingled into the mainstream of Indian Culture, and had become part of the common cultural heritage and Philosophers of India" (Dr.Zakir Hussain, (1897-1969) Former President of India).

10. "There are a great number of problems, economic, political and social, standing in the way of a ruler! Solutions and guidance for such problems can be found in 'Kuralism', the maxims of Thirukkural" (Mrs.Indira Gandhi, (1917-1984), Former Prime Minister of India.

11. "Thirukkural is considered to provide the code of conduct for the humanity of the planet Earth, for all times, which makes the past meet the present and creates the future!" (Dr.A.P.J.Abdul Kalam (1931-2015), Scientist, Former President of India).

12. "I bow to the great Thiruvalluvar! Simple and vast in scope, his thoughts and writings have been a strong influence on humanity, for centuries.

Thirukkural does not refer to any nation, leader, society, language, religion, or caste in the entire book, which is why it has been called the Universal Veda!" (Narendra Damodardas Modi, 1950—xx, Prime Minister of India).

13. "Thirukkural is a standing repute to modern Tamil" (Rev.John Lazarus, Christian Missionary, 1845-1925)..

14. "Thiruvalluvar is rightly considered as Chief d'oeuvre of both Indian and World literature. This is due to not only to the great artistic merits of the work, but also the lofty humane Ideas permeating it, which are equally precious to the people all over the world, of all periods and countries" (Alexander Piatigorsky, Russian Philosopher, 1929-2009).

15. "Humility, charity, and forgiveness of injuries, being Christian qualities are not described by Aristotle! Now these three are everywhere forcibly inculcated by the Tamil Moralist… (Thiruvalluvar)!" (Sir Alexander Grant, (1826-1884), Principal of the University of Edinburgh, (1868- 1884), a British Historian of repute, who had strong links with India)..

16. "No translation can convey any idea of its charming effect! It (Thirukkural) is an apple of gold in a network of silver!!" (Dr.KarlGraul (1814-1864), German Lutheran Missionary, Translator of Thirukkural into Latin & German).

17. "Everyone knows the Thirukkural, one of the World's greatest works on Ethics! There is not a facet of human existence that is not explored and illuminated by this great literature"(Padmashri George L. Hart,III, Professor of Tamil, University of California, Berkeley, United States of America, 1945- xx)

18. "Almost every readings at its freshness and relevance to the problems of our times –for such is its Universality and Humanism ….in Thirukkural" (Yu His, (1951—xx) Taiwanese Poet, Translator of Thirukkural into Mandarin Language, Founder-President of Tamil Sangam in Taiwan).

19. "A work of literary art, Thirukkural reveals a single structural plan, and looks like a Work of a single master!" Kamil Zvelebil (1927-2009), Czech Scholar in Indian Literature and Linguistics).

20. "Tamilnadu gave Thiruvalluvar to the benefit of the World, thereby earning Sky- high Fame!" (Mahakavi Subramania Bharathi, Tamil Poet and Indian Nationalist, 1882-1921)

21. "The best known classical Tamil work is the Kural (Aphoristic stanzas) by the weaver Thiruvalluvar!" (W.Norman Brown (1892-1975), American Ideologist and Sanskritist.

22. "He (Thiruvalluvar) has entirely avoided in the work, everything that savours sectarianism, in order to harmonize the suffrages of all the sects!" (Simon Casie Chetty, Ceylonese Author, 1807-1860).

23. "The Kural's sentences are as binding as the Ten Commandments on the Jews. Kural is as important and influential on the Tamil mind as Dante's great work on the language and thought of Italy". (Charles Edward Gover, English Folklorist. 1835-1872; worked in Chennai; Translated Thirukkural into English; one of the earliest translations).

24. "The future of every country lies at the hands of younger generation.It is the duty of the State to show them the rightful path, and there is no other philosophy than what is preached in Thirukkural!"(Madras High Court, Ashok, K.M., (1 May, 2016):"Teach Thirukkural in Schools to build a Nation with Moral Values: Madras High Court tells Government.

25. "The Kural is the core of the spirit of the Tamil people. And the most remarkable point is that it is threaded through with "Love to the others" (Shuzo Matsunaga, First Japanese translator of the Thirukkural, 1921—xx).

26. "The universal humanism and eclectic spirit that breathe through Thirukkural makes this a masterpiece, defying time, so ancient, yet so contemporary! It overwhelms the reader by its depth of insight and sensitivity!"....Albert Schweitzer, German Theologian (1875-1965).

27. "Thiruvalluvar was a social-scientist who upheld justice for all".... Thirumuruga Kirubananda Vaariyar Swamigal (1906-1993), celebrated as the 64th 'Nayanmaar' in spreading 'Saivite Philosophy'!). "Thirukkural-Kathaigal", meaning "Thirukkural-Stories" was his version of Thirukkural which he preached around the world to propagate 'Valluvarism'!

28. "Thiruvalluvar preached for the path of virtues to be followed by every human being with kindness and compassion to all to deserve the Blessings of the Almighty God!" Kavi Yogi Maharishi Dr.Shuddhananda Bharati Vanmeegar (1897-1990). (He is hailed as the First Translator of

Thirukkural, to have done both verse and prose renderings of Thirukkural into English ("Thirukkural with English-Meaning", 2005, Shree Shenbagha Pathippagam, Chennai).

29. "Thiruvalluvar is, perhaps, the earliest 'dissenter'* in Tamil Society. He is looked upon as a poet and a philosopher who laid down norms for the 'art of living'...His denunciation of the roots of the caste-system, condemning animal- sacrifices, prescribing chastity as a virtue common to both (sexes)... ('kaRpu' in one-case (females), and; 'Pae-raaN- mai' in the case of the other (males). are a few of the instances of his reform-effort!" Dr.V.C.Kulandaiswamy, 1929-2016, Indian Academic, Educationist, Writer, Orator. (Former Vice Chancellor of Madurai Kamarajar University, Anna University, Indira Gandhi National Open University, Member of University Grants Commission, New Delhi, First Vice Chancellor of Tamil Virtual University, Vice Chairman of the Institute of Asian Studies)..

    (Ref: "They Thought Differently"....2004, ISBN 81-7735-160-5; Pavai Printers, Chennai-600014). (Note: karpu=chastity=(Kural 54); PaeraaNmai= steadfast determination against temptation= (Kural 148. (*Note: The term 'dissenter' means 'disagreement with a concept or philosophy or dogma'!).

    In Kural 972, describing the equality of human beings, there is aconflicting-difference, with reference to what has been said in Rig-Veda,with reference to the Four-Varnas-Society, 'by-birth': vide Rig Veda (10:90).

    (Thiruvalluvar's 'Equality theory' contained in Kural 972 was the only one reference in the entire (ancient) writings of Indian origin! Political leaders like Rettamalai-Srinivasan, M.C.Rajah, N.Sivaraj, Mrs. 'Annai' Meenambal Sivaraj, took pleasure in quoting this Kural-couplet 972, while arguing in favour of social-equality, while interacting with Dr.B.R.Ambedkar and Mahatma Gandhi, on topics related to equality among Indians of Independent India! 'Thanthai Periyar' E.V.Ramasamy admired the wisdom behind the 'equality-theory' pronounced by Thiruvalluvar some 2000-years ago!

    i. Diwan Bahadur Rettamalai Srinivasan (1860-1945) (https://en.m.wikipedia.org>wiki>Rett...

    ii. Rao Bahadur M.C.Rajah (1883-1943) (https://en.m.wikipedia.org>wiki>m.c.rajah

iii. Rao Bahadur N.Sivaraj (1892-1864) (https://en.m.wikipedia.org>wiki>n.sivaraj

iv. Mrs. Annai-Meenambal-Sivaraj(1904-1992). (https://en.m.wikipedia.org>wiki>Annai...

v. Thanthai-Periyar-E.V.Ramasamy (1879-1973). (https://en.m.wikipedia.org>wiki>Periyar E.V.Ramasamy

30. "Thirukkural is complete in itself. It is a treatise par excellence on the art of living........Books that talk about Gods and Kings have forgotten the common man in the society.But Thirukkural places man at the forefront, and guides him. Hence, it is a newVedham"....'Mahaa-Sannidhanam ThavaththiruKundrakkudiAdigalaar'. (1925-1995). (https://en.m.wikipedia.org>wiki>Kundrakudi Adigalar. (Citation: "Thirukkural-il TholkaappiyaMeip-paadu-gaL", Dr.C.Sethupathi, 2009,Paavai Publications, Chennai. Page 20)

31. "Thirukkural is a reference book for shaping our attitudes towards fellow-men"....Prof. K.Sivathamby, 1930-2011, Tamil Scholar of Sri Lanka.

32. "Thirukkural must be taught to children right from school-days, so that they become smart and intelligent"..... S.J.V.Selvanayagam, 1898-1977, *'Thanthai-Selva'*, Political leader, Lawyer in Sri Lanka.

33. "There is a treasure of knowledge hidden in Thirukkural. It is an enjoyable experience to study it in depth"..... S.Rajaratnam, 1915-2006, Former Deputy Prime Minister of Singapore.

34. "Thirukkural is a prestigious treasure of world literature. We have got a share in its pride. We must learn it to understand it ourselves"....Yang Amat Berbahagia Tun S.SamiVellu, Malaysian Politician, 1936—xx, Former Minister, and Parliamentarian in Malaysia.

35. "Thirukkural shows the path of life, teaching how to lead a meaningful and purposeful life"...... Prof.Dr.P.Ramasamy, 1949—xx, Malaysian Politician, Former Deputy Chief Minister II of Penang State, Malaysia, Parliamentarian.

36. "Thirukkural recognizes the need for showing kindness and compassion towards the poor and the weak. It is a form of justice",.....Mahakavi Sri Kumaran Asan (Aasaan), (1873-1924), Great Poet of Malayalam language.

37. "The service to people you do to peoples' welfare will be long remembered for many generations. You will find evidence for it, in the great book: Thirukkural"....Diwan Bahadur Arcot Ramasamy Mudaliar, 1887-1976, Indian Lawyer, Diplomat, Statesman, Senior Leader of Justice Party (India),....(tallies with kural 233).

38. "The friends you make in College will be your friends for life! I've met the best people here! It is mentioned in Thirukkural, claiming 'friendship' as wealth and protection",.....Quaid-e-Millat' M.Muhammad Ismail Sahib Rowther, 1896-1972, Indian Politician, Parliamentarian, Social Activist, Former Member of the Constituent Assembly of India....(tallies with kural 783)..

39. "The students in the class-room will get the inspiration to learn, if a kural-couplet is recited once, before commencing the lessons in the day!"... Prof.M.Ruthnaswamy, Educationist, Statesman and Writer, Bar-at-Law, Former Vice Chancellor of Annamalai University (1942-'48).

40. "Tamil Communities living around the world take pride in displaying the portrait of Thiruvalluvar, as a symbol of pride. It makes a sensible relevance!"............

    C.Subraminam, Independence Activist, Member of Constituent Assembly, Statesman, 1910-2000.

41. "Thirukkural is a source of inspiration for promoting intellectual and moral solidarity of mankind!" Dr.Malcom Adiseshaiya, 1921-1994,

    Former Vice Chancellor of Madras University, Former Associate General Secretary of the World University Service in Geneva; Former Assistant Director General of UNESCO.

42. "Thirukkural vouches for patience to endure insults; for promoting the great human quality of magnanimity in protecting one's own self-respect"... Dr.M.Santappa, Former Vice Chancellor of Madras University and Sri Venkateswara University of Tirupathi, a world-renowned research (scientific) contributor in Science and Technology, 1923-2017.

43. "Thiruvalluvar prescribes the norms for imbibing admirable human qualities, to be cultivated from childhood and to be practiced throughout one's lifetime to qualify for fame in life, which would be remembered for

a long time!",. Dr.Mu.Karunanithi, 1924-2018, Social Reformer, Tamil Scholar, Writer, Statesman, Former Chief Minister Of Tamil Nadu.

44. "Thirukkural teaches human justice, without differentiating between the rich and the poor",.......Rao Bahadur Sir A.T.Pannirselvam, 1888-1940, Indian Attorney, Politician, Former Minister of Home & Finance, Madras Presidency.

45. "Thirukkural needs to be made popular in the rural area through lectures, as it shows the way of life"......Diwan Bahadur Agaram Subbarayalu Reddiar, 1855-1921, Former (First) Chief Minister of Madras Presidency.

46. "Thirukkural represents the richness of literature in Tamil Language. Efforts must be made to popularize its contents in rural areas of India, as it shows the way for human interactions in an orderly society"....... Mrs. Ammu Swaminathan, 1894-1978, Former Member of the Constituent Assembly of India, Indian Politician, Indian Social Worker, Political Activist, Indian Independence Activist.

47. "Thirukkural teaches social justice. Charity is insisted upon as a commitment for the privileged persons born in rich families. This helps promoting human sympathy. It reflects a command which other poets could not give to the society. It is a rare literature which describes virtuous human life. It preaches human equality. That is the nobility!".... Prof. 'Naavalar' SomasundaraBharathiar, 1879-1959. Writer, Lawyer, Professor, Social Activist.

48. "The conduct and character of a young person can be moulded through a systematic training, based on the knowledge derived from Thirukkural", V.Nadimuthu Pillai, of Pattukkottai, Parliamentarian, and Member of the Constituent Assembly of India.

49. "The drama, as a popular medium was promoted to spread knowledge from literature, and history, for which Thirukkural gives the command in kural 411"..... Avvai-T.K.Shanmugam Pillai, 1912-1973, Innovative Artist in Tamil Theatre..

50. "Thirukkural was a source of inspiration to spread literature-knowledge in order to be appealing to the people who did not have exposure to letters; and we remember this point while composing songs and dialogues for our

plays, to spread ethics and righteousness"... Sankaradas Swamigal, 1867-1922, a pioneer in Tamil Drama production, Writer, Song-composer, Actor.

51. "Thirukkural teaches the path of love, kindness, compassion and forbearance to the whole humanity, for maintaining peace, happiness,health and prosperity in the world", ...Rev. Fr. Dr. Xavier S. Thani Nayagam, (Thani NayagamAdigalaar), Sri Lankan Tamil Scholar, with exposure to multi-lingual capabilities, 1913-1980, Author of "Tamil Culture and Civilisation", Asia Publishing House, N.Y., 1970.

52. "Thirukkural gives encouragement for those who endeavour hard for achieving success, in their ventures!", SwamiVipulananda (VipulanadaAdigal), 1892-1947, Sri Lankan Scholar, Social Reformer, Poet, Literary critic.

53. "Thirukkural teaches patience, non-violence, grace, and all other good qualities a man must practice in human interactions",...Arumuga Naavalar, Sri Lankan Tamil Scholar, 1822-1879,

54. "Thirukkural offers solace and preaches for practicing endurance for those who meet with hardships or unexpected failures in their experiences in life, and helps to rebuild their lives!', ...Abraham Pandithar, 1859-1917, a Tamil scholar, Tamil musicologist, Composer, Social Reformist.

55. "Thirukkural preaches for human equlaity. Freedom from foreign rule must ensure equality among fellow citizens of India" -. V.I.Muniswamy Pillai (1889-1953) Social Activist, Member of the Constituent Assembly of India (Tallies with Kural 972).

56. "Thirukkural preaches for the creation of a society of disciplined citizens who follow a dignified virtuous path in all their actions", V.Veeraswamy, Former Member of Parliament in India (1952-1957).

57. "Thirukkural offers education to all people, the rich and the poor, insisting on virtuous path, based on the ancient Tamil Culture"..... A.M.Rathnasamy,Indian Independence Activist, Member of the Constituent Assembly (1946-1952).

58. "Kindness to all, and belief in human equality are supreme virtues as glorified in Thirukkural..." C.Iyothee Thass, 1845-1914, Philosopher, Anthrapologist, Journalist... (tallies with kurals 72; 972).

APPENDIX-3 A

COMPARISON OF THIRUKKURAL WITH WORLD-LITERATURE

1. "Words are leaves, the substance consists of deeds which are the true fruits of good tree" .....Queen Elizabeth I (1533-1603): Address to Parliament. Quoted in G.R.Elton,"Renaissance and Reformation 1300-1648)", 2nd Edition, 1968. p.134.... (Tallies with Kural 97: Uttering Pleasant Words).
2. "Chastity is the Ermine of woman's soul. To be a king and wear a crown is a thing more glorious to them that see it than it is pleasant to them that bear it!"...... Queen Elizabeth I: "Collected Works", p.97, University of Chicago Press, 2002. ...... (Tallies with Kural 54: Woman's Honour).
3. "When we hang on to resentments, we poison ourselves, as compulsive over-eaters, we cannot afford resentment, since it exacerbates our disease" - Queen Elizabeth I: "The Public Speaking of the Queen Elizabeth: Selection from Her Majesty's Official Address"...... (Tallies with Kural 853: Healthy attitude towards others).
4. "My loving people, we have been persuaded by some that are careful of our safety, to take heed how we commit ourselves to armed multitudes for fear of treachery; but I assure you, I do not desire to live to distrust my faithful and loving people".... Queen Elizabeth I: (azquotes.com). Speech to the Troops at Tilbury, awpc.cattcente.iastate.edu, August 19, 1588. ..... (Tallies with Kural 388: Glory of ruler).
5. "The stone often recoils on the head of the thrower"... Queen Elizabeth_I... (Tallies with Kural 319: No harm to others).
6. "Heard-melodies are sweet! But, those unheard are sweeter!"....John Keats (1795-1821) (Tallies with Kural 416: Affection in silence).

7. "Before man can be free, and equal, and truly wise, he must cast aside the chains Of habit and superstition, he must strip sensuality of its pomp, and selfishness, Of its excuses, and contemplate action and objects as they really are!" Percy Bysshe Shelley, English Poet (1792-1822), "Shelly on "Love: An Anthology", 1980, p.83, University of California Press. .... (Tallies with Kural 983: Righteousness in action).

8. "The Young are always in extremes!. " Ms. Mary Wollstonecraft Shelley, English novelist, 1797-1851; "Ladore", 1835, p.62........... (Tallies with Kural 976: Need for respecting elders).

9. "I could not understand why men who knew all about good and evil, could hate and kill each other?"..... Ms. Mary Wollstonecraft Shelley, "The Last Man", 1833, p.51. (Tallies with Kural 856: Avoidance of hatred),

10. "Hatred is the madness of the heart!", Lord Byron, English Poet, 1788-1824,. (tallies with Kural 851: Hateful attitude).

11. "That music in itself, whose sounds are strong, the poetry of speech!" Lord Byron; "Byron: Selected Poetry and Prose", 2013, p.375; Routledge. .... (Tallies with Kural 641: Pleasant eloquence).

12. "Love is flower-like! Friendship is like a sheltering tree!" .... Samuel Taylor Coleridge, English Poet, 1772-1834, (Tallies with Kurals 781: 1289 Friendship as a protection).

13. "Gratitude is heaven itself! There could be no heaven without gratitude!" ... William Blake, 1757-1827, English Poet,... (tallies with ...Kural 110: Realisation of gratitude).

14. "The end of all learning is to know God! And out of that knowledge to love and imitate Him!!" .... John Milton .... an English poet, and an intellectual who served as Civil Servant for the Commonwealth of England, 1608-1674,... (tallies with Kural 2: Benefit of education).

15. "The mind is its own place, and in itself can make a heaven of hell, a hell of heaven"....John Milton, (tallies with kural 505 which states that one's action will decide the happiness or sufferings of a person!

16. "As God loves a cheerful giver, so also he loves a cheerful taker; who takes hold of his gifts with a glad heart!",. John Donne,English Poet, 1572- 1631,. (tallies with Kural 1057: pleasure of giving).

17. "Have a heart that never hardens and a temper that never tires, and a touch that never hurts!" .... Charles Dickens (Charles John Huffam Dickens), English Writer and Social critic, 1812-1870, "Our Mutual Friend", 2009, p.415, Cosimo.Inc. ...(tallies with Kural 317): Avoidance of evil acts.

18. "A very little key will open a very heavy door!" Charles Dickens,.. "The Mystery of Edwin Drood and other Stories", 1998, p.358, Peter Preston, Woodworth Editions. ... (tallies with Kural 667: Firmness in action).

19. "The world belongs to those who set out to conquer it armed with self-confidence and good humour". Charles Dickens,. "David Copperfield", 2006,p.160. Penguin..... (Tallies with Kural 540: Avoidance of forgetfulness).

20. "I have been bent and broken; But I hope into a better shape" (Charles Dickens (Tallies with Kural 621).

21. "My advice is never do tomorrow what you can do today. Procrastination is the thief of time!" ..... Charles Dickens,... "David Copperfield", 2006,p.160. Penguin... (tallies with Kural 605: Freedom from laziness).

22. "There can be no friendship without confidence; and no confidence without integrity!" Samuel Johnson (Dr.Johnson), an English Writer, Poet, Lexicographer, Critic, 1709-1784, ... (tallies with Kural 802: Intimacy in Friendship).

23. "Few things are impossible to diligence and skill. Great works are performed, not by strength, but by perseverance!" .... Samuel Johnson (tallies with Kural 666: Firmness in action).

24. "Integrity without knowledge is weak and useless; and knowledge without integrity is dangerous and dreadful".... Samuel Johnson (tallies with Kural 300: Truthfulness; Kural 962: Personal honour).

25. "Knowledge is of two kinds: We know a subject ourselves; or we know where we can find information on it!"...... Samuel Johnson.. (tallies with Kural 677: Methodology for action; Kural 724: Willingness to learn from others).

26. "There is too much of negativity in this world: Do your best to make sure that you aren't contributing to it!" ... Ms. Germany Kent, American print and broadcast journalist, Social Media Expert, 1975-xx, (tallies with Kural 891: Avoidance of causing harm to wise-persons).

27. "For a friend with an understanding heart is worth no less than a Brother!"... Homer, An ancient Greek author and epic poet, (born during 8th Century BC,..quoting from the Odyssey.... (tallies with Kural 801: Intimacy in friendship).

28. "Sleep, delicious and profound, the very counterfeit of death!" ... Homer,.. quoting from The Odyssey... (tallies with Kural 339: Impermanence).

29. "And empty words are evil"... Homer,...quoting from The Odyssey..... (tallies with Kural 200: Avoidance of uttering useless words).

30. "Let me not die ingloriously, and without a struggle, but let me first do some great things that shall be told among men hereafter!"... Homer,.. quoting from The Iliad..... (tallies with Kural 233: Fame; Kural 335: Good deeds before death could occur).

31. "No man or woman born, coward or brave, can shun his/her destiny!".... Homer,..quoting from The Iliad ... (tallies with Kural 380: Destiny).

32. "Beauty! Terrible Beauty! A deathless Goddess-so she strikes our eyes"!...... Homer,...quoting from The Iliad.... (tallies with Kural 1081: Admiration of feminine charm; beauty).

33. "A man who has been through bitter experiences and travelled far, enjoys even his sufferings after a time"....Homer,. quoting from The Odyssey (Tallies with Kural 628: Endurance during hardships in life).

34. "There is no great genius without some touch of madness"....Aristotle, Greek philosopher (384-324 BC)....... (tallies with Kural 503: Clarity based on analysis).

35. "Hate is a bottomless cup; I will pour and pour!"...Euripides (Greek philosopher 480-406 BC), in 'Medea'...... (tallies with Kural 851).

36. "A bad beginning makes a bad ending"...Euripides, a Greek philospher, 480-406 BC,. in 'Medea'...(tallies with Kural 491).

37. "The great pleasure of life is love" ....Euripides, in 'Medea' (tallies with Kural 75),

38. "Friends show their love in times of trouble; not in happiness!"..... Euripides,... in 'Medea' (tallies with Kural 787).

39. "Our wisdom varies in proportion to our failure or achievements",... Euripides, in 'Hippolytus'..... (tallies with Kural 676).

40. "There is no greater evil than one's failure to consult and consider"...... Sophocles, Greek philosopher, 497-406 BC, author of 'Antigone', 'Ajax', 'Electra', 'Oedipus Rex',etc. (tallies with Kural 893).

41. "Tomorrow is tomorrow! Future cares have future cures; and we must mind today!"......Sophocles... (tallies with Kural 605).

42. "I was born to join in love; not in hate!....that is my nature"....Sophocles, ... (tallies with Kural 858).

43. "That man is sharp who can say what he wants in a minimum of words", Aristophanes, Greek philosopher, 446-386 BC, author of 'Lesistrata',.... (tallies with Kural 649).

44. "The greater wealth is to live with content with little!" Plato, Greek philosopher, author of 'Meno', 428/427-348/347 BC........ (tallies with Kural 430).

45. "In peace, sons bury their fathers. In war, fathers bury their sons!"... Herodotus, Greek philosopher, Writer, Geographer and Historian, 484-425 BC... (tallies with Kural 780).

46. "Courage conquers all things: it even gives strength to the body", ... Ovid, (Publius Ovidius Naso), 43 BC-17/18 AD,....author of 'The Metamorphoses....(tallies with Kural 591).

47. "Anger is momentary madness! So, control your passion, or it will control you!"....Horace (Quintus Horatius Flaccus), Roman Lyric Poet (Latin), 65BC-8BC, (tallies with Kural 305).

48. "What wisdom can you find greater than kindness?",.... (Jean Jacquis) Rousseau, Swiss-born Philosopher, 1712-1778,.. (tallies with 75).

49. "Everything is good as it comes from the maker of the world! But (it) degenerates, once it gets into the hands of man!"... (Jean Jacquis) Rousseau,... (tallies with Kural 1062).

    (Note: Thiruvalluvar puts the blame on the Creator of the World, for the poverty responsible for promoting the practice of begging (by the economically-disabled) poor people! Rousseau puts the blame on the ruler of the land, for improper distribution of wealth. It is a socioeconomic problem! It needs a wider debate, including the creation of job opportunities to cater to the needs of various categories of people,such as the skilled, the unskilled, the educated sections of society!).

50. "It is difficult to free fools from the chains they revere!... Voltaire (Francois-Marie Arouet), French Philosopher and Writer (1694-1778),... (tallies with Kural 37).

51. "Our greatest glory is not in never-falling, but in rising every time we fall", Oliver Goldsmith, Anglo-Irish Novelist (1728-1774).........(tallies with Kural 625).

52. "An honest man is the noblest work of God!",..Alexander Pope (English Poet and Satirist, 1688-1744).... (tallies with Kural 34).

53. "We praise those who love their fellow-men", Aristotle, (tallies with Kural 71).

54. "If, knowing God, they lift not hands of prayer, both for themselves and those who call them friends!"... Alfred Tennyson (British poet, 1809- 1892) .... (tallies with Kural 789).

55. "The sovereign cure for worry is prayer!", William James, American Philosopher (1842-1910).... (tallies with Kural 7).

56. "Success depends on a 'plus' condition of mind and body, on power of work, on courage!" ...Ralph Waldo Emerson (1803-1882, American essayist).... (tallies with Kural 661),

57. "Those who love-not their fellow-beings, live unfruitful lives", Percy Bysshe Shelley (British poet, 1792-1822),...... (tallies with Kural 78).

58. "To err is human; to forgive, divine"....Alexander Pope (British Poet and satirist, 1688-1744)..... (tallies with Kural 987).

59. "A contended mind is the greatest blessing a man can enjoy in this world!", Joseph Addison (British Essayist, 1672-1719), ... (tallies with Kural 430).

60. "Enjoy your life without comparing it with that of others!", ... Marquis de Condorcet (known as Marie Jean Antoine Nicolas de Caritat, Nichlas de Condorcet, a French philosopher and mathematician, 1743-1794).... (tallies with Kural 162).

61. "To be happy, at home, is the ultimate result of all ambitions!",..Samuel Johnson (always referred to as Dr.Johnson, English writer, poet, playwright, essayist, moralist, literary-critic, biographer, editor, and lexicographer, 1709-1784)….. (tallies with Kurals 45; 49; 47).

62. "The family is the nucleus of civilisation!", Will Durant (William James Durant, 1885-1981, American Writer, historian and philosopher)…….. (tallies with Kural 60).

63. "I firmly believe that the future of civilization is absolutely dependent upon finding some way of resolving international differences without resorting to war!", … President Dwight D. Eisenhower (American Military Officer, a War-Hero of World War-II, 1890-1969), and the 34th President of the United States of America)… (tallies with Kurals 734; 861).

64. "We have learned that we cannot live alone, at peace; that our well-being is dependent upon the well-being of other nations, far away" … President Franklin D. Roosevelt (American Politician, 1882-1945, 32nd President of the United States of America)…… (Tallies with Kurals 734; 425).

65. "We are free, free to choose our government. To speak out our minds, to observe different religions; because we are generous with our freedom,.., we share our rights with those who disagree with us; because we hate no people and covet no-people's land; because we are blessed with a natural and varied abundance; because we set no limit to a man's achievement, regardless of class, creed, can realize his ambition; because we have great dreams,…, and because we have the opportunity to make those dreams come true!",. Wendell Willkie (American Politician, 1892-1944, Lawyer and Corporate Executive, and the 1940th year nominee for Presidential candidature in the United States)… (Tallies with Kurals 731; 736; 737; 738; 739; 733; 732). (Ref: Lillian Eichler Watson, 1951, "Light from many Lamps", A Fireside Book, Published by Simon & Schuster. p.318.

    (Note: These contents in the statements given by an American Politician, to enthuse and motivate the younger generation, the future hope of Humanity. It is applicable in India Too! in India too!).

66. "Consider your origin. You were not formed to live like brutes; but to follow virtue, And knowledge" Durentedelgi Alighieri (Dante), Italian

philosopher, 1265-1321, Author of 'Divine comedy', referred to as "Father of Italian Language" (tallies with Kural 952: good family-virtues).

67. "Love insists the loved loves back"....Dante Alighieri, Italian poet, writer and philosopher (tallies with kural 1204).

68. "The first method of estimating the intelligence of a ruler is to look at the men he has around him" Niccolo Machiavelli, 1469-1527), Italian Diplomat.... (tallies with Kural 446).

69. "Everyone sees what you appear to be; few experience what you really are",....Niccolo Machiavelli,. (tallies with kural 826).

70. "Surround yourself with people who make you happy; people who make you laugh; who help you when you are in need; People who genuinely care! They are the ones worth keeping in your life; everyone else is just passing through!"....Karl Marx (1818-1883).... (tallies with Kurals 786; 787; 781; 783; 792).

71. "Good, better, best; never let it rest! Till your good is better; your better is best!"...St. Jerome (Jerome Of Stridon), Latin Priest, 342/347-420 A.D,. (tallies with Kural 666).

72. "Compassion is the basis of morality"...Arthur Schopenhauer ...1822-1893, German philosopher... (tallies with Kural 242).

73. "Your attitude, not your aptitude, will determine your altitude"...Zig Ziglar, 1926-2012, American Author, Salesman, and motivational speaker (tallies with Kural 595).

74. "The best preparation for tomorrow is doing your best today"...H.Jackson Brown, Jr., (Harriet Jackson Brown Jr.).1940—xx, author of "Life's Little Instruction Book",.. (tallies with Kural 605).

75. "Beauty is Power! A smile is its sword!" ...John Ray, English Naturalist, 1627-1705... (tallies with Kural 93).

76. "Once you replace negative thoughts with positive ones, you start having positive results"...William Nelson (Willie Hugh Nelson).1932—xx, American Musician... (tallies with Kural 798).

77. "It is not what you have lost; but what you have left that counts"....Harold Russel, 1914-2002, American-Canadian Film Actor,....(tallies with kural 114).

78. "Every generation enjoys the use of a vast hoard bequeathed to it by antiquity, and transmits the hoard, augmented by fresh acquisitions, to future ages"...Lord Thomas Macaulay (Thomas Babington Macaulay), 1800-1859, who served on the Governor General's Council, in India, and was instrumental in making English the medium of instruction for higher education in India......(tallies with kural 725).

79. "Those who bring sunshine to the lives of others, cannot keep it from themselves"!..... James Mathew Barrie, Scottish Novelist, 1860-1937.... (tallies with kurals 101; 103).

80. "The main aim of religion is not to get a man into heaven,but to get heaven into him",.....Thomas Hardy, 1840-1920, an English Novelist and Poet,.... (tallies with kural 50).

81. "There is no greater hell than to be a prisoner of fear",...Ben Johnson,English Playwright, and Poet, 1572-1637.....(tallies with kural 382.

82. "The best portion of a good man's life: his little, nameless unremembered acts of kindness and love",...... William Wordsworth... (in Lyrical Ballads), 1770-1850, English Poet.....(tallies with kural 975).

83. "Life of great men all remind us,we can make our lives sublime, and departing, leave behind us,foot prints on the sands of time",... Henry Wordsworth Longfellow, 1807-1882, an American poet and Educator,....... (tallies with kurals 114; 50).

84. Spanish-Proverb: "Love can do it all!".....(tallies with kural 75; 71).

85. Italian Proverb: "The poor man is lacking many things; A greedy man lacks all things!".........(tallies with kural 368).

86. Irish Proverb: "May the hinges of our friendship never grow rusty!".... (talles with kural 425).

87. Turkish Proverb: "Whoever gossips you, will gossip of you too!"....(tallies with 188).

88. Mexican Proverb: "Show me whom you are with; I 'll show you who you are!"...(tallies with kural 452).

89. Brazilian Proverb: "There's no good thing that lasts for ever; nor evil that never ends!...(tallies with kural 376).

90. Columbian Proverb: "Clean hands offend no one"....(tallies with kural 995; 978).

91. Proverb in Egypt: "Seek to perform your duties to your highest ability; this way, your actions will be blameless!"......(tallies with kural 616; 665).

92. Arabian proverb.1: "He who eats alone, chokes alone!'....(tallies with kural 82).

93. Arabian Proverb.2: "Your degree is a piece of paper; your education is seen in your behaviour!"......(tallies with kural 391).

94. Proverb from Netherlands: "Fools get the best cards!"....(meaning: Luck can overcome intelligence!).......(tallies with kural 1072).

95. Russian Proverb: An old friend is better than two new friends! (tallies with kural 508).

96. Proverb(1) from Portugal: "Who sees face does not see heart!", meaning: Do not judge a book by its cover!.........(tallies with kural 355).

97. Proverb(2) from Portugal: "Hear no evil; See no evil; Speak no evil"..... (tallies with kural 202).

98. Proverb from Czechoslovakia: "Good advice is better than gold!".... (tallies with kural 462).

99. Proverb from Hungary: "Your lies will come to light sooner than you think!"...(tallies with kural 293).

100. Proverb from Romania: "Adversity makes a man wise, not rich!",...(tallies with kural 796).

101. Proverb from Switzerland: "It is easier to criticize than to do better!".... (tallies with kural 664).

102. Proverb from Finland: "What comes singing, leaves whistling"....(tallies with kural 332). (The coming-in and going-out, applicable to wealth!).

103. Proverb from Sweden: "We notice faults of others, and easily forget our own!'....(tallies with kural 436).

104. Proverb from Poland: "You become whom you befriend!"..(tallies with kural 452).

105. Proverbs from Greece: "When a person in authority is not present, the others enjoy their freedom!"....(tallies with kural 520)..

106. Proverb from Austria: "Nothing ventured,nothing gained!"...(tallies with kural 449).

107. It is a capital mistake to theorize before one has data! Insensibly, one begins to twist facts to suit theories, instead of theories to suit facts"..... Sir Arthur (ignatius) Conan Doyle, tallies with kurals 423, 1079).

108. "Believe nothing that you hear!,.. and only half that you see!"...Edgar Allan Poe, American Novelist, and Literary Critic, 1809-1849, (tallies with kurals 355; 423).

109. "I must learn to be content with being happier than I deserve!"...Jane Austen, 1775-1817, British Novelist,....Author of 'Pride and Prejudice', 'First Impression', etc... (tallies with kural 430).

110. "If you tell the Truth, you don't have to remember anything!'...Mark Twain, 1835-1910, American Writer, Humorist and Entrepreneur,..... (tallies with kural 294).

111. "Always forgive your enemies; nothing annoys them so much!",...Oscar Wilde, 1854-1900, Irish Poet, Playwright, author of 'The Importance of Being Earnest',etc......(tallies with kural 314).

112. "I always advise people never to give advice!",...P.G.Wodehouse (Sir Pelham Grenvile Wodehouse), 1881-1975)...English Writer, Playwright,... (tallies with kural 664).

113. "A friend is a gift you give yourself ",...Robert Louis Stevenson, 1850-1894, Scottish Novelist, Essayist, Poet,... (tallies with kural 781).

114. "Fear is the mother of Foresight"..Thomas Hardy (Thomas Hardy OM), 1840-1928, English Novelist, Actor, Producer,... (tallies with kural 428).

115. "If a man deceives me once shame on him; if he deceives me twice, shame on me" Edgar Allen Poe, American Novelist Actor, Literary Critic, 1809-1849,... (tallies with Kural 655)..

116. "All things must be examined,debated, investigated, without exception and without regard for anyone's feelings", ...Denis Diderot, 1713-1784, French philosopher,...(tallies with kurals 355 and 423).

117. "Peace is not the absence of war. It is a virtue: a state of mind; a disposition of benevolence, confidence and justice" Baruch Spinoza, 1623-1677, Dutch- Portuguese philosopher,......(tallies with kural 734).

118. "When angry, count ten, before you speak; If very angry, (count) a hundred!",...Thomas Jefferson, 1743-1826, Third President of the United States of America, Dipolmat,Statesman, Lawyer, Archtect, Philosopher,.... (tallies with kural 303).

119. "I have to remember that, for the most part, people will see me for what I do; and not for what I say I do!",.... Ms.Jemima Jo Kirke, 1985-xx, English-American Artist, Actress, Director....(tallies with kural 26).

120. "Tyranny and anarchy are never apart",.....Samuel Bentham, 1757-1831, British Mechanical Engineer and Naval Architect......(tallies with kural 551).

121. "There is nothing more artistic than to love people",....Vincent van Gogh, 1853-1890,..Dutch Painter......(tallies with kural 73).

122. "All mankind, being all equal and independent, no one ought to harm another in his life, health, liberty or possessions", ...John Locke, 1632-1704, English philosopher,physician, an Enlightenment Thinker,........ (tallies with kural 204).

123. "People who know little are usually great talkers; while men who know much say little"...... Jean Jacques Rousseau, 1712-1778, Genevan Philosopher, Writer, Author of Social Contact,. (Tallies with Kural 26).

124. "Truth is the cry of all; but the game of few",... George Berkeley, 1685-1753, Anglo-Irish philosopher,... (tallies with kural 300; 997).

125. "No society can surely be flourishing and happy of which by far the greater part of the numbers are poor and miserable"....Adam Smith, 1723-1790, British Economist, Philosopher,...(tallies with kural 734).

126. "Beauty is no quality in things themselves. It exists merely in the mind which contemplates them; and each mind perceives a different beauty",... David Hume, 1711-1776, Scottish Enlightened Philosopher, Historian... (tallies with kurals 73; 982).

127. "Reasoning draws a conclusion; but it does not make the conclusion certain, unless the mind discovers it by the path of experience",....Roger Bacon, 1220-1292,medieval English Phlosopher and Franciscan friar, ...(tallies with kural 352).

128. "Crimes are more effectively prevented by the certainty than the severity of punishment", Cesare Beccaria, 1738-1794, Italian Thinker, ...(tallies with kurals 549; 562);

129. "and to every action, there is always an equal and opposite or contrary reaction"....Isaac Newton, 1643-1727), English Mathematician, Physicist, Astronomer, Theologian, Writer,,...(tallies with kural 319).

130. 'Inspiration exists! But, it has to find you working!",... Plato Picaso, 1881-1973, Spanish Painter, Sculptor, Theatre Designer,... (tallies with kural 616).

131. "That is only one thing that matters: Customer satisfaction!", ...Ms. Raphael, (Sanzio da Ulbino) 1483-1520,Italian Painter,....(tallies with kural 120).

132. "I am going to live for ever! Geniuses do not die"!. Salvador Dali, 1904-1989, Spanish surrealist artist, expert in draughtmanship (tallies with kural 665).

133. "It is not enough to be nice! You have to be good!"...Roger Scruton (Sir Roger Vermon Scruton), 1944-2020, English Philosopher, ...(tallies with kural 818).

134. "To know how to wait is the secret of success!", Joseph de Maistre, 1753-1821, French Philosopher,Lawyer, Writer, Diplomat,......(tallies with kural 490).

135. "A person may cause evil to others not by his action, but by his inaction, and in either case, he is justly accountable to them for the injury",...John Stuart Mill, 1806-1873, English Political Philosopher and Economist,....... (tallies with kurals 818; 824).

136. "Everybody feels the evil; but, no one has courage or energy enough to seek the cure"..Alexis de Torqueville, 1805-1859, French Aristocrat, Diplomat, Political Scientist, Historian, (tallies with kurals 870; 561; 784).

137. "It cannot be precisely known how anything is good or bad, till it is precisely known what it-is!",... James-Mill, 1773-1834, Scottish-Philosopher,,,,,,,,,,(tallies with kural 355).

138. "Every block of stone has a statue inside it! And, it is the task of the sculptor to discover it!"...Micheangelo, 1475-1564, Italian Sculptor,... (tallies with kural 355).

139. To think is to confine yourself to a single thought that one day stands like a star in the world's sky!",....Martin Heidegger, 1885-1976, German Philosopher,....(tallies with kural 975).

140. "The world is my country! All mankind are my brothren! And To do good is my religion!!....Thomas Paine, 1737-1809, English-born-American Political Activist, Political Theorist, (tallies with kurals425; 426; 140).

141. "The real man smiles in trouble! Gathers strength from distress; and grows brave by reflection",... Thomas Paine, English - born American Political Activist (1737 - 1809) ......(tallies with kurals 621; 622).

142. "There is no greater tyranny that which is perpetrated under the shield of law, and in the name of law"....Motesquieu, 1689-1755, French Philosopher, Judge, Man of Letters,..(tallies with kurals 551; 552).

143. "The reading of all good books is like conversation with the finest men of past centuries!",...Rene Descartes, 1596-1650, French Philosopher, Mathematician, Scientist.... (tallies with kurals 724; 717; 399).

144. "Every man is the architect of his own fortune!",...Sallust, 86 BCE-35 BCE, Roman Historian, ...(tallies with kural 759).

145. "There is no witness so dreadful, no accuser so terrible, as the conscience that dwells in the heart of every man!",.... Polybius, 200 BC, Greek Philosopher, Author of "Rise of Roman Empire", (tallies with kural 293).

146. "I don't need a friend who changes when I change, and who nods when I nod; my shadow does that much better", Plutarch, Greek Philosopher, 46 AD-119 AD., (tallies with kural 784).

147. "The secret to happiness is freedom! And secret to freedom is courage!!"... Thucydides, Athenian Historian, 460 BC – 400 BC........(tallies with kural 591).

148. "Self confidence must always ride side by side with strong sense of humility!",......Xenophon of Athens, a Military Leader, Philosopher,Historian, 430 BC – 355/354 BC......(tallies with kurals 985; 125; 979).

149. "To spare oneself from grief at all cost can be achieved only at the price of total detachment which excludes the ability to experience happiness",... Eric Fromm (Eric Seligmann Fromm), 1900-1980, German Social Psychologist, Philosopher, author of "The Art of Living", "Escape from Freedom", "Man for Himself ", "Psychoanalaysis and Religion', "The Sane Society", "The Nature of Man", "The Art of Being", "The Heart of Man", "The Anatomy of Human Destructiveness"...,......(tallies with kural 341).

150. "Human it is to have compassion on the unhappy", Giovanni Boccaccio, 1313-1375, Italian Writer, Poet, Renaissance Humanist, ...(tallies with kural 571).

151. "Education is the art of making man ethical",...George Wilhelm (Fredrich) Hegel, 1770-1831, German Philosopher, ...(tallies with kurals391; 400).

152. "To those who, no longer, have a homeland, writing becomes home!",... Theodor W. Adorno, German philosopher, 1903-1969, (tallies with kural 397).

153. "The only person with whom you have to compare yourself is you in the past",....Sigmund Freud, 1856-1939, Austrian Neurologist,... (tallies with kural 436).

154. "Everything has been figured out, except how to live!",... Jean Paul Charles Aymard Sartre, 1905-1980, French Philosopher, Playwright,Political Activist, (tallies with kurals 45; 50).

155. "It is for those without hope, that hope is given",....Walter Benjamin, 1892-1940, German Philosopher,...(tallies with kural 221).

156. "No one is free until we are all free!",...Jurgen Habermas, 1929-xx, German Philosopher, Sociologist,... (tallies with kural 37).

157. "Being first virtues of human activities, truth and justice are uncompromising"...John Bordley Rawls, 1921-2002, American Philosopher,... (tallies with kurals 300; 388; 541).

158. "Our patience will achieve more than our force", Edmond Burke, 1729-1797, Irish - born British Statesman,, Economist, Philosopher, ... (tallies with kural 156).

159. "Kind words don't cost much. Yet they accomplish much", ...BlaisePascal, 1623-1662, French Mathematician, Physicist, Philosopher,Writer, Catholic Theologian, ...(tallies with kural 100).

160. "Nature has placed mankind under the governance of two sovereign masters: pain and pleasure! It is for them alone to point out what we ought to do, as well as to determine what we shall do!"...Jeremy Bentham, 1748-1832, English Philosopher, Jurist, Social Reformer, Founder of Modern Utilitarianism......(tallies with kurals 137; 628; 505).

161. "Reading maketh a full man; Conference a ready-man; and writer an exact man!"...Sir Francis Bacon, 1561-1626, English Statesman, Philosopher,.....(tallies with kurals 396; 394; 717).

162. "One who makes himself a worm,cannot complain afterwards, if people step on him", Immanuel Kant, 1724-1804, German Philosopher,....(tallies with kurals 37; 967).

163. "May be the target nowadays is not to discover what we are! But to refuse what we are!!".... Paul Michel Foucault, 1926-1984, French Philosopher, Writer, Political Activist,....(tallies with kurals 435; 190).

164. "Three passions, simple, but overwhelmingly strong, have governed my life: i) the longing for love, ii) the search for knowledge, and iii) unbearable pity for the suffering of mankind!"........Bertrand (Arthur William) Russel, 1872-1970, British philosopher, (tallies with kural 578).

165. "Failure is instructive"......John Dewey, American philosopher, Psychologist, 1859-1952, (tallies with kurals 473; 539).

166. "That is what I consider true generosity! You give 'your' all! And, yet, you always feel as if it costs you nothing" Simone de Beauvoir, French Writer, Social theorist, 1908-1986, tallies with kural 235).

167. "The first step towards non-violence, which is surely an absolute obligation we all bear, is to begin to think critically, and to ask others to do the same!"......Ms. Judith Pamela Butler, 1956-xx, American Philosopher, Gender Theorist, (tallies with kural 317).

168. "Talent is a flame; Genius is a fire!"....Bernard Williams (Sir Bernard Arthur Owen Williams), 1929-2003, English Philosopher (tallies with kural 421).

169. "Society means unity in diversity!",......George Herbert Mead, 1863-1931, American Scientist, Sociologist, ... (tallies with kural 140).

170. "Our greatest glory is not in never-failing; but, in rising-up, every time we fall"........Ralf Waldo Emerson.1803-1882, American Essayist, ...(tallies with kural 628).

171. "Change will not come, if we wait for some other person, or some other time! We are the ones, we have been waiting for! We are the change that we seek! ",.....Charles Sanders Peirce, 1839-1914, American Philosopher, Logician, Mathematician, Scientist,.......(tallies with kurals 605; 466; 505; 609).

172. "Unless you can find some sort of loyalty, you cannot find unity and peace, in your active living!", ...Josiah Royce, 1855-1916, American Objective Idealist, Philosopher, ...(tallies with kural 462).

173. "The great aim of education is not knowledge; but action!",. Herbert Spencer, 1820-1903, English Philosopher, ...(tallies with kuarl 391).

174. "The ethic of conviction and the ethic of responsibility are not opposites; they are complementary to one another"......Max Weber, German Sociologist, 1864-1920,... (tallies with kural 994).

175. "If I had my life to live ever again, I would have made a rule to read some poetry, and listen to some music, at least once a week!",...... Charles (Robert) Darwin, Naturalist, 1809-1882,... (tallies with kurals 411; 420).

176. "melancholy suicide— This is connected with a general state of extreme depression and exaggerated sadness, causing the patient no longer to realize sanely the bonds which connect him with people and things, about him. Pleasures no longer attract...".…, Emile Durkheim, French Sociologist, 1858-1917,... (tallies with kural 999).

177. "The sacred formula of positivism; love as a principle, the order as foundation, and progress as a goal",....Auguste Comte, 1798-1857, French Philosopher, and Writer, ...(tallies with kural 47; 45; 540).

178. "He is educated who knows how to find out what he does not know"..... Georg Simmel, German Sociologist, Anthropologist, Philosopher, 1858-1918... (tallies with kural 978; 399).

179. "Self-trust is the first secret of success", Ralph Wado Emerson, American poet, 1803-1882,. (tallies with kural 595).

180. "Culture, the acquainting ourselves with the best that has been known and said in the world, and thus with the history of human kind", Mathew Arnold, English poet and cultural critic, 1822-1888,. (tallies with kural 140; 725).

181. "Unity is strength.....when there is team-work and collaboration... Wonderful things can be achieved", Mattie J.T.Stepanek, 1990-2004, American poet and writer,. who died at the age of 13, after authoring 7 best-selling books of poetry and peace-essays. (tallies with kural 651).

182. "Eventhough the future seems to be far away, it is actually beginning right-now!", Mattie J.T.Stepanek,. (tallies with kural 611).

183. "While we are living in the present, we must celebrate life every day, knowing that we are becoming history with every work, every action,every deed",....Mattie J.T.Stepanek,. (tallies with kural 975).

184. "People are capable, at any time in their lives, of doing what they dream of "...Paulo Coelho, 1947—xx, a Brazilian lyricist and novelist..author of a novel "The Alchemist", in Portuguese language (tallies with kural 609; 471).

185. "Words are, of course, the most powerful drug used by mankind", Joseph Rudyard Kipling, 1865-1936, (born in Mumbai), an English journalist, story-writer, poet, novelist,....(tallies with kural 91).

186. "Intelligence without ambition is a bird without wings",... Salvador Dali, 1904-1989, a Spanish painter of repute, creator of 'The Persistence of Memory', a piece of Art, presently being kept in the Museum of Modern Art in New York... (tallies with kural 592).

187. "No person is your friend who demands your silence, or denies your right to grow",....Alice Walker (Alice Malsenior Telluah-Kate Walker), 1944—xx, American Novelist, Poet, and Political activist, author of 'The Color Purple', Winner of Pulitzer Prize for Fiction, (tallies with kural 825).

188. "If you haven't got it, you can't show it',...Ms. Zora Neale Hurston, 1891-1960, American Writer, Folklorist and Anthropologist, author of 'Their Eyes Were Watching God', 1937... (tallies with kural 849).

189. "The only way get a thing done is to start to do it; then, keep on doing it, and finally, you will finish it",....Langston Hughes, (James Mercer Langston Hughes) 1902-1967, American Poet, Social activist, author of 'The Big Sea', 1940......(tallies with kural 611).

190. "When your rage is choking you, it is best to say nothing", Ms. Octavia E. Butler, 1947- 2006), American Science Fiction Writer, ...(tallies with kural 305).

191. "Don't leave inferences to be drawn, when evidence can be presented", ... Richard Nathaniel Wright, 1908-1960, American writer of novels, short stories, and poems .....(tallies with kural 355).

192. "The world is a possibility, if only you'll discover it",...Ralph Waldo Ellison, 1914-1994, American Writer, and Social activist, author of 'Invisible Man',... (tallies with kural 472).

193. "In every conceivable manner, the family is the link to our past, bridge to our future", ...Alex Halley (Alex Murray Palmer Halley), 1921-1992, American Writer, author of 'Roots: The Saga of an American Family', ...(tallies with kural 522).

194. "It is for God to punish wicked persons; we should learn to forgive"... James Arthur Baldwin, 1924-1987, American Writer and Social Activist, ...(tallies with kural 987).

195. "You can do some rather extraordinary thing, if that is what you believe in"......... Ms. Toni Morrison (Chloe Anthony Wofford Morrison), 1931-2019,American novelist,Nobel Prize Winner in Literature (1993), Winner of Pulitzer Prize for Fiction, author of 'Song of Solomon', etc. ....(tallies with kural 26).

196. "Love recognizes no barriers; It jumps hurdles; Leaps fences;penetrates walls; to arrive at its destination, full of hope",.....Ms. Maya Angelou, 1928-2014, American Poet,Social Activist... (tallies with kural 71).

197. "Leaders must invoke an alchemy of great vision" Dr. Henry Kissinger, 1923-xx, Former Secretary of States, U.S.A. (tallies with kural 648).

198. "Success is more permanent when you achieve it without destroying your principles" Mr. Walter Cronkite, Jr., and American Broadcast Journalist 1916-2006). (tallies with kural 989).

APPENDIX—3B

COMPARISON OF THIRUKKURAL WITH SHAKESPEAREAN IDEOLOGY

William Shakespeare, 1564-1616, Poet, Play Wright, Dramatist, and actor)

1. "If music be the food of love, play on; give me excess of it" Twelfth Night,(Act I. Scene 1).. … (Tallies with Kural 412: Pleasure of listening).
2. "Besides that he is a fool, he is a great quarreler; and but he hath the gift of a coward to ally the gust he hath in quarreling, 'tis thought that among the prudent he would quickly have the gift of a grave", Twelfth Night, Act I, Scene 3…(Tallies with Kural 305: angry person inviting danger),
3. "What's a drunken man like? Like a drowned man. A fool and a mad man; one draught above heat makes him a fool; the second mads him; and a third drowns him!" Twelfth Night, Act I, Scene.5.. (Tallies with Kural 929: drunken person loses control over his senses).
4. "Fate! Show thy force; ourselves we do not owe; What is decreed must be, - and be this so!" (Twelfth Night: Act I; Scene.5)….. (Tallies with Kural 377: Inescapable situations).
5. "Her will is, it should be so returned: If it be worth stooping for, there it lies in your eye! If not, be it his that finds it!" (Twelfth Night; Act II; Scene II)…… (Tallies with Kural 709: Eyes as index of the mind).
6. "O Time, thou must untangle this, not I; It is too hard a knot for me to untie!", Twelfth Night, Act I, Scene 2,… (Tallies with Kural 676: cleverness to escape a tough situation).
7. "Unnatural deeds/ Do breed unnatural troubles!" Macbeth, Act V, Scene.1,.. (Tallies with Kural 319: Tit for Tat).

8. "You know that Love/Will creep in service/Where it cannot go!", Two Gentlemen of Verona; Act IV, Scene.2,... (Tallies with Kural 71: Greatness of kindness).

9. "Cowards die many times before their deaths!/The valiant never taste of death but once!", Julius Caesar, Act II, Sc.2,... (Tallies with Kural 244: Courage embraces conviction to serve others).

10. "Live a Thousand years, I shall not find myself so apt to die!",...Julius Caesar, Act III, Scene.1,.... (Tallies with Kural 245: Purposeful life promises longevity).

11. "Out, out, brief candle!/ Life is but a walking shadow, a poor player/ That struts and frets his hour upon the stage/ And then is heard no more; It is a tale/ Told by an idiot, full of sound and fury/ Signifying nothing!", Macbeth, Act V, Scene. 5... (Tallies with Kural 337: Fear of impermanence).

12. "For where thou art, there is the world itself! With every pleasure in the world/ And where thou art not,desolation!" Henry VI (2nd Part), Act III, Scene.2, ... (Tallies with Kural 379: Never to lose heart at times of crisis).

13. "What a piece of work is a man! How noble in reason/how infinite in faculty/ In form and moving, how he expresses and admirable, in action how like An angel, in apprehension, how like a god—the beauty of the world, The paragon of animals!", (Hamlet, Act II, Scene.2, (Tallies with Kural 34: an ideal person).

14. "All the world's a stage! And all the men and women merely players; They have their exits and entrances!", As You Like It; Act II,Scene.7.... (Tallies with Kural 336: human life is mortal).

15. (recovering from failure) "What can be avoided / Whose end is purposed by the mighty gods?" Julius Caesar, Act II, Sc.3......... (Tallies with Kural 380: the might of destiny).

16. "Wise men never sit and wail their loss, but cheerily seek how to redress their harms", Henry VI, Part 3, Act 4, Scene4,... (Tallies with Kural 625: Endurance helps).

17. "There is a tide in the affairs of men which taken at the flood, leads on to fortune; omitted, all the voyage of their life is bound in shallow and in

miseries", Julius Caesar, Act 4, Scene 3,.... (Tallies with Kural 671: careful and bold approach helps; Kural473: Knowing one's own strength).

18. "How, in one house, should many people under two commands hold amity? It is hard; almost impossible", King Lear, Act 2, Scene 4.. (Tallies with Kural 885: Internal rivalry to be avoided).

19. "To business that we love we rise betimes and go to 't with delight", Antony and Cleopatra, Act 4, Scene 4,... (Tallies with Kural 512: happy undertakings will yield results).

20. "It is not the stars to hold our Destiny! But in ourselves", Julius Caesar, Act 1, Scene2, page 6,.. (Tallies with Kural 619: Will to win materializes).

21. "Strong reasons make strong actions", King John, Act 3, Scene4... (Tallies with Kural 661: Justified approach helps).

22. "Go wisely and slowly; Those who rush, stumble and fall", Romeo and Juliet, Act 2, Scene 3, page 4....(Tallies with Kural485; 473: systematic approach helps; hap-hazard planning will end in misery).

23. "Brevity is the soul of wit", Hamlet, Act 2, Scene 2 ... (Tallies with Kural 649: Apt words will convey the correct sense).

24. "Things won are done! Joy's soul lies in the doing", Troilus and Cressida, Act 1, Scene 2...... (Tallies with Kural 26: Achievers deserve merit).

25. "how far the little candle throes his beams? So shines a good deed in a naughty world", The Merchant of Venice, Act 5, and Scene 1... (Tallies with Kural1022: Dedication gives strength to achieve).

26. "And oftentimes excusing of a fault doth make the fault the worse by the excuse", King John, Act 4, Scene 2,... (Tallies with Kural 466: Decision must be logical).

27. "Love sought is good; but given unsought is better", Twelfth Night, Act 3, Scene 1, page 8,.... (Tallies with Kural 462: depends on persons concerned).

28. "Though this be madness, yet there is method in't", Hamlet, Act 2, Scene 2, page 9, ... (Tallies with Kural 873: rational thinking matters).

29. "The purest treasure mortal times afford Is spotless reputation; that away! Men are but gilded loam, or painted clay....Mine honor is my life; Both

grow in one; Take honor from me; and my life is done", Richard II, Act 1, Scene 1,...(Tallies with Kural 982: greatness has its own value).

30. "If we should fail? We fail. But screw your courage to the sticking place, and we'll not fail", Macbeth, Act 1, Scene 7, page 3, ... (Tallies with Kural 597: Boldness during crisis will yield benefit).

31. "Talking isn't doing! It is a kind of good deed to say well; and yet words are not deeds", King Henry VIII, Act 3, Scene 2,... (Tallies with Kural 596: Think first. Endeavour next: Kural 662).

32. "See first that the design is wise and just; that ascertained, pursue it resolutely; do not for one repulse forego the purpose that you resolved to effect",... (Tallies with Kurals 675; 671).

33. "Our doubts are traitors; and make us lose that we oft might win, by fearing to attempt",Measure-for-Measure, https://www.quotes.net/ quote/37871>. Quotation #28791: ... (Tallies with Kural 512; 467).

34. "If you have poison for me, I will drink it! I know you do not love me, for your sisters/ Have, as I do remember, done me wrong', you have some cause; they have not!" (King Lear, Act IV, Sc.6) ... (Kural 580: Poison will kill, if taken knowingly or unknowingly).

35. "The quality of mercy is not strained; It droppeth as the gentle rain from Heaven; Upon the place beneath / It is twice blessed; /It blesseth Him that gives, and him that takes!" (The Merchant of Venice; Act IV; Sc, 1) .... (Tallies with Kurals 571, 241, 242, 243: Grace and mercy, if shown, will benefit the giver and receiver).

36. "I have forgiven and forgotten all" (All's Well That Ends Well, Act V, Sc.3) William Shakespeare ... (Tallies with Kural 108: Forgetting offence done, and forgiving the same are noble qualities).

37. "Parting is such sweet sorrow! That I shall say good night till it be morrow! .....Romeo and Juliet Act I, Sc.1).... (Tallies with Kural 1302: Happiness prevails in self-control of emotions).

38. "Sad hours seem long" (Romeo and Juliet, Act I, Sc.1)....(Tallies with Kural 1269: It is all in the mind).

39. "Time's pace is so hard that it seems the length of seven years! (As You like It, Act II, Sc.2) .... (Tallies with Kural 1269: Endurance is the solution).

40. "Ah! My tender babes! My unblown flowers; new-appearing sweets!", (Richard III, Act IV; Sc.4) .... (Tallies with Kural 64: Happiest moments).

41. "O World! How apt the poor are to be proud/ if one should be a prey, how Much better/ To fall before the lion than the wolf!" Twelfth Night, Act IV, Sc.1)..... (Tallies with Kural 1041; 1045 Entangled between the devil on one side and the deep sea on the other side).

42. "She is mine own/and I as rich in having such a jewel/ As twenty seas, If all their sand were pearl /The water nectar, and the rocks pure gold!"...Two Gentlemen of Verona; Act II; Sc.4) .... (Tallies with Kural 60: Happiness and prosperity made available by surprise).

43. "Shake off this downy sleep, death's counterfeit!),, Macbeth, Act II; Sc.3). (Tallies with Kural 339).

44. "Kindness nobler than revenge!".... (As You Like It; Act IV, Sc.3),..... (Tallies with Kural 314).

45. "His words are bonds,his oaths are oracles/ His love sincere, his thought immaculate/ His tears pure messengers sent from his heart, and His heart is far from fraud as heaven from Earth!".... (Two Gentlemen of Verona; Act II, Sc.7, page 4)... (Tallies with Kural 983).

46. "My purse, my person, my extremist means, Lie all unlocked to your occasions!".... (The Merchant of Venice; Act I; Sc.1).... (Tallies with Kural 787).

47. "Charity itself fulfills the law; and who can sever love from charity?".... (Love's Labour's Lost; Act IV; Sc.3)... (Tallies with Kural 221).

48. "Like one that draws the model of a house Beyond his power to build it, who, half through Gives o'er and leaves his part—created cost A naked subject to the weeping clouds And Waste for churlish winter's tyranny!".... (Henry IV; Part II, Act I; Sc.3)...(Tallies with Kural 473).

49. My chastity's the jewel of our house, Bequeathed down from many ancestors; Which are the greatest obloquy I' the world In me to lose", ... All's well That Ends Well, Act IV, Scene 2, ... (Tallies with Kural 54).

50. "I have lost my reputation! I have lost the immortal part of myself! And What remains is bestial"...(bestial=savagely cruel: derived from the Latin word, 'bestin', meaning 'beast').Othello, Act II, Scene 3. (Tallies with Kural 969).

51. "He hath borne himself beyond the promise of his age, doing in a figure of a lamb the feats of a lion", (Much Ado about Nothing, Act I, Sc.1),... (Tallies with Kural 667).

52. "And think him as a serpent's egg/which when hatched, would, As his kind grow mischievous/ And kill him in the shell!" (Julius Caesar, Act II; Sc.1).. (Tallies with Kural 879).

53. "(We) observed his courtship to the common people; How he did seem to dive into their hearts/ With humble and familiar Courtesy; When reverence he did throw away on slaves/Wooing poor Craftsmen with the craft of smiles!" (Richard *II; Act I; Sc.4),... (Tallies with*Kurals 386, 387).

54. "O mighty Caesar! dost thou lie so low? Are all thy conquests, glories, triumphs, spoils. Shrunk to this little measure? Fare thee well!" (Julius Caesar, Act III, Sc.1),.. (Tallies with Kurals 647; 388; 544; 780).

55. "Be not too tame neither! But let your own discretion be your tutor! Suit the action to the word, the word to the action" Hamlet, Act.3; Sc..2.,... (Tallies with Kural 294).

56. "Forgive us our sins!....Do not think, gentlemen, I am drunk; ...I can stand well-enough! And speak well-enough!....Othello, Act II, Sc.3,........ (Tallies with Kural 928).

57. "How poor are they that have not patience! What wound did ever heal, but by degrees? Thou know'st we work by wit; and not, by witchcraft! And wit depends on dilatory time!"... Othello. Act II, Sc.3. (William Shakespeare). (Tallies with Kurals 484; 490).

58. "Let us not burden our remembrance with/ A heaviness that's gone! ... has just expressed his regret for past actions.." The Tempest, Act V, Sc 1,. (Tallies with Kural 108).

59. "Forget, forgive; conclude, and be agreed! Our doctors say this is no month to bleed....Let this end where it begun".....Richard II, Act 1, Sc 1... (William Shakespeare). (Tallies with Kural 108).

60. "Poor and content is rich, and rich enough! But riches fineless is as poor as winter; to him that ever fears he shall be poor! Good Heaven, the souls of all my tribe defend, from jealousy!'....Othello. Act III, Sc 3... (Tallies with Kural 430). .

61. "To be or not to be is the question; Whether it is nobler in the mind to suffer,. or to be take arms against sea of troubles And by opposing, End them!..." Hamlet, Act III, Sc 1.. (Ref: Kural 1048, as applied to poverty).815

(Note: Situational quotes may be improved upon by referring to the exact context when the words were uttered. The purpose will be served if a comparative study is attempted) - Author.

APPENDIX-3 C

COMPARISON OF THIRUKKURAL WITH ASIAN IDEOLOGY

1. “A superior man is modest in his speech, but excels in actions”,... (Confucius)... (Tallies with Kurals 985; 26; 125).
2. “Real knowledge is to know the extent of one's ignorance”... (Confucius)...... (Tallies with Kural 844).
3. “When it is obvious that the goals cannot be reached, don't adjust the goals; adjust the action-steps”... (Confucius) (Tallies with Kural 673).
4. “The object of superior man is Truth!” (Confucius).... (Tallies with Kural 295).
5. “What you do not want done to yourself, do not do to others”. (Confucius)...... (Tallies with Kural 206).
6. “We should feel sorrow, but not sink under its oppression”... (Confucius)...... (Tallies with Kural 622).
7. “In a country well governed, poverty is something to be ashamed of. In a country badly governed, wealth is something to be ashamed of ”.... (Confucius) (Tallies with Kural 1062).
8. “Only the wisest and the stupidest men never change”..... (Confucius)..... (Tallies with Kural 1073).
9. “Without feelings of respect, what is there to distinguish men from beasts?”... (Confucius) .... (Tallies with Kural 80).
10. “When you are laboring for others, let it be with the same zeal, as if it were for yourself ”...... (Confucius)... (Tallies with Kural 72).
11. “The strength of a nation derives from the integrity of the home”.... (Confucius) ...... (Tallies with Kural 731).

12. "A superior man thinks always of virtues; the common man thinks of comfort". (Confucius). .... (Tallies with Kural 26).

13. "Heaven means to be one with God"... (Confucius) .... (Tallies with Kural 3).

14. "Speak the truth; do not yield to anger; Give, if thou art asked for little; By these three steps, thou wilt go near the Gods! (Confucius)....... (Tallies with Kural 50).

15. "An oppressive Government is to be feared than a tiger"... (Confucius)...... (Tallies with Kural 551).

16. "Wisdom, compassion and courage are the three universally recognized moral qualities of men"...... (Confucius)... (Tallies with Kural 422; 600; 983)

17. "The quality of decision is like the well-timed swoop of a falcon which enables it to strike and destroy its victim" (Tsu Quotes) ... (Tallies with Kural 490).

18. "When envoys are sent with compliments in their mouths, it is a sign that the enemy wishes for a truce".... (TsuQuotes)... (Tallies with Kural 680)

19. "When anger rises, think of the consequences"... (Confucius)... (Tallies with Kural 303).

20. "To know what is right and not to do it, is the worst cowardice".... (Confucius)....(Tallies with Kurals 384; 511).

21. "Study the past, if you would define the future". (Confucius) .... (Tallies with Kural 422).

22. "To practice five things under all circumstances constitutes perfect virtue; these are: gravity, generosity of soul, sincerity, earnestness, and kindness" (Confucius)... Tallies with Kural 983;).

23. "By three methods we may learn wisdom: First by Reflection, which is noblest; second by Imitation, which is easiest; and third, by Experience, which is the bitterest... (Confucius)... (Tallies with Kural 636; 637; 640).

24. "It does not matter how slowly you go, so long as you do not stop"....... (Confucius)... (Tallies with Kural 594).

25. "When you know a thing, to hold that you know it; and when you do not know a thing, to allow that you do not know it: This is knowledge"...... (Confucius)......(Tallies with Kural 986; 352; 294).

26. "It is only the enlightened ruler or the wise general who will use the highest intelligence of the army for the purpose of spying, and thereby they achieve great results"....... (Confucius). (Tallies with Kural 581).

27. "Forget injuries; never forget kindness"...(Confucius)... (Tallies with Kurals 806; 807)

28. "Success depends upon previous preparations. and without such preparation, there is sure to be failure! (Confucius)... (Tallies with Kurals 491; 465).

29. "The superman understands what is right; the inferior man understands what will sell!"..... (Confucius Quotes)... (Tallies with Kurals 981; 1018; 979; 430).

30. "A gentleman would be ashamed should his deed not match his words!".... (Confucius)...... (Tallies with Kurals 1016; 664).

31. "The will to win, the desire to succeed, the urge to reach your full potential, these are keys that will unlock the door to personal excellence!"...... (Confucius Quotes).... (Tallies with Kurals 1021; 1022; 1023; 1024; 661).

32. "By nature, men are all alike; by practice, they get to be wide apart!".... (Confucius)... (Tallies with Kurals 1071; 503; 504; 505).

33. "He who will not economize will have to agonize!"... (Confucius)......... (Tallies with Kural 479).

34. "What we see men of a contrary character, we should turn inwards and examine ourselves!".... (Confucius). (Tallies with Kurals 436).

35. "It is easy to hate; and it is difficult to love. This is how the whole scheme of things works. All good things are difficult to achieve; bad things are easy to get" ... (Confucius).... (Tallies with Kurals 856; 860).

36. "The superior man acts before he speaks; and afterwards, speaks according to his actions!"..... ... (Confucius). (Tallies with Kural 663).

37. "Life is simple; but, we insist on making it complicated!". (Confucius) ... (Tallies with Kural 843).

38. "Friends are the siblings, God never gave us!".... (Mencius Quotes) (Tallies with Kural 781).

39. "India conquered and dominated China culturally for 20 Centuries without ever having to send a single soldier across her border!".... (Shi Quotes: Category: Chinese Philosopher Quotes).... (Tallies with Kural 425).

40. "Music is a fantastic peace keeper of the world; and it is integral to harmony, and it is required fundamental of human emotions"... (Zi Quotes)... (Tallies with Kural 411).

41. "Pride and excess bring disaster for man" .... (Zi Quotes).... (Tallies with Kural 868).

42. "Wise men talk about ideas, intellectuals about facts, and the ordinary man talks about what he eats". ....Mongolian Proverb. .... (Tallies with Kurals 430: 427; 841): wisdom versus innocence are compared).

43. "If you kick a stone in anger, you will hurt your own foot" North Korean Proverb...... (Tallies with Kural 307: anger will give punishment to the self).

44. "There is nothing superior to an act of giving food to a hungry man!" Telugu Poetry by Kavi Vermana (Born in 1652 AD). (Tallies with Kural 226: feeding the poor is a method of saving wealth).

45. "You must not trample a speck of dust, assuming that it is small; it will hurt your eyes. Similarly, do not oppress the weak people assuming that it is easy to do. If the weaker person retaliates, it will be harmful to you"..... Hindi poetry by Saint Kabir Das (1398-1518)... (Tallies with Kural 204; 205; 250).

46. "Among the crores of knowledge-base, knowledge in agriculture is the best. With its strength, regular life-cycle of people continues. If it is disturbed in a country, its decline would follow"... Kannada-language poetry by Saint Sarvajna of Karnataka State, India (16th Century A.D.)... (Tallies with Kurals 731; 1032; 1034: wealth through agriculture brings prosperity to a country. Knowledge on agriculture must be protected).

47. "Human body is covered by a beautiful skin, hiding the bone, nerves, flesh, blood, etc. This structure is common to all of us. Then, where is the upper class and lower class formed? "Kannada language poetry of Saint Sarvajna of Karnataka State, India (16th Century)... (Tallies with Kural 972: human equality by birth).

48. "Dear children, you must all know that there is nothing called caste-difference, among you! Observing superiority or inferiority based on caste is a sin against God!"... Tamil Poetry by Mahakavi Subramaniya Bharathi, Indian Nationalist and Tamil Poet (1882-1921)... (Tallies with Kural 972).

49. "Our fingers, hands, and feet should always find work. They are like restless horses. If we do not keep them engaged in (sufficient) work, we shall fall ill!"...Sri Narayana Guru, (1856-1928), (Indian Philosopher).... (Tallies with Kurals 619; 620; 608).

50. "One caste, one religion, one God, for all people of the world: One Form and the same blood in all: I cannot find any differences!"....Sri Narayana Guru (Indian philosopher) .... (Tallies with Kural 972).

51. "Tears overflow my eyes / When I muse of that Hand's might/ Which this enduring beauty of dawn/ The blue expanse deep and the Sun/ Glorifying by itself",... Mahakavi Kumaran Asan (1873-1924), Indian Social Reformer, Philosopher and Poet in Malayalam,... (tallies with kurals 1, 2, 9).

52. "Freedom is Nectar itself/ Freedom alone is Life;/ Slavery, to the Self-Respecting / is Fearful far than Death!":....Mahakavi Kumaran Asan,...... (tallies with kurals 37, 967, 970).

53. "Love is on earth the Essence all inclusive/ Love's essence is sole Truth/ Worldly ties are bewitching, / Pure one And I left being in love with it" ..... Mahakavi Kumaran Asan,... (talies with kurals 71, 73).

54. "The moment my body ceases to stir/ So soon my mind and instinct lapse/ As to the ground descends the falling flower/ So!.. Lord, refuge to Thee, I seek".....Mahakavi Kumaran Asan... (tallies with kurasl 340, 34, 50).

55. "At times, muddy flows the river/ And at other times, pure and transparent/ Grieve not, intelligent one, needlessly/ Pining that thy timing is up"..... Mahakavi Kumaran Asan,... (tallies with kural 622).

56. "Haven't thee seen now, because of it/ The changeableness of prosperity?".... Mahakavi Kumaran Asan,......(tallies with kural 332).

57. "The riches of intenal peace/ No thief can steal!/ And the illumined mind, Cupids arrows can't wound"....Mahakavi Kumaran Asan......(tallies with kurals 352, 267, 348, 344, 350)

58. "Cultivation of Mind should be the ultimate aim of human existence!"....... Dr.B.R.Ambedkar, (1891-1956), Indian Political Leader, The Architect of the Indian Constitution ... (Tallies with Kural 132).

59. "If you cannot feed a hundred persons, then, feed just one person!"....... St. Mother Teresa. (Mother Mary Teresa Bojaxhiu, 1910—1997)....... (Tallies with Kural 226: Feeding a hungry person is considered as a service).

60. "There is nothing more horrifying than stupidity in action", Jawaharlal Nehru, (1889-1964). Indian Freedom Fighter, Writer and the First Prime Minister of India... (Tallies with Kural. 843: harm caused to the self-due to one's own stupid action).

61. "If someone insults me, I only feel infinite pity for him", Dr.K.R. Narayanan (1921-2005), Former President of India, (Source: 'A Remarkable Life Story', By Gopala Krishna Gandhi) ... (Tallies with Kural 151) Patience as a Virtue.

62. "We come nearest to the great when we are great in humility", Rabindranath Tagore... (Tallies with Kural 125).

63. "The issue of inequality and that of poverty not separable" Dr. Amartya Sen, 1933—xx, Nobel Memorial Prize Winner in Economic Sciences (1998); ... (Tallies with Kural 1045).

64. "Anything is possible in human-Nature! Love, Madness, Hope, Infinite Joy!"....... Ms. Arundhati Roy, (1961—xx), Indian Novelist... (Tallies with Kural 628).

65. "No matter how much success you are having, you cannot continue working together, if you cannot communicate",.. Dr. Montek Singh Ahuliwalia, Indian Economist, (1943—xx)...... (Tallies with Kural 724).

66. "Lack of education leads to lack of wisdom,...,lack of morals,....lack of progress,....leading to oppression of lower castes!",...' Mahatma' Jyoti Rao Govindrao Phule, Social Reformer in Maharashtra, India (1827- 1890)... (Tallies with Kural 409).

67. "Everything is easy when you are busy! But, nothing is easy when you are lazy!".....Swami Vivekananda, Indian Saint (1863-1902). (Tallies with Kural 602).

68. "Where the mind is without fear, and the head is held high; Where the knowledge is free; Where the world has not been broken into fragments by narrow domestic walls; Where words come out from the depth of truth; Where tireless striving stretches its arms towards perfection; Where the clear stream of reason has not lost its way into the dreary desert sand of dead habit; Where the mind is led forward by thee into ever-widening thought and action—into that heaven of freedom, my Father, let my country awake!"....Poem XXXV, in Gitanjali, by Rabindranath Tagore...... (Tallies with Kurals 600; 430; 352; 291; 972; 294; 994; 735; 425; 50; 983; 1).

69. "That is my prayer to thee, my Lord! Strike, strike at the root of penury in my heart; Give me strength lightly to bear my joys and sorrows; Give me strength to make my love fruitful in service; Give me strength never to disown the poor or bend my knees before insolent might; Give me strength to raise my mind high above daily trifles; And Give me strength to surrender my strength to thy will with love!", poem XXXVI, in Gitanjali, by Rabindranath Tagore (Tallies with Kurals 3; 34; 628; 571; 600; 221; 428; 628; 625; 4), Nobel Laureate.

70. "Having taken the time to think, venture to act; once you have done so, stop thinking", Japanese-quote: (kobejones.com.au).... (Tallies with Kural 467).

71. "He who strongly desires to rise up will think of a way to build a ladder!'.... Japanese-quotes (kobejones.com.au)... (Tallies with Kural 443).

72. "Do everything that you can, and leave the rest to Fate!' Japanese-quotes (ko bejones.com.au)...... (Tallies with 619).

73. "Learning without thinking is useless; but thinking without learning is very dangerous"....Dr.Sukarno, (1901-1977), Former President of Indonesia... (Kurals 391; 401).

74. "Whatever can the mind of man can conceive, and believe, it can achieve"...a Proverb in Thailand: Team ThaiPod 101.com (Top 10 Inspirational quotes)... (tallies with kural 596).

75. "Life loses half its interest, if there is no struggle; if there are no risks to be taken" Nethaji Subhas Chandra Bose (1897-1945),...Indian Freedom Fighter,.... (Tallies with Kural 628).

76. "Books are the means by which we build bridges between cultures", Dr.S.Radhakrishnan, 1988-1975, Former President of India... (Tallies with Kural 396).

77. "There are days where you do everything right, and nothing goes in your favour!" Harbhajan Singh, 1920-2002), Punjabi Poet, Critic, and Political Commentator,...(Tallies with Kural 628).

78. "Exposure to literature gives you refinement in understanding!", Rasigamani T.K.C. (T.K.ChidambaranathaMudaliar), 1882-1954, Tamil Literary Critique (Tallies with Kurals 725; 396).

79. "Even in the midst of hardships, you have to remain dedicated to duty, with dignity, and discipline, in serving the people" C.N.Annadurai (Paerarigner Anna), Social Reformist, Mass-leader, Former Chief Minister of Tamil Nadu, India (1909-1969). (Tallies with Kural 669).

80. "When suffering of others is brought to your notice, it is your duty to help them" K.Kamaraj, (1903-1975), Indian Freedom Fighter, National Leader, and Former Chief Minister of Tamil Nadu, Former Member of the Constituent Assembly of India. (Tallies with Kural 315).

81. "Honesty in serving the people will grant all happiness you need!"... P.Kakkan, (1908-1981)....... (Indian Freedom Fighter, Political Leader, Former Home-Minister in Government of Tamil Nadu, Former Member of the Constituent Assembly of India. (Tallies with Kural 294).

82. "You cannot expect good things happening to you all the time. You must have endurance to bear it with patience, if something bad happens!"... P.Jeevanantham (Jeeva), 1907-1963, Social-Activist, Orator, Political Leader (Tallies with Kural 628).

83. "It is a service to God, if you help the poor, and treat them with honour"..... Sir P.T.Rajan, 1892-1974, Politician, Social Reformist, Former Chief Minister of Madras Presidency,.(Tallies with Kural 221).

84. "Do not insult others, if you are highly placed. Do not let others to ill- treat you, if your status gets declined" W.P.A.Soundarapandian Nadar, 1893-1953, Social Reformist, Politician. (Tallies with Kural 963).

85. "You have to sacrifice many things, including your comforts, in the service of others towards whom you feel dedicated" Dr.T.M.Nair (1868- 1919), Indian Politician and Political Activist identified with Justice Party (India), as one of the Founders. (Tallies with Kural 235).

86. "You have to help the poor. That is a privilege given to you by God, as you are placed in a position to give!"....Sir PitiTheagaroyar (1852-1925),.. Industrialist, Social Reformist, Political Leader.. Philanthropist, identified with Justice Party (India), as one of the Founders. (Tallies with Kural 231).

87. "Regulating your eating habits is a method of increasing your life- span! You have to live long, in order to serve the people" Dr.C. Natesa Mudaliar, (1875-1937), Political Leader, identified with Justice Party (India).as one of the Founders. (Tallies with Kural 943).

88. "A man must not insult anybody, if he does not want to be insulted, in turn! Is it not relevant to protecting one's self-respect?" Rao Bhadur, Prof.M.C.Rajah (1883-1943), Freedom Fighter, Politician. (Tallies with Kural 316).

89. "Oh Gracious God! Help me to avoid making friendship with those persons who have got ill-will towards me in their minds, and yet manage to show a friendly face to me, when they interact with me!" Swami Vadalur Ramalingam Adigalar (1823-1874), Social Reformer and Philosopher,. (Tallies with Kural 824).

90. "It is my duty to educate the poor people and serve them. It is my ambition in my life!".... Sahajananda Swamigal (1890-1959), Indian Politician, Legislator, and Social Activist. (Tallies with Kural 211).

91. "All young persons must develop courage and confidence in them, to liberate themselves from diversions, and to earn success in all their endeavors!" V.O.Chidambaram Pillai, 1872-1936, Freedom-Fighter, Swadesi-Entrepreneur in Shipping,Tamil Scholar, Lawyer (Tallies with Kural 591). Founder of Swadesi Steam Navigation Company.

92. "In the present life, you need to be driven by a lofty objective, as otherwise, your inborn potentials cannot be put into the benefit of the society" Prof. Manonmaniyam Sundaram Pillai, (1855-1897), author of 'Manonmaniyam', a Tamil-Drama-Classic, and author of 'Thamizh-th-thaai-Vaazhththu (Invocation-Song)', in honour of Tamil-Goddess........ (Tallies with Kural 596).

93. "Jealousy is evil-producing; it is bad for you! Do not develop desire for snatching away another person's wealth; it is capable of ruining you; Do not show your anger on others; it will bring harm to you; Do not insult any person, nor cause mental agony to others; You will harvest evil; If you are free from these evils in your mind, Virtues will grow in you, to yield benevolence!.......Poet Puratchi-kavigner- Bharathi-Dasan (1891-1964).... Poem:"Dravidar-Virtues"(Dravidar-Ozhukkam)..... (Tallies with Kurals 161; 178; 303; 852).

94. "A person entrusted with responsibility by the people, must realize the value of the trust that they have invested in him! He must do whatever good things he is capable of doing for them, with firmness",..O.P.Ramaswamy Reddiyar, (1895-1970), Freedom Fighter, Writer, Lawyer, Former Chief Minister of Madras Presidency, Former Member of the Constituent Assembly of India. (Tallies with Kural 634).

95. "I do have the privilege of working out any scheme, in consultation with others, and carry out scheme for all, both the poor and the rich, taking help from all my colleagues",. Dr.P.Subbarayan (1889-1962), Freedom- Fighter, Diplomat, Former Chief Minister of Madras Presidency,Member of the Constituent Assembly of India (Tallies with Kural 975).

96. "Whoever is a rich person among us, can join together, with others, to start an industrial venture, either alone, or as a group, so that we can create job-opportunities in our region, so that the country will prosper!" P.S.Kumaraswamy Rajah, (1989-1957), Former Chief Minister Of Madras Presidency (Tallies with Kural 651).

97. "No guns, but only brotherhood can solve our problems!",. Atal Bihari Vajpayee, (1924-2018)…. Former Prime Minister of India….(tallies with kural 71).

98. "Education must be a great equalizer in our society",...Rajiv Gandhi, (1944-1991) Former Prime Minister Of India, ...(tallies with kural 400).

99. "The creative personality needs an emotional zeal. The ethical one ordains the the approval of one's conscience!".... V.P.Singh (Viswanath Pratap Singh), 1931-2008,..Former Prime Minister of India....(tallies with kural 294).

100. "What we need is a dialogue among civilizations; and we need multi-culturism, respect for diversity, tolerance, respect for diverse faiths!",.... Dr.Manmohan Singh, 1932—xx, Former Prime Minister of India,..... (tallies with kural 140; 425).

101. "We believe in the dignity of man as an individual, whatever his race, colour, or creed, and his right to a better, fuller and richer life",....Lal Bahadur Shastri, 1904-1966, Former Prime Minister of India,.....(tallies with kural 972).

102. "About the government,...I think it is for the people,..the journalists, commentators, and intellectuals have to comment,..which they have done copiously! And, all I would say, is: I am grateful!",..... P.V.Narasimha Rao, 1921-2004), Former Prime Minister of India,...(tallies with kural 872).

103. "I love meeting people! That is how, I will come to know their needs! For a person, in public service, it brings pleasure to the mind and soul! I find it as a social commitment towards my countrymen"... H.D.Deva Gowda, 1933—xx, Former Prime Minister of India.........(tallies with kural 386).

104. "Anybody can pilot a ship when the sea is calm",... Giani Zail Singh, 1916-1994, Former President of India, ...(tallies with kural 676).

105. "True politics is about promotion of human happiness".... Jayaprakash Narayan, An Indian Independence Activist, 1902-1979),.......(tallies with kural 545).

106. "Non-violence is the greatest force at the disposal of mankind. It is mightier than the mightiest weapon devised by the ingenuity of man",... Babu Jagjivan Ram, 1908-1986, Indian Independence Activist, Former Deputy Prime Minister of India ....(tallies with kural 987).

107. "If we do not want to be pained by anybody, we must not cause pain to others;and how can a man consider himself humane, if he wants to live

at the cost of others?".... Morarji Desai, 1896-1995, Indian Independence Activist, Former Deputy Prime Minister of india,.......(tallies with kural 206).

108. "We cannot fight new wars with old weapons"...Vinoba Bhave, 1895-1982, Philosopher and Social Activist,.......(tallies with kural 465).

109. "By common endeavour, we can raise the country to a new greatness! While a lack of unity will expose us to new calamities!"....... Sardar Vallabai Patel, 1875-1950,Indian Statesman, Indian Independence Activist, Former Deputy Prime

110. "Development means nothing, if it does not lead for human development,in its broadest sense! It must have components of health-care, for everybody; and food-security for everybody; and in this, the role of the State is vital"....Prof.Dr.C.T.Kurien, Economist, Scholar of Social Conscience, 1932—xx, ...(tallies with kurals 226; 734; 738; 950; 1062).

111. "Every person should show mercy to another human being who is affected with poverty" Dr. M.G.Ramachandran (1917-1987), Film Actor, Politician, Former Chief Minister of Tamil Nadu...........(tallies with kural 221)

112. "Every person must practice a habit of speaking out purposeful words. It will reflect the wholesomeness of constructive thinking stored in the mind"... M.Bhakthavatchalam, (1897-1987), Indian independence Activist, Former Chief Minister of Tamil Nadu,.........(tallies with kural 200).

113. "However much you strain yourself, with well-planned thoughts, and tireless efforts, you will harvest the yields proportionate to your efforts! Lack of sincere efforts will take you to nowhere!"...Dr. Ms.J.Jayalalithaa, 1948-2016, Film Actress,Politician, Former Chief Minister of Tamil Nadu, ...(tallies with kural 616).

114. "You must earn fame through your good works and philanthropy. Futures generations will remember you with gratitude!".... A.Nagappa Chettiar, 1915-1982, Pioneer in Indian Leather Industry......(tallies with kural 231).

115. "Every person must start feeling how difficult it is to bear the harms caused by others, on the self. This will deter him to cause harm to others!"... V.Ramaiah, Former Parliamentarian, Member of Constituent the Assembly of India, Former Minister in the Government of Madras State (1957-1967)......(tallies with kural 318).

116. "A lot of reading is needed to comprehend ideas, before lecturing on it to others!".... O.V.Alagesan, 1911-1992, Parliamentarian, Former Member of Constituent Assembly of India, Former Minister in Union Government of India, ...(tallies with kural 725).

117. "It is the human willingness which is needed to understand the sufferings of others. Once you understand the genuineness of it, the Almighty will make you sympathize with them, and come to their rescue!"... A.Y.S.Parisutha Nadar, 1909-1985,..Former Politician and Legislator,...... (tallies with kural 578).

118. "Listening to those who experience hardship in life helps a person to understand the needs of others! It helps us to help them!".... M.Bakthavathsalam,, (1897-1987), Indian Independence Activist, Former Chief Minister of Tamil Nadu,.....(tallies with kural 571).

119. "Every day, you must be looking forward to help others! Your acts of benevolence will be remembered for a long time, in our society of innocent people!".. N.T.S. Arumugam Pillai, Philanthropist, 1917-1992.,......(tallies with kural 33).

120. "Nothing is impossible to achieve, if a decision is taken, after carefully analyzing the pros and cons of a target, and decide to act, with determination to achieve it".. Sir Dr. R.K.Shanmukham Chettiar, 1892-1953, Indian Lawyer, Economist, First Finance Minister of India, Former Diwan of Cochin Kingdom, Member of the Constituent Assembly of India, Former Vice Chancellor of Annamalai University.....(tallies with kural 611).

121. "The theory of human equality is not meant for preaching; it must be shown in action, in every aspect, every day, every moment, remaining watchful to extend the unfailing-courtesy".....Dr.Kalaignar Mu.Karunanithi, 1924-2018, Tamil Scholar, Poet, Writer, Orator, Playwright, Leader of Dravidian Movement, Reputed Script-Writer for Tamil Movies, Statesman, Former Chief Minister of Tamil Nadu......(tallies with kural 664).

122. "Human starvation is an unbearable pain. Those who help the poor in feeding the hungry people will deserve all merits of human virtues! A rich person need not experience hunger to understand the pains of it! On fasting-days, it becomes a test for every one to learn it: how hard it is to bear the pain of starvation!" ...Dr.M.G.Ramachandran (MGR), 1917-1987, Indian Politician, Actor, Film-Maker,Politician, Social Activist, Former Chief Minister of Tamil Nadu,... (tallies with kural 226).

123. "Past is gone; Present is Going; and Tomorrow is 'day-after-tomorrow's Yesterday'!"....R.K.Narayan (Rasipuram Krishnaswami Iyer Narayanaswami), 1906-2001, Indian Writer known for his work set in fictional South Indian Town of 'Malgudi'!.....(tallies with kural 605, implying that a work which must be done today must not be postponed!).

124. "One must learn to learn from others whatever we missed to learn!".... Ma.Po.Sivagnanam, 1906-1995)... Indian Politician and Independence Activist,...(tallies with kural 724).

125. "The challenge of success in any undertaking will be in finding appropriate personnel to handle the intended task"... C.Subramaniam, 1910-2000, Indian politician, and Independence Activist, Former Member of The Constituent Assembly of India......(tallies with kural 517).

126. "Thirukkural preaches for 'universal brotherhood', insisting upon kindness, compassion and charity,with the purpose of promoting peace in human society",..Padma Bhushan, Chevalier, 'NadigarThilagam' Sivaji Ganesan, Indian Film Actor, Politician, 1928-2001..........(tallies with kural 244).

127. "Thirukkural preaches for mutuality in doing good things to others, as well as in extending respect to others. Whatever you do to others will be returned to you!",. 'NadigavaeL' M.R.Radha (Raathaa), Indian Film Actor and Social Reformist, 1907-1979. (talles with kural 206).

128. "Thirukkural preaches for equality among the human beings.It must be practiced while interacting with one another", M.Singaravelar, 1860-1946, Activist in Indian Independence Movement, Social Reformist, Politician,....(tallies with kural 972).

129. "Thirukkural advocates for human justice being delivered without showing partiality. People will accept this theory of human equality. People will reject any theory which preaches for showing differentiation in delivering justice based on various classes in human society",..Prof. 'Manonmaniyam' Sundaram Pillai, 1855-1897, an Indian scholar. The famous Tamil Drama classic: "Manonmaniyam".... (tallies with kurals 972, 541 and 118).

130. "A judge should muster courage to deliver a judgment based on the facts and law without fear or favour" .... Justice S. Ratnavel Pandian (1929-2018), Former Judge of the Supreme Court of India..... (tallies with Kural 41)

131. "A successful judicial system is a hallmark of any developed civilization" Justice Dr. Ar. Lakshmanan (1942-2020). Former Judge of the Supreme Court of India (tallies with Kural 544)

132. "Concern, Sharing, Empathy for the pains and sufferings of others are the hallmarks of a true Civilization", Maathaa Amirthanandamayi, "Ammaa", (1953----xx). (tallies with Kural 315).

133. "The Court should be guided by Gandhi who advocated for the interests of the weaker sections of the Society", ... Justice V.R.Krishna Iyer, (1915-2014), Former Justice of the Supreme Court of India ...... (tallies with Kural 250).

134. "A sense of humour and cheerfulness are essential for a healthy mind".... "Kalai-vaaNar" N.S. Krishnan, Indian Actor, Comedian and Social Reformer, (1908-1957) ...... (tallies with Kural 999).

135. "If you have a heart to bear that endures anything, you will have peace of mind throughout your lifetime", "Kavi-Arasar" Kannadasan, Indian Philosopher, Poet, Lyricist, Writer, Actor (1927-1981)....... (tallies with Kural 628).

136. "Human equality and secularism must be practiced in rural India so that the nation marches towards unity and prosperity." --- Thaa. Pandian (D. Pandian), Parliamentarian (1932-2021)... (tallies with Kural 972).

137. "Love All; Serve All; Help Ever; Hurt Never" ..... Sri Satya Sai Baba (1926 – 2011).... (tallies with Kurals 71; 72; 571; 209).

APPENDIX- 3D

COMPARISON OF THIRUKKURAL WITH THE IDEOLOGY OF WORLD-LEADERS

1. "Living isn't just about doing to yourself; but what you do for others as well!", Dr. Nelson Mandela (1918-2013), Former President of South Africa ...... (Tallies with Kural 72: Great persons with kindness will live for the welfare of others).

2. "Freedom is never given voluntarily by the oppressor; it must be demanded by the oppressed!", Martin Luther King Jr., American Baptist Minister, (1929-1968). .... (Tallies with Kural 37: rider in a palanquin and those who carry the palanquin will not have a mindset to bother about human freedom).

3. "I have decided to stick with love! Hate is too great a burden to bear!!"..... Martin Luther King Jr., (1929-1968), American Baptist Minister. ...... (Tallies with Kural 75: Love and Kindness towards others will yield the valuable friendship and goodwill in this world).

4. "The best way to predict your future is to create it! Your elevation depends on the quantum of your efforts." President Abraham Lincoln, (1809-1865), 16th President of the United States of America ...... (Tallies with Kural 595).

5. "Do I not destroy my enemies when I make them my friends?"....... Abraham Lincoln, (Tallies with Kural 874: making friends with enemies as a strategy?).

6. "Whenever I have anyone arguing for slavery, I feel a strong impulse to see it tried on him personally" Abraham Lincoln, Lincoln's "House- Divided" Speech, in Springfield, Illinois, June 16, 1858. (Tallies with Kural 37). If the quote is applied, the question will be like: "What would happen, if the rider has to become a person as one among those who carry the palanquin?").

7. "I do not like that man. I must get to know him better!" Abraham Lincoln, ... (Tallies with Kural 876: The person whom I did not like could be my enemy; so must be studied better! (For my own safety).

8. "Those who deny freedom to others, deserve it not for themselves; and under the rule of a just God, cannot long retain it!" Abraham Lincoln... (Tallies with Kural.37: (The quote refers to the mind-set of palanquin riders).

9. "Don't worry when you are not recognized! But strive to be worthy of recognition"...Abraham Lincoln.... (Tallies with Kural 619).

10. "As I would not be a slave, so I would not be a master! This is my idea of democracy!"...Abraham Lincoln... (Tallies with Kural 37).

11. "My dream is of a place and time where America will once again be seen last best hope on earth".......Abraham Lincoln,......(The quote can be applied to India as well, as the best place to live in, with freedom, prosperity, equality, in the lines indicated in Kural 733: "An ideal country is the land which is capable of bearing the financial burden, in excess of what could the country normally bear, and is having the potential to provide the necessary resources to the Government, inclusive of taxes, to set right the treasury!" (Note: The 'excessive burden' may include unexpected expenses arising out of war, feeding the poor during famines or during natural calamities, providing relief-measures during natural disasters, in accommodating refugees from another country, or related to economic crisis faced during epidemics/pandemics, etc!).

12. "I remember my mother's prayers and they have always followed me. They have clung to me all my life!'.. Abraham Lincoln... (Tallies with Kural 69).

13. "Thepriceofgreatnessisresponsibility",SirWinstonChurchill,(1856-1965) Statesman and Orator, United Kingdom. (Tallies with Kural 383: Alertness, learning and courage as qualities for a leader). (13.b). We make a living by what we get; but we make life by what we give!".....Sir Winston Churchill, (tallies with kural 228).

14. "If you are walking down the right path, and if you are willing to keep walking, eventually, you will make progress!"...... President Barack Obama, (1961-xx), 44th U.S. President, author of "Promised Land", 2020... (Tallies

with Kural 594: success will come to a person who constantly pursues in the righteous path).

15. "Ability is what you are capable of doing; Motivation determines what you do; Attitude determines how well you do it!"...Lou Holtz (Louis Leo Holtz), (Former) American Foot Ball Player (1937-xx) ... (Tallies with Kurals 594; 591; 592: victory will come to a person who works with determination to win).

16. "Life is not to be easy, my child! But, take courage—It can be delightful", George Bernard Shaw (1856-1950). Irish Playwright, Critic, Political Analyst, Nobel Prize Winner in Literature (1925).........(Tallies with Kural 592: courage can be acquired in order to make efforts towards success and prosperity).

17. "Music is the shorthand of emotions..(Leo Tolstoy)...(Tallies with Kural 411).

18. "Everyone thinks of changing this world; but no one thinks of changing himself,... (Leo Tolstoy)...... (Tallies with Kural 436).

19. "A man can live and be healthy, without killing animals for food; therefore, if he eats meat, he participates in taking animal life, merely for the sake of his appetite; And to act so, is immoral...... (Leo Tolstoy)....(Tallies with Kural 251).

20. "Let us forgive each other; only then, we live in peace (Leo Tolstoy) ...... (Tallies with Kural 108).

21. "Each person's task in life is to become an increasingly better person"... (Leo Tolstoy) (Tallies with Kural 137; 138).

22. "There is no greatness where simplicity, goodness and truth are absent"......... (Leo Tolstoy).... (Tallies with Kural 983).

23. "When work is a pleasure, life is a joy! When work is a duty, life is slavery!!".... Maxim Gorky, Russian & Soviet writer, 1868-1900...(tallies with kural 37)

24. "The only thing to do with good advice is to pass it on! It is never of any use to oneself!). (A satire by Oscar Wilde, British Playwright, 1854-1900)... (Tallies with Kural 664).

25. "Be not simply good; Be good for something!!"…….(Henry David Thoreau, American Philosopher and Poet, 1817-1862)…(Talli with Kurals 472; 591; 5 98; 614). (This saying reiterates the concept that a person must be good by character; but at the same time, must be a capable person, with skills and intelligence, the central idea stressing which this book is being released!)!

26. "Literature is the art of discovering something extraordinary about ordinary people, and saying with ordinary words, something extraordinary". (Boris Pasternak, Russian Poet, Author of "Doctor Zhivago", 1890-1960).

    (Note: This saying becomes a tribute to Thirukkural itself!).

27. "Responsibilities gravitate to the person who can shoulder them", Elbert Hubbard, (1856-915), American Philosopher, Writer, Artist……….

    (Tallies with Kural 613: a generous person with administrative capacity; and Kural 1026: a person's administrative capacity to take care of the family, with responsibility).

28. "Nothing great is ever achieved without enthusiasm"… Ralph Waldo Emerson (1803-1882), American Essayist… (Tallies with Kural 598: combination of perseverance and will-power enhances moral strength to success).

29. "If you want to live a happy life, you tie it to a goal; not to people or things!"… (Albert Einstein, Theoretical Physicist, 1879-1955)… (Tallies with Kural 540).

30. "To be true to ourselves, we must be true to others!" President Jimmie Carter, 39th President of the United States of America, (1924—xx)….. (Tallies with Kural 294).

31. "Victory belongs to the most persevering!"…Napoleon Bonaparte, French Emperor (1769 - 1821)...Talies with (kurals 666:771).

32. "The greatest discovery of my generation is that a human being can alter his life by altering his attitudes!" …William James, American Philosopher, (1842-1910)… (Tallies with Kural 609).

33. "It is today that our best work can be done; not some future day, or future year!", W.E.B. Du Bois(1868-1963), American Sociologist, Socialist, Historian, Civil Rights Activist… (Tallies with Kural 605).

34. "Associate yourself with people of good quality, for it is better to be alone than to be in bad company"...Booker T. Washington, 1856-1915, Educator, Author of "Character Building", Civil Rights Leader..... (Tallies with Kural 460).

35. "....without education, you are not going anywhere in this world!".... Malcolm-X, 1925-1965, African-American Muslim Minister, Civil Rights Activist....... (Tallies with Kural 395).

36. "Books and ideas are the most effective weapons against intolerance and ignorance", ... President Lyndon B. Johnson, 1908-1973, 36th President of The United States of America,......(tallies with kural 396).

37. "We cannot build our own future without helping others to build theirs",... President Bill Clinton (William Jefferson Clinton), 1946—xx, 42nd President of the United States of America, ...(tallies with kural 72).

38. "The greatest gift is the ability to forget bad things and focus on the good".... President Joseph R. Biden Jr., 1942—xx, 46th President of the United States of

39. "Our engagement with the world, on natural resources and on services and on diversity of our citizens has always been a tremendous advantage for us" .... Justin Trudeau, 1971—xx,Prime Minister of Canada,.... (tallies with kural 731).

40. "Anyone who claims to be a leader must speak like a leader! That means speaking with integrity and truth", Ms.Kamala D. Harris, 1964—xx, 49th and current Vice President of the United States of America, ...tallies with kural 648).

41. "Judge me on my actions. That is all that counts",.... President Emmanuel Macron, 1977—xx,President of France, (tallies with kural 234).

42. "It is easy to make promises! It is hard work to keep them"... Boris Johnson (Alexander Boris de Pfeffel Johnson), 1964—xx, Prime Minister of the United Kingdom,......(tallies with kural 664). (Note: It means that whatever is being proposed to be done, must be done, without giving any excuse!).

43. "Disciplining yourself to do what you know is right and important, although difficult, is the high road to pride, self-esteem, and personal satisfaction"... Ms.MargaretThatcher (Margaret Hilda Thatcher), 1925-2013, Former Prime Minister of the United Kingdom...... (tallies with kural 661).

44. When it comes human dignity, we cannot make compromises"..... Ms.Angela Merkel (Angela Dorothea Merkel), 1954—xx, Former Chancellor of the Federal Republic of Germany,... (tallies with kural 972).

45. "Efforts must be pursued,. aiming to realize a sustainable economy and society that is resilient against all kinds of crises, where all people flourish and reap the benefit of economic growth",.. Yoshihide Suga, 1948—xx, Former Prime Minister of Japan (tallies with kural 731).

46. "..Generous in spirit, we have to share our good fortune with others, both at home and overseas, out of compassion and a desire for justice!"..... Scott Morrison, 1959—xx, Australian Prime Minister,.......(tallies with kural 733).

47. "I refuse to believe that you cannot be compassionate and strong"... Ms.Jacinda Ardern, 1980—xx, 40th Prime Minister of New Zealand, ... (tallies with kural 578).

    (Note: It means that a person can be a stern administrator, while remaining compassionate, and sympathetic towards tricky issues, in order to take decisions in accordance with norms of justice and righteousness!).

48. "Never let your fears hold you back from pursuing your hopes" President John F. Kennedy, 1917-1963), 35th President of the United States of America... (Tallies with Kural 594).

49. "Great men simplify great principles, and make them easily intelligible to ordinary men".... Tungu Abdul Rahman, 1903-1990, Malaysian Statesman. (Tallies with Kural 975).

50. "We have learned that we cannot live alone, at peace; that our well-being is dependent upon the well-being of other nations, far away" President Franklin D. Roosevelt (American Politician, 1882-1945, 32nd President of the United States of America)...(Tallies with Kural 213; 734).

51. "I firmly believe that the future of civilization is absolutely dependent upon finding some way of resolving international differences without resorting

to war!", President Dwight D. Eisenhower (American Military Officer, a War-Hero of World War-II, 1890-1969), and the 34th President of the United States of America)... (Tallies with Kural 861; 425).

52. "A critical issue for women is the possibility to be a mother, and the ability to participate in the workforce", ...Ms.Erna Solberg, 1961—xx, Prime Minister of Norway, 1961—xx,.......(tallies with kural 60).

53. "I always make list of things I need to get done! I like the sense of having completed one thing, so that I can move on to the next"...Ms.Mette Frederiksen, 1977—xx,Prime Minister of Denmark,......(tallies with kurals 663; 493; 612; 484).

54. "Education is the promise of progress, in every society, in every family"...... Dr.Kofi Annan, (1938-2018), 7th Secretary General of The United Nations, Nobel Laureate (Peace Prize),Diplomat, Founder of Kofi-Annan-Foundation,.........(tallies with kural 400).

55. "Never give up, and sit down and grieve! Find another way!"... President Richard M.Nixon, 1913-1994, 37th President of the United States of America... (tallies with kural 673).

56. "Reading is the basics for all learning!",... President George W. Bush,..1946—xx, 43rd President of the United States of America,........ (tallies with kural 396).

57. "We are a nation of communities....a brilliant diversity spread like stars! Like a Thousand Points of Light in a broad and Peaceful Sky!"... President George H.W.Bush, 1924-2018, 41st President of the United States of America......(tallies with 731; 738).

58. "You don't walk away, if you love someone! You help the person", Ms. Hillary Clinton Queen's University, Belfast,... (tallies with 789).

59. "Surround yourself with the best people you can find, delegate authority, and don't interfere as long as the policy you've decided upon is being carried out" President Ronald Reagan, 1911-2004, 40th President of the United States of America, ...(kurals 441; 445; 446; 517; 518).

60. "Always, aim high! Work hard!! And, care deeply what you believe in"...... Ms. Hillary Clinton, 1947—xx, 67th Secretary of State of the United States of America,. (tallies with kural 596).

61. "Every accomplishment starts with the decision to try",. President John F. Kennedy, 1917-1963,the 35th President of the United States of America,… (tallies with kural 594).

62. "As we express our gratitude, we must never forget that the highest form of appreciation is not to utter words, but to live by them",. President John F. Kennedy….(tallies with kural 110).

63. "Ask not what your country can do for you! Ask what you can do for your country",......President John F. Kennedy,.......(talles with kurals 696; 981; 765; 731; 735).

64. "There is no more important task in a democracy than resolving the differences among people and finding a course of action that will be supported by a sufficient number to permit the nation to achieve a better life for all" Robert McNamara, 1916-2009, 8th Secretary of Defence,of the United Stares, ….(tallies with kural 735).

65. "It is better to be alone than in bad company".… President George Washington, 1732-1799, First President of the United States of America, ……..(tallies with kural 814).

66. "Truth is the glue that holds government together," President Gerald R. Ford, 1913-2006, 38th President of the United States of America.... (tallies with kural 556).

67. "Everything we see in this world is the creative work of women" Mustafa Kemal Pasha (Kemal Ataturk), 1881-1938, First President of the Republic of Turkey (tallies with Kural 60).

68. "You can tell whether a man is clever by his answer; you can tell a man is wise, by his questions" Naguib Mahfouz, (1911-2006), Egyptian Writer, Nobel Prize Winner,. (tallies with kural 725).

69. "Service to others is the rent you pay for your room here on Earth",..... Muhammad Ali, American Boxer and Philanthropist, (1942 - 2016)... (tallies with kural 211).

APPENDIX3-E

COMPARISON OF THIRUKKURAL WITH THE IDEOLOGY OF BUSINESS MAGNATES

1. "A second opinion (and hopefully frank opinion) from someone who knows your strengths and weaknesses can be especially helpful", Shiv Khera, (1961-xx), author of "You Can Win: Step by Step Tool for Top Achievers", Boomsbury Business Publishing, 2018. ... (Tallies with Kural 677: getting the views of a person who is already familiar with the proposed plan/work).

2. "Get your advice from successful people, and not from living-failures, who will tell you how to succeed!", Shiv Khera(1961-xx).... (Tallies with Kural 462:taking advice from known-persons and analyzing the pros and cons; Kural 516: with advice from persons familiar with the task; Kural 677: in consultation with experts who are familiar with the methodology to be adopted; and Kural 473: after learning the painful experiences of those who met with failure half-way through in a similar undertaking).

3. "Education teaches us what we can do, and also teaches what we cannot do. I am looking for men with infinite capacity for not knowing what cannot be done", Henry Ford (1863-1947), American Industrialist........ (Tallies with Kural 517: Identifying a person capable of carrying out an act, and entrusting the work to him/her).

4. "Life is not fair; Get used to it!",.. Bill Gates, American Business Magnate, (1955-xx)... (Tallies with Kural 628: an able person will consider that it is normal to face crisis; will not be looking for pleasant things always).

5. "Chains of habits are too light to be felt, until they are too heavy to be broken", Warren (Edward) Baffett (1930-xx), American Investor and Business Tycoon, & Philanthropist... (Tallies with Kural 475: if light weight feathers of a bird (peacock) go on being loaded into a cart, at some stage, the axle of the moving cart will break due to overweight).

6. “Never invest in any business you cannot understand!”, Warren Buffet (Warren Edward Buffet), 1930—xx,. (tallies with kural 832).

7. “Only invest in simple business that you understand!”, Warren E. Buffett (1930-xx),. (tallies with Kural 472: Choosing a work which suits the person and can be sustainably managed; &Kural 832: avoiding a work which will not be suitable for the self).

8. “Sometimes, life hits you in the head with a brick. Do not lose faith. I’m convinced that the only thing that kept me going was that I loved what I did” ....Steve Jobs (Steven Paul Jobs, 1955-2011, American Business Magnate, co-founder of Apple Computer Inc., and pioneer of the ‘personal computer era’ (Tallies with Kural 624).

9. “We must be open to criticism and respect divergent and different views and interests”....George Soros, 1930—xx, American billionaire investor and philanthropist,. (tallies with kural 389).

10. “High expectations are the key to everything”,. Samuel Moore Walton, 1918-1992, American Businessman and Entrepreneur, Founder of Wal Mart,. (tallies with kural 596).

11. “All our dreams can come true, if we have the courage to pursue them”.... Walt Disney (Walt Elias Disney) 1901-1966, a pioneer in the American Animation Industry,..(tallies with kural 594).

12. “All the problems in the world can be settled easily if men were only willing to think” Thomas J. Watson, Sr., American Businessman, Former Chairman of the IBM (International Business Machines Corporation), 1874-1956,. (tallies with kural 676).

13. “There is a time and place for creativity” William Redington Hewlett, American Businessman, co-founder of Hewlett Packard Company, 1913-2001.,. (tallies with kural 482).

14. “Lying is the greatest of all sins”... Alfred Bernhard Nobel, 1833-1896, a Swedish Chemist, Engineer, Inventor, Businessman and philanthropist, best known for having bequeathed his fortune to establish the ‘Nobel Prize’, after having made several contributions to science, with the fame of holding 355- ‘patents’ during his lifetime....(tallies with kural 293).

15. "I do not think that there is any other quality so essential to success of any kind as the quality of perseverance. It overcomes almost everything, even nature",.... John Davidson Rockefeller Sr., 1839-1937, American Businessman and philanthropist, (tallies with kurals 591; 619).

16. "Think of giving, not as a duty; but as a privilege!"...John D. Rockefeller, Sr., American Business Magnate, (1839-1937).......(tallies with kural 231).

17. "People are capable, at any time in their lives, of doing what they dream of"...Paulo Coelho, 1947—xx, a Brazilian lyricist and novelist..author of a novel "The Alchemist", in Portuguese language (tallies with kural 601).

18. "Words are, of course, the most powerful drug used by mankind", Joseph Rudyard Kipling, 1865-1936, (born in Mumbai), an English journalist, story-writer, poet, novelist,....(tallies with kural 91).

19. "Intelligence without ambition is a bird without wings",... Salvador Dali, 1904-1989, a Spanish painter of repute, creator of 'The Persistence of Memory', a piece of Art, presently being kept in the Museum of Modern Art in New York... (tallies with kural 592).

20. "Ignore people who tell you it won't work, and hire people who embrace your vision",..... Michael Saul Dell, 1965—xx, American Billionaire Businessman, founder-chairman and CEO of Dell Technologies, and philanthropist, (tallies with kural 517).

21. "I have tried **to make the men around me** feel as I do, that we are embarked as pioneers upon a new science and industry, in which our problems are so new and unusual that it behooves no one to dismiss any novel idea with the statement: 'it cannot be done'...", ...William Edward Boeing, 1881-1956, founder of The Boeing Company, one of the largest aerospace manufacturers in the world....(tallies with kural 651).

22. "I have only had two rules: Do all you can; and do it the best you can",... Colonel Hartland Sanders, the founder of Kentucky Fried Chicken (KFC), an American Entrepreneur....(tallies with kural 661).

23. "The most important requirements for major success are: first, being in the right place, at the right time, and second,doing something about it", ... Ray Kroc (Raymond Albert Kroc), 1902-1984, American Businessman,

McDonald's Corporation Founder and Former CEO,.... (tallies with kural 484; 491)

24. "Your first job is to turn out quality merchandise that consumers will buy, and keep on buying it",...... William Cooper Procter, 1862-1934, American manufacturer who established the nation's first profit-sharing plan for employees, Disability pension plan, life insurance plan, and employee-representation in the Board of Directors....... (the quote is a statement made by Mr.Procter in 1887:Ref: 'The Life of William Cooper Procter, from Industrial Statesman: discerning readers.com)......(tallies with kural 120).

25. "If you want to walk fast, walk alone! But if you want to walk far, walk together!"... Ratan Tata (1937- xx), Indian Industrialist ... (Tallies with Kural 462).

26. "None can destroy Iron, but its own rust can! Likewise, none can destroy a person, but his own mind-set can!"..... Ratan Tata (1937-xx), Indian Industrialist...(Tallies with Kurals 434; 505)

27. "Ups and downs in life are important to keep us going! Because, a straight-line in an E.C.G. means we are not alive!"... Ratan Tata..... (Tallies with Kural 628).

28. "The important thing which I have really learned is how you do not give up, because you never succeed in the first attempt" Mukesh Ambani (1957-xx), Indian Industrialist... (Tallies with Kural 616; 666; 669).

29. "Success is achieved twice: Once, in the mind! And the second time, in the real world!" Azim Premji (1945- xx), Indian Industrialist...... (Tallies with Kural 309).

30. "Every economic opinion is associated with a set of assumptions".... Gautam Adani (1962- xx), Indian industrialist... (Tallies with Kural 423).

31. "Everyone experiences tough times, it is a measure of your determination how you deal with them, and how you can come through them!", Lakshmi Mittal, Indian industrialist (1950 - xx)......(Tallies with Kural 621).

32. "We have to and understand the countries, their cultures and the markets in which we operate", Gopichand P. Hinduja (1940 - xx), Indian-born British Businessman... (Tallies with Kurals 425; 426).

33. "I do not want India to be an economic super power; I want India to be a happy country!" J.R.D.Tata (1904-1993), Indian Industrialist, (Tallies with Kurals 738;

34. "At the end of the day, everybody has to take the right decisions for the right reasons". Cyrus Pallonji Mistry (1068 - xx), Irish Businessman of Indian origin)….. (Tallies with Kural 520; 1039).

35. "The trouble with opportunity is, it never announces when it comes. It is only after it is gone, you would realise that you have missed it!", Uday Suresh Kotak (1959 - xx), Indian Businessman, (Tallies with Kural 466).

36. "The important factor that keeps me going is the kind of people I work with",…. Kumar Mangalam Birla (1967 - xx), Indian Industrialist, (Tallies with Kural 651).

37. "Our nation is growing not because of its size, or democracy, but because of its outstanding entrepreneurs, and hardworking people", Rahul Bajaj (1938 - xx), I*ndian Businessman… (Tallies with Kural 731).*

38. "Everyone has a purpose in life, and a unique talent to give to others. And when we blend this unique talent with service to others, we experience the ecstasy and exaltation of own spirit which is the ultimate goal of all goals", …..Dr.Kallam Anji Reddy (1939 - xx), Scientist, Founder-Chairman of Dr.Reddy's Laboratories, Hyderabad, India……. (Tallies with Kural 611).

39. "Wealth earned by human efforts must be properly utilised for social benefits in addition to family commitments, so that it gives a wholesome pleasure", Dr.Rajah Sir Annamalai Chettiar, Philanthropist, First Founder-Pro Chancellor of Annamalai University, Tamil Nadu, India (1881-1948)… .. (Tallies with Kurals 754; 385).

40. "Any Government must consult public opinion on any project. " Dr. Rajah Sir MuthiahChettiar,Philanthropist Second Founder-Pro Chancellor of Annamalai University (1905-1984), Member, Constituent Assembly of India, Proceedings of Legislative Council, of Madras Presidency, on 17th August 1938… (Tallies with Kurals 384; 544).

41. "In any establishment, human resource potential becomes an important capital itself!"…. Dr.M.A.M. Ramaswamy Chettiar, (1931-2015), Philanthropist Third Founder-Pro Chancellor of Annamalai University,

Former Member of Parliament, Tamil Nadu... (Tallies with Kurals 758; 675; 651)

42. "We must promote education among the masses, so that they are able to work with confidence in India and abroad (to) wherever they migrate!".... Dr. Sir Rm. Alagappa Chettiar, Industrialist and Educationist and Philanthropist, 1909-1957... (Tallies with Kurals 397; 400).

43. "I've survived things that have tested hard on others. My life is a message of hope, as I endured the testing times, with all possible patience in the world!".....A.V.MeyyappaChettiar, Indian Film Producer (1907-1979).... (Tallies with Kurals 624; 625; 620).

44. "Your dream does not have an expiration date! Take a deep breath, and try again!".....Dr.N.Mahalingam, Industrialist and Educationist (1923-2014).... (Tallies with Kural 593; 598)

45. "Education deals with the human growth in mind, spirit, character and effective behaviour"...Dr.G.R.Damodaran, (1914-1986)...Industrialist and Educationist.... (Tallies with Kural 400; 140; 391).

46. "It is important to keep your head up, and follow what you believe is right!"... G.D.Naidu, Industrialist, 1893-1874 ... (Tallies with Kural 384).

47. "Every man reaches his destination, if he keeps on walking!" .... G.D.Naidu... (Tallies with Kurals 616; 637).

48. "You have to work with what you are given, even (a role) in Shakespeare! We have our form, and it is important that we free ourselves through it!"...... G.D.Naidu... (Tallies with Kurals 472; 512; 600).

49. "Exposure to literature gives you refinement in understanding!" Rasigamani T.K.C. (T.K.Chidambaranatha Mudaliar), 1882-1954, Tamil Literary

50. "A clear vision of a scheme must start with proper planning"..... KarumuthuThiyarajanChettiar, Industrialist and Educationist, 1893-19740....

51. "Always do your best. What you plant now, you will harvest later!". ...M.Ct.M.ChidambaramChettiar, Founder of Indian Overseas Bank, India, (1908-1954).... (Tallies with Kural 675; 677; 666).

52. “Capital, methodology, capability, place and time have to be combined with team work, for earning success in industry”, ... A.M.M.MurugappaChettiar, Indian Industrialist (1902-1965)...... (Tallies with Kural 675).

53. “Small capital and affordable hard work will yield success in any undertaking!” H.Vasanthkumar, Parliamentarian and Businessman, 1950-2020.... (Tallies with Kural 594).

54. “Vision looks inward and becomes duty; Vision looks outward and becomes aspiration; Vision looks upward and becomes faith!”.....P.A.C.Ramasamy Raja, Industrialist and Educationist, (1894—196)2... (Tallies with Kural 661).

55. “Intimacy in interaction brings pleasure among sportsmen, as well as among the learned, out of mutual admiration!”...... M.A.ChidambaramChettiar, Industrialist and Cricket Administrator (1918-2000)....... (Tallies with 394).

56. “Success in industry depends on identifying skills in the working-force!’...... T.V.Sundaram Iyengar, Indian Industrialist (1877—1958),.... (Tallies with Kural 517).

57. “Every small incident needs to be reported and made known to all the people, to verify whether it needs corrective action by appropriate authorities. Let us do it with care!”.... S.Kasturi Ranga Iyengar, (1859-1923), Indian Lawyer and Indian Independence Activist, the Founder of The Hindu (Newspaper)..... (Tallies with Kural 583; 582; 549).

58. “Simplicity and humility are tokens of greatness in the mind, in spite one’s personal achievements”... S.P.Aditanar, Lawyer, Politician and Industrialist, 1905-1981, (Tallies with Kural 124).

59. “T task of learning skills and earning capabilities depends on how much of hard work you put in, to fulfill the task in front of you! Will-power and perseverance are the keys”.....Padmashri Dr.B.SivanthiAdityan (Sivanthi Adhithanar), 1936-2013, Newspaper Media Baron and Sports Administrator, Former President of the Indian Olympic Association and Vice-President of the Olympic Council of Asia... (tallies with kural 661).

60. “If you are calm, about your ambitions, you become confident of achieving what you set out to do!’.... Shiv Nadar, Intrenational Industrialist, Founder Chairman Emeritus of HCL, 1945—xx... (Tallies with Kural 472).

61. "Collaboration is a key part of the success of any organization, executed through a clearly defined vision and mission based on transparency and constant communication".... Dinesh C. Paliwal, Indian American business Executive, 1957— xx... (Tallies with Kural 651).

62. "Growth is painful; Change is painful; But, nothing is as painful as staying stuck where you do not belong!"...... N.R.Narayana Murthy, Indian Business Magnate, 1946-xx... (Tallies with Kural 473; 511; 670; 673; 832).

63. "Innovative ideas in business, executed with sincerity and honesty, will yield benevolent success",..... V.G.Panneerdas, 1932-1998, a pioneer in introducing 'hire-purchase scheme', in Chennai City,. (tallies with kural 120).

64. "A person is happy, not because everything is right in his life! He is happy because his attitude towards everything in his life is right".... Sundar Pitchai, (1972—xx),... (tallies with kural 628).

65. "Don't stop chasing your dreams, because dreams do come true!"... Sachin Tendulkar,...1973—xx, Former Captain of Indian Cricket Team....(tallies with kural 596).

66. "When you have to work, work with a smile", Kapil Dev (Kapil Dev Ramlal Nikkhanj), 1959—xxx, Indian Cricketer of the Century in 2002,....... (tallies with kural 483).

67. "The need for practice will be better appreciated when you exasperate while running fast in the field, and end up winning"....Sunil Gawaskar, 1949—xx, Reputed Indian Cricket Player......(tallies with kural 676).

68. "Every fraction of a second is important in your alertness; in order to prove your valour in the field! For that, you have to go on trying to synchronize your physique and mind together",... M.S.Dhoni, 1981—xx, Former Captain of Indian Cricket Team,... (tallies with kural 616).

69. "I am an optimist by nature, and I reserve the right to be wrong".. Rakesh Jhunjhunwala, Indian Stock Trader, (1960—xx) ... (Tallies with Kural 628)

70. "A team is the most important part of a start-up", Ashok Soota, Chairman of Happiest Minds Technology Private Limited, India, (1942-- xx) ... (tallies with kural 462)

71. "Nobody programmes the brain. But it keeps on learning",.......Senapathy (Kris) Gopalakrishnan, Executive Vice Chairman of Infosys, Indian businessman, (1955-- xx), ...(tallies with kural 396).

APPENDIX- 3F

COMPARISON OF THIRUKKURAL WITH IDEOLOGY OF AFRICAN THINKERS

1. "Fear has many titles; but no honour! Hatred has many forms; but no soul. Agony has many hands; but no heart! Ego has many forms; but no soul!"..... (Matsona Dhliwayo, a Canadian based Philosopher and Entrepreneur, born in Harere, Zimbabwe, author of "Art of Winning" (Tallies with Kurals 428; 8 54; 621; 978).

2. "Envy has great strength; but no brains! Malice has many heads; but no heart! Lust has many titles; but no honour! Evil has many forms; but no soul!".... (Matshona Dhliwayo) (Tallies with Kurals 161; 851; 434; 202).

3. "The ignorant learn from none! The curious learn from many! The simple learn from some! The intelligent learn from many! But the enlightened learn from all!" ... (Matshona Dhliwayo)...... (Tallies with Kurals 414; 424; 394; 724).

4. "A strongmindisgreaterthanastrongfist!"......... (Matshona Dhliwayo).... (Tallies with Kural 861: clever moves to avoid enmity with anybody).

5. "The prettiest flowers earn their honour from the ugliest dirt!" (Matshona Dhliwayo)... (Tallies with Kural 973).

6. "The Seven Secrets of Happiness: Think positively; Do work you love; Avoid anger; Give generously; be grateful; Overcome negativity; Develop thick skin!"..... (Matshona Dhliwayo) .... (Tallies with Kurals 596; 1022; 305; 223; 103; 600; 159; 389).

7. "The heart is a class room! The soul is a teacher! The mind is a student! And the Life is the exam!"...... (Matshona Dhliwayo).... (Tallies with Kurals 75; 80; 426; 33; 40)

8. "The world Intelligence tells you what you to do! Insight tells you how to do it! Understanding tells you when to do it! Wisdom tells you why you 493 do it!" ... (Matshona Dhliwayo) .... (Tallies with Kurals 616; 461; 501; 512; 483; 1026)

9. "When perplexed, God appears to you in the form of Wisdom!"..... (Matshona Dhliwayo)..... (Tallies with Kurals 631; 636; 668).

10. "Learn from friends; and you are intelligent! Learn from family; and you are clever! Learn from your enemies; and you are wise!"....... (Matshona Dhliwayo).... (Tallies with Kurals 787; 524; 533).

11. "The world owes you nothing, because the universe has given you everything!"..... (Matshona Dhliwayo)..... (Tallies with Kurals 430; 211).

12. South African Proverb: "A crocodile's strength is in water!"....(tallies with kural 495).

13. Ethiopian proverb: "An eye and a friend are quickly hurt"....(tallies with kural 90).

14. Tanzanian Proverb: "Every bird flies on its own wings".....(tallies with kural 591).

15. Kenyan Proverb: "Blind belief is dangerous"....(tallies with kural 423).

16. Algerian Proverb: "A friend is someone who shares your happiness and your pains".........(tallies with kurals 787; 784; 788).

17. Proverb from Ghana: "If you are on the road to nowhere, find another road!'...(tallies with kural 673).

18. Proverb from Madagascar: "Truth is like sugarcane! Even if you chew it for a long time, it is still sweet"......(tallies with kural 300).

19. Proverb from Zambia: "He who keeps on trying, gets the reward!"... (tallies with kural 595).

20. Proverb from Congo: "The snake and the crab don't sleep in the same hole"....(tallies with kural 890).

21. Kenyan proverb: "How easy it is to defeat people who do not kindle fire for themselves!".....(tallies with kural 863).

22. Proverb from Uganda: "Old men sit in the shade, because they planted a tree many years before!"…..(tallies with kural 760).

23. Proverb from Cameroon: "It is better to be the victim of injustice than to be unjust yourself "….(tallies with kural 203).

24. Proverb from Cyria: "A little spark can kindle a great fire"……(tallies with kural 674).

25. Proverb from Somalia: "He, who does not seize the opportunity today, will be unable to seize tomorrow's opportunity…..(tallies with kural 466).

26. Proverbs from Morocco: "It is worse to be wounded by words than a sword!"….(tallies with kural 129).

27. Proverb from Sudan: "Relatives are a dense forest"……(tallies with kural 524).

28. Proverb from Angola: "Actions speak louder than words" (tallies with Rural 664)

29. Nigerian Proverb: "The same sun that melts wax is also capable of hardening clay"… (tallies with kurals 593; 483).

30. Proverb from Liberia: "An elephant will never get tired of carrying its Tusks"……(tallies with kural 597).

APPENDIX -3G

COMPARISON OF THIRUKKURAL WITH NATIVE - AMERCAN IDEOLOGY

1. "When you were born, you cried; and the world rejoiced! Live your life, so that when you die, the world cries!" (Cherokee Saying) (Tallies with Kurals 50; 974; 114; 72).

2. "Our first teacher is our own heart!".....(Cheyenne Saying).... (Tallies with Kurals 293; 294; 296; 300).

3. "Treat all men alike! ...Give them all the same law. Give the all an even chance to live and grow"...Dee Brown, Bury My Heart at Wounded knee, ..An Indian History of the American West...Native AmericanWisdomQuotes... (https://www.goodreads.com/quotes/tag/nativeamericanwisdom)... (tallies with kural 541).

4. "At the end of our lives, when our bodies are about to be laid in Mother Earth, we will know for ourselves whether we are a Two-legged being full of light or a Two-legged being full of darkness"....Anasazi-Foundation: The Seven Paths, Changing One's Way of Walking in the World....(https:// www.goodreads.com/quotes/tag/anasazi-foundation.....(tallies with kural 114).

APPENDIX- 3H

COMPARISON OF THIRUKKURAL WITH PERSIAN IDEOLOGY:

1. "Woman is the Light of God!"... [Rumi (Maulana Jalaludin Rumi), (1207-1273, 13th century Persian Poet hailing from Greater Iran]..... (Tallies with Kurals 54; 974).
2. "Yesterday, I was clever; so, I wanted to change the world! Today, I am wise; so I am changing myself!.Rumi.... (Tallies with Kurals 436).
3. "Don't grieve; anything you lose, comes around, in another form" ....Rumi... (Tallies with Kurals 376; 659).
4. "Raise your words; not the Voice! It is the rains that grows flowers; not Thunders",.....(Rumi)... (tallies with kural 93).
5. "The lion is most handsome when looking for food!"...Rumi....(tallies with kural 824)
6. "Living Life Tomorrow's fate, though thou be wise, Thou canst tell nor yet surmise; Pass, therefore, not today in vain, For it will never come again",.. Omar Khayyam (1048-1131)...... (Tallies with Kural 334).
7. "Although all religions promise paradise, take care to create your own paradise, here, and now, on the earth!",......Omar Khayyam, 1048- 1131,. (tallies with kural 50).
8. "If you hope for eternal rest, feel the pain yourself; but do not hurt others".... Omar Khayyam,. (tallies with kural 209).

APPENDIX-4

THIRUKKURAL AS A VALUE EDUCATION PROGRAMME:

At the level of school education, some ideas of Thiruvalluvar have to be introduced, to the young minds of the children, in several phases, depending on the mental maturity of the child. The following schemes may be considered:

a. By the time the child completes the school-final class (Tenth Standard), the following topics are to be made familiar to the child, choosing one poem (couplet) in each chapter, to motivate the child, aiming at "Personality-building effort". In this relevance, the chapters to be considered are: 1. Avoidance of Laziness/Lethargy (Ch.61); 2.Firmness in Strenuous Acts(Ch.62); 3. Freedom from Stage Fear (Ch.73); 4. Learning/ Education (Ch.40); 5. Possession of Kindness (Ch.8); 5. *Friendship (Ch.79); 6. Avoidance of Slandering/ Back-biting (Ch.19); 7. Avoidance of Useless Words (Ch.20); 8. Uttering Pleasant Words (Ch.10); 9.Good Conduct/ Character (Ch.14); 10.Power* of Speech (Ch.65); 11.Link with Great Persons as Patrons (Ch.45); 12. Avoidance of Anger (Ch.31); 13.Medicine and Eating Habits (Ch.95); 14. Patience as a Virtue (Ch.16); 15. Avoidance of Envy (Ch.17).15. Truth fulness (Ch.30).

b. When students reach senior classes, they can refer to the full contents of each chapter, on topics such as, Judging the Audience (Ch. 72), Freedom from Stage Fear(Ch. 73), Purity of Action (Ch. 66), Excellence in Action (Ch. 67), Methodology for Action (Ch.68), Carelessness out of Foolishness (Ch.84), Charity(Ch.23), Fame (Ch.24), Forbidden Friendship(Ch.83).

c. Persons interested in research in the disciplines of human psychology will be able to find materials from many Kural couplets, in various chapters of Thirukkural. Best of Luck to those who wish to try!

APPENDIX-5A

APPLICATION IN PROFESSIONAL DEVELOPMENT

There is rich material in Thirukkural for students of many different disciplines of learning:

a. The Students of Civil Engineering and Architecture will admire the contents of Chapter 2 which describes the process of raining, its importance in relevance to the hydrology involved in the benevolence of raining as described by the poet! Many concepts of the process of raining are described, related to hydrology. Also in Chapter 75 (Defense Fortification), Kural 742 describes the layout of a Fort needed for a King, to be designed in such a way that the boundaries are marked by a garland-shaped layout, with a main entrance-gate to be provided at the neck portion of the garland, the fort being surrounded by a garland- shaped canal containing deep waters, adjoining which, on the outer side, a dense forest with shady trees will be grown. Also, Chapter 75 describes the various other facilities to be provided inside the Fortress-building to ensure the safety of persons(inmates), materials, arms and ammunition! The structure inside the fort must be safe against intrusion by tunneling!

b. Students of Engineering and Technology, who have a desire for Entrepreneurship, will be impressed to be guided by Chapter76 (Ways of Earning Wealth), Chapter 47 (Action After Deep Thinking), Chapter 48 (Knowing One's Own Strength), Chapter 50 (Choice of Place for Action), Chapter 49(Choice of Time for Action), Chapter 51 (Clarity based on Analysis), Chapter 52 (Initiation of Action After Clarity), Chapter 66 (Purity of Action), Chapter 67 (Excellence in Action), Chapter 68 (Methodology for Action), Chapter 60 (Perseverance as a Strength), Chapter 61 (Avoidance of Laziness/Lethargy), Chapter

62 (Firmness in Strenuous Acts), Chapter 63 (Endurance during Hardships in Life),Chapter 79 (Friendship), Chapter 80 (Assessment of Friendship), Chapter 81(Intimacy in Friendship), Chapter 82 (Harmful Friendship), Chapter 83(Forbidden Friendship), Chapter 84 (Carelessness out of Foolishness, especially Kural 831), Chapter 40(Learning/ Education), and Chapter 12 (Neutrality), especially Kural 120!

c. Students of Health Sciences will appreciate the contents of Chapter 95, describing the methods of diagnosis (Kural 948, 941, 949), the hospital infrastructure (Kural 950), and eating habits (Kurals 942 to 947), especially the couplet relating to allergic foods (Kural 945)!

d. Students of Agricultural Sciences will appreciate the contents of Chapter 104 which describes the need for ploughing the land, application of manure, removal of weeds, need for irrigation and protection of crops in Kurals 1031 to 1040. Kurals 11 to 20 describe the importance of rain for the farmers, correlating the rain with wealth and prosperity of farmers, and their duty-bound obligations in supporting the ascetics, vagabonds, helpless-people, and local deities!

e. For Research scholars / senior students at College level, in any discipline: All chapters listed in items (b) to (d), plus the contents in Chapter 72 (Judging the Audience), Freedom from Stage Fear (Chapter 73), Power of Speech (Chapter 65), etc., have to be gone through! Kural 717 refers to: "The greatness of vast learning of the speaker will be revealed while addressing the audience of persons who have learned the words free from faults, and who are strong in gathering information"! This kind of tradition is being followed in institutions of higher learning around the world during the modern times! Kural 711 to 720 relating to the Chapter-72 (Judging the Audience), and Kural 721 to 730 relating to the Chapter 73 (Freedom from Stage Fear) form a treasure of information in the academic field in assessing the capability of academic scholars at higher level of learning, such as Masters level and Doctoral level in all disciplines of study! The yardstick indicated by Thiruvalluvar, in assessing the calibre of scholars, remains valid during the 21st Century relating to international practice in all universities around the world!

f. Students of General Administration, Political Science, Legal studies can peruse chapters: 4, 8, 12, 14, 15, 18, 19, 21, 28, 29, 30, 32, 33, 39, 43, 44, 45, 46, 55, 56, 57, 58, 59, 64, 65, 66, 69, 70, 72, 74, 76, 80, 89, 90, 92, 94, 95, 99, 100, 104, 105, 106, 107, 108, etc., with an inquisitive approach!

APPNDIX-5B

BENEFITWISE CONSIDERATIONS

1. Personality Development:

   Kural 396(Study habits); Kural 641(speaking pleasant words); Kural 643 (ability to convince others); Kural 642(avoidance of bad words); Kural 711 (facing elders in Interviews); Kural 646(knowledge-sharing with others); Kural 728(avoidance of stage fear); Kural 1100 (body-language orientation; remaining watchful); Kural 124 (making a good appearance); Kural 455 (remaining watchful about the circle of friendship and acquaintance); Kural 34 (training the mind and action to be free from bad thoughts); Kural 72 (showing kindness to all); Kural 95(pleasant words and modest behaviour); Kural 131 (desire to acquire good habits and behaviours); Kural 158 (remaining vigilant about the harm likely to be done by others, and taking advice from elders as to how to handle it); Kural 161 (to remain cautious about developing jealousy); Kural 177(determination not to develop a desire to get wealth from others); Kural 186 (to be totally free from back-biting habit;); Kural 578(to develop a sympathetic attitude towards persons who deserve help); Kural 595(to develop a taste for hard work and perseverance); Kural 610 (avoidance of laziness in order to deserve prosperity); Kural 636(desire to earn to strength of theoretical and practical knowledge); Kural 652(avoiding useless activities); Kural 673(to think the right way to achieve right things); Kural 781(to select a friend who will remain trustworthy); Kural 853(avoidance of hatred towards anybody); Kural 946(to take care in practising good eating habits); Kural 952 (to maintain a good character and truthfulness to uphold the honour of the family); Kural 963(to maintain magnanimity commensurate with elevated status); Kural 975 (to carry out activities which will bring glory); Kural 301 and Kural 306 (avoiding anger for personal welfare and honour); Kural 314 (doing a benevolent act to whoever did harm to the self, to discourage enmity); Kural 982(to acquire good virtues and be useful to the society); Kural 992(to practice kindness and upgrade the fame of the family); Kural 1015(to develop a natural desire to avoid bad activities of the self and associates); Kural 1022(perseverance and hard work to the benefit of the family); Kural 1071 (to remain vigilant about the differentiation between good people and bad people, by watching their activities, and taking care to support the innocent, as the poet says that by appearance, it is not easy to judge who is good and who is bad!).

2. Choice of Employees in all cadres: Kural 517 (judging the person's capabilities); Kural 514 (certain persons are not capable of carrying out certain activities, for reasons best known to them); Kural 506(not to believe strangers); Kurals 508, 509, 510(caution to be exercised in interacting with staff for the chosen work);

3. Allotment of Responsibility in Work: Kural 517 (after confirming that a person is capable of carrying out the desired work, the responsibility is given to that person); Kural 516 (timely execution, when guaranteed, the work is entrusted to that person); Kural 518 (full trust on the person, if confirmed; full freedom can be given to that person to execute work);

4. Avoidance of worrying too much during hardships:Kural 625 (to endure the difficulties and sufferings with patience); Kural 621(to feel cheerful at the time of crisis, in order to avoid anxiety which will aggravate the feelings).

5. Concession to those who did not have opportunity to learn: Kural 414 (to compensate the loss of opportunity to learn by schooling, the privilege of hearing is considered as a great blessing to acquire knowledge); Kural 411 (knowledge earned through hearing is considered as a superior treasure of knowledge); Kural 413 (a pleasure of listening to music to get peace of mind; listening to lectures and discourses to earn knowledge); Kural 416 (it is possible to hear and learn about good things); Kural 417(those who have learned through hearing are considered to possess a good knowledge);

6. Happiness of Married Life: Kural 45 (a married life with kindness by following the virtuous path will yield a praiseworthy life, satisfying cultural perfection in the society, yielding benevolent benefits); Kural 48(married life in virtuous path will be admired on par with the life of ascetics); Kural 60(virtuous wife is considered as a pride for the entire family; added to

that will be the benefit of good children); Kural 67 (the duty of a father is to give the benefit of education to the child so that the child earns the meritorious upcoming in life); Kural 70 (if the child comes up in life, with better achievements, the good name comes to the father/parent, for having earned the divine blessings to give birth to such a meritorious child); Kural 69(when a child proves the merit in the society, it gives a greater joy to the mother than the joy she would have enjoyed at the time of giving birth to the child); Kural 64 (simple food of boiled grain-gruel dabbled by the playful tiny fingers of a baby will taste sweeter to a parent, more than a divine food of ambrosia!); Kural 65(the tender touch of a child is more blissful to the parent, and the lisping words of the child will be more pleasant to hear through the ears!; Kural 66 (the pleasant music of flute or lyre/guitar (a string instrument) will be blissful only to a parent who has not listened to the sweeter babbling words of his/her own child!

7. Importance of knowledge: Kural 421(knowledge is a great wealth; it cannot be destroyed by anybody, including one's own enemies). Kural 423 the right kind of knowledge is ascertained, only after evaluating and examining whatever is being told by others! Kural 424 (sharing knowledge with others will be beneficial to know more); Kural 428 (certain things which must be feared for, must be examined with care); Kural 429 (necessity to foresee any probable dangers and taking preventive actions will correspond to a safe knowledge); Kural 430 (sense of satisfaction with whatever you are provided with, corresponds to a superior knowledge); Kural 391 (learn without errors; practice what has been learned; Only then, it deserves merit as knowledge); Kural 664(practice what you preach for); Kural 398 (knowledge earned through education during one birth will be benevolent for seven generations in the future: it will lead to an intelligent dynasty of off-springs; there is an interpretation that the knowledge is transferred to subsequent generations through DNA/RNA genetic transfer!) (Note: If it is asked whether intelligence (Intelligent Quotient, IQ) is determined by genetic factors, the answer is: Like any other aspects of human behaviour and cognition, intelligence is a complex phenomenon which seems to be influenced by two factors, namely, i) genetic factors and ii) environmental factors, such as parental guidance, schooling resources, external contacts, etc., apart from nutritional resources. This needs further research.

8. Thought process: Kural 505(good benefits and bad effects are produced from one's own actions; do not entertain bad thoughts); Kural 666(right kind of thoughts will help you to achieve better benefits: so, think about high ideals); Kural 34 (absence of bad thoughts in the mind corresponds to a great virtue; It will bring benefits); Kural 137 (persons with good character will earn fame; persons without a good character will earn only abuses; therefore, everybody is advised to earn a good name);

9. Motivation: Kural 593 (Never give up self-confidence, when you happen to lose something which you possessed; make efforts to re-build confidence): Kural 591(those who have got hope in themselves only will prosper!); Kural 596 (Always think high about great ambitions; you will achieve them!); Kural 597(even after being hurt heavily in the war, an elephant will not lose hope! Think about it); Kural 484(even if you desire to own the world, you will succeed, if you make moves choosing the right time and right place); Kural 619(even if it not possible to achieve it through the blessings of god, it may be possible to achieve it through hard labour and sustained efforts);

10. Link with good person: Kural 783 (the more you move with good people, the more will be enjoyable their link); Kurals 451 to 460 in Chapter 46, give a caution about the bad effects of having link with bad persons!

APPENDIX-6

MULTI-DISCIPLINARY RELEVANCE OF THIRUKKURAL

Astronomy: Kural 1031: the earth as a planet revolving 'around its own axis'?

Climatology /meteorology: Kurals 11-to 20, describing the atmospheric/ hydrologic processes involved in the raining phenomenon! Also, interdependence of life process of living creatures on the donation of Nature, in the form of rain, for their very survival (Kural 20).

Mathematics/Theory of Numbers: The importance of Numbers and Letters is highlighted as the two eyes of a living person in Kural 392; Use of number one (Kurals 1, 24, 40 etc); number two (Kurals 5, 23, 374 etc); number three (Kural 41, 360, 383 etc.); number four (Kurals 35, 382, 390 etc); number five (Kurals 24, 25, 27 etc.); number six(Kural 381); number seven (Kurals 62, 107, 126 etc.); number eight (Kural 9); number ten (Kurals 450, 817); concept of fraction (Kural 1037); Multiple-digit numbers: one hundred (Kural 932): One thousand (Kural 259); single or multiple crores (multiples of ten millions):Kural 337, 377, 639, 816, 817, 954, 1005; 1061; Concept of infinity: countless number: Kural 22; concept of zero Kural 270 (the term "ilar"). (Note: Number 9 has not been used).

Physical Sciences: Use of a physical weighing-balance (Kural 118); unit of time (Kural 29); benefit of using axle-pin (Kural 667, 1032); Image-reflecting mirror (Kural 706); One's own shadow due to solar light (Kural 208), Shade under the Umbrella(Kural 1034); sound waves from musical instruments, namely, lyre and flute (Kural 66); Sceptre (542; 543; 544; 545; 546; 554; 556; 558).

Metallurgical sciences: use of steel (Kural 759, 773, 279); spears made of steel (Kurals 500, 546, 552, 774, 775); arrows (Kurals 279, 597), swords (Kurals 727, 882); rods (24); and files (Kural 567, 997); Process of combustion/heat: (Kurals 129, 308, 435, 674, 691, 896);

Gold materials/jewellery (Kurals 1081, 267, 931; touch stone (Kurals 505, 986); iron-cutting base (Kural 821); vessels made of copper ((Kurals 887, 1000); Chemical materials/aspects: salt (Kurals 802, 1050, 1302); yeast (1050); poison (Kural 580, 926); Lime as a whitening agent (Kural 714); Toddy (liquor in Kural 922).

Agricultural sciences: soil fineness (Kural 1037), manure application (1038), irrigation (Kural 1038); removal of weeds (Kurals 1038, 550); protection of crops (Kural 1038); constant care of land (Kural 1040); moisture and plant growth (Kural 16).

Knowledge on water quality (Kural 452); Uncultivable land (Kural 406); desert land (Kural 78); Fertility of soil which can sustain a crop (Kural 959)

There is a mention about Lotus flower, an aquatic plant (Kurals 595, 617); extinct species: Anicham flower (Kurals 90, 1111, 1120); a thorny bush:Nerunchi, cow's thorn (1120); millet seed (Kurals 104, 144, 433, 1282); Seasame seed(Kural 889); kundrimaniseed (Kural 277); sugar cane (Kural 1078); Yeast(Kural 1050); Green grass (Kural 16); edible fruit(Kural 216); poisonous fruit (Kural 1008); thorny shrub(Kural 879). Palm tree seed (Kurals 104, 433,).Shady trees (Kural 742); Water bodies (Kural 742; 215; 595); Hill (Kural 29, 742, 758); Flat land (Kural 742); River (Kural 278);

Many species of animals, birds and insects are mentioned: Elephant (Kural 500, 599, 774,); Lion (59, 381); Tiger (Kural 273, 599); cow (1066, 481); goat (486); fox(Kural 500); rat (763); snake (Kural 763); tortoise(Kural 126); crocodile (Kural 495); crow (Kural 527, 481); Bird crane/heron (274, 490); Owl (Kural 481); Peacock (Kural 475); Swan bird (1120); Boneless animal species(Invertebrates) in Kural 77.

Health Sciences: five senses of human organs (Kural 27); Personal hygiene(Kural 298); Food habits (Kurals 942, 943, 946, 947); allergic food (Kurals 943, 945); diagnosis of diseases(Kurals 941, 948, 949), Hospital infrastructure(Kural 950).

Psychology: Human conscience (Kurals282, 293, 318, 335, 484, 668, 930, 932, 1080, 1081, 1270, 1295).

Management Sciences: (Kurals 385, 390, 431, 443, 447, 449, 461 to 470, 477, 479, 485, 491 to 500, 506 to 510, 511 to 520, 531 to 540, 596, 609, 611 to

620, 621 to 630, 639, 651, 653, 661 to 663, 669, 670, 671 to 680, 691, 740, 750, 758, 770, 819, 825, 831, 834, 848, 863, 876, 891, 902, 960, 962, 986, 994, 1014, 1028, 1039).

Trade and Financial management: Kurals 120; 113; 177; 212; 300; 385; 449; 462; 466; 477; 478; 479; 480; 485; 491; 506, 507, 508; 509; 510; 517; 518; 519; 520; 524; 534; 578; 596; 613; 621; 758;

Academicfields: 391-400, 411, 421-430, 431-440, 441, 451, 462, 471, 484, 534, 567, 578, 595, 605, 615, 621, 631, 641-650, 654, 661, 675, 677, 698, 711-720, 721-730, 751, 781, 853, 892, 975, 981, 994, 1022.

APPENDIX-7

COMPARISON OF THIRUKKURAL WITH RELIGIOUS PHILOSOPHIES

I. **Comparison of Thirukkural with Jainism:**

The Reader has to compare the Kural-couplets relating to Avoidance of killing (Chapter 33), Refusal to eat flesh (Chapter 26), Insistence on virtues (Chapter 4), Possessing kindness (Chapter 8), Good Conduct and Character (Chapter 14), Patience as a Virtue (Chapter 16), Avoidance of envy (Chapter 17), Fear for Evil Acts (Chapter 21), Charity(Chapter 23), Renunciation of desires (Chapter 35), Realization of True knowledge (Chapter 36), etc, to understand the major principles of Jainism. Certain additional quotes are given below:

i. "Do not injure, abuse, oppress, enslave, insult, torment, or kill any creature or living-being"! —Lord Mahavira..... (Tallies with Kural 321; 323; 327; 1018).

ii. "Do unto others you would like to be done to you (by others). Injury or violence done by you to any life, in any form, animal or human, is as harmful as if caused to your own self "!—Lord Mahavira... (Tallies with Kural 206; 209).

iii. "It is a friend's duty that he does not leave his friend in a difficult position, but provide intimacy and support to him. In difficulty, whoever leaves is a false friend, and he who is not quitting is a true friend".....Aacharya Shri Mahashraman..... (Tallies with Kural 787; 789).

Hints: (a) Jainism does not believe in a creator of the world. (b) There is no practice of casteism among the Jains. (c) No killing of animals is permitted in Jainism. (d) Total Vegetarianism is practiced by the Jains.(e) Jains believe in Rebirths. Moksha/Samsara/Karma

(Ref: https://byjus.com>...>UPSC Preparation Strategy: Difference between Hindus and Jains)

SUMMARY:

Core Values of Jainism: (i).Ahimsa (non-violence, in thoughts, words, and deeds; (ii). Anekantavada (respect for different view-points and beliefs); (iii). Aparigraha (non-materialism and simplicity of living); (iv). Asteya (non-stealing and abidance of the law); (v). Satya (Truthful living with sincerity and integrity), and (vi). Brahmacharya (Restraint in sensual indulgence). (Ref: 50be10cb9.pdf; http://www.anekant.org; http://www.jaina.org).

II. Comparison of Thirukkural with Buddhist-Literature:

(Reader has to compare the Kural-couplets relating to Avoidance of killing (Chapter 33), Refusal to eat flesh (Chapter 26), Insistence on virtues (Chapter 21), Possessing kindness (Chapter 8), Good Conduct and Character (Chapter 14), Patience as a Virtue (Chapter 16), Avoidance of Envy (Chapter 17), Fear for Evil Acts (Chapter 21), Charity (Chapter 23), Renunciation of Desires (Chapter 35), Realization of True knowledge (Chapter 36), Curtailment of Desires (Chapter 37) etc, to have a broader understanding on Buddhism). Certain additional quotes are given below:

Lord Buddha taught the famous 'Four-Noble Truths" and "Eightfold Path". The Four-Noble Truths will correspond to: i) Dhukka (suffering), ii) Samudaya (desire), iii) Nirodha (cessation of desire), and Margha (Noble Eightfold Path).

The Eight-fold Path will correspond to: i) Right Understanding (Wisdom), ii) Morality (sila), iii) Right Speech, iv) Right Action, v) Right Livelihood, vi) Right Effort, vii) Right mindfulness, and viii) Right concentration (withdrawal from sensuality, one-pointedness of awareness, free from directed-thought and evaluation-internal assurance, pleasurable abiding, and abandoning of pleasure and pain!

(Ref:https://en.wikibooks.org>Introduction to philosophy. What is Buddhist Philosophy?)

The Blessed One: (Ref: http://www.sacred-texts.com/bud/bits009.htm)

Gautama Buddha, immediately after attaining Buddhaship, described the 'Brahman-making'- qualities:

"The Brahman who his evil-traits hath banished; Is free from pride; is self-restrained and spotless; Is learned; and the holy life hath followed;

'T is he alone may claim the name of Brahman;

With things of earth he hath no point of contact" ...... Then, Gautama Buddha described the Blessed One: "How blest the happy solitude,

Of Him hears and knows the Truth! How Blest is harmlessness towards all, And self-restraint towards living things! How blest from passion to be free,

All sensuous joys to leave behind! Yet far the highest bliss of all

To leave the pride which says, "I am"!

(Tallies withKurals 300; 350; 316; 322; 342; 341; 346; 343; 357).

By way of tribute to Lord Buddha the following poem is given by Sir Edwin Arnold.

"For peace and pureness, those Four Noble Truths Which hold all wisdom as shores shut the seas,

Those Eight right Rules whereby who will may walk-Monarch or slave

-upon the Perfect Path;

That hath its Stages Four and Precepts Eight, Whereby whoso will live-mighty or mean,

Wise or unlearned, man, woman, young or old— Shall soon or late break from the wheels of life,

Attaining blest Nirvana!" (Ref: Sir Edwin Arnold, "Light of Asia", 2010, Pilgrims Publishers, Varanasi, India). Page 150.

Important: Devotees confirm their faith in the Five-Principles called "Panch-Sheel, as described below:

1. Do not take Life; 2. Do not steal; 3.Do not commit adultery; 4. Do not lie; 5.Do not consume liquor or any other intoxicant. (These five commands tally with many Kural couplets: 321 to 330; 281 to 290; 141 to 150; 293 & 294; 921 to 930, respectively, in about 42-couplets!).

(Ref: 49786.pdf; Bhikkhu Bodhi, "The Noble Eightfold Path. The Way To End Suffering", Buddhist Information (http://www.buddhistinformation.com); Essentials of Buddhism (http://www.buddhaweb.org).

Highlights Of "The Dhammapada", as quoted by Dr.Sarvapalli Radhakrishnan:

(Ref: "The Dhammapada, authored by Dr.S.Radhakrishnan, published by Pilgrims Publishing, Varanasi,India, 2007). Page 1.

i. All that we are is the result of what we have thought: all that we are is founded on our thoughts and formed of our thoughts..(tallies with kural 505).

ii. If a man speaks or acts with a pure thought, happiness pursues him like his own shadow that never leaves him.....(tallies with kural 208).

iii. "He reviled me, he beat me, and conquered me and then plundered me", who express such thought, tie their mind with the intention of retaliation. In them, hatred will not cease....(tallies with kural 858).

iv. "He reviled me, he beat me, and conquered and the plundered me, who do not express such thoughts, in them hatred will cease!.....(tallies with kural 987).

v. "In this world, never is enmity appeased by hatred; enmity is appeased by LOVE! This is the Law eternal!......(tallies with kural 998).

vi. (vi) The many who know not this also forget that in this world we shall one day die. They do not restrain themselves. But those who recognize the Law end their quarrels soon!...(tallies with kural 334).

vii. Whose lives pursuing pleasures, his senses unrestrained, immoderate in eating, indolent, devitalized—him verily doth Mara uproot as a gale a weak tree!....(tallies with kural 368).

viii. Whoso lives disciplining himself, unmindful of pleasures, his senses restrained, moderate in eating, full of faith and dauntless energy (Virya)—him verily Mara doth overturn as a gale overturn a rocky mountain!.....(tallies with kural 628).

ix. He may display it on himself but he has not merited the yellow robe who has purged away depravities and is well grounded in virtues, who is regardful of temperance and truth!...... .....(tallies with kural 365).

x. He indeed has merited the yellow robe who has purged away depravities and well-grounded in virtues, who is regardful of temperance and truth....(tallies with kural 367).

xi. Those who live in the pleasure-ground of fancy see truth in the unreal and untruth in the real. They never arrive at truth!....... (tallies with kural 344).

xii. Those who abide in the world of right thought see truth in the real and untruth in the unreal.They arrive at truth!......(tallies with kural 352).

xiii. Rains pour into an ill-thatched house; desired pour into an ill- trained mind!..(tallies with kural 368).

xiv. Rains wet not a well-thatched house; desires enter not the disciplined mind!...(tallies with kural 369).

xv. The evil doer suffers in this world and he grieves in the next; he mourns in both. Afflicted, he grieves in the visualization of his sinful deeds! .....(tallies with kural 204).

xvi. The virtuous rejoices in this world, and he rejoices in the next! And he rejoices in both. He rejoices, rejoices exceedingly, in the visualization of his pure deeds!......(tallies with kural 243).

xvii. The evil-doer laments here, and laments hereafter! "Evil have I done?, he soliloquizes. Greater is his torment when he is in the place of evil!.....(tallies with kural 116).

xviii. The righteous man is happy here, he is happy hereafter! "I have done well", he soliloquizes. Greater is his delight, in the blissful place!..... (tallies with kural 50)

xix. He who quotes the sacred texts but is lazy and will not apply, he is like a cowherd counting the cows of others. He shares not the blessings of the Good Life!...(tallies with kural 606).

xx. He who forsakes lust, hatred and folly is possessed of true knowledge and a serene mind, craves nought of this world, or of any other, applies to himself the teachings of the sacred texts he recites, even though a few in number—such a one shares in the blessings of the Good Life!.....(tallies with kural 983).

III. Thirukkural and the Sikhism Ideology:

(Reader has to compare the Kural-couplets relating to Possessing kindness, Good Conduct and Character, Patience as a Virtue, Avoidanceof envy, Fear for Evil Acts, Charity, etc). Certain additional quotes are given below:

i. "As fragrance dwells in a flower, And Reflection in a mirror, So does God dwell in every soul: seek Him therefore, in thy self!"— Guru Nanak (1469-1539). (Tallies with Kural 3).

ii. "There is one supreme being, the eternal reality, the creator, without fear and devoid of enmity, immortal, never incarnated, self-existent, known by grace through the true Guru". This philosophy Tallies with Kural 4 which says "For those who reach the Almighty who is free from feelings of likes and dislikes, there will never be any sufferings".

iii. "Your mercy is my social-status!"....Guru Nanak, Sri Guru Granth Sahib.. (Tallies with Kural 3).

iv. "What should the yogi have to fear? Trees, Plants, and all that is inside and outside, is he himself"! Guru Nanak, Sri Guru Granth Sahib..... (Tallies with Kural 350).

v. "He himself makes the mortals anxious; and he himself takes the anxiety away"......Guru Amar Das, Sri Guru Granth Sahib..... (Tallies with Kural 348)

(Similarities and differences between Hinduism and Sikhism are given below):

Refer: https://www.asiahighlights.com>hinduism-vs-sikhism.

Sikhs are not Hindus. They have got their own Scriptures: Sri Guru Grant Sahib. They practice a separate religious appearance. Place of worship for them is the Gurudwara. The place of worship for the Hindus is the Temples/Mandirs. Hindus worship many gods of their choice, whereas the Sikhs worship only one God. Hindus practice the worship of statues/ images/idols, etc., whereas Sikhs do not use idol or image for their worship. Hindus believe in Moksha. Sikhs believe in Mukthi. Diet habits are either vegetarianism or non-vegetarianism.

SUMMARY:

The Mool Mantar: (basic belief written by Guru Nanak):

A. Ik Onkar: There is only One God;

B. Sat Nam: Truth is his name!

C. Karta Purakh: The Creator;

D. Nir Bhau: Without fear

E. AkaalMoorat: Immortal; Indestructive;

F. Ajooni: Beyond Births and Deaths!

G. Saibhang: Self-Illuminated, the Enlightener!

H. Gur Parsaad: Realised by the kindness of the True Guru (God)!

PRAYER WRITTEN BY GURU GOBIND SINGH:

Grant me this boon, O God, from thy Greatness; May I never refrain from righteous acts; May I fight without fear with All foes in life's battle; With Confident courage claiming the victory; May thy glory be grained in my mind; And my highest ambition be singing Thy Praise; When this mortal life reaches its limits, May I die with limitless courage! (Tallies with Kurals 7, 34, 497; 382; 5; 10; 50 reflecting the life of an idealist!).

(Ref: https://core.ac.uk>pdf;https://www.sikhcoalition.org>pdf).

IV. Thirukkural and the Bible:

i. Kural couplet 1 states: The first alphabet 'Akaram' (pronounced as 'A') marks the origin of all letters in a language; similarly, for all activities of the world, the origin is the blessings from the ancient God! (There is another interpretation that God created the language, first, as the first entity, before creating the world!).

   This is comparable with the Bible: 'The Gospel according to John':1.1, which reads as "In the beginning, was the Word, and the Wordwas with God, and the Word was God!"

ii. "Do not judge (others), or you too will be judged. For in the same way you judge others, you will be judged, and with the measure youuse, it will be measured to you"! Mathew 7:1-2 (Holy Bible, King James Version……. (Tallies with Kural 204).

iii. "Blessed are those who mourn; they will be comforted".... Matt 5.4, (Holy Bible, King James Version)…… (Tallies with Kural 622).

iv. "Love knows no limit to its endurance; no end to its trust; no fading away of its hope; it can outlast anything. Love never fails"… ..1Corinthians 13(Holy Bible, King James Version)… (Tallies with Kural 71).

v. "God is Love; and he who abides in love abides in God and Godin him"….1 John (Holy Bible, King James Version)… (Tallies with Kural 3).

vi. "Finally, brothers and sisters; whatever is true, whatever is noble, whatever is right, whatever is pure, whatever is lovely, whatever is admirable—if anything is excellent or praiseworthy—think about such things"….Philippians 4:8 (Holy Bible, King James Version)….. (Tallies with Kural 34).

vii. "If you had two weeks to live, how would you treat people? And will you speak to people? ….Because, no one knows neither the day nor the hour? Mathew 24:36… (Holy Bible. King James Version). …..(Tallies with Kural 335).

viii. "Not to us, O Lord, not to us; but your name gives us glory! For the sake of your steadfast-love and your faithfulness"……Psalm 115:1 (Holy Bible, King James Version)……. (Tallies with Kural 4).

ix. "Seek good, and not evil; so that, you may live, and the Lord will be with you"… Amos 5:14 (Holy Bible, King James Version)…. (Tallies with Kural 31).

x. "Thou shalt love thy neighbour as thyself ", Leviticus 19:18… (Tallies withKural 75).

xi. "False teachers come to you, dressed like sheep, but in their hearts they are dangerous wolves!"…… (Mathew 7: 15) (Tallies with Kural 273).

xii. “He scatters abroad, he give to the poor; his righteousness endures for ever”...2 Corinthians 9:9... (Tallies with Kural 226).

xiii. “Knowing this beforehand, beware lest you be carried away with the error of lawless men and lose your own stability!”...2 Peter 2:17..... (Tallies with Kural 460).

xiv. “you shall love your neighbour as yourself ”..... Galatians 4:14...... (Tallies with Kural 71).

xv. “He is like a tree planted by streams of water, that yields its fruits in its season, and itself does not wither. In all that does, he prospers.... The Psalm, Book I, 1:3... (Tallies with Kural 216).

xvi. Refrain from anger, and forsake wrath! Fret not yourself; it tends only to evil Psalms 36:8....(Tallies with Kural 307).

xvii. “The wicked draw the sword and bend their bows to bring down the poor and needy; to slay those who walk uprightly; their sword shall enter their own heart, and their bows will be broken”...Psalms 37: 14 & 15......(Tallies with Kurals 204, 205 & 1079).

xviii. “The mouth of the righteous utters wisdom, and his tongue speaks justice”... Psalms 37:30... (Tallies with Kural 119).

xix. “It is not an enemy who taunts me —then I could bear it; it is not an adversary who deals insolently with me —then I could hide from him; But it is you, my equal, my companion, my familiar friend”... Psalms 55:12 &13..... (Resembles Kural 884; but the hero gives a counselling and clears the difference of opinion between the two persons, and converts him to jointly fight against the enemy).

xx. “His speech was smoother than butter, yet war was in his heart; his words were softer than oil, yet they were drawn-swords!”... Psalms 55:21...... (Tallies with Kural 811).

xxi. “A prudent man conceals his knowledge; but fools proclaim their folly”...Proverbs 12:23......(Tallies with Kural 979).

xxii. “Without counsel, plans go wrong; but with many advisers they succeed! “...Proverbs 15: 22... (Tallies with Kural 462).

xxiii. "A man of understanding sets his face toward wisdom; but the eyes of a fool are on the end of the earth".....proverbs 17:24...(Tallies with Kural 978).

xxiv. Do not rob the poor, because he is poor, or crush the afflicted at the gate; for the LORD will plead their cause and despoil the life of those who despoil them! Proverbs 22:22... (Tallies with Kural 205).

xxv. She opens her mouth with wisdom, and the teaching of kindnesses on her tongue; She looks well to the ways of her household, and does not eat the bread of idleness. Her children rise up and call her blessed; her husband also, and he praises her; Many women have done excellently, but you surpass them all....! Proverbs 31: 26-29....

.... (Tallies with Kural 60 which states as: The wife's wholesome excellence in virtues is considered as the splendour and pride of the family; and will be further glorified by the treasure of good children!)

xxvi. "When you give a feast, invite the poor, the maimed, the lame, the blind, and you will be blessed, because they cannot repay you. You will be repaying" Luke 14:13-14. (Tallies with Kural 221).

xxvii. "Him slanders his neighbour secretly, I will destroy", Psalms 101:5... (Tallies with Kural 183).

V. Comparison of Thirukkural with the Quran:

i. Quran says: "Kind words and forgiveness are better than charity followed by injury"...Surah Al-Baqarah, 2:263...(Tallies with Kural 92 which reads as "Uttering pleasant words, with a cheerful face, to a person is considered to be better than giving a gift of material value. to a person with wholehearted willingness").

ii. Kural 478 reads as: "There is no harm to any person, even if the income is limited, provided that the expenditures are not excessive/ expanded. (Tallies with: Quran...Al-Isra, 17:26: which reads as "Give relatives their due, and the needy, and travellers: do not squander your wealth wastefully").

iii. Quran says: "Whoever does righteousness, man or woman, we will grant them happy life": (Surah An-Nahi 16:97)... This Tallies with

Kural 31 which states: "Following the virtuous path (ARam) in all actions will bring glory and wealth. There could be no other strength which could prove to be better than the force of righteousness/ virtues/ ethics. (The integrated concept of the three qualities is called"ARam").

iv. Quran says: "The good deed and the bad deed are not the same. Return evil with good!" (Quran 41; 34).This Tallies with Kural 314, which reads as: "The best way to punish a person who has done harm to you, will be to do something beneficial to that person, thus making that person to feel ashamed of his/her act. Also, later on, youforget all about it, to feel relieved (and have peace of mind).

v. Quran says: "And do not let your dislike of people lead you to be unjust!' Surah Al-Ma idah 5:8).

This tallies with Kural 852 which reads as: "If a stranger (who is neither a friend nor a foe), does harm to a person due to some inexplicable reason or conflicting interest, to prevent others from coming closer to you, it will be appreciated if the affected person does not develop hatred (discordance) and retaliate in doing harm to that offender".Also. It is closer to kural 111 which reads as: "Practicing impartiality (neutrality) is the only one virtuous policy in situations warranting the interactions with people who remain divided among themselves on issue-based problems!". It implies one's response in a secular society!

vi. Quran says: "Do not lose hope; nor be sad!' (Quran 3:139). This Tallies with Kural 621 which reads as "When trouble comes to any person, it is better to give a gentle smile, and bear it with patience! There is no other way to make it move away".

vii. Quran says: "Oh, you who have believed, indeed, intoxicants... are but defilement from the work of Satan, so avoid it that you may be successful." (Surah 5, Ayat 90) – Tallies with Kural 921 which states: "Those persons who consume liquor will lose their reputation in the society, and their enemies will lose fear for them, for ever. (Enemies will give them trouble!)".

viii. Quran says: "Do not come near adultery; it is indeed an abomination and an evil- way." (Surah 17, Ayat 32) – Tallies with Kural 145 which reads as "If a man commits an immoral act with another man's wife, thinking that the the act is easy to be done, the sense of guilt will haunt his conscience, and the blame will stay imperishable with him, throughout his life-time, and beyond"!.

ix. Quran says: "And the servants of the Most Merciful are those who walk upon the earth in humility; and when the ignorant address them (harshly), they reply with (words of) peace." - Surah 25, Verse 63.... (Tallies with Kural 978). (under the topic: Humility), which reads as "Great persons will not exhibit their pride while interacting with others, taking care to practice humility, on those occasions. On the contrary, mean-minded-persons, will decorate themselves, in self-flattery, all the time. (They will not extend courtesy to others!).

    It also, tallies with kural 125, which reads as: "Practicing humility is good for all persons. Among them, it is more important for rich persons, to be valued as wealth, within wealth (which corresponds to additional wealth!).

x. Quran says: "Enjoin the believing men to cast down their looks and be modest: that is purer for them." - Surah 24, Verse 30... (Tallies with Kural 148)... (under the topic: Modesty), which reads as "If a man maintains moral strength of not being attracted by another man's wife, the merit reflects not only the strength of virtue, but also the greatness of an exemplary character"!

xi. Quran says: "Good and evil cannot be equal. Respond (to evil) with (the deed) what is better; thereupon the one you are in a feud with (will become) as though he is a devoted friend. - Surah 41, Verse 34....... (Tallies with Kural 314)... Under the topic: kindness

xii. Quran says: "Let not a people ridicule (another) people; perhaps they may be better than them; nor let women ridicule (other) women; perhaps they may be better than them. And do not insult one another, and do not call each other-by (offensive) nicknames." - Surah 49, Verse 11........(Tallies with Kural 972)... (under the topic: Equality), which reads as: "All human beings are equal to one another, on birth! The importance/dignity assigned to each of them varies, depending on the quality-characteristics of their actions/ activities!".

It also tallies with kural 100 which reads as "Uttering unpleasant words, is not warranted, when pleasant words are available. If you do it, it is like being attracted by unripe-fruit, when ripe-fruits are readily available. It is not a wise-thing to do. It will bring down your image!".

It also tallies with kural 995 which reads as "Even while interacting with each other in a humorous way, the practice of extending insult to any person is harmful! Even among enemies, this courteous tradition is being entertained, by virtuous persons who are capable of understanding the probable feelings of the insulted-persons"!

xiii. Quran says: "Righteousness is (in) one who gives wealth, in spite of love for it, to relatives, orphans, the needy, the traveler, those who ask (for help), and for freeing slaves." - Surah 2, Verse 177 ...(Tallies with Kural 221).... (under the topic: Charity, which reads as "Giving material-help to poor persons, typically qualifies for being called as charity! Giving to all others will correspond to reciprocal acts enacted in anticipation of (expected) returns").

It also tallies with kural 227 which reads as "Hunger which is also known as a fiery (fire-like) disease will not touch a person who has become habituated to share his/her food with others".

xiv. Quran says: "Those will be given their reward twice for what they patiently endured, and (because) they avert evil through good." - Surah 28, Verse 54... (Tallies with Kural 154)...under the topic: Patience). It reads as "If a person decides that the wholesomeness of greatness should not depart from the self, it becomes necessary for that person, to practice patience, with pride and conviction, in his/her life!".

It also tallies with kural 314 which reads as "The best way to punish a person who has done harm to you will be to do something beneficial to that person, thus making that person to feel ashamed of his/her act! Also, later on, you must forget all about it, to feel relieved (to have peace of mind!).

xv. Quran says: "Humanity is but a single brotherhood; so make peace and reconciliation with your brethren." - Surah 49, Verse 10...........

(Tallies with Kural 140)……under the topic: Brotherhood, which reads as “Those who do not learn to live in peace with other people of the world, in agreement with the prescribed norms of the society around them are considered as ignorant persons, lacking worldly wisdom, even if they learned many things”!

It also tallies with kural 74 which reads as “Kindness (love) towards another person yields a desire towards a ‘link’ (bondage), which, in turn, emerges as a friendship, called a rare asset, for any person to acquire!”.

xvi. Quran says:” I worship not that which you worship; nor will you worship that which I worship; to you, be your religion; and to me, my religion!” (Surah Al-Kafirun, 109:1-6).This Tallies with Kural 426 which reads as “Wisdom requires that a person must follow the path in life, synchronizing with whatever path along which the peopleof the world align themselves. This understanding will correspond toan element of wisdom”!

VI.a. Comparison of Thirukkural with Bhagavad Gita:

(Note: The time by which Thirukkral was written and the time by which Baghvat Gita was written were chronologically different. Those doing research on this area have to give consideration for this factor).

i. Hell has got three gates: Lust, anger, and Greed. (Tallies with Kural 35). (https://www.quora.com>How does Lord Krishna explain.).

ii. Man is made by his belief.As he believes, so he is! (Tallies with Kural 5).

iii. When meditation is mastered, the mind is unwavering like the flame of a lamp in a windless place. (Tallies with Kural 352).

iv. There is neither this world, nor world beyond, nor happiness for the one who doubts… (Tallies with Kural 10).

v. We are kept from our Goal, not by Obstacles, but by Clear Path to a Lesser Goal. (Tallies with Kural 511).

vi. A man's own self is his friend. A man's own self is his foe! (Tallies with Kural 204).

(Ref: https://www.indiatimes.com/culture/who-we-are/11-simple-lessons- from-the-bhagavadgita-that-all-you-need-to-know-about-life-244390.html).

VI.b. The term "aRam" used in Thirukkural is different from "Dharma" usedin Manu Smriti, or Bhagvad Gita. The virtuous human qualities enshrined in Thirukkural are applicable to all human beings, whereas the human duties in Manu Smriti or Bhagvad Gita, to be practiced, are dictated, depending upon a particular 'varna' (category of birth of persons). A Brahmin has to perform one set of duties which are different from the duties to be performed by a member of the Kshatriya (land-ruling) class, which are different from the duties dictated for either a Vaisya or Sudra! As a result, the duties (dharma) to be performed by a person belonging to a Shudra-family is totally different from that of all the other three varnas!

(Lord Krishna says that these duties based on 'Varnashra-Dharmam' cannot be exchanged-or- interchanged; and that He will not permit it, even if asked for!). (Ref:https:www.quora.com/Is_Bagavat_Geetha_better_than_ Thirukkural).

In Kural 972, the poet has formulated a new theory: "All are created equal by birth". This can be claimed as an amendment to Rig-Vedic provision of the four-varna system of society. There is provision for such a new ideology, in Rig- Veda, itself, vide sloka I-89-1, which reads as "Let noble thoughts come to us from every side!", as cited by Sri C.Rajagoplachari, in his book "KURAL: The Great Book of Tiru-Valluvar!. If at all, Sri Rajagoplachari's liberal interpretation could have been given consideration by the British Colonial Government, the contents of Manusmriti could have been amended in the Hindu-Law enacted by the British Government in the year 1772 itself! (This is a hypothetical imagination).

(Ref:https://en.wikipedia.org/wiki/Hindu_Law).

During the period from 1772 to 1828, Sanskrit-'pandits' (interpreters) were employed in legal-courts to assist the British judges in deciding the degree of punishment to be given to the accused-person, depending on the 'varna' to which he/she belonged, as spelled out in Manusmriti!

VI.c. Similarities in the philosophies of Thirukkural and Bhagvad Gita:

(Comparison by Rev.G.U.Pope and V.R.R. Dikshita, compiled by London Swaminathan: 'Chanakya and Valluvar', Post No. 4530): (presented below, for comparing similarities):

i. Kural 126 states on self-conrol: "If a person exercises control over the five senses, like the tortoise controlling its limbs, within its shell, it will bring merit/glory during all his/her seven births".The Bhagvad Gita (2-58) states: "As a tortoise will restrain all limbs into itself, he who would restrain his sense will attain wisdom".

ii. Kural 299 states on Truthfulness: 'All lamps cannot be considered as useful lamps which could show the way in one's life! For noble persons, avoidance of falsehood (implementation/practice of truthfulness) is the real lamp which can show the way in life!"

   Bhagvad Gita (6-19) states: "The Yogi (saint) controlled, self-engaged, in meditation, is likened to a lamp that is still in a windless place!"

iii. Kural 339 states (on impermanence): "The occurrence of death is like going to sleep! The birth of a person is like waking up from sleep! (both events) are unpredictable!"

   The Bhagvad Gita (in 6-63) states: "There is certain death to one who isborn, and there is certain birth to one dead!"

VI.d. Similarites between Thirukkural and Manu Smriti:

i. Kural 226 (on Charity) states: "The act of feeding the poor people with timely food,to save-them-from 'killing-hunger' is considered as the store-house (repository/warehouse), for the safe-keeping of the material-wealth of the fortunate (wealthy) persons!!"

   Manu (3-106) rules to this effect: "One must not eat by self, without feeding the guest first! Feeding of guest leads to wealth, health, fame and heaven".

ii. Kural 256 states on 'refusal to eat meat(flesh)': "If the people of the world decide not to kill the living-creatures, for the purpose of eating the flesh, there will not be anybody to kill the life of those creatures and offer it for sale!".

Manu (5-51) states: "He who approves of the killing of an animal, he who preserves the slaughtered-body, he who buys and sells it, he who cooks itand who serves it, and who makes a meal of it are to be termed 'Killers'!"

iii. Kural 257 states (on vegetarianism): "Determination not to eat meat (flesh) is recommended, as it becomes essential to realize that, after all, the flesh is the wounded-portion of another living creature!"

Manu (5-49, 52) states: "..having learned the origin of flesh (meat) and the killing of creatures, one will refrain from any kind of meat!".

iv. Kural 259 (on vegetarianism) states: "The practice of 'not-killing' a living creature, and 'not-eating' its flesh is far more beneficial than performing a thousand ritualistic sacrifices by pouring voluminous quantities of ghee (derivative of butter) to the burning fire!".

Manu (in 5-53) states: "He who would perform a hundred 'Aswamedha'- sacrifices, year after year, and he who would refrain from flesh-eating are equal, in so far as the attainments of fruits are concerned!".

(Note: However, there is a subtle difference between the two statements: Manu equates the two persons, as equals. Thirukkural gives a higher merit to the person who avoids eating flesh!".

v. Kural (on Penance) states: "All other forms of life (souls) in this world will worship a person who has liberated himself from the sensation of 'me' and 'my-life', from his mind, relinquishing all that belongs to the self, thus qualifying himself, as an ideal ascetic/ saint!".

Manu (in 7-44) states: "one should endeavour any day and night to conquer the senses; and one who conquers his senses is able to have all people under his control!".

(Note: There is a subtle difference: Thiruvalluvar's saint becomes a person worshiped by all souls in the world, with reverence! Manu's saint becomes successful in enforcing submissiveness!).

vi. Kural 330 states: "It is generally believed by people that those persons who indulge in the activity of killing (separating the life from a living-creatures) would be destined to suffer from a life of chronic sufferings, in the form of diseases and tortures!"

Manu (in 5-45) states: "He who causes the killing of 'prohibited' animals, for his own happiness, is considered to be dead, though living, for he never attains happiness!"

(Note: There is a subtle difference. Kural 330 refers to killers who kill any form of life!Manu refers to those who kill prohibited-animals!).

VI.e. Similarities between Chanakya and Thiruvalluvar:

(Ref:https://tamilandvedas.com/2017/12/22/chanakya-and-valluvar-post-no-4530/).

a. Kural 381 states: "A king who possesses the six things, namely, powerful army, loyal subjects, decent wealth, capable ministers, reliable friends (allies)-and a protected fort is considered as a lion among the kings".

Chanakya says in Arththa-sastra (Book 6-1. of Kamandaka 1-18): "The king, minister,fort treasury, army friends constitute the elements of a state.....He who possesses these and who follows the righteouspolicy is able to conquer the whole earth and is never defeated".

(Note: Here too, Kural makes a distinctive difference, in making a mention about 'loyal subjects', specifically, to be a major element! The necessity for the king to take care of the safety, satisfaction (welfare), and proper administration,etc., are highlighted in Kurals 384, 386., 387, 388, 389, 390, 552, 554, 555, 558 and 560.

b. Kural 385 states: "A king must be capable of devising the methods of generating wealth, in the normal (righteous) way, and safeguarding the wealth so earned, and distributing the wealth equitably to the benefit of the citizens (subjects/people).Chanakya says in Arththa-sastra (Kamandaka 1-20): "The four-fold functions of the king are to acquire wealth by equitable means, to preserve it, to augment it, and expend it on the 'deserving'!"

c. Kural 390 states: "A king is considered to be a guiding-light (beacon) of all other kings, if he does carry out the four duties in ruling the land, namely,

d. philanthropy/charity/beneficence, ii)gracious attitude while interacting with people, iii) righteous rule (depicted by the symbolic Scepter), and iv) bestowing care for people's welfare and protection!"

   Chanakya (in Kamandaki 3-2) states: "Pleasant speech, grace-gifts, protection of the poor and the distressed, and association with men of character are recognized by the people of the world as the right thing!"

e. Kural 391 states: "Let every person learn;learning it thoroughly, without errors; and after learning, whatever has been learned, must be put into practice, in accordance with what has been learned!"

   (Note: If educated persons do not follow the norms which they have learned, orderliness in society will not prevail").

   Chanakya (in Book 1-5 of Arththasastra) says: "Sciences should be studied under qualified teachers and their precepts duly followed... Discipline is the fruit of learning!"

f. Kural 411 states: "Knowledge of any person gained by listening through the ears is considered as the most precious wealth (top in the list) among all other forms of wealth".Chanakya (in Arththasastra, Book 1 Chapter 5) says: "Hearing opens the door to knowledge, knowledge to right action, and to knowledge of one's self. This is what constitutes 'Vidyaa"!

g. Kural 427 (on Knowledge) says: "Wise persons will be able to know before hand what exactly is going to happen in future! Unwise persons will lack that knowledge".

Chanakya (in Arthasastra Book 9, Chapter 1) says: "He who possesses the eye of knowledge and science, is able to discern the true thing with a little effort!".

h. Kural 441 (on Great men) says: "Practical wisdom (prudence) suggests that a smart person must select and earn the relationships of wise persons, in consideration of their virtues and great wisdom, and earn their patronage!".

Chanakya (in Arththasastra Book 1-8) says: "The prescription of Bharadwaja is that companions whose honesty and skill have been put to satisfactory tests must be appointed as ministers!"

(Note: Kural 441 recommends the patronage of wise-elders for promoting the welfare of the self of any person. In contrast, Chanakya talks about recruiting a suitable person for the minister's role!' However, Chanakya's advice is reflected by Kural 635; 445).

i. Kural 447 (describing Great men) says: "Who can do a harm to a king who rules the land, with assistants (who are) empowered with freedom of pin-pointing the errors (committed by the king), whenever committed or likely to commit!"

Chanakya (In Arththasastra, Book 1-8) says: "A king should select such ministers whose loyalty has been tried and who would protect him from risks involving danger to life!"

(Note: Kural introduces a concept of the king's alertness in giving freedom to advisers to unhesitatingly warn the king in advance (in a confidential manner) about policy-issues before and during implementation, so that nobody is enabled to find fault with the king's style of administration! This corresponds to a relaxation in the 'cautious-methods of approach', prescribed to be followed by personnel serving in close proximity of the king, described inChapter 70, under the title, 'Co-ordination with the King' in Kurals 691-700!).

j. Kurals 462 and 470 (on Consideration/ the right of fore-thought) says: "462:There cannot be anything too hard to acquire, if a person desires to undertake an activity, with known person(s), and with selective thoughts!". "470: Perform any act which would not be despised (hated, not-relished) by others, because, the world will not approve of anything that is not acceptable!"

Chanakya (in Arththasatra, Book 1-5) says: "All undertakings are to be preceded by mantra or counsel.....Let the king review the works with the- ministers present....That which gives fruition and is advocated by the best men, must be done!".

VI.f. Difference between Tirukkural and Manusmriti:

a. Some researchers in the web-site

https:// oneamongyou.wordpress.com have listed the following Kural-couplets to disagree with the contents of Manusmriti: Kurals 229; 259; 297; 328; 409; 423; 541; 978 and 1031.

They have identified that the following Manusmriti slokas do not agree with the ideology preached by Thirukkural, namely, Manusmritislokas: 4-80; 10-106; 8-112; 5-32; 1-103; 1-109; 1-99; 2-31; 8-270; 8-373-379; 10-84. (Note: 10-84 relates to Agriculture).

b. The following are the Manu Smriti slogans differing from the concepts of Thirukkural:(Ref: The Laws pf Manu, Translated by Wendy Doniger and Brian K.Smith, Penguin Classics, 2000. ISBN 9780140445404). Classics, 2000... 5404. Also, refer to: Srimani Ganth: Manu Smriti's Text in Sanskrit with English Translation: https://www.academia.edu/31478379...

1. MS.ch.1.100: "All of this belongs to the priest, whatever there is in the universe; The priest deserves all of this because of his excellence and his high birth".

2. MS.ch.8.270: "If a man of one birth has not undergone the initiation that is the second birth; he may be a servant, a man with a high-caste father and low caste mother, or a man of any class who has failed to ...for he was born from the rear end!; 271: If he mentions their name or caste maliciously, a red hot iron nail ten fingers long should be thrust into his mouth; 272: If he is so proud to instruct priests about their duty, the king should have hot oil poured into his mouth and ears; 273: If in his

pride he tells lies about (their) knowledge of the revealed canon, their district, their caste, or the ritual perfection of their bodies, he should be made to pay a fine of two hundred pennies."

3. MS.ch.2:31: "The name of a priest should have a word for auspiciousness, of a ruler strength, of a commoner property, and the name of a servant should breed disgust".
4. MS.ch.1:103: "A learned priest –but no one else—should study it (the Veda) carefully and explain it to his pupils properly".
5. MS.ch.4:80:" He (the twice-born Vedic graduate) should not share his opinions with a servant, nor the left-overs from his (the priest's) meals, or oblations, nor should he instruct him (the servant) about his (the priest's) duty, or assign a vow to him (the servant)."
6. MS.ch.6:43: "The hermit should have no fire and no home, but should go to a village to get food, silent, indifferent, unwavering and deep in concentration.
7. MS.ch.10:84: "Some people think that "Farming is a virtuous trade"; but as a livelihood, it is despised by good people, for the wooden-plough with the iron-mouth injures the earth and creatures that live in the earth".
8. MS.ch.8:112: "But there is no crime in a false-oath about women whom one(he) desires, marriages, fodder for cows, fuel, and helping a priest".
9. MS.ch.10:105: "Ajigarta, famished, stepped forward to kill his own son, but was not smeared with evil, for he was acting to remedy his hunger".
10. MS.ch:9:248:" But if a man born of a lower class intentionally bothers a priest, the king should punish him physically with various forms of corporal and capital punishment that make men shudder".
11. MS.ch.8:379: "Shaving the head is ordained as the punishment consisting in the loss the life's breath, for a priest; but for the

other classes, the punishment should be the actual-loss of life's breath".

12. MS.ch.8:380: "The king should never kill a priest, even one who persists in every sort of evil; he should banish such a man from the kingdom, unhurt and with all his wealth".
13. MS.Ch:8:381: "There is no greater act of irreligion on earth than priest-killing! Therefore, the king should not even conceive in his mind of killing that man!

c. In this analysis, the farming-profession is rated low in esteem in the Manusmriti, in Chapter 10, verse 84 which states as "Some declare that agriculture is something excellent; but, that means of existence is blamed by the virtuous (persons); for the reasonthat wooden implement with iron point injures the earth andthe living organisms in the earth! This is in direct conflict withKural 1031 which states as: "Although the people of the worldrevolve around many other works, all those persons involvedin various other works are dependent on the farming work, for satisfying their requirement of food. Farming is the best work, although several hardships are involved in doing it! (Note: Itis upto the reader to understand the relative importance.It isto be noted that the saints who formulated Manu Smriti were themselves dependent upon farmers for their food-requirements(vide kurals 18 and 19). (Note:Manu worries about the injury about the harm being done by wooden implement (used in agricultural practice) with iron point which 'injures the earth and the living organisms' in the earth! However, a similar sympathy is not being shown towards women and fellow-men, in the Manu Smrithi slogans. It is not understandable!).

On the topic of Justice, Kural 541 states:"Norms to be followed by any king relating to punishment for crime are listed as follows: (i) investigating any occurrence of crime, (ii) examining the details without showing partiality (either liking or hatred), whoever it may be, and (iii) selecting a solution to render justice!This is the proper way to give punishment to offenders.

d. In this relevance, Manu says in Chapter 8, Verse 379, that: "Tonsure of the head is ordained for a brahmana*, instead of capital punishment; but men of other castes shall suffer capital punishment, for murder- charges".

(*Ref:page.12. in "Makers of Indian Literature: THIRUVALLUVAR", authored by Justice S.Maharajan, published by Sakitya Akademi, 1979).

(Note: Researchers have to remain contented that what is said in Thirukkural remains valid during the 21st Century, and will remain valid for ever, irrespective of time and space, whereas illogical practices recommended by other literature will not be held relevant!).

VI. g. As Indians, we have to feel proud that we have shifted to the Constitution of India, and every one citizen becomes equal to another person, in enjoying individual freedom, and in deserving equality before law.

Past is past! We have to protect this Constitution of India, treating it as a divine instrument! To maintain our dignity and self respect as Indians, with a sense of unity in diversity!and to achieve a sense of unity and brotherhood.

CONCLUSION: Thirukkural spells out a code of conduct for human behaviour, aiming at a harmonious life-style, in the path of human-life, for practicing co-existence and co-ordination, in peace, without initiating any war, or suffering from any war!

There are similarities in the 'sara' (essence) of all religious philosophies listed above, but for subtle differences. Therefore, it is necessary to develop and promote a conviction of 'Mutual Respect' for the faiths of one another, in order to build up a sense of universal brotherhood, as Lord Vivekananda aspired for! And as, Dr.A.P.J. Abdul Kalam was dreaming for!! This could have been the dream of the great poet Thiruvalluvar, too!

In the year 2000, Swami Dayananda Saraswati insisted that 'mutual respect" for the religious faiths of one another must be practiced, instead of referring to it as "religious tolerance!", in his capacity as the head of the Hindu-Delegation to the United Nation's Millennium Religion Summit 2000! (Ref.7, cited below).Dr. Rajiv Malhotra played a pivotal role in the summit! Dr.Kofi Annan, UN-Secretary-General, appealed to the leaders to help the UN bring world peace!

There should be some efforts from various countries of the world toward this direction. One way of achieving it will be to organize World Religious Conferences annually, in various regions of the Globe, similar to conducting the World Olympic Meets, on a rotation basis. Another method will be to read out citations from the scriptures of all religions in public functions participated by the Heads of States,in their respective countries, in accordance with the number of religions prevailing in that State! Third suggestion will be to circulate the highlights of norms spelled out in each religion, commensurate with the 'Constitution of the State- concerned, in order to promote general understanding of their brothren- cum-fellow-citizens!(References:1-12).

It is suggested also that the United Nations Organization (U.N.O) may co-ordinate in the enforcement of human equality, with its own mechanism, of Human Rights Organization, in the member-countries, based on international cooperation, mediation, dialogue, auditing, etc. It will be a noble service to global community, to protect the self-respect of the affected people who do not have the human ability to protest or speak for themselves, as they are just 'surviving' along with other-privileged brothren who are not exposed to any ill-treatment or hardships arising out of 'human- inequality'!.

In India, the Indian Constitution supports and encourages religious harmony (13). Every citizen has a right to choose and practice the religion of his/her choice (14). The Rig Veda supports plurality of religious thoughts (15), vide Rig Veda 1.64.46, "Ekam-sad-vipra-bahudha- vadanti", meaning that 'wise people explain the same truth in different manners'!

According to His Holiness Dalai Lama, 'India is a model for religious harmony......In the last 2000-3000 years (of history), different religious traditions, such as Jainism, Islam, Sikhism, and others, have flourished!' (16). It reflects the urge that the youth around the world must and shall work towards developing a harmonious universal-brotherhood, for safeguarding the humanity, without war, any more, any further, during the future!

His Excellency the 29th Sultan of Brunei, Hassanal Bolkiah has released an appeal to the world: "Future Peace, prosperity, and confidence depend on the success of all nations! Hence, we are all partners, no matter what our backgrounds, cultures, faiths and histories(17)". This great ideology is in resonance with Kural 425, which reads as: "Wisdom of a person requires ability to make friendship at global level, and manoeuvre it at comfortable status, in such a way that the petals of the flower do not close down or get withered away."

REFERENCES:

1. Difference between Buddhism and Hinduism, UPSC Prelims Syllabus (UPSC2021) (pdf).
2. Differences between Hinduism and Jainism, UPSC Notes. (pdf).
3. induism-Hinduism-Islam/Britannica (https://www.britannica.com>topic(Hinduism and Christianity: covered).
4. Wikipedia: Hinduism; Wikipedia: Islam.
5. Hinduism and Sikhism (From Wikipedia, the Free Encyclopedia)
6. Religious Harmony in India: en.m.wikipedia.org/wiki/Religous_harmony_in_India
7. Rajiv Malhotra, Infinity foundation. 2021, "Tolerance Isn't Good Enough: The Need For Mutual Respect In Interfaith Relations
8. Dayananda Saraswati (Arsha Vidya), Wikpedia.
9. Ram Mohan Roy, Wikipedia.
10. Parliament of the World's Religions, en.m.wikipedia.org.
11. Towards a Global Ethic: An Initial Declaration, en.m.wikipedia.org.
12. The Church in the wider world-Ecumenism-Practices in Christianity-GCSE Religious Studies Revision-OCR BBC Bitesize (https://www.bbc.co.uk/ bitesize/guides/zdcbcj6/revision/11;

13. Article 51(A)e: The Constitution of India', Retrieved 27 June 2017. "51A. Fundamental duties.It shall be the duty of every citizen of India to abide by the Constitution and respect its ideals and institutions,the National Flag, and National Anthem; ….. (e) to promote harmonyand the spirit of common brotherhood amongst all the people of India transcending religious, linguistic and regional, or sectional diversities; to renounce practices derogatory to the dignity of women; (f) to value and preserve the rich heritage of our composite culture".

14. "Indian Culture", MapsofIndia.com. Retrieved 24 June 2013.

15. "Religious Harmony in India", Wikipedia.

16. "India is a Model for Religious Harmony", Dalai Lama, NDTV.com. 25 November 2012. Retrieved 24 June 2013.

17. https://en.m.wikipedia.org>wiki>Hassanal Bolkiah.

APPENDIX-8

HIGHLIGHTS OF THIRUKKURAL (TOPICWISE -QUICK REFERENCE)

(Useful hints for those who prepare forparticipationin Oratorical Competitions)

1. Praising the almighty:Kurals 1; 2; 3
2. Blessings of Rain: Kurals 11-20
3. Merit of Ascetics: Kurals 21; 22; 26; 29; 30
4. Aram: Righteousness/Virtue/Ethics:Kurals 32; 33; 34; 35; 36; 39
5. Good Householder: Kurals 41; 45; 46; 47; 49; 50.
6. Life-Partner (Ideal Wife): 51; 54; 57; 58; 60
7. Good Children: Kurals 61; 64; 65; 66; 67; 68; 69; 70
8. Love/Kindness:Kurals 71; 72; 73; 74; 75; 76; 77; 78; 80
9. Generous Hosts: Kurals 81; 82; 85; 88; 89; 90 10.
10. Soft Words: Kurals 91; 92; 93; 94; 95; 99; 100
11. Sense of Gratitude: Kurals 101; 102; 108; 109
12. Rectitude (Neutrality): Kurals 112; 113; 114; 116; 117; 120 13.
13. Self-Control: Kurals 121; 122; 125; 126; 127; 129; 130
14. Character: Kurals 131; 132; 133; 134; 137; 138; 140
15. Immoral Desire: Kural 141
16. Forbearance(Patience as a Virtue):
17. Kurals 151; 152; 155; 156; 158; 159
18. Do Not Envy: Kurals 161; 162; 163; 165; 167; 168; 170

19. Do not covet: Kurals 171; 173; 174; 175; 176; 177; 179; 180
20. Do not speak ill of others: Kurals 184; 190
21. 11. Avoid Worthless Talk: Kurals 191; 192
22. Conscience (Fear for Evil Acts): Kurals 201; 202; 203; 204; 207; 208; 209
23. Social-Cooperation(Desire-to-help-others): Kurals 211-220.
24. Helping the Poor (Charity): Kurals 221-230
25. Public Esteem (Fame): Kurals 235; 237
26. Compassion (Gracious Attitude): Kurals 242; 244; 247; 248; 249; 250 27.
27. Eat Not Meat:Kurals 251; 253; 254; 256; 257; 259; 260
28. Penance: Kurals 261; 262; 263; 267; 268
29. Impure Life (Bad Conduct): Kurals 271-280
30. Avoidance of Stealing: Kurals 282; 285
31. Truthfulness:Kurals 291-300
32. Avoidance of Anger: Kurals 301-310
33. Do not cause harm to others: Kurals 314; 315; 318; 319
34. Avoidance of Killing:Kurals 322; 324
35. Non-Permanence:Kurals 332; 324; 325; 326; 327; 328; 330
36. Renunciation of Desires: Kurals 341; 344; 345; 347; 348; 349; 350
37. Realisation oif True Knowledge: Kurals 351; 353; 354; 355; 356; 360
38. Freedom from Greed: Kurals364; 366
39. Destiny (Fate): Kurals 371; 374; 377; 380
40. Greatness of Leadership of Kings: Kurals 383; 385; 388; 389 41.
41. Learning: Kurals 391; 392; 394; 395; 396; 397; 399; 4 00
42. Illiteracy: Kurals 401; 409
43. Listening Pleasure: Kuarl 411; 412; 414; 416
44. Wisdom: Kurals 423; 425; 426; 428; 430

45. Condemning Faulty Acts: Kurals 434; 435; 436; 437
46. Link with Elders: Kurals 441; 442; 448; 450
47. Avoidance of Bad Company: Kural 451; 457; 460
48. Actions after Deep Thinking: Kural 481; 482; 466; 467; 468
49. Knowing One's Own Strength: Kurals 471; 474; 476; 476; 477; 479
50. 40. Choosing Time For Action: Kurals 482; 484; 489; 490
51. Choice of Place for action: Kurals 491; 497
52. Clarity based on Analysis: Kural 504; 505; 508
53. Initiation of Action After Clarity: Kurals 511; 513; 517; 520
54. Link with Relatives:Kurals 524; 526; 527
55. Caution against forgetfulness: 531; 533; 539
56. Righteous Governance: 541; 544
57. Rule of Tyranny: Kurals 553; 556
58. Avoidance of Hateful Acts: Kurals 561; 567
59. Kind outlook: Kurals 571; 573; 578
60. Spying information: Kurals 581; 588
61. Courage: Kurals 591; 594; 595
62. Avoidance of Laziness: Kurals 602; 605; 609
63. Firmness in Strenuous Acts: Kurals 611; 616; 618; 619; 620
64. Endurance during hardships: Kurals 621; 625; 628
65. Ideal Minister: Kurals 631; 632; 636
66. Power of Speech: Kurals 641; 642; 643; 648; 649; 650
67. Purity of Actions: Kurals 651; 654; 656
68. Perfection in Action: Kurals 664; 666; 667; 669
69. Methodology for action: Kurals 672; 675; 676; 677; 679
70. Envoy Service; Kurals 683; 685

71. Coordination with the King: Kurals 691; 697; 700
72. Mind-Reading:Kurals 701; 705; 706
73. Judging the Audience: Kurals 711; 712; 717; 718
74. Freedom from Stage-Fear: Kurals 722; 724; 725; 728; 730 75.
75. Ideal Country: Kurals 731; 734; 737; 738; 739; 740
76. Defense Fortification: Kural 742; 750
77. Ways of Earning Wealth: Kurals 751; 754; 759
78. Excellence of an Army: Kurals 769; 770
79. Pride of an Army: Kurals 773; 780
80. Friendship: Kurals 781; 784; 786; 788; 789
81. Assessment of Friendship: Kurals 792; 795
82. Intimacy in Friendship: Kurals 801; 803; 810
83. Harmful Friendship: Kurals 811; 812; 820
84. Forbidden Friendship: Kurals 821; 828; 830
85. Carelessness out of Foolishness: Kurals 83; 832; 834; 835
86. Lack of Knowledge: Kurals 841; 843
87. Hateful Attitude: Kurals 853; 856
88. Merits of an Army:Kurals 861; 870
89. Appraisal of Enemy's Strength: Kurals 874; 878
90. Internal Enmity: Kurals 881; 882; 888; 890
91. Avoidance of harming Elders: Kurals 891; 895
92. Henpecked Husband: Kural 901; 907
93. Wanton women: Kural 920
94. Avoidance of Consuming Liquor: Kurals 922; 923
95. Gambling: Kurals 931; 932
96. Medicine and Eating Habits: Kurals 941-950

97. Family Background: Kurals 954; 960
98. Self-Respect (Honour): Kurals 962; 963; 964; 969
99. Greatness of Persons: Kurals 972; 973; 978
100. Righteous Persons:Kurals 983; 987; 988
101. Cultured Courteousness: Kurals 994; 996; 998
102. Worthless Wealth: Kurals 1005; 1008; 1009
103. Shyness against Evil Acts:Kurals 1014; 1015; 1018
104. Promoting Family Welfare: Kurals 1022; 1023; 1026
105. Farming (Agriculture): Kurals 1031; 1033; 1039; 1040
106. Poverty: Kurals 1041; 1047; 1049; 1050
107. Begging: Kurals 1053; 1054; 1060
108. Shyness for Begging: Kurals 1061; 1062; 1067; 1070
109. Unscrupulous persons (Meanness):Kurals 1071-108
110. Self-correction of life-style towards prosperity: kural 609.
111. Army strategy: kurals 471; 861; 487; 488; 489.
112. Protection of welfare of employees: kurals 519; 520.

A. PRIORITY OF APPRECIATION BY THIRUVALLUVAR:

a. Melancholic Personality: Kural 999.
b. Humour: Kurals 839; 842; 844; 907; 1071; 1073; 1077; 1183
c. Enjoyable examples: Kurals 757; 490; 226; 215
d. Regrettable examples: Kurals 890; 780; 1049; 374; 1077
e. Human rights: Kurals 37; 972; 1067
f. Self-respect: Kural 1061; 1065; 656; 969
g. Advice to monarchs: Kurals 544; 549; 382; 388; 389; 610
h. Advice to youth: Kurals 73; 95; 108; 121; 131; 151; 161; 177; 181; 191; 202, 212; 221;

231; 282; 294; 305; 314; 355; 391;

411; 425; 434; 441; 458; 467;

472; 484; 497; 504; 517; 525; 537;

578; 596; 605; 611; 621; 641; 651;

666; 673; 691; 706; 717; 724;

754; 786; 791; 814; 824; 831; 853;

891; 931; 944; 951; 963; 975; 981;

994; 1018; 1021; 1040; 34.

i. Advice to agriculturists: Kurals 1039; 1040

j. Encouragement to Philanthropists: Kurals 211; 215; 216; 217; 226; 231; 242

k. Thiruvalluvar's testmiony: Kural 300 (vouching for Truthfulness).

l. Thiruvallvar's regret:Kural 1062 (lamenting for poverty of poor people).

m. Regret for the fate of certain folks: Kural 1007 (regretting for the ignorance of rich persons who do not believe in charity and the fame yielded from it; at the same time, feeling the pains of a pathetic (yet virtuous) woman who remains a sinister until she gets old. In the example, the poet records the sympathy towards such virtuous women whose precious life could have been made brighter, through the efforts of some elders to get the young woman married.

n. Regretting for the hardened attitudes of others:Kural 1080 (which reads as "What is the use of persons whose human quality is low? They will speedily sell themselves, in order to protect themselves, if any trouble comes to them!". Thiruvalluvar is disappointed in those unscrupulous persons, in his expectations from them, that they would practice virtues and righteousness, in order to promote peace in the society!

o. The Poet's disappointment in well-informed persons:Kural 278 which reads as "It is surprising to note that there are persons living in this world, possessing dirt in their minds, and yet pretending as honourable persons in society, doing tricks such as disappearing in the flowing river-water to claim a show of strength, and still practicing a hideous conduct in the background!"

p. The poet is unhappy with some people: Kural 823: which relates to persons who have got fixed-ideas in their minds who refuse to develop a refined attitude towards others, in spite of their having received significant levels of education!

q. In kural 828, the horrors of concealed-enmity is revealed by the poet, in exposing the weapon hidden within the folded arms, to caution the victim! (before it is too late!).

r. The pride of women in self-control is hightlighted: kurals 54; 57; 58; 60; 974; 1137).

APPENDIX-9

EQUALITY AMONG THE HUMANS:

William Henry Drew (19th Century Christian Missionary, who translated the first 630 couplets of Thirukkural into English, made the following observations on Thirukkural:

"Cural (The (Kural) has a strong claim upon our attention, as a literature of the country, and as a work of intrinsic excellence. The author, passing over what is peculiar to particular classes of society, and introducing such ideas only as are common to all, has avoided the uninteresting details of observances found in Menu and the other shastras; and thus, in general, maintains a dignified style"....

(Note: William Henry Drew, the 19th Century Theologian, compares the concept of equality by birth contained in Kural 972, to be in conflict with what have been mentioned in Manu Smriti and Rig Veda (Rig vedic Purusha Sukta. (RV.10.90.11-12; Ref; D.R.Jatava, 2011, 'The Hindu Sociology', p.92, Surabhi Publications; Yajnik, Acyuta and Sheth, Suchitra, 2005', 'Shaping of Modern Gujarat', Plurality, Hindutva and Beyond".Penguin Books).

According to Rig Veda, a Brahmin child is born from the mouth of Purusha; a Kshatriya child is born from both arms of Purusha; a Vaishya child is born from both the thighs of Purusha; a Shudra Child is born from the feet of Purusha.

There is a fifth category called 'Avarna'. A commentary on the Varna system, as spelt out in Manu Smriti is found in the book by Davidson Lorenzen, 2006, 'Who Invented Hinduism: Essays on Religion and History', pp.147-149 (Yoda Press, ISBN 978-81-902272-6-1).

In kural 972, the poet has formulated a new theory: "All are created equal by birth". This can be claimed as an amendment to Rig-Vedic provision of the four-varna system of society.

There is provision for such a new ideology, in Rig-Veda, vide sloka I-89-1, which reads as "Let noble thoughts come to us from every side!", as cited by Sri C.Rajagoplachari, in his book" KURAL: The Great Book of Tiru-Valluvar). In such a case, kural 972 must have been appended to Rig Veda, for ensuring 'equality of humans, by birth', and kurals 541 and 561, for ensuring 'equality in justice, irrespective of Varna'. Also kural 436 to ensure that a faultless (bias-less) person sits as the king to deliver judgement on crimes!

If at all, Sri Rajagoplachari's liberal interpretation could have been given consideration by the British Colonial Government, the contents of Manusmriti could have been amended in the Hindu-Law enacted by the British Government in the year 1772 itself! (This is a hypothetical imagination).

(Ref:https://en.wikipedia.org/wiki/Hindu_Law).

During the period from 1772 to 1864, sanskrit pandits were employed in courts to assist the British judges in deciding the degree of punishment to be given to the accused-persons, depending on the varna to which he/she belonged, as spelled out in Manusmriti!

However, in the year 1862, the Indian penal code passed by the Imperial Legislative Council came into force, in India, through the efforts of Thomas Babington Macaulay, the Chairman of the First Law Commission of India.

Not only because of the fact that the equality-theory of Thiruvalluvar is convincing and genuine, but also there is a provision in the Rig Veda to accommodate it, vide the verse quoted above! (This is a wild imagination, on a hypothetical basis!).

Once inequality among humans is believed in, and practiced by humans, it will have an adverse sociological impact, on human interactions.

'The Print' dated 27th March 2018 reported an article by Kenneth J. Kooper, on the topic "Indians have imported 'casteism' into the United States". In this relevance, Kural 972 becomes the solution, to resolve the misunderstanding, if practiced by all.

Isabel Wilkerson (2020) stated that the racism 'in the United States', the caste-system of India, and the Nazism (which prevailed in Hitler's Germany) are similar, originating from notions, such as, 'hierarchy, inclusion, exclusion and purity' (of genes?). (Ref: "Caste", by Isabel Wilkerson, 2020, published by Random House). Here too, the human equality theory of Thiruvalluvar becomes a tool for harmonizing human relations!

The equality theory, proposed 2000 years ago, as found in kural couple 972 reads as "All human beings are equal to one another by birth. The importance / dignity assigned to each of them varies, depending upon the difference in the quality-characteristics of their actions/activities of virtues".

This concept could serve as a solution to resolve the problem of inequality prevailing around the world, in human interactions.

To avoid any adverse sociological impact, Thiruvalluvar suggests a few steps to improve the human understanding as follows: i) In Kural 140, it is said: "Those who do not learn to live with other people of the world, in agreement with the prescribed norms of the society (around them), are considered as ignorant persons, lacking worldly wisdom, even if they have learned many things!". Secularism and co-existence, with tolerance and mutual respect for one another, in a cosmopolitan society, could be a solution;ii)Kural 425 states: "Wisdom of a person requires ability to make friendship at world-level and manoeuvre (maintain) it at a comfortable status, in such a way that the petals of the flower do not close down or get withered away!". The magic formula is 'kindness towards all, and malice towards none', as Abraham Lincoln proclaimed/prompted!; iii)Kural 71 reads: "Is it possible at all to have a bolt to stop the true love (kindness) being shown to others? The sympathetic tears of an affectionate person appearing over the eyes, on seeing the distress of another person in grief, will reveal the true love (kindness) which is in store"; and iv) Kural 426 reads: "Wisdom requires that a person must follow the path in life, synchronizing with whatever path along which the people of the world align themselves".

William Shakespeare describes human equality by comparing a common-man and a king: "The king is but a man; the violet smells to him as it doth to me! The elements show to him as it doth to me" (Ref: 'William Shakespeare', Henry V, p.211, Oxford University Press, U.S.A).

Isabel Wilkerson (2020) dreams about the probable emergence of a 'World Without Caste', with the following wishes: "Once awakened, i)we can be born to the dominant caste, but choose not to dominate!..., or, ii) we can be born to a subordinated caste, but resist the box others force upon us" (Ref: Caste:

The Lies That Divide Us", authored by Isabel Wilkerson, 2020, Allen Lane, an Imprint of Penguin Books, page 380).

The human-equality theory proposed by Thiruvalluvar 2000 years ago, vide Kural 972, helps to maintain a harmonious relationship among the people of the world, forgetting the differences based on religion, race, ethnicity, caste or creed.

However, the adjustment and understanding has to come from the privileged beneficiaries of the 'inequality-theory', so that Thirukkural 972 becomes operative, not only to remove caste-based inequalities, but also race-based inequalities, or ethnicity-based inequalities. Such a person,who comes forward to accept the equality theory of Thiruvalluvar, forgetting the sense of superiority assigned to him/her, by birth in a privileged class, will be equated with the brotherly calibre of Abraham Lincoln, the big brother of humanity!

This is the topic on which the United Nations Organization (U.N.O) have to bestow their attention, in order to achieve a meaningful and 'harmonious human-rights' intact, for being practiced everywhere around the world, with the cooperation of the member-countries of The UNO! The key is: "love and compassion towards universal brotherhood" as yearned by many philosophers around the world!

APPENDIX-10

NOTES ON HIGHLIGHTS

(RELEVANT TO WORLD - PEACE)

I. "Thirukkural does not refer to any nation, leader, society, language, religion, or caste in the entire book, which is why it has been called the Universal Veda!" (Sri Narendra Modi, 1950—xx, Prime Minister of India)… (Appendix-2, item 12) .

II. "My loving people, we have been persuaded by some that are careful of our safety, to take heed how we commit ourselves to armed multitudes for fear of treachery; but I assure you, I do not desire to live to distrust my faithful and loving people"…Queen Elizabeth I, (tallies with kural 388)… (Appendix-3A, item 4).

III. "The greatest gift is the ability to forget bad things and focus on the good"…. President Joseph R. Biden Jr., 1942—xx, 46th President of the United States of America, (tallies with kural 108)……………

IV. (Appendix-3 D, item 38).

V. "Anyone who claims to be a leader must speak like a leader! That means speaking with integrity and truth", Ms.Kamala D. Harris, 1964—xx, 49th and current Vice President of the United States of America, ……tallies with kural 648)……(Appendix-3 D, item 40).

VI. H.E.,the 29th Sultan of Brunei, Hassanal Bolkiah has released an appeal to the world: "Future Peace, prosperity, and confidence depend on the success of all nations! Hence, we are all partners, no matter what our backgrounds, cultures, faiths and histories". This great ideology is in resonance with Kural 425…(Appendix-7;p.532).

VII. Kurals 250 and 861 offer a solution to world-peace: THIS CONCEPT, IF PRACTICED, WILL PREVENT WAR, AND ENABLE WORLD- PEACE!). Leo Tolstoy highlighted on this point… (Appendix 1, item 13; Appendix 2, item 3). The poet puts the responsibility, on the shoulders of righteous persons in the world, in kural 989, to prevent a world-war leading to 'apocalypse' of the world which is likely to be initiated by a cranky-tyrant ruler of an anonymous country!.(Apocalypse=Greek word, meaning, 'remove the lid'. Is it from a pressure vessel? It tallies with 'releasing an atom-bomb' to cause the catastrophe!). Refer kurals 880; 989; 990; 996.

VIII. Equality of human beings, by birth, as a concept in Thirukkural, vide Kural 972, becomes a solution to solve and eradicate inequalities prevailing among the humans, in various parts of the world, such as racism, casteism and Nazism, wherever it exists… (Appendix-9)..

IX. Rajaji (Sri C.Rajagopalachari) was of the opinion that there is provision for adding supplement to the ideology of Rig-Veda,vide verse 1-89-1 which states: "Let noble thoughts come to us from every side". Perhaps, he might have wanted to give a liberal interpretation of the verses relating to the 4-varna ideology of Rig Veda! in consideration of the Human Equality Theory of Thiruvalluvar in Kural 972. Please see Appendix -9;p.542).

X. In the year 2000, Swami Dayananda Saraswati insisted that 'mutual respect" for the religious faiths of one another must be practiced,…, in

XI. his capacity as the head of the Hindu-Delegation to the United Nation's Millennium Religion Summit 2000! Dr. Rajiv Malhotra played a pivotal role in the summit! (Appendix-7;p.531).

XII. United Nations Organization (U.N.O) may co-ordinate in the enforcement of human equality, with its own mechanism, of Human Rights Organization, in the member- countries, based on international cooperation, mediation, ……….(Appendix-9;p.544).

APPENDIX-11

ABOUT THE BOOK: THIRUKKURAL RESEARCH 2021

(Author: Prof.M.P.Chockalingam of Annamalai University, India).

A. Individual Appendix describes the following topics:

Appendix-1:My Findings:New Interpretations on 21- kural couplets, pp.408-431;

Appendix-2:Tributes to Thirkkural updated (58 entries), pp.427--435);

Appendix-3A:Comparison of Thirukkural with Quotes from Western Literature (198 entries), pp.432-460;

Appendix-3B:Situational Quotes from Shakespearean Plays and its similarity with Thirukkural (61 entries), pp.461-467;

Appendix-3C: Comparison of Thirukkural concepts with Asian ideology (129 entries), pp.468-482;

Appendix-3D: Comparison of Thirukkural concepts with the quotes from World leaders (69 entries), pp.483-490;

Appendix-3E: Comparison of Management concepts found in Thirukkural with the quotes from Business Magnates of the Twentieth and Twenty First centuries (71 entries), pp.491-499;

Appendix-3F: Comparison of Thirukkural with African ideology (30 entries), pp. -500-502;

Appendix-3G: Comparison of Thirukkural with Native-American ideology (4- entries), p.503;

Appendix-3H: Comparison of Thirukkural with Persian ideologies (8 entries), p.504.

Appendix-4: Thirukkural as a Value-Education Programme, p.505;

Appendix-5A:Application of Thirukkural concepts for Professional Development/ Career Making, pp. 506-508;

Appendix-5B: Benefitwise Considerations in Thirukkural,pp. 509-512;

Appendix-6: Thirukkural's relevance to core-concepts in multidisciplinary areas of study, pp.513-515;

Appendix-7: Comparison of Thirukkural ideology with philosophies found in some Religious Literature (Jainism, Buddhism, Sikhism, Islam, Christianity and Hinduism), pp. 516-542;

Appendix-8: Highlights of Thirukkural (Topicwise Quick Reference),

for developing self-skill in oratory, pp.543- 549.

Appendix-9: Equality among the Humans, as preached by Thirukkural, pp. 550-553;

Appendix-10: Notes on Highlights, Relevant to World Peace, pp.554-555;

Appendix-11: About the Book, THIRUKKURAL RESEARCH 2021, pp.556-564;

Appendix-12: About the Author, pp.565-566.

Appendix-13: CITATION INDEX, pp.567-573.

Appendix-14: Key to Pronunciation of Tamil Words (Lata Font): Standardization of Pronunciation of 'Kural'-couplets in English- script! .. pp.574-575).

Appendix-15: World Tamil Conferences which promoted the awareness about Thirukkural, p.576

B. Notes on Special Aspects: Suggestions for Future Research:

1. Hints from History to be researched: i) Sri C.Rajagopalachari (Rajaji) quotes a slogan from Rig Veda: Vide verse 1-89-1 which reads as "let noble thoughts come to us from every side!". Perhaps, he might have wanted to give a liberal interpretation for the verses relating to the 4-'varna'-ideology of Rig Veda! (p.551).

2. The poet takes up the initiative, in kural 205, to caution such of those mightier persons with muscle-power, advising them not to cause harm to the poor-people!, warning them that they would (themselves) would become poor, if they violate the norms of justice, described in kural 204!....(p.410). (Note: this is a new interpretation in comparison to all other earlier interpreters!).

3. 'Contribution of knowledge by an individual person to the field of his/ her own profession is considered important to the development of the specific field!...(p.411).

4. In the case of the majority of the people believing in superstition, the man who does not believe in that superstition qualifies for being called as the 'Aloe' (katraazhai), a herbal plant which serves as the cure for the illness!.....(p.423, in relevance to kural 850).....(This is a new interpretation, compared to all other earlier interpreters, during the past 2000 years!.This needs further research).

5. 'Heraclitus of Ephasus, an ancient Greek philosopher (6th century BC), as cited in 'Fragments', states: "Many fail to grasp what they have seen, and cannot judge what they have learned, although they tell themselves, 'they know!'...".This observation tallies with kural 849!.... (p.422).

6. 'The queries raised by Rev. Dr.G.U.Pope on kurals like 897, 899 and 900 must be studied further, considering the socio-political situations which prevailed in Tamil-country, during the lifetime of Thiruvalluvar, the poet!"....(p.427).

7. 'The couplet (kural 763) signifies the enmity between unequal enemies! Perhaps, highlighting the lack of unity among the weaker-party in the fight!'....(p.421).

8. The poet is a peace-maker! Not a poet who encourages the strong person to attack a small person to crush him, just because the the small person has not received education (*kal-laan*!) ....(p.425, in relevance to kural 870).

9. 'Thiruvalluvar has used a term "*ve-nh-thup-pin*" which means 'based on severe spying report'...because of which a person (the offender) has earned the fury of the king!'......(kural 895; p.425). This is a new interpretation, in contrast to earlier interpretations given during the past 2000 years! It amounts to what happens to those who involve themselves in espionage activities in a country. If this interpretation is accepted, it gives a new dimension, in respect of international importance.

10. 'The fundamental logic for the kural-couplet 972, relating to human equality by birth, could have emerged from the scientific reality that all babies are born 'to mothers', and hence are equal to one another!'...... (p.430).

11. "It is worthwhile to remember the famous quote from Kamil Zvelebil, a Czech scholar who carried out extensive research on Indian-languages:

    ..."Tamil culture is independent! And not imitative!! It is pre-Sanskrit!!!.. and from this point of view, Tamil alone stands apart! When compared to major languages and literature of India'....(p.418, in relevance to kural 543).

12. "There is no great genius without some touch of madness!"...Aristotle, Greek philosopher(384-324 BC).....tallying with kural 503, in the Chapter-51 dealing with "Clarity based on Analysis'.......(p.151).

13. "It is a unique literature in which justice-without-bias is demanded! The poet insists that a person sitting in judgement of any offence committed by an individual person must be free from faults or biases! (please see kural 436!"....(p.134).

14. "Knowledge on the religious philosophies of Jainism,Buddhism and the Cult of Vedas were available to the poet, in the background of the ancient Tamil beliefs and practices, for the purpose of reference! The poet had freedom to compare them, in the light of Tamil traditions and beliefs prevailing in the land,while composing Thirukkural. He has made it as a world-document! To deserve the treatise being hailed as 'the Universal scriptures!"......(p.420).

15. “Some interpreters have described the pathetic part of the story depicted in kural 1270, and left it there, in which case, it is categorized as a tragedy, in the Shakespearean sense! However, Manakkudavar Urai has made it a Comedy, as it was described that it was a story of a worried-husband, blabbering about the his wife's plight affected by the separation of the couple, for a long time! When the man decides to return home speedily, it becomes a Comedy, as it is established that the wife is all safe! This is an example of an ‘anti-climax’ in the art of Drama!!....(p.431, in relevance to kural 1270!).

16. ‘Ancient Tamil music is the historical predecessor of ‘Carnatic’ music, during the ‘Sangam’ -period which spanned over 500 years from 500 BCE to 200 BCE. The ‘Tholkappiam’ makes a mention about ‘*yaazh*’, a melodic instrument and ‘*paRai*’, a percussion instrument, while correlating a particular mood of the poem to be synchronized with a corresponding musical mood (*paN)* pertaining to each of the five landscapes (‘t*hiNai*’).... (p.332. with relevance to kural 1115).

17. ‘Ignorance, false beliefs and superstition may prevail in the mind of a person, in spite of higher education’...(p 115, with relevance to kural 373).

18. ‘The poet does not specify any age-limit for learning (receiving education). He seems to believe in adult-education too! ‘...(p.123, in relevance to kural 397.

19. ‘He (the poet) fixes the responsibility on the individual person, for earning education, knowing fully well that that the king or his favourite ‘wise men’ will not take steps to promote education among the masses!’....p.121.

20. ‘Laziness is not a crime; Laziness is an innocent weakness! It must be watched in children very carefully by parents. A child must be taught to avoid it, to remain active and alert!!’....p.179.

21. ‘Human qualities such as lack-of-patience, lack of self-confidence, practice of back-biting, jealousy, using harsh-words, desire to pick up bad habits, etc., must be and silently watched in the behavioral response of the child, so that it becomes possible to correct it, when the signal shows emerging!’...p.251.

22. 'He (the poet) encourages defense-build-up, vide kural 878, permitting every country to remain strong enough! However, nobody must initiate the war, so that the world remains safe!! That describes the balance-of- power!!!....(p.258;p.259).

23. 'The poet laments! With care!! To find an alternative, rehabilitation scheme for the gamblers' (kural 932; p.276).

24. Kural 950 broadly specifies the infrastructure needed for an ideal health- care-facility!...(p.281).

25. The scenario depicted in kural 724 simulates Symposiums/Conferences conducted at National /International Levels which help the objective of sharing of knowledge among the stake-holders, specific to any discipline of study, or multi-disciplinary relevance!......(p.212).

26. The scenario described under kural 722 simulates the speech given by a student-candidate appearing for the viva-voce (oral) examination for the award of a degree or diploma, in front of a learned group of examiners!... (p.212).

27. The poet highlights on the need for a genuine foreign policy, in kural 734, for promoting good relationship with the neighbouring countries! To have peace in the Land!!...(p.216).

28. The poet speaks, on behalf of army-personnel and the people to caution the rulers! In kural 769!!, stressing the need for courteous treatment extended to soldiers, and the need to give good food to the soldiers... (p.226).

29. 'The ideal-ruler of the land, according to the poet, is a monarch who runs the Government in the style of a welfare-state, being focused on the 'protection and welfare' of the people, with an obligation to earn a good name from the people of the country, ensuring an upright rule! Research is needed to compare it with the ideology of Plato's Republic!!'....(p.169, relating to kural 570).

30. The poet is an optimist! He is a consultant who offers advice to his client, depending upon the needs felt by the client: He describes an eight-fold path to keep on trying, until achieving success!...(p. 184), in relevance to kural 620! ....(He takes 'this-much' precaution to

ensure that youngsters must not be discouraged by the Fate - theories recorded in kurals 377 and 380!)......(p.116). (These ideas will help those who want to become Entrepreneurs).

31. 'Anichcham'-flower mentioned in kural 1111 gets mentioned in Sanskrit literature by Poet Kalidaasaa (p.330).

32. A scientific hint is conveyed in kural 1116, about the constant motion of stars in the sky (p.333).

33. The brightness of the face of a young woman is compared with the brightness of the moon. Recent scientific studies reveal that the intensity of the illumination on the face of the moon varies from 0.05 lux units to 0.10 lux, depending on the lunar phase!(p.334, in kural 1118).

34. In kural 1170, the speed of 'thought' strikes a scientific flavour of imagination! in respect of time required to reach a distant location!! (p.351).

35. Taste of water 'under the shade of a tree' relates to a scientific hint! It must be researched!(p.400; kural 1309).

36. The maid advises her (heroine) to exercise caution while selecting a life- partner! (kural 1195; p.359).

37. The maid speaks out: 'Next time, when he (your husband) visits here, I am going to tell him that he has to take his wife along with him, to wherever he goes, ignoring the social taboo which the superstitious society has imposed, banning the travel of women across the sea! (kural 1205; p.363).

    (Research is needed to verify whether traders from foreign countries such as Egypt, Greece, Arabian countries, China etc., brought their wives to the Tamil-speaking-Country, 2000 years ago, when they travelled to Tamil Country which had established-trade links with those countries, by land-route and sea-route! (p.364).

    The maid laments: 'This separation between a husband and wife exerts a sociological impact, in the sense that the family-growth (the privilege of having children) is arrested during the period of their separation! (p.364).

'Tholkaappiyam' indicates a historical note that women do not accompany their husbands when they go on business trips (across the sea),... and stay far away from home for many years.The plight of women becomes miserable, as well as the that of men!....(p.364).

38. The maid is an intelligent person! She believes that a man must devote sufficient time to earn wealth, sacrificing personal pleasures, if necessary, as otherwise, some undesirable effect could result as indicated in kural 902! (p.268).

39. 'It is always the woman who must start the dialogue, as recommended in kural 51, which empowers a woman as the head of the portfolio of home management!' (p.400, in kural 1308).

40. The maid says: 'After all, the husband and wife do not live for themselves alone! The life, as such, has got a greater purpose: to generate a dynasty of good off-springs! That will be their contribution to the world!! (p.401, in kural 1310).

41. 'Kurals 250 and 861 offer a solution to world-peace! This concept, if practiced, will prevent war and enable world-peace! Leo Tolstoy highlighted on this point. The poet puts the responsibility on the shoulders of righteous persons in the world, in kurals 989 and 990, to prevent a world-war leading to 'apocalypse' of the world!', meaning a calamitous destruction... (pp.88; 254; 259; 260; 292; 293).

42. Kurals related to Management Sciences (p.514);

43. Kurals related to Trade and Financial Management (p.515).

44. Kural related to Academic Fields (p.515).

45. Kurals related to Health Sciences, Psychology (p.514).

46. "Surround yourself with people who make you happy; people who make you laugh!;Who help you when you are in need; People who genuinely care! They are the ones worth keeping in your life! Everyone else is just passing through!"... Karl Marx,...(tallies with kural 786; 787; 781; 783; 791).... (p.448).

47. The poet fixes the responsibility on good persons to show interest in the welfare of the people in the country! Perhaps, the poet expects the

virtuous persons to intervene, if the ruler of the land goes wrong! To impress upon the ruler, to give an upright rule, in the light of reasons explained in kurals 445, 446, 447, 448, 555, 556)......(p.260).

48. "Books that talk about Gods and Kings have forgotten the common man in society; But Thirukkural places man at the forefront, and guides him; Hence, it is a new 'Vaedham'!"...Mahasannithaanam, Thavath-Thiru Kundrakkudi Adigalaar Swamigal, ...(p.437).

49. "The United Nations Organization (UNO) has to bestow their attention, in order to achieve a meaningful and 'harmonious human rights', in-tact, for being practiced everywhere, around the world, with the co-operation of the Member-Countries of the U.N.O....The key is "love and compassion towards universal brotherhood, as yearned by many philosophers around the world!.........(p.553).

50. His Holiness Dalai Lama opined: "India is a model for religious harmony!"....(p.540).

51. His Excellency the 29th Sultan of Brunei, Hassanal Bolkiah has released an appeal to the world: "Future Peace, Prosperity, and Confidence depend on the success of all nations! Hence, we are partners, no matter what our backgrounds, cultures, faiths and histories!!"....(p.541.).

52. Booker T. Washington suggests that a person must strive hard to come up in life against several hardships that may occur in his/her life, in tune with Chapter 30 Promoting Family Welfare) of Thirukkural. (p. 16).

53. The poet speaks about a monarch who runs the Government in the style of a welfare state, similar to an ideology of a democracy (p.419).

APPENDIX-12

ABOUT THE AUTHOR

Full Name: Maniam Palaniswamy CHOCKALINGAM

Place of Birth: Sevalur Village, Thirumayam Taluk, Pudukkottai District. Tamil Nadu, India.

Father: Maniam Palaniswamy Mandore Mother: Mrs. Avathaal Palaniswamy.

Qualifications: B.E. (Civil Engineering); M.Sc. Engg (Public Health); M.S. (Environ. Engg; WSU); Ph.D. (Air Pollution) (Washington State University, Pullman); M.I.S.T.E., F.I.E.

A. Institutions served as a member of Teaching Faculty:

Central Polytechnic, Adyar, Chennai (1967-1969); College of Engineering, Guindy, Anna University, Chennai (1969-1985); Annamalai University (1985-2001); Self-Financing Engineering Institutions in Chennai (2001-2021).

PhDs guided in Civil Engineering and Architecture: 12 (Awarded)

B. Honorary Positions held:

Chairman, Advance Enviornmental Planning Group for Godavari Valley Coalfields, Ministry of Coal, Government of India, New Delhi (1988-1991); Member, Enviornmental Appraisal Committee for New Thermal Power Plant Projects in India, Dept of Environment and Forests, Government of India, New Delhi, under the Chairmanship of Sri. Sunil K. Roy, IFS, Former Indian Diplomat (1986-1989); Member, Standing Sub-Committee on Environment & Ecology, Ministry of Coal, Government of India, New Delhi, under the Chairmanship of Sri.K.C.S. Acharya, IAS (1993-1996); Member, Technical Advisory Committee, Tamil Nadu Pollution Control Board, Chennai (1992- 1995; 2003-2006).

C. Role in academic bodies:

Member of Senate: i) University of Madras (1992-1998); Algappa University (1992-1995); Annamalai University (1985-2001); Member of Syndicate, Annamalai University (1995-1999).

Email ID: chockalingammp@gmail.com….WhatsApp; +918838901884 Residential Address:Plot No.3, Second Cross Street, Dr. Radhakrishnan Nagar, Thiruvanmiyur, Chennai - 600 041. Tamil Nadu, India.

APPENDIX-13

CITATION INDEX

(PAGE NUMBERS SHOWN WITHIN PARENTHESES)

I. **Quotes from India:**

QUOTES FROM MALAYSIA, SINGAPORE,SRI LANKA:

i. **Quotes from foreign countries:**

ii. **Quotes from Proverbs**

iii. **General Citations:**

APPENDIX- 14

KEY TO PRONUNCIATION OF TAMIL WORDS

(LATHA FONT)

உயிர் எழுத்து:

(அ=a); (ஆ=aa); (இ= i); (ஈ= ee); (உ= u); (ஊ=oo);

(எ=ye; e); (ஏ=yae; ae); example: yaetRam;kaNNae); (ஐ=ai; ay);

(ஒ=o); (ஓ=O); example: koL; pOl; nhOkku;

(ஔ=av);(ஃ=a-h); example: a-h-thu; ஓஒ=Oh, oh (exclamatory)

இன - conjunct ஒற்று.

(க்;=k); (ச்=ch, s); (ட்=t, d); (த்=th); (ப்;=p);

(ர்=r); (வ்;=v); (ற்=tR);

மெய் எழுத்து

(க்;=k); (ங்=ng); (ச்;=ch); ((ஞ்=gn); (l;=t, tt); (ண்=N); (த்=th); (ந்=nh); (ப்=p); (ம்=m); (ய்=y); (ர்=r); (ல்;=l); (வ்=v); (ழ்=zh); (ள்=L); (ற்=R);(ன்=n)

உயிர்- மெய் எழுத்து:

க (ka); ங (nga); ச (cha, sa Example: sollu, chollu); ஞ (gna); ஞா (gnaa); ட (ta, da; ண (Na); ன (na); த (tha); ந (nha); ப (pa, ba); ம (ma); ய (ya); ர (ra); ல (la); வ (va); ழ (zha); ள (La); ற (Ra); இன்று=indRu; பெற்று=petRu; அறம்= aRam; ந = nha நன்று = nha-ndRu; வெற்றி =vetRi; எஞ்ஞான்றும்;=yegn-gnaa-ndRum; சொல்=sol, chol;

ஆங்கு=aangku; எழிலி=yezhili; ஐந்தின்;=ai-nh-thin; ஒளி=oLi; நோக்கு=nhO-kku; குறிக்கோள்;=kuRi-kkOL; என்ப=yenba; enba; பெருங்கடல்=perung-kadal; நின்று=nhi-ndRu; எழுமை=yezhu-mai; ஊக்கி=ookki; ஓங்கு=Ong-ku. ஒற்று=otRu

APPENDIX-15

WORLD TAMIL CONFERENCES

World Tamil Conferences promoting awareness about Thirukkural :

1. First World Tamil Conference held in Kuala Lumpur, Malaysia, 1966.
2. Second World Tamil Conference held in Chennai, 1968. (Organised by M.Baktavatchalam, Chief Minister; C.N.Annadurai, Chief Minister, Tamil Nadu).
3. Third World Tamil Conference held in Parrys, France, 1970.
4. Fourth World Tamil Conference held in Jafna, Sri Lanka, 1974.
5. Fifth World Tamil Conference held in Madurai, 1981 (Organised by Dr.M.G.Ramachandran, Chief Minister, Tamil Nadu)
6. Sixth World Tamil Conference held in Kuala Lumpur, Malaysia, 1987.
7. Seventh World Tamil Conference held in Port Louis, Maritius, 1989.
8. Eighth World Tamil Conference held in Thanjavur, India, 1995 (Organised by Dr.J.Jayalalithaa, Chief Minister, Tamil Nadu)
9. Ninth World Tamil Conference held in Kuala Lumpur, Malaysia, 2015.
10. Tenth World Tamil Conference held in Chicago, U.S.A, 2019 (Organised by International Association for Tamil Research: FeTNA & Chicago Tamil Sangam).
11. World Classical Tamil Conference held in Coimbatore, India, 2010. (Organised by Dr. Kalaignar Mu. Karunanithi, Chief Minister, Tamil Nadu).

www.ingramcontent.com/pod-product-compliance
Lightning Source LLC
LaVergne TN
LVHW041135150826
845673LV00001B/9

* 9 7 9 8 8 8 9 8 6 9 1 1 5 *